THE LIFE OF FRIEDRICH SCHILLER

THE LIFE OF FRIEDRICH SCHILLER

THOMAS CARLYLE

ISBN: 978-93-89614-49-7

Published: -

LECTOR HOUSE LLP
E-MAIL: lectorpublishing@gmail.com

THOMAS CARLYLE'S COLLECTED WORKS.

LIBRARY EDITION.

IN THIRTY VOLUMES.

VOL. V.

LIFE OF FRIEDRICH SCHILLER.

From a Miniature in the Possession of the Hofdame Fräulein von Kalb, in Berlin, taken
while Schiller lived with the Körners in Dresden.

THE LIFE OF FRIEDRICH SCHILLER

COMPREHENDING AN EXAMINATION OF HIS WORKS.

BY

THOMAS CARLYLE.

Quique pii vates et Phœbo digna locuti.

Virgil.

WITH A SUPPLEMENT OF 1872

PREFACE TO SECOND EDITION.

THE excuse for reprinting this somewhat insignificant Book is, that certain parties, of the pirate species, were preparing to reprint it for me. There are books, as there are horses, which a judicious owner, on fair survey of them, might prefer to adjust by at once shooting through the head: but in the case of books, owing to the pirate species, that is not possible. Remains therefore that at least dirty paper and errors of the press be guarded against; that a poor Book, which has still to walk this world, do walk in clean linen, so to speak, and pass its few and evil days with no blotches but its own adhering to it.

There have been various new *Lives* of Schiller since this one first saw the light;—great changes in our notions, informations, in our relations to the Life of Schiller, and to other things connected therewith, during that long time! Into which I could not in the least enter on the present occasion. Such errors, one or two, as lay corrigible on the surface, I have pointed out by here and there a Note as I read; but of errors that lay deeper there could no charge be taken: to break the surface, to tear-up the old substance, and model *it* anew, was a task that lay far from me,—that would have been frightful to me. What was written remains written; and the Reader, by way of constant commentary, when needed, has to say to himself, "It was written Twenty years ago." For newer instruction on Schiller's Biography he can consult the *Schillers Leben* of Madame von Wolzogen, which Goethe once called a *Schiller Redivivus*; the *Briefwechsel zwischen Schiller und Goethe*;—or, as a summary of the whole, and the readiest inlet to the general subject for an English reader, Sir Edward Bulwer's *Sketch of Schiller's Life*, a vigorous and lively piece of writing, prefixed to his *Translations from Schiller*.

The present little Book is very imperfect:—but it pretends also to be very harmless; it can innocently instruct those who are more ignorant than itself! To which ingenuous class, according to their wants and tastes, let it, with all good wishes, and hopes to meet afterwards in fruitfuler provinces, be heartily commended.

T. CARLYLE.

London, 7th May 1845.

CONTENTS

SUMMARY AND INDEX.

PART I.

SCHILLER'S YOUTH (1759-1784).

AMONG the writers of the concluding part of the last century there is none more deserving of our notice than Friedrich Schiller. Distinguished alike for the splendour of his intellectual faculties, and the elevation of his tastes and feelings, he has left behind him in his works a noble emblem of these great qualities: and the reputation which he thus enjoys, and has merited, excites our attention the more, on considering the circumstances under which it was acquired. Schiller had peculiar difficulties to strive with, and his success has likewise been peculiar. Much of his life was deformed by inquietude and disease, and it terminated at middle age; he composed in a language then scarcely settled into form, or admitted to a rank among the cultivated languages of Europe: yet his writings are remarkable for their extent and variety as well as their intrinsic excellence; and his own countrymen are not his only, or perhaps his principal admirers. It is difficult to collect or interpret the general voice; but the World, no less than Germany, seems already to have dignified him with the reputation of a classic; to have enrolled him among that select number whose works belong not wholly to any age or nation, but who, having instructed their own contemporaries, are claimed as instructors by the great family of mankind, and set apart for many centuries from the common oblivion which soon overtakes the mass of authors, as it does the mass of other men.

Such has been the high destiny of Schiller. His history and character deserve our study for more than one reason. A natural and harmless feeling attracts us towards such a subject; we are anxious to know how so great a man passed through the world, how he lived, and moved, and had his being; and the question, if properly investigated, might yield advantage as well as pleasure. It would be interesting to discover by what gifts and what employment of them he reached the eminence on which we now see him; to follow the steps of his intellectual and moral culture; to gather from his life and works some picture of himself. It is worth inquiring, whether he, who could represent noble actions so well, did himself act nobly; how those powers of intellect, which in philosophy and art achieved so much, applied themselves to the every-day emergencies of life; how the generous ardour, which delights us in his poetry, displayed itself in the common intercourse between man and man. It would at once instruct and gratify us if we could understand him thoroughly, could transport ourselves into his circumstances outward and inward, could see as he saw, and feel as he felt.

But if the various utility of such a task is palpable enough, its difficulties are not less so. We should not lightly think of comprehending the very simplest character, in all its bearings; and it might argue vanity to boast of even a common acquaintance with one like Schiller's. Such men as he are misunderstood by their daily companions, much more by the distant observer, who gleans his information from scanty records, and casual notices of characteristic events, which biographers are often too indolent or injudicious to collect, and which the peaceful life of a man of letters usually supplies in little abundance. The published details of Schiller's history are meagre and insufficient; and his writings, like those of every author, can afford but a dim and dubious copy of his mind. Nor is it easy to decipher even this, with moderate accuracy. The haze of a foreign language, of foreign manners, and modes of thinking strange to us, confuses and obscures the sight, often magnifying what is trivial, softening what is rude, and sometimes hiding or distorting what is beautiful. To take the dimensions of Schiller's mind were a hard enterprise, in any case; harder still with these impediments.

Accordingly we do not, in this place, pretend to attempt it: we have no finished portrait of his character to offer, no formal estimate of his works. It will be enough for us if, in glancing over his life, we can satisfy a simple curiosity, about the fortunes and chief peculiarities of a man connected with us by a bond so kindly as that of the teacher to the taught, the giver to the receiver of mental delight; if, in wandering through his intellectual creation, we can enjoy once more the magnificent and fragrant beauty of that fairy land, and express our feelings, where we do not aim at judging and deciding.

Johann Christoph Friedrich Schiller was a native of Marbach, a small town of Würtemberg, situated on the banks of the Neckar. He was born on the 10th of November 1759,—a few months later than our own Robert Burns. Schiller's early culture was favoured by the dispositions, but obstructed by the outward circumstances of his parents. Though removed above the pressure of poverty, their station was dependent and fluctuating; it involved a frequent change of place and plan. Johann Caspar Schiller, the father, had been a surgeon in the Bavarian army; he served in the Netherlands during the Succession War. After his return home to Würtemberg, he laid aside the medical profession, having obtained a commission of ensign and adjutant under his native Prince. This post he held successively in two regiments; he had changed into the second, and was absent on active duty when Friedrich was born. The Peace of Paris put an end to his military employment; but Caspar had shown himself an intelligent, unassuming and useful man, and the Duke of Würtemberg was willing to retain him in his service. The laying-out of various nurseries and plantations in the pleasure-grounds of Ludwigsburg and Solitude was intrusted to the retired soldier, now advanced to the rank of captain: he removed from one establishment to another, from time to time; and continued in the Duke's pay till death. In his latter years he resided chiefly at Ludwigsburg.

This mode of life was not the most propitious for educating such a boy as Friedrich; but the native worth of his parents did more than compensate for the disadvantages of their worldly condition and their limited acquirements in knowledge. The benevolence, the modest and prudent integrity, the true devoutness of these good people shone forth at an after period, expanded and beautified in the character of their son; his heart was nourished by a constant exposure to such influences, and thus the better part of his education prospered well. The mother was a woman of many household virtues; to a warm affection for her children and husband, she joined a degree of taste and intelligence which is of much rarer occurrence. She is said to have been a lover of poetry; in particular an admiring reader of Utz and Gellert, writers whom it is creditable for one in her situation to have relished.[1] Her kindness and tenderness of heart peculiarly endeared her to Friedrich. Her husband appears to have been a person of great probity and meekness of temper, sincerely desirous to approve himself a useful member of society, and to do his duty conscientiously to all men. The seeds of many valuable qualities had been sown in him by nature; and though his early life had been unfavourable for their cultivation, he at a late period laboured, not without success, to remedy this disadvantage. Such branches of science and philosophy as lay within his reach, he studied with diligence, whenever his professional employments left him leisure; on a subject connected with the latter he became an author.[2] But what chiefly distinguished him was the practice of a sincere piety, which seems to have diffused itself over all his feelings, and given to his clear and honest character that calm elevation which, in such a case, is its natural result. As his religion mingled itself with every motive and action of his life, the wish which in all his wanderings lay nearest his heart, the wish for the education of his son, was likely to be deeply tinctured with it. There is yet preserved, in his handwriting, a prayer composed in advanced age, wherein he mentions how, at the child's birth, he had entreated the great Father of all, "to supply in strength of spirit what must needs be wanting in outward instruction." The gray-haired man, who had lived to see the maturity of his boy, could now express his solemn thankfulness, that "God had heard the prayer of a mortal."

Friedrich followed the movements of his parents for some time; and had to gather the elements of learning from various masters. Perhaps it was in part owing to this circumstance, that his progress, though respectable, or more, was so little commensurate with what he afterwards became, or with the capacities of which even his earliest years gave symptoms. Thoughtless and gay, as a boy is wont to be, he would now and then dissipate his time in childish sports, forgetful that the stolen charms of ball and leapfrog must be dearly bought by reproaches: but occasionally he was overtaken with feelings of deeper import, and used to express the agitations of his little mind in words and actions, which were first rightly interpreted when they were called to mind long afterwards. His schoolfellows can *now* recollect that even his freaks had sometimes a poetic character; that a certain earnestness of temper, a frank integrity, an appetite for things grand or moving, was discernible across all the caprices of his boyhood. Once, it is said, during a tremendous thunderstorm, his father missed him in the young group within doors; none of the sisters could tell what was become of Fritz, and the old man grew at length so anxious that he was forced to go out in quest of him. Fritz was scarcely past the age of infancy, and knew not the dangers of a scene so awful. His father found him at last, in a solitary place of the neighbourhood, perched on the branch of a tree, gazing at the tempestuous face of the sky, and watching the

[1] She was of humble descent and little education, the daughter of a baker in Kodweis.

[2] His book is entitled *Die Baumzucht im Grossen* (the Cultivation of Trees on the Grand Scale): it came to a second edition in 1806.

flashes as in succession they spread their lurid gleam over it. To the reprimands of his parent, the whimpering truant pleaded in extenuation, "that the lightning was very beautiful, and that he wished to see where it was coming from!"—Such anecdotes, we have long known, are in themselves of small value: the present one has the additional defect of being somewhat dubious in respect of authenticity. We have ventured to give it, as it came to us, notwithstanding. The picture of the boy Schiller, contemplating the thunder, is not without a certain interest, for such as know the man.

Schiller's first teacher was Moser, pastor and schoolmaster in the village of Lorch, where the parents resided from the sixth to the ninth year of their son. This person deserves mention for the influence he exerted on the early history of his pupil: he seems to have given his name to the Priest 'Moser' in the *Robbers*; his spiritual calling, and the conversation of his son, himself afterwards a preacher, are supposed to have suggested to Schiller the idea of consecrating himself to the clerical profession. This idea, which laid hold of and cherished some predominant though vague propensities of the boy's disposition, suited well with the religious sentiments of his parents, and was soon formed into a settled purpose. In the public school at Ludwigsburg, whither the family had now removed, his studies were regulated with this view; and he underwent, in four successive years, the annual examination before the Stuttgard Commission, to which young men destined for the Church are subjected in that country. Schiller's temper was naturally devout; with a delicacy of feeling which tended towards bashfulness and timidity, there was mingled in him a fervid impetuosity, which was ever struggling through its concealment, and indicating that he felt deeply and strongly, as well as delicately. Such a turn of mind easily took the form of religion, prescribed to it by early example and early affections, as well as nature. Schiller looked forward to the sacred profession with alacrity: it was the serious daydream of all his boyhood, and much of his youth. As yet, however, the project hovered before him at a great distance, and the path to its fulfilment offered him but little entertainment. His studies did not seize his attention firmly; he followed them from a sense of duty, not of pleasure. Virgil and Horace he learned to construe accurately; but is said to have taken no deep interest in their poetry. The tenderness and meek beauty of the first, the humour and sagacity and capricious pathos of the last, the matchless elegance of both, would of course escape his inexperienced perception; while the matter of their writings must have appeared frigid and shallow to a mind so susceptible. He loved rather to meditate on the splendour of the Ludwigsburg theatre, which had inflamed his imagination when he first saw it in his ninth year, and given shape and materials to many of his subsequent reveries.[3] Under these circumstances,

---

[3] The first display of his poetic gifts occurred also in his ninth year, but took its rise in a much humbler and less common source than the inspiration of the stage. His biographers have recorded this small event with a conscientious accuracy, second only to that of Boswell and Hawkins in regard to the Lichfield *duck*. 'The little tale,' says one of them, 'is worth relating; the rather that, after an interval of more than twenty years, Schiller himself, on meeting with his early comrade (the late Dr. Elwert of Kantstadt) for the first time since their boyhood, reminded him of the adventure, recounting the circumstances with great minuteness and glee. It is as follows: Once in 1768, Elwert and he had to repeat their cat-

his progress, with all his natural ability, could not be very striking; the teachers did not fail now and then to visit him with their severities; yet still there was a negligent success in his attempts, which, joined to his honest and vivid temper, made men augur well of him. The Stuttgard Examinators have marked him in their records with the customary formula of approval, or, at worst, of toleration. They usually designate him as 'a boy of good hope,' *puer bonæ spei.*

This good hope was not, however, destined to be realised in the way they expected: accidents occurred which changed the direction of Schiller's exertions, and threatened for a time to prevent the success of them altogether. The Duke of Würtemberg had lately founded a Free Seminary for certain branches of professional education: it was first set up at Solitude, one of his country residences; and had now been transferred to Stuttgard, where, under an improved form, and with the name of *Karls-schule*, we believe it still exists. The Duke proposed to give the sons of his military officers a preferable claim to the benefits of this institution; and having formed a good opinion both of Schiller and his father, he invited the former to profit by this opportunity. The offer occasioned great embarrassment: the young man and his parents were alike determined in favour of the Church, a project with which this new one was inconsistent. Their embarrassment was but increased, when the Duke, on learning the nature of their scruples, desired them to think well before they decided. It was out of fear, and with reluctance that his proposal was accepted. Schiller enrolled himself in 1773; and turned, with a heavy heart, from freedom and cherished hopes, to Greek, and seclusion, and Law.

His anticipations proved to be but too just: the six years which he spent in this establishment were the most harassing and comfortless of his life. The Stuttgard system of education seems to have been formed on the principle, not of cherishing <u>and correcting nature, but of rooting it out, and supplying its place</u> with something echism together on a certain day publicly in the church. Their teacher, an ill-conditioned, narrow-minded pietist, had previously threatened them with a thorough flogging if they missed even a single word. To make the matter worse, this very teacher chanced to be the person whose turn it was to catechise on the appointed day. Both the boys began their answers with dismayed hearts and faltering tongues; yet they succeeded in accomplishing the task; and were in consequence rewarded by the mollified pedagogue with two kreutzers apiece. Four kreutzers of ready cash was a sum of no common magnitude; how it should be disposed of formed a serious question for the parties interested. Schiller moved that they should go to Harteneck, a hamlet in the neighbourhood, and have a dish of curds-and-cream: his partner assented; but alas! in Harteneck no particle of curds or cream was to be had. Schiller then made offer for a quarter-cake of cheese; but for this four entire kreutzers were demanded, leaving nothing whatever in reserve for bread! Twice baffled, the little gastronomes, unsatisfied in stomach, wandered on to Neckarweihingen; where, at length, though not till after much inquiry, they did obtain a comfortable mess of curds-and-cream, served up in a gay platter, and silver spoons to eat it with. For all this, moreover, they were charged but three kreutzers; so that there was still one left to provide them with a bunch of St. John grapes. Exhilarated by such liberal cheer, Schiller rose into a glow of inspiration: having left the village, he mounted with his comrade to the adjacent height, which overlooks both Harteneck and Neckarweihingen; and there in a truly poetic effusion he pronounced his malediction on the creamless region, bestowing with the same solemnity his blessing on the one which had afforded him that savoury refreshment.' *Friedrich von Schillers Leben* (Heidelberg. 1817), p. 11.

better. The process of teaching and living was conducted with the stiff formality of military drilling; every thing went on by statute and ordinance, there was no scope for the exercise of free-will, no allowance for the varieties of original structure. A scholar might possess what instincts or capacities he pleased; the 'regulations of the school' took no account of this; he must fit himself into the common mould, which, like the old Giant's bed, stood there, appointed by superior authority, to be filled alike by the great and the little. The same strict and narrow course of reading and composition was marked out for each beforehand, and it was by stealth if he read or wrote any thing beside. Their domestic economy was regulated in the same spirit as their preceptorial: it consisted of the same sedulous exclusion of all that could border on pleasure, or give any exercise to choice. The pupils were kept apart from the conversation or sight of any person but their teachers; none ever got beyond the precincts of despotism to snatch even a fearful joy; their very amusements proceeded by the word of command.

How grievous all this must have been, it is easy to conceive. To Schiller it was more grievous than to any other. Of an ardent and impetuous yet delicate nature, whilst his discontentment devoured him internally, he was too modest and timid to give it the relief of utterance by deeds or words. Locked up within himself, he suffered deeply, but without complaining. Some of his letters written during this period have been preserved: they exhibit the ineffectual struggles of a fervid and busy mind veiling its many chagrins under a certain dreary patience, which only shows them more painfully. He pored over his lexicons and grammars, and insipid tasks, with an artificial composure; but his spirit pined within him like a captive's, when he looked forth into the cheerful world, or recollected the affection of parents, the hopes and frolicsome enjoyments of past years. The misery he endured in this severe and lonely mode of existence strengthened or produced in him a habit of constraint and shyness, which clung to his character through life.

The study of Law, for which he had never felt any predilection, naturally grew in his mind to be the representative of all these evils, and his distaste for it went on increasing. On this point he made no secret of his feelings. One of the exercises, yearly prescribed to every scholar, was a written delineation of his own character, according to his own views of it, to be delivered publicly at an appointed time: Schiller, on the first of these exhibitions, ventured to state his persuasion, that he was not made to be a jurist, but called rather by his inclinations and faculties to the clerical profession. This statement, of course, produced no effect; he was forced to continue the accustomed course, and his dislike for Law kept fast approaching to absolute disgust. In 1775, he was fortunate enough to get it relinquished, though at the expense of adopting another employment, for which, in different circumstances, he would hardly have declared himself. The study of Medicine, for which a new institution was about this time added to the Stuttgard school, had no attractions for Schiller: he accepted it only as a galling servitude in exchange for one more galling. His mind was bent on higher objects; and he still felt all his present vexations aggravated by the thought, that his fairest expectations from the future had been sacrificed to worldly convenience, and the humblest necessities of life.

Meanwhile the youth was waxing into manhood, and the fetters of discipline lay heavier on him, as his powers grew stronger, and his eyes became open to the stirring and variegated interests of the world, now unfolding itself to him under new and more glowing colours. As yet he contemplated the scene only from afar, and it seemed but the more gorgeous on that account. He longed to mingle in its busy current, and delighted to view the image of its movements in his favourite poets and historians. Plutarch and Shakspeare;[4] the writings of Klopstock, Lessing, Garve, Herder, Gerstenberg, Goethe, and a multitude of others, which marked the dawning literature of Germany, he had studied with a secret avidity: they gave him vague ideas of men and life, or awakened in him splendid visions of literary glory. Klopstock's *Messias*, combined with his own religious tendencies, had early turned him to sacred poetry: before the end of his fourteenth year, he had finished what he called an 'epic poem,' entitled *Moses*. The extraordinary popularity of Gerstenberg's *Ugolino*, and Goethe's *Götz von Berlichingen*, next directed his attention to the drama; and as admiration in a mind like his, full of blind activity and nameless aspirings, naturally issues in imitation, he plunged with equal ardour into this new subject, and produced his first tragedy, *Cosmo von Medicis*, some fragments of which he retained and inserted in his *Robbers*. A mass of minor performances, preserved among his papers, or published in the Magazines of the time, serve sufficiently to show that his mind had already dimly discovered its destination, and was striving with a restless vehemence to reach it, in spite of every obstacle.

Such obstacles were in his case neither few nor small. Schiller felt the mortifying truth, that to arrive at the ideal world, he must first gain a footing in the real; that he might entertain high thoughts and longings, might reverence the beauties of nature and grandeur of mind, but was born to toil for his daily bread. Poetry he loved with the passionateness of a first affection; but he could not live by it; he honoured it too highly to wish to live by it. His prudence told him that he must yield to stern necessity, must 'forsake the balmy climate of Pindus for the Greenland of a barren and dreary science of terms;' and he did not hesitate to obey. His professional studies were followed with a rigid though reluctant fidelity; it was only in leisure gained by superior diligence that he could yield himself to more favourite pursuits. Genius was to serve as the ornament of his inferior qualities, not as an excuse for the want of them.

But if, when such sacrifices were required, it was painful to comply with the dictates of his own reason, it was still more so to endure the harsh and superfluous restrictions of his teachers. He felt it hard enough to be driven from the enchant-

[4] The feeling produced in him by Shakspeare he described long afterwards: it throws light on the general state of his temper and tastes. 'When I first, at a very early age,' he says, 'became acquainted with this poet, I felt indignant at his coldness, his hardness of heart, which permitted him in the most melting pathos to utter jests,—to mar, by the introduction of a fool, the soul-searching scenes of *Hamlet, Lear,* and other pieces; which now kept him still where my sensibilities hastened forward, now drove him carelessly, onward where I would so gladly have lingered * * He was the object of my reverence and zealous study for years before I could love himself. I was not yet capable of comprehending Nature at firsthand: I had but learned to admire her image, reflected in the understanding, and put in order by rules.' *Werke*, Bd. viii 2, p. 77.

ments of poetry by the dull realities of duty; but it was intolerable and degrading to be hemmed-in still farther by the caprices of severe and formal pedagogues. Schiller brooded gloomily over the constraints and hardships of his situation. Many plans he formed for deliverance. Sometimes he would escape in secret to catch a glimpse of the free and busy world to him forbidden: sometimes he laid schemes for utterly abandoning a place which he abhorred, and trusting to fortune for the rest. Often the sight of his class-books and school-apparatus became irksome beyond endurance; he would feign sickness, that he might be left in his own chamber to write poetry and pursue his darling studies without hindrance. Such artifices did not long avail him; the masters noticed the regularity of his sickness, and sent him tasks to be done while it lasted. Even Schiller's patience could not brook this; his natural timidity gave place to indignation; he threw the paper of exercises at the feet of the messenger, and said sternly that "*here* he would choose his own studies."

Under such corroding and continual vexations an ordinary spirit would have sunk at length, would have gradually given up its loftier aspirations, and sought refuge in vicious indulgence, or at best have sullenly harnessed itself into the yoke, and plodded through existence, weary, discontented, and broken, ever casting back a hankering look upon the dreams of youth, and ever without power to realise them. But Schiller was no ordinary character, and did not act like one. Beneath a cold and simple exterior, dignified with no artificial attractions, and marred in its native amiableness by the incessant obstruction, the isolation and painful destitutions under which he lived, there was concealed a burning energy of soul, which no obstruction could extinguish. The hard circumstances of his fortune had prevented the natural development of his mind; his faculties had been cramped and misdirected; but they had gathered strength by opposition and the habit of self-dependence which it encouraged. His thoughts, unguided by a teacher, had sounded into the depths of his own nature and the mysteries of his own fate; his feelings and passions, unshared by any other heart, had been driven back upon his own, where, like the volcanic fire that smoulders and fuses in secret, they accumulated till their force grew irresistible.

Hitherto Schiller had passed for an unprofitable, a discontented and a disobedient Boy: but the time was now come when the gyves of school-discipline could no longer cripple and distort the giant might of his nature: he stood forth as a Man, and wrenched asunder his fetters with a force that was felt at the extremities of Europe. The publication of the *Robbers* forms an era not only in Schiller's history, but in the Literature of the World; and there seems no doubt that, but for so mean a cause as the perverted discipline of the Stuttgard school, we had never seen this tragedy. Schiller commenced it in his nineteenth year; and the circumstances under which it was composed are to be traced in all its parts. It is the production of a strong untutored spirit, consumed by an activity for which there is no outlet, indignant at the barriers which restrain it, and grappling darkly with the phantoms to which its own energy thus painfully imprisoned gives being. A rude simplicity, combined with a gloomy and overpowering force, are its chief characteristics; they remind us of the defective cultivation, as well as of the fervid and harassed feelings of its author. Above all, the latter quality is visible; the tragic interest of the *Robbers* is deep throughout, so deep that frequently it borders upon horror. A grim inexpiable Fate is made the ruling principle: it envelops and overshadows the whole; and under its louring influence, the fiercest efforts of human will appear but like flashes that illuminate the wild scene with a brief and terrible splendour, and are lost forever in the darkness. The unsearchable abysses of man's destiny are laid open before us, black and profound and appalling, as they seem to the young mind when it first attempts to explore them: the obstacles that thwart our faculties and wishes, the deceitfulness of hope, the nothingness of existence, are sketched in the sable colours so natural to the enthusiast when he first ventures upon life, and compares the world that is without him to the anticipations that were within.

Karl von Moor is a character such as young poets always delight to contemplate or delineate; to Schiller the analogy of their situations must have peculiarly recommended him. Moor is animated into action by feelings similar to those under which his author was then suffering and longing to act. Gifted with every noble quality of manhood in overflowing abundance, Moor's first expectations of life, and of the part he was to play in it, had been glorious as a poet's dream. But the minor dexterities of management were not among his endowments; in his eagerness to reach the goal, he had forgotten that the course is a labyrinthic maze, beset with difficulties, of which some may be surmounted, some can only be evaded, many can be neither. Hurried on by the headlong impetuosity of his temper, he entangles himself in these perplexities; and thinks to penetrate them, not by skill and patience, but by open force. He is baffled, deceived, and still more deeply involved; but injury and disappointment exasperate rather than instruct him. He had expected heroes, and he finds mean men; friends, and he finds smiling traitors to tempt him aside, to profit by his aberrations, and lead him onward to destruction: he had dreamed of magnanimity and every generous principle, he finds that prudence is the only virtue sure of its reward. Too fiery by nature, the intensity of his sufferings has now maddened him still farther: he is himself incapable of calm reflection, and there is no counsellor at hand to assist him; none, whose sympathy might assuage his miseries, whose wisdom might teach him to remedy or to endure them. He is stung by fury into action, and his activity is at once blind and tremendous. Since the world is not the abode of unmixed integrity, he looks upon it as a den of thieves; since its institutions may obstruct the advancement of worth, and screen delinquency from punishment, he regards the social union as a pestilent nuisance, the mischiefs of which it is fitting that he in his degree should do his best to repair, by means however violent. Revenge is the mainspring of his conduct; but he ennobles it in his own eyes, by giving it the colour of a disinterested concern for the maintenance of justice,—the abasement of vice from its high places, and the exaltation of suffering virtue. Single against the universe, to appeal to the primary law of the stronger, to 'grasp the scales of Providence in a mortal's hand,' is frantic and wicked; but Moor has a force of soul which makes it likewise awful. The interest lies in the conflict of this gigantic soul against the fearful odds which at length overwhelm it, and hurry it down to the darkest depths of ruin.

The original conception of such a work as this betrays the inexperience no less than the vigour of youth: its execution gives a similar testimony. The characters of the piece, though traced in glowing colours, are outlines more than pictures: the few features we discover in them are drawn with elaborate minuteness; but the rest are wanting. Every thing indicates the condition of a keen and powerful intellect, which had studied men in books only; had, by self-examination and the perusal of history, detected and strongly seized some of the leading peculiarities of human nature; but was yet ignorant of all the minute and more complex principles which regulate men's conduct in actual life, and which only a knowledge of living men can unfold. If the hero of the play forms something like an exception to this remark, he is the sole exception, and for reasons alluded to above: his character resembles the author's own. Even with Karl, the success is incomplete: with the other personages it is far more so. Franz von Moor, the villain of the Piece, is an amplified copy of Iago and Richard; but the copy is distorted as well as amplified. There is no air of reality in Franz: he is a villain of theory, who studies to accomplish his object by the most diabolical expedients, and soothes his conscience by arguing with the priest in favour of atheism and materialism; not the genuine villain of Shakspeare and Nature, who employs his reasoning powers in creating new schemes and devising new means, and conquers remorse by avoiding it,—by fixing his hopes and fears on the more pressing emergencies of worldly business. So reflective a miscreant as Franz could not exist: his calculations would lead him to honesty, if merely because it was the best policy.

Amelia, the only female in the piece, is a beautiful creation; but as imaginary as her persecutor Franz. Still and exalted in her warm enthusiasm, devoted in her love to Moor, she moves before us as the inhabitant of a higher and simpler world than ours. "*He* sails on troubled seas," she exclaims, with a confusion of metaphors, which it is easy to pardon, "he sails on troubled seas, Amelia's love sails with him; he wanders in pathless deserts, Amelia's love makes the burning sand grow green beneath him, and the stunted shrubs to blossom; the south scorches his bare head, his feet are pinched by the northern snow, stormy hail beats round his temples—Amelia's love rocks him to sleep in the storm. Seas, and hills, and horizons, are between us; but souls escape from their clay prisons, and meet in the paradise of love!" She is a fair vision, the *beau idéal* of a poet's first mistress; but has few mortal lineaments.

Similar defects are visible in almost all the other characters. Moor, the father, is a weak and fond old man, who could have arrived at gray hairs in such a state of ignorance nowhere but in a work of fiction. The inferior banditti are painted with greater vigour, yet still in rugged and ill-shapen forms; their individuality is kept up by an extravagant exaggeration of their several peculiarities. Schiller himself pronounced a severe but not unfounded censure, when he said of this work, in a maturer age, that his *chief* fault was in 'presuming to delineate men two years before he had met one.'

His skill in the art of composition surpassed his knowledge of the world; but that too was far from perfection. Schiller's style in the *Robbers* is partly of a kind with the incidents and feelings which it represents; strong and astonishing, and sometimes wildly grand; but likewise inartificial, coarse, and grotesque. His sentences, in their rude emphasis, come down like the club of Hercules; the stroke is often of a crushing force, but its sweep is irregular and awkward. When Moor is involved in the deepest intricacies of the old question, necessity and free will, and has convinced himself that he is but an engine in the hands of some dark and irresistible power, he cries out: "Why has my Perillus made of me a brazen bull to roast men in my glowing belly?" The stage-direction says, 'shaken with horror:' no wonder that he shook!

Schiller has admitted these faults, and explained their origin, in strong and sincere language, in a passage of which we have already quoted the conclusion. 'A singular miscalculation of nature,' he says, 'had combined my poetical tendencies with the place of my birth. Any disposition to poetry did violence to the laws of the institution where I was educated, and contradicted the plan of its founder. For eight years my enthusiasm struggled with military discipline; but the passion for poetry is vehement and fiery as a first love. What discipline was meant to extinguish, it blew into a flame. To escape from arrangements that tortured me, my heart sought refuge in the world of ideas, when as yet I was unacquainted with the world of realities, from which iron bars excluded me. I was unacquainted with men; for the four hundred that lived with me were but repetitions of the same creature, true casts of one single mould, and of that very mould which plastic nature solemnly disclaimed. *** Thus circumstanced, a stranger to human characters and human fortunes, to hit the medium line between angels and devils was an enterprise in which I necessarily failed. In attempting it, my pencil necessarily brought out a monster, for which by good fortune the world had no original, and which I would not wish to be immortal, except to perpetuate an example of the offspring which Genius in its unnatural union with Thraldom may give to the world. I allude to the *Robbers*.'[5]

Yet with all these excrescences and defects, the unbounded popularity of the *Robbers* is not difficult to account for. To every reader, the excitement of emotion must be a chief consideration; to the mass of readers it is the sole one: and the grand secret of moving others is, that the poet be himself moved. We have seen how well Schiller's temper and circumstances qualified him to fulfil this condition: treatment, not of his choosing, had raised his own mind into something like a Pythian frenzy; and his genius, untrained as it was, sufficed to communicate abundance of the feeling to others. Perhaps more than abundance: to judge from our individual impression, the perusal of the *Robbers* produces an effect powerful even to pain; we are absolutely wounded by the catastrophe; our minds are darkened and distressed, as if we had witnessed the execution of a criminal. It is in vain that we rebel against the inconsistencies and crudities of the work: its faults are redeemed by the living energy that pervades it. We may exclaim against the blind madness of the hero; but there is a towering grandeur about him, a whirlwind force of passion and of will, which catches our hearts, and puts the scruples of criticism to silence. The most delirious of enterprises is that of Moor, but the vastness of his mind renders even that interesting. We see him leagued with desperadoes directing their savage strength to actions more and more audacious; he is in arms

---

[5] *Deutsches Museum v. Jahr* 1784, cited by Doering.

against the conventions of men and the everlasting laws of Fate: yet we follow him with anxiety through the forests and desert places, where he wanders, encompassed with peril, inspired with lofty daring, and torn by unceasing remorse; and we wait with awe for the doom which he has merited and cannot avoid. Nor amid all his frightful aberrations do we ever cease to love him: he is an 'archangel though in ruins;' and the strong agony with which he feels the present, the certainty of that stern future which awaits him, which his own eye never loses sight of, makes us lenient to his crimes. When he pours forth his wild recollections, or still wilder forebodings, there is a terrible vehemence in his expressions, which overpowers us, in spite both of his and their extravagance. The scene on the hills beside the Danube, where he looks at the setting sun, and thinks of old hopes, and times 'when he could not sleep if his evening prayer had been forgotten,' is one, with all its improprieties, that ever clings to the memory. "See," he passionately continues, "all things are gone forth to bask in the peaceful beam of the spring: why must I alone inhale the torments of hell out of the joys of heaven? That all should be so happy, all so married together by the spirit of peace! The whole world one family, its Father above; that Father not *mine*! I alone the castaway, I alone struck out from the company of the just; not for me the sweet name of child, never for me the languishing look of one whom I love; never, never, the embracing of a bosom friend! Encircled with murderers; serpents hissing around me; riveted to vice with iron bonds; leaning on the bending reed of vice over the gulf of perdition; amid the flowers of the glad world, a howling Abaddon! Oh, that I might return into my mother's womb;—that I might be born a beggar! I would never more—O Heaven, that I could be as one of these day-labourers! Oh, I would toil till the blood ran down from my temples, to buy myself the pleasure of one noontide sleep, the blessing of a single tear. There *was* a time too, when I could weep—O ye days of peace, thou castle of my father, ye green lovely valleys!—O all ye Elysian scenes of my childhood! will ye never come again, never with your balmy sighing cool my burning bosom? Mourn with me, Nature! They will never come again, never cool my burning bosom with their balmy sighing. They are gone! gone! and may not return!"

No less strange is the soliloquy where Moor, with the instrument of self-destruction in his hands, the 'dread key that is to shut behind him the prison of life, and to unbolt before him the dwelling of eternal night,'—meditates on the gloomy enigmas of his future destiny. Soliloquies on this subject are numerous,— from the time of Hamlet, of Cato, and downwards. Perhaps the worst of them has more ingenuity, perhaps the best of them has less awfulness than the present. St. Dominick himself might shudder at such a question, with such an answer as this: "What if thou shouldst send me companionless to some burnt and blasted circle of the universe; which thou hast banished from thy sight; where the lone darkness and the motionless desert were my prospects—forever? I would people the silent wilderness with my fantasies; I should have Eternity for leisure to examine the perplexed image of the universal woe."

Strength, wild impassioned strength, is the distinguishing quality of Moor. All his history shows it; and his death is of a piece with the fierce splendour of his life. Having finished the bloody work of crime, and magnanimity, and horror, he thinks that, for himself, suicide would be too easy an exit. He has noticed a poor man toiling by the wayside, for eleven children; a great reward has been promised for the head of the Robber; the gold will nourish that poor drudge and his boys, and Moor goes forth to give it them. We part with him in pity and sorrow; looking less at his misdeeds than at their frightful expiation.

The subordinate personages, though diminished in extent and varied in their forms, are of a similar quality with the hero; a strange mixture of extravagance and true energy. In perusing the work which represents their characters and fates, we are alternately shocked and inspired; there is a perpetual conflict between our understanding and our feelings. Yet the latter on the whole come off victorious. The *Robbers* is a tragedy that will long find readers to astonish, and, with all its faults, to move. It stands, in our imagination, like some ancient rugged pile of a barbarous age; irregular, fantastic, useless; but grand in its height and massiveness and black frowning strength. It will long remain a singular monument of the early genius and early fortune of its author.

The publication of such a work as this naturally produced an extraordinary feeling in the literary world. Translations of the *Robbers* soon appeared in almost all the languages of Europe, and were read in all of them with a deep interest, compounded of admiration and aversion, according to the relative proportions of sensibility and judgment in the various minds which contemplated the subject. In Germany, the enthusiasm which the *Robbers* excited was extreme. The young author had burst upon the world like a meteor; and surprise, for a time, suspended the power of cool and rational criticism. In the ferment produced by the universal discussion of this single topic, the poet was magnified above his natural dimensions, great as they were: and though the general sentence was loudly in his favour, yet he found detractors as well as praisers, and both equally beyond the limits of moderation.

One charge brought against him must have damped the joy of literary glory, and stung Schiller's pure and virtuous mind more deeply than any other. He was accused of having injured the cause of morality by his work; of having set up to the impetuous and fiery temperament of youth a model of imitation which the young were too likely to pursue with eagerness, and which could only lead them from the safe and beaten tracks of duty into error and destruction. It has even been stated, and often been repeated since, that a practical exemplification of this doctrine occurred, about this time, in Germany. A young nobleman, it was said, of the fairest gifts and prospects, had cast away all these advantages; betaken himself to the forests, and, copying Moor, had begun a course of active operations,—which, also copying Moor, but less willingly, he had ended by a shameful death.

It can now be hardly necessary to contradict these theories; or to show that none but a candidate for Bedlam as well as Tyburn could be seduced from the substantial comforts of existence, to seek destruction and disgrace, for the sake of such imaginary grandeur. The German nobleman of the fairest gifts and prospects turns out, on investigation, to have been a German blackguard, whom debauchery and riotous extravagance had reduced to want; who took to the highway, when he could take to nothing else,—not allured by an ebullient enthusiasm, or any heroical and misdirected appetite for sublime actions, but driven by the more palpable stimulus of importunate duns, an empty purse, and five craving senses. Perhaps in his later days, this philosopher *may* have referred to Schiller's tragedy, as the source from which he drew his theory of life: but if so, we believe he was mistaken. For characters like him, the great attraction was the charms of revelry, and the great restraint, the gallows,—before the period of Karl von Moor, just as they have been since, and will be to the end of time. Among motives like these, the influence of even the most malignant book could scarcely be discernible, and would be little detrimental, if it were.

Nothing, at any rate, could be farther from Schiller's intention than such a consummation. In his preface, he speaks of the moral effects of the *Robbers* in terms which do honour to his heart, while they show the inexperience of his head. Ridicule, he signifies, has long been tried against the wickedness of the times, whole cargoes of hellebore have been expended,—in vain; and now, he thinks, recourse must be had to more pungent medicines. We may smile at the simplicity of this idea; and safely conclude that, like other specifics, the present one would fail to produce a perceptible effect: but Schiller's vindication rests on higher grounds than these. His work has on the whole furnished nourishment to the more exalted powers of our nature; the sentiments and images which he has shaped and uttered, tend, in spite of their alloy, to elevate the soul to a nobler pitch: and this is a sufficient defence. As to the danger of misapplying the inspiration he communicates, of forgetting the dictates of prudence in our zeal for the dictates of poetry, we have no great cause to fear it. Hitherto, at least, there has always been enough of dull reality, on every side of us, to abate such fervours in good time, and bring us back to the most sober level of prose, if not to sink us below it. We should thank the poet who performs such a service; and forbear to inquire too rigidly whether there is any 'moral' in his piece or not. The writer of a work, which interests and excites the spiritual feelings of men, has as little need to justify himself by showing how it exemplifies some wise saw or modern instance, as the doer of a generous action has to demonstrate its merit, by deducing it from the system of Shaftesbury, or Smith, or Paley, or whichever happens to be the favourite system for the age and place. The instructiveness of the one, and the virtue of the other, exist independently of all systems or saws, and in spite of all.

But the tragedy of the *Robbers* produced some inconveniences of a kind much more sensible than these its theoretical mischiefs. We have called it the signal of Schiller's deliverance from school tyranny and military constraint; but its operation in this respect was not immediate; at first it seemed to involve him more deeply and dangerously than before. He had finished the original sketch of it in 1778; but for fear of offence, he kept it secret till his medical studies were completed.[6] These, in the mean time, he had pursued with sufficient assiduity to merit

[6] On this subject Doering gives an anecdote, which may perhaps be worth translating. 'One of Schiller's teachers surprised him on one occasion reciting a scene from the *Robbers*, before some of his intimate companions. At the words, which Franz von Moor addresses to Moser: *Ha, what! thou knowest none greater? Think again! Death, heaven, eternity, damnation, hovers in the sound of thy voice! Not one greater?*—the door opened, and the master saw Schil-

the usual honours;[7] in 1780, he had, in consequence, obtained the post of surgeon to the regiment *Augé*, in the Würtemberg army. This advancement enabled him to complete his project, to print the *Robbers* at his own expense, not being able to find any bookseller that would undertake it. The nature of the work, and the universal interest it awakened, drew attention to the private circumstances of the author, whom the *Robbers*, as well as other pieces of his writing, that had found their way into the periodical publications of the time, sufficiently showed to be no common man. Many grave persons were offended at the vehement sentiments expressed in the *Robbers*; and the unquestioned ability with which these extravagances were expressed, but made the matter worse. To Schiller's superiors, above all, such things were inconceivable: he might perhaps be a very great genius, but was certainly a dangerous servant for his Highness the Grand Duke of Würtemberg. Officious people mingled themselves in the affair: nay, the graziers of the Alps were brought to bear upon it. The Grisons magistrates, it appeared, had seen the book: and were mortally huffed at being there spoken of, according to a Swabian adage, as *common highwaymen*.[8] They complained in the *Hamburg Correspondent*; and a sort of Jackal, at Ludwigsburg, one Walter, whose name deserves to be thus kept in mind, volunteered to plead their cause before the Grand Duke.

Informed of all these circumstances, the Grand Duke expressed his disapprobation of Schiller's poetical labours in the most unequivocal terms. Schiller was at length summoned to appear before him; and it then turned out, that his Highness was not only dissatisfied with the moral or political errors of the work, but scandalised moreover at its want of literary merit. In this latter respect, he was kind enough to proffer his own services. But Schiller seems to have received the proposal with no sufficient gratitude; and the interview passed without advantage to either party. It terminated in the Duke's commanding Schiller to abide by medical subjects: or at least to beware of writing any more poetry, without submitting it to *his* inspection.

We need not comment on this portion of the Grand Duke's history: his treatment of Schiller has already been sufficiently avenged. By the great body of man-

ler stamping in desperation up and down the room. "For shame," said he, "for shame to get into such a passion, and curse so!" The other scholars tittered covertly at the worthy inspector; and Schiller called after him with a bitter smile, "A noodle" (ein confiscirter Kerl)!'

[7] His Latin Essay on the *Philosophy of Physiology* was written in 1778, and never printed. His concluding *thesis* was published according to custom: the subject is arduous enough, "the connection between the animal and spiritual nature of man," — which Dr. Cabanis has since treated in so offensive a fashion. Schiller's tract we have never seen. Doering says it was long 'out of print,' till Nasse reproduced it in his Medical Journal (Leipzig, 1820): he is silent respecting its merits.

[8] The obnoxious passage has been carefully expunged from subsequent editions. It was in the third scene of the second act; Spiegelberg discoursing with Razmann, observes, "An honest man you may form of windle-straws; but to make a rascal you must have grist: besides, there is a national genius in it, a certain rascal-climate, so to speak." In the first edition, there was added: "*Go to the Grisons, for instance: that is what I call the thief's Athens.*" The patriot who stood forth on this occasion for the honour of the Grisons, to deny this weighty charge, and denounce the crime of making it, was not Dogberry or Verges, but 'one of the noble family of Salis.'

kind, his name will be recollected, chiefly, if at all, for the sake of the unfriended youth whom he now schooled so sharply, and afterwards afflicted so cruelly: it will be recollected also with the angry triumph which we feel against a shallow and despotic 'noble of convention,' who strains himself to oppress 'one of nature's nobility,' submitted by blind chance to his dominion, and—finds that he cannot! All this is far more than the Prince of Würtemberg deserves. Of limited faculties, and educated in the French principles of taste, then common to persons of his rank in Germany, he had perused the *Robbers* with unfeigned disgust; he could see in the author only a misguided enthusiast, with talents barely enough to make him dangerous. And though he never fully or formally retracted this injustice, he did not follow it up; when Schiller became known to the world at large, the Duke ceased to persecute him. The father he still kept in his service, and nowise molested.

In the mean time, however, various mortifications awaited Schiller. It was in vain that he discharged the humble duties of his station with the most strict fidelity, and even, it is said, with superior skill: he was a suspected person, and his most innocent actions were misconstrued, his slightest faults were visited with the full measure of official severity. His busy imagination aggravated the evil. He had seen poor Schubart[9] wearing out his tedious eight years of durance in the fortress of Asperg, because he had been 'a rock of offence to the powers that were.' The fate of this unfortunate author appeared to Schiller a type of his own. His free spirit shrank at the prospect of wasting its strength in strife against the pitiful constraints, the minute and endless persecutions of men who knew him not, yet had his fortune in their hands; the idea of dungeons and jailors haunted and tortured his mind; and the means of escaping them, the renunciation of poetry, the source of all his joy, if likewise of many woes, the radiant guiding-star of his turbid and obscure existence, seemed a sentence of death to all that was dignified, and delightful, and worth retaining, in his character. Totally ignorant of what is called the world; conscious too of the might that slumbered in his soul, and proud of it, as kings are of their sceptres; impetuous when roused, and spurning unjust restraint; yet wavering and timid from the delicacy of his nature, and still more restricted in the freedom of his movements by the circumstances of his father, whose all depended on the pleasure of the court, Schiller felt himself embarrassed, and agitated, and tormented in no common degree. Urged this way and that by the most powerful and conflicting impulses; driven to despair by the paltry shackles that chained him, yet forbidden by the most sacred considerations to break them, he knew not on what he should resolve; he reckoned himself 'the most unfortunate of men.'

Time at length gave him the solution; circumstances occurred which forced him to decide. The popularity of the *Robbers* had brought him into correspondence with several friends of literature, who wished to patronise the author, or engage him in new undertakings. Among this number was the Freiherr von Dalberg, superintendent of the theatre at Mannheim, under whose encouragement and countenance Schiller remodelled the *Robbers*, altered it in some parts, and had

---

[9] See Appendix I., No. 1.

it brought upon the stage in 1781. The correspondence with Dalberg began in literary discussions, but gradually elevated itself into the expression of more interesting sentiments. Dalberg loved and sympathised with the generous enthusiast, involved in troubles and perplexities which his inexperience was so little adequate to thread: he gave him advice and assistance; and Schiller repaid this favour with the gratitude due to his kind, his first, and then almost his only benefactor. His letters to this gentleman have been preserved, and lately published; they exhibit a lively picture of Schiller's painful situation at Stuttgard, and of his unskilful as well as eager anxiety to be delivered from it.[10] His darling project was that Dalberg should bring him to Mannheim, as theatrical poet, by permission of the Duke: at one time he even thought of turning player.

Neither of these projects could take immediate effect, and Schiller's embarrassments became more pressing than ever. With the natural feeling of a young author, he had ventured to go in secret, and witness the first representation of his tragedy, at Mannheim. His incognito did not conceal him; he was put under arrest during a week, for this offence: and as the punishment did not deter him from again transgressing in a similar manner, he learned that it was in contemplation to try more rigorous measures with him. Dark hints were given to him of some exemplary as well as imminent severity: and Dalberg's aid, the sole hope of averting it by quiet means, was distant and dubious. Schiller saw himself reduced to extremities. Beleaguered with present distresses, and the most horrible forebodings, on every side; roused to the highest pitch of indignation, yet forced to keep silence, and wear the face of patience, he could endure this maddening constraint no longer. He resolved to be free, at whatever risk; to abandon advantages which he could not buy at such a price; to quit his step-dame home, and go forth, though friendless and alone, to seek his fortune in the great market of life. Some foreign Duke or Prince was arriving at Stuttgard; and all the people were in movement, occupied with seeing the spectacle of his entrance: Schiller seized this opportunity of retiring from the city, careless whither he went, so he got beyond the reach of turnkeys, and Grand Dukes, and commanding officers. It was in the month of October 1782.

This last step forms the catastrophe of the publication of the *Robbers*: it completed the deliverance of Schiller from the grating thraldom under which his youth had been passed, and decided his destiny for life. Schiller was in his twenty-third year when he left Stuttgard. He says 'he went empty away,—empty in purse and hope.' The future was indeed sufficiently dark before him. Without patrons, connexions, or country, he had ventured forth to the warfare on his own charges; without means, experience, or settled purpose, it was greatly to be feared that the fight would go against him. Yet his situation, though gloomy enough, was not entirely without its brighter side. He was now a free man, free, however poor; and his strong soul quickened as its fetters dropped off, and gloried within him in the dim anticipation of great and far-extending enterprises. If, cast too rudely among the hardships and bitter disquietudes of the world, his past nursing had not been delicate, he was already taught to look upon privation and discomfort as

---

[10] See Appendix I., No. 2.

his daily companions. If he knew not how to bend his course among the perplexed vicissitudes of society, there was a force within him which would triumph over many difficulties; and a 'light from Heaven' was about his path, which, if it failed to conduct him to wealth and preferment, would keep him far from baseness and degrading vices. Literature, and every great and noble thing which the right pursuit of it implies, he loved with all his heart and all his soul: to this inspiring object he was henceforth exclusively devoted; advancing towards this, and possessed of common necessaries on the humblest scale, there was little else to tempt him. His life might be unhappy, but would hardly be disgraceful.

Schiller gradually felt all this, and gathered comfort, while better days began to dawn upon him. Fearful of trusting himself so near Stuttgard as at Mannheim, he had passed into Franconia, and was living painfully at Oggersheim, under the name of Schmidt: but Dalberg, who knew all his distresses, supplied him with money for immediate wants; and a generous lady made him the offer of a home. Madam von Wolzogen lived on her estate of Bauerbach, in the neighbourhood of Meinungen; she knew Schiller from his works, and his intimacy with her sons, who had been his fellow-students at Stuttgard. She invited him to her house; and there treated him with an affection which helped him to forget the past, and look cheerfully forward to the future.

Under this hospitable roof, Schiller had leisure to examine calmly the perplexed and dubious aspect of his affairs. Happily his character belonged not to the whining or sentimental sort: he was not of those, in whom the pressure of misfortune produces nothing but unprofitable pain; who spend, in cherishing and investigating and deploring their miseries, the time which should be spent in providing a relief for them. With him, strong feeling was constantly a call to vigorous action: he possessed in a high degree the faculty of conquering his afflictions, by directing his thoughts, not to maxims for enduring them, or modes of expressing them with interest, but to plans for getting rid of them; and to this disposition or habit,—too rare among men of genius, men of a much higher class than mere sentimentalists, but whose sensibility is out of proportion with their inventiveness or activity,—we are to attribute no small influence in the fortunate conduct of his subsequent life. With such a turn of mind, Schiller, now that he was at length master of his own movements, could not long be at a loss for plans or tasks. Once settled at Bauerbach, he immediately resumed his poetical employments; and forgot, in the regions of fancy, the vague uncertainties of his real condition, or saw prospects of amending it in a life of literature. By many safe and sagacious persons, the prudence of his late proceedings might be more than questioned; it was natural for many to forbode that one who left the port so rashly, and sailed with such precipitation, was likely to make shipwreck ere the voyage had extended far: but the lapse of a few months put a stop to such predictions. A year had not passed since his departure, when Schiller sent forth his *Verschwörung des Fiesco* and *Kabale und Liebe*; tragedies which testified that, dangerous and arduous as the life he had selected might be, he possessed resources more than adequate to its emergencies. *Fiesco* he had commenced during the period of his arrest at Stuttgard; it was published, with the other play, in 1783; and soon after brought upon the Mannheim theatre, with universal approbation.

It was now about three years since the composition of the *Robbers* had been finished; five since the first sketch of it had been formed. With what zeal and success Schiller had, in that interval, pursued the work of his mental culture, these two dramas are a striking proof. The first ardour of youth is still to be discerned in them; but it is now chastened by the dictates of a maturer reason, and made to animate the products of a much happier and more skilful invention. Schiller's ideas of art had expanded and grown clearer, his knowledge of life had enlarged. He exhibits more acquaintance with the fundamental principles of human nature, as well as with the circumstances under which it usually displays itself; and far higher and juster views of the manner in which its manifestations should be represented.

In the *Conspiracy of Fiesco* we have to admire not only the energetic animation which the author has infused into all his characters, but the distinctness with which he has discriminated, without aggravating them; and the vividness with which he has contrived to depict the scene where they act and move. The political and personal relations of the Genoese nobility; the luxurious splendour, the intrigues, the feuds, and jarring interests, which occupy them, are made visible before us: we understand and may appreciate the complexities of the conspiracy; we mingle, as among realities, in the pompous and imposing movements which lead to the catastrophe. The catastrophe itself is displayed with peculiar effect. The midnight silence of the sleeping city, interrupted only by the distant sounds of watchmen, by the low hoarse murmur of the sea, or the stealthy footsteps and disguised voice of Fiesco, is conveyed to our imagination by some brief but graphic touches; we seem to stand in the solitude and deep stillness of Genoa, awaiting the signal which is to burst so fearfully upon its slumber. At length the gun is fired; and the wild uproar which ensues is no less strikingly exhibited. The deeds and sounds of violence, astonishment and terror; the volleying cannon, the heavy toll of the alarm-bells, the acclamation of assembled thousands, 'the voice of Genoa speaking with Fiesco,'—all is made present to us with a force and clearness, which of itself were enough to show no ordinary power of close and comprehensive conception, no ordinary skill in arranging and expressing its results.

But it is not this felicitous delineation of circumstances and visible scenes that constitutes our principal enjoyment. The faculty of penetrating through obscurity and confusion, to seize the characteristic features of an object, abstract or material; of producing a lively description in the latter case, an accurate and keen scrutiny in the former, is the essential property of intellect, and occupies in its best form a high rank in the scale of mental gifts: but the creative faculty of the poet, and especially of the dramatic poet, is something superadded to this; it is far rarer, and occupies a rank far higher. In this particular, *Fiesco*, without approaching the limits of perfection, yet stands in an elevated range of excellence. The characters, on the whole, are imagined and portrayed with great impressiveness and vigour. Traces of old faults are indeed still to be discovered: there still seems a want of pliancy about the genius of the author; a stiffness and heaviness in his motions. His sublimity is not to be questioned; but it does not always disdain the aid of rude contrasts and

mere theatrical effect. He paints in colours deep and glowing, but without sufficient skill to blend them delicately: he amplifies nature more than purifies it; he
omits, but does not well conceal the omission. *Fiesco* has not the complete charm of
a true though embellished resemblance to reality; its attraction rather lies in a kind
of colossal magnitude, which requires it, if seen to advantage, to be viewed from
a distance. Yet the prevailing qualities of the piece do more than make us pardon
such defects. If the dramatic imitation is not always entirely successful, it is never
very distant from success; and a constant flow of powerful thought and sentiment
counteracts, or prevents us from noticing, the failure. We find evidence of great
philosophic penetration, great resources of invention, directed by a skilful study
of history and men; and everywhere a bold grandeur of feeling and imagery gives
life to what study has combined. The chief incidents have a dazzling magnificence;
the chief characters, an aspect of majesty and force which corresponds to it. Fervour of heart, capaciousness of intellect and imagination, present themselves on
all sides: the general effect is powerful and exalting.

Fiesco himself is a personage at once probable and tragically interesting. The
luxurious dissipation, in which he veils his daring projects, softens the rudeness
of that strength which it half conceals. His immeasurable pride expands itself not
only into a disdain of subjection, but also into the most lofty acts of magnanimity:
his blind confidence in fortune seems almost warranted by the resources which he
finds in his own fearlessness and imperturbable presence of mind. His ambition
participates in the nobleness of his other qualities; he is less anxious that his rivals
should yield to him in power than in generosity and greatness of character, attributes of which power is with him but the symbol and the fit employment. Ambition in Fiesco is indeed the common wish of every mind to diffuse its individual
influence, to see its own activity reflected back from the united minds of millions:
but it is the common wish acting on no common man. He does not long to rule,
that he may sway other wills, as it were, by the physical exertion of his own: he
would lead us captive by the superior grandeur of his qualities, once fairly manifested; and he aims at dominion, chiefly as it will enable him to manifest these.
'It is not the arena that he values, but what lies in that arena:' the sovereignty is
enviable, not for its adventitious splendour, not because it is the object of coarse
and universal wonder; but as it offers, in the collected force of a nation, something
which the loftiest mortal may find scope for all his powers in guiding. "Spread out
the thunder," Fiesco exclaims, "into its single tones, and it becomes a lullaby for
children: pour it forth together in *one* quick peal, and the royal sound shall move
the heavens." His affections are not less vehement than his other passions: his
heart can be melted into powerlessness and tenderness by the mild persuasions of
his Leonora; the idea of exalting this amiable being mingles largely with the other
motives to his enterprise. He is, in fact, a great, and might have been a virtuous
man; and though in the pursuit of grandeur he swerves from absolute rectitude,
we still respect his splendid qualities, and admit the force of the allurements which
have led him astray. It is but faintly that we condemn his sentiments, when, after
a night spent in struggles between a rigid and a more accommodating patriotism,
he looks out of his chamber, as the sun is rising in its calm beauty, and gilding the
waves and mountains, and all the innumerable palaces and domes and spires of

Genoa, and exclaims with rapture: "This majestic city—mine! To flame over it like the kingly Day; to brood over it with a monarch's power; all these sleepless longings, all these never satiated wishes to be drowned in that unfathomable ocean!" We admire Fiesco, we disapprove of him, and sympathise with him: he is crushed in the ponderous machinery which himself put in motion and thought to control: we lament his fate, but confess that it was not undeserved. He is a fit 'offering of individual free-will to the force of social conventions.'

Fiesco is not the only striking character in the play which bears his name. The narrow fanatical republican virtue of Verrina, the mild and venerable wisdom of the old Doria, the unbridled profligacy of his Nephew, even the cold, contented, irreclaimable perversity of the cutthroat Moor, all dwell in our recollections: but what, next to Fiesco, chiefly attracts us, is the character of Leonora his wife. Leonora is of kindred to Amelia in the *Robbers*, but involved in more complicated relations, and brought nearer to the actual condition of humanity. She is such a heroine as Schiller most delights to draw. Meek and retiring by the softness of her nature, yet glowing with an ethereal ardour for all that is illustrious and lovely, she clings about her husband, as if her being were one with his. She dreams of remote and peaceful scenes, where Fiesco should be all to her, she all to Fiesco: her idea of love is, that *'her* name should lie in secret behind every one of his thoughts, should speak to him from every object of Nature; that for him, this bright majestic universe itself were but as the shining jewel, on which her image, only *hers*, stood engraved.' Her character seems a reflection of Fiesco's, but refined from his grosser strength, and transfigured into a celestial form of purity, and tenderness, and touching grace. Jealousy cannot move her into anger; she languishes in concealed sorrow, when she thinks herself forgotten. It is affection alone that can rouse her into passion; but under the influence of this, she forgets all weakness and fear. She cannot stay in her palace, on the night when Fiesco's destiny is deciding; she rushes forth, as if inspired, to share in her husband's dangers and sublime deeds, and perishes at last in the tumult.

The death of Leonora, so brought about, and at such a time, is reckoned among the blemishes of the work: that of Fiesco, in which Schiller has ventured to depart from history, is to be more favourably judged of. Fiesco is not here accidentally drowned; but plunged into the waves by the indignant Verrina, who forgets or stifles the feelings of friendship, in his rage at political apostasy. 'The nature of the Drama,' we are justly told, 'will not suffer the operation of Chance, or of an immediate Providence. Higher spirits can discern the minute fibres of an event stretching through the whole expanse of the system of the world, and hanging, it may be, on the remotest limits of the future and the past, where man discerns nothing save the action itself, hovering unconnected in space. But the artist has to paint for the short view of man, whom he wishes to instruct; not for the piercing eye of superior powers, from whom he learns.'

In the composition of *Fiesco*, Schiller derived the main part of his original materials from history; he could increase the effect by gorgeous representations, and ideas preëxisting in the mind of his reader. Enormity of incident and strangeness of situation lent him a similar assistance in the *Robbers. Kabale und Liebe* is destitute of these advantages; it is a tragedy of domestic life; its means of interesting are comprised within itself, and rest on very simple feelings, dignified by no very singular action. The name, *Court-Intriguing and Love*, correctly designates its nature; it aims at exhibiting the conflict, the victorious conflict, of political manœuvering, of cold worldly wisdom, with the pure impassioned movements of the young heart, as yet unsullied by the tarnish of every-day life, inexperienced in its calculations, sick of its empty formalities, and indignantly determined to cast-off the mean restrictions it imposes, which bind so firmly by their number, though singly so contemptible. The idea is far from original: this is a conflict which most men have figured to themselves, which many men of ardent mind are in some degree constantly waging. To make it, in this simple form, the subject of a drama, seems to be a thought of Schiller's own; but the praise, though not the merit of his undertaking, considerable rather as performed than projected, has been lessened by a multitude of worthless or noxious imitations. The same primary conception has been tortured into a thousand shapes, and tricked out with a thousand tawdry devices and meretricious ornaments, by the Kotzebues, and other 'intellectual Jacobins,' whose productions have brought what we falsely call the 'German Theatre' into such deserved contempt in England. Some portion of the gall, due only to these inflated, flimsy, and fantastic persons, appears to have acted on certain critics in estimating this play of Schiller's. August Wilhelm Schlegel speaks slightingly of the work: he says, 'it will hardly move us by its tone of overstrained sensibility, but may well afflict us by the painful impressions which it leaves.' Our own experience has been different from that of Schlegel. In the characters of Louisa and Ferdinand Walter we discovered little overstraining; their sensibility we did not reckon very criminal; seeing it united with a clearness of judgment, chastened by a purity of heart, and controlled by a force of virtuous resolution, in full proportion with itself. We rather admired the genius of the poet, which could elevate a poor music-master's daughter to the dignity of a heroine; could represent, without wounding our sense of propriety, the affection of two noble beings, created for each other by nature, and divided by rank; we sympathised in their sentiments enough to feel a proper interest in their fate, and see in them, what the author meant we should see, two pure and lofty minds involved in the meshes of vulgar cunning, and borne to destruction by the excess of their own good qualities and the crimes of others.

Ferdinand is a nobleman, but not convinced that 'his patent of nobility is more ancient or of more authority than the primeval scheme of the universe:' he speaks and acts like a young man entertaining such persuasions: disposed to yield everything to reason and true honour, but scarcely anything to mere use and wont. His passion for Louisa is the sign and the nourishment rather than the cause of such a temper: he loves her without limit, as the only creature he has ever met with of a like mind with himself; and this feeling exalts into inspiration what was already the dictate of his nature. We accompany him on his straight and plain path; we rejoice to see him fling aside with a strong arm the artifices and allurements with which a worthless father and more worthless associates assail him at first in vain: there is something attractive in the spectacle of native integrity, fearless though inexperienced, at war with selfishness and craft; something mournful, because the victory will seldom go as we would have it.

Louisa is a meet partner for the generous Ferdinand: the poet has done justice to her character. She is timid and humble; a feeling and richly gifted soul is hid in her by the unkindness of her earthly lot; she is without counsellors except the innate holiness of her heart, and the dictates of her keen though untutored understanding; yet when the hour of trial comes, she can obey the commands of both, and draw from herself a genuine nobleness of conduct, which secondhand prudence, and wealth, and titles, would but render less touching. Her filial affection, her angelic attachment to her lover, her sublime and artless piety, are beautifully contrasted with the bleakness of her external circumstances: she appears before us like the '*one* rose of the wilderness left on its stalk,' and we grieve to see it crushed and trodden down so rudely.

The innocence, the enthusiasm, the exalted life and stern fate of Louisa and Ferdinand give a powerful charm to this tragedy: it is everywhere interspersed with pieces of fine eloquence, and scenes which move us by their dignity or pathos. We recollect few passages of a more overpowering nature than the conclusion, where Ferdinand, beguiled by the most diabolical machinations to disbelieve the virtue of his mistress, puts himself and her to death by poison. There is a gloomy and solemn might in his despair; though overwhelmed, he seems invincible: his enemies have blinded and imprisoned him in their deceptions; but only that, like Samson, he may overturn his prison-house, and bury himself, and all that have wronged him, in its ruins.

The other characters of the play, though in general properly sustained, are not sufficiently remarkable to claim much of our attention. Wurm, the chief counsellor and agent of the unprincipled, calculating Father, is wicked enough; but there is no great singularity in his wickedness. He is little more than the dry, cool, and now somewhat vulgar miscreant, the villanous Attorney of modern novels. Kalb also is but a worthless subject, and what is worse, but indifferently handled. He is meant for the feather-brained thing of tags and laces, which frequently inhabits courts; but he wants the grace and agility proper to the species; he is less a fool than a blockhead, less perverted than totally inane. Schiller's strength lay not in comedy, but in something far higher. The great merit of the present work consists in the characters of the hero and heroine; and in this respect it ranks at the very head of its class. As a tragedy of common life, we know of few rivals to it, certainly of no superior.

The production of three such pieces as the *Robbers*, *Fiesco*, and *Kabale und Liebe*, already announced to the world that another great and original mind had appeared, from whose maturity, when such was the promise of its youth, the highest expectations might be formed. These three plays stand related to each other in regard to their nature and form, as well as date: they exhibit the progressive state of Schiller's education; show us the fiery enthusiasm of youth, exasperated into wildness, astonishing in its movements rather than sublime; and the same enthusiasm gradually yielding to the sway of reason, gradually using itself to the constraints prescribed by sound judgment and more extensive knowledge. Of the three, the *Robbers* is doubtless the most singular, and likely perhaps to be the most widely popular: but the latter two are of more real worth in the eye of taste, and will better bear a careful and rigorous study.

With the appearance of *Fiesco* and its companion, the first period of Schiller's literary history may conclude. The stormy confusions of his youth were now subsiding; after all his aberrations, repulses, and perplexed wanderings, he was at length about to reach his true destination, and times of more serenity began to open for him. Two such tragedies as he had lately offered to the world made it easier for his friend Dalberg to second his pretensions. Schiller was at last gratified by the fulfilment of his favourite scheme; in September 1783, he went to Mannheim, as poet to the theatre, a post of respectability and reasonable profit, to the duties of which he forthwith addressed himself with all his heart. He was not long afterwards elected a member of the German Society established for literary objects in Mannheim; and he valued the honour, not only as a testimony of respect from a highly estimable quarter, but also as a means of uniting him more closely with men of kindred pursuits and tempers: and what was more than all, of quieting forever his apprehensions from the government at Stuttgard. Since his arrival at Mannheim, one or two suspicious incidents had again alarmed him on this head; but being now acknowledged as a subject of the Elector Palatine, naturalised by law in his new country, he had nothing more to fear from the Duke of Würtemberg.

Satisfied with his moderate income, safe, free, and surrounded by friends that loved and honoured him, Schiller now looked confidently forward to what all his efforts had been a search and hitherto a fruitless search for, an undisturbed life of intellectual labour. What effect this happy aspect of his circumstances must have produced upon him may be easily conjectured. Through many years he had been inured to agitation and distress; now peace and liberty and hope, sweet in themselves, were sweeter for their novelty. For the first time in his life, he saw himself allowed to obey without reluctance the ruling bias of his nature; for the first time inclination and duty went hand in hand. His activity awoke with renovated force in this favourable scene; long-thwarted, half-forgotten projects again kindled into brightness, as the possibility of their accomplishment became apparent: Schiller glowed with a generous pride when he felt his faculties at his own disposal, and thought of the use he meant to make of them. 'All my connexions,' he said, 'are now dissolved. The public is now all to me, my study, my sovereign, my confidant. To the public alone I henceforth belong; before this and no other tribunal will I place myself; this alone do I reverence and fear. Something majestic hovers before me, as I determine now to wear no other fetters but the sentence of the world, to appeal to no other throne but the soul of man.'

These expressions are extracted from the preface to his *Thalia*, a periodical work which he undertook in 1784, devoted to subjects connected with poetry, and chiefly with the drama. In such sentiments we leave him, commencing the arduous and perilous, but also glorious and sublime duties of a life consecrated to the discovery of truth, and the creation of intellectual beauty. He was now exclusively what is called a *Man of Letters,* for the rest of his days.

PART II.

FROM SCHILLER'S SETTLEMENT AT MANNHEIM TO HIS SETTLEMENT AT JENA.
(1783-1790.)

IF to know wisdom were to practise it; if fame brought true dignity and peace of mind; or happiness consisted in nourishing the intellect with its appropriate food and surrounding the imagination with ideal beauty, a literary life would be the most enviable which the lot of this world affords. But the truth is far otherwise. The Man of Letters has no immutable, all-conquering volition, more than other men; to understand and to perform are two very different things with him as with every one. His fame rarely exerts a favourable influence on his dignity of character, and never on his peace of mind: its glitter is external, for the eyes of others; within, it is but the aliment of unrest, the oil cast upon the ever-gnawing fire of ambition, quickening into fresh vehemence the blaze which it stills for a moment. Moreover, this Man of Letters is not wholly made of spirit, but of clay and spirit mixed: his thinking faculties may be nobly trained and exercised, but he must have affections as well as thoughts to make him happy, and food and raiment must be given him or he dies. Far from being the most enviable, his way of life is perhaps, among the many modes by which an ardent mind endeavours to express its activity, the most thickly beset with suffering and degradation. Look at the biography of authors! Except the Newgate Calendar, it is the most sickening chapter in the history of man. The calamities of these people are a fertile topic; and too often their faults and vices have kept pace with their calamities. Nor is it difficult to see how this has happened. Talent of any sort is generally accompanied with a peculiar fineness of sensibility; of genius this is the most essential constituent; and life in any shape has sorrows enough for hearts so formed. The employments of literature sharpen this natural tendency; the vexations that accompany them frequently exasperate it into morbid soreness. The cares and toils of literature are the business of life; its delights are too ethereal and too transient to furnish that perennial flow of satisfaction, coarse but plenteous and substantial, of which happiness in this world of ours is made. The most finished efforts of the mind give it little pleasure, frequently they give it pain; for men's aims are ever far beyond their strength. And the outward recompense of these undertakings, the distinction they confer, is of still smaller value: the desire for it is insatiable even when successful; and when baffled, it issues in jealousy and envy, and every pitiful and painful feeling. So keen a temperament with so little to restrain or satisfy, so much to distress or tempt it, produces contradictions which few are adequate to reconcile. Hence the unhappiness of literary men, hence their faults and follies.

Thus literature is apt to form a dangerous and discontenting occupation even for the amateur. But for him whose rank and worldly comforts depend on it, who does not live to write, but writes to live, its difficulties and perils are fearfully increased. Few spectacles are more afflicting than that of such a man, so gifted and so fated, so jostled and tossed to and fro in the rude bustle of life, the buffetings of which he is so little fitted to endure. Cherishing, it may be, the loftiest thoughts, and clogged with the meanest wants; of pure and holy purposes, yet ever driven from the straight path by the pressure of necessity, or the impulse of passion; thirsting for glory, and frequently in want of daily bread; hovering between the empyrean of his fancy and the squalid desert of reality; cramped and foiled in his most strenuous exertions; dissatisfied with his best performances, disgusted with his fortune, this Man of Letters too often spends his weary days in conflicts with obscure misery: harassed, chagrined, debased, or maddened; the victim at once of tragedy and farce; the last forlorn outpost in the war of Mind against Matter. Many are the noble souls that have perished bitterly, with their tasks unfinished, under these corroding woes! Some in utter famine, like Otway; some in dark insanity, like Cowper and Collins; some, like Chatterton, have sought out a more stern quietus, and turning their indignant steps away from a world which refused them welcome, have taken refuge in that strong Fortress, where poverty and cold neglect, and the thousand natural shocks which flesh is heir to, could not reach them any more.

Yet among these men are to be found the brightest specimens and the chief benefactors of mankind! It is they that keep awake the finer parts of our souls; that give us better aims than power or pleasure, and withstand the total sovereignty of Mammon in this earth. They are the vanguard in the march of mind; the intellectual Backwoodsmen, reclaiming from the idle wilderness new territories for the thought and the activity of their happier brethren. Pity that from all their conquests, so rich in benefit to others, themselves should reap so little! But it is vain to murmur. They are volunteers in this cause; they weighed the charms of it against the perils: and they must abide the results of their decision, as all must. The hardships of the course they follow are formidable, but not all inevitable; and to such as pursue it rightly, it is not without its great rewards. If an author's life is more agitated and more painful than that of others, it may also be made more spirit-stirring and exalted: fortune may render him unhappy; it is only himself that can make him despicable. The history of genius has, in fact, its bright side as well as its dark. And if it is distressing to survey the misery, and what is worse, the debasement of so many gifted men, it is doubly cheering on the other hand to reflect on the few, who, amid the temptations and sorrows to which life in all its provinces and most in theirs is liable, have travelled through it in calm and virtuous majesty, and are now hallowed in our memories, not less for their conduct than their writings. Such men are the flower of this lower world: to such alone can the epithet of great be applied with its true emphasis. There is a congruity in their proceedings which one loves to contemplate: 'he who would write heroic poems, should make his whole life a heroic poem.'

So thought our Milton; and, what was more difficult, he acted so. To Milton, the moral king of authors, a heroic multitude, out of many ages and countries, might be joined; a 'cloud of witnesses,' that encompass the true literary man throughout his pilgrimage, inspiring him to lofty emulation, cheering his solitary thoughts with hope, teaching him to struggle, to endure, to conquer difficulties, or, in failure and heavy sufferings, to

> 'arm th' obdured breast
> With stubborn patience as with triple steel.'

To this august series, in his own degree, the name of Schiller may be added.

Schiller lived in more peaceful times than Milton; his history is less distinguished by obstacles surmounted, or sacrifices made to principle; yet he had his share of trials to encounter; and the admirers of his writings need not feel ashamed of the way in which he bore it. One virtue, the parent of many others, and the most essential of any, in his circumstances, he possessed in a supreme degree; he was devoted with entire and unchanging ardour to the cause he had embarked in. The extent of his natural endowments might have served, with a less eager character, as an excuse for long periods of indolence, broken only by fits of casual exertion: with him it was but a new incitement to improve and develop them. The Ideal Man that lay within him, the image of himself as he *should* be, was formed upon a strict and curious standard; and to reach this constantly approached and constantly receding emblem of perfection, was the unwearied effort of his life. This crowning principle of conduct, never ceasing to inspire his energetic mind, introduced a consistency into his actions, a firm coherence into his character, which the changeful condition of his history rendered of peculiar importance. His resources, his place of residence, his associates, his worldly prospects, might vary as they pleased; this purpose did not vary; it was ever present with him to nerve every better faculty of his head and heart, to invest the chequered vicissitudes of his fortune with a dignity derived from himself. The zeal of his nature overcame the temptations to that loitering and indecision, that fluctuation between sloth and consuming toil, that infirmity of resolution, with all its tormenting and enfeebling consequences, to which a literary man, working as he does at a solitary task, uncalled for by any pressing tangible demand, and to be recompensed by distant and dubious advantage, is especially exposed. Unity of aim, aided by ordinary vigour of character, will generally insure perseverance; a quality not ranked among the cardinal virtues, but as essential as any of them to the proper conduct of life. Nine-tenths of the miseries and vices of mankind proceed from idleness: with men of quick minds, to whom it is especially pernicious, this habit is commonly the fruit of many disappointments and schemes oft baffled; and men fail in their schemes not so much from the want of strength as from the ill-direction of it. The weakest living creature, by concentrating his powers on a single object, can accomplish something: the strongest, by dispersing his over many, may fail to accomplish anything. The drop, by continual falling, bores its passage through the hardest rock; the hasty torrent rushes over it with hideous uproar, and leaves no trace behind. Few men have applied more steadfastly to the business of their life, or been more resolutely diligent than Schiller.

The profession of theatrical poet was, in his present circumstances, particu-

larly favourable to the maintenance of this wholesome state of mind. In the fulfilment of its duties, while he gratified his own dearest predilections, he was likewise
warmly seconded by the prevailing taste of the public. The interest excited by the
stage, and the importance attached to everything connected with it, are greater in
Germany than in any other part of Europe, not excepting France, or even Paris.
Nor, as in Paris, is the stage in German towns considered merely as a mental recreation, an elegant and pleasant mode of filling up the vacancy of tedious evenings:
in Germany, it has the advantage of being comparatively new; and its exhibitions
are directed to a class of minds attuned to a far higher pitch of feeling. The Germans are accused of a proneness to amplify and systematise, to admire with excess, and to find, in whatever calls forth their applause, an epitome of a thousand
excellencies, which no one else can discover in it. Their discussions on the theatre
do certainly give colour to this charge. Nothing, at least to an English reader, can
appear more disproportionate than the influence they impute to the stage, and the
quantity of anxious investigation they devote to its concerns.

With us, the question about the moral tendency of theatrical amusements is
now very generally consigned to the meditation of debating clubs, and speculative
societies of young men under age; with our neighbours it is a weighty subject of
inquiry for minds of almost the highest order. With us, the stage is considered
as a harmless pastime, wholesome because it occupies the man by occupying his
mental, not his sensual faculties; one of the many departments of fictitious representation; perhaps the most exciting, but also the most transitory; sometimes
hurtful, generally beneficial, just as the rest are; entitled to no peculiar regard,
and far inferior in its effect to many others which have no special apparatus for
their application. The Germans, on the contrary, talk of it as of some new organ
for refining the hearts and minds of men; a sort of lay pulpit, the worthy ally of
the sacred one, and perhaps even better fitted to exalt some of our nobler feelings;
because its objects are much more varied, and because it speaks to us through
many avenues, addressing the eye by its pomp and decorations, the ear by its har-
monies, and the heart and imagination by its poetical embellishments, and heroic
acts and sentiments. Influences still more mysterious are hinted at, if not directly
announced. An idea seems to lurk obscurely at the bottom of certain of their abstruse and elaborate speculations, as if the stage were destined to replace some
of those sublime illusions which the progress of reason is fast driving from the
earth; as if its pageantry, and allegories, and figurative shadowing-forth of things,
might supply men's nature with much of that quickening nourishment which we
once derived from the superstitions and mythologies of darker ages. Viewing the
matter in this light, they proceed in the management of it with all due earnestness.
Hence their minute and painful investigations of the origin of dramatic emotion,
of its various kinds and degrees; their subdivisions of romantic and heroic and ro-
mantico-heroic, and the other endless jargon that encumbers their critical writings.
The zeal of the people corresponds with that of their instructors. The want of more
important public interests naturally contributes still farther to the prominence of
this, the discussion of which is not forbidden, or sure to be without effect. Literature attracts nearly all the powerful thought that circulates in Germany; and the
theatre is the great nucleus of German literature.

It was to be expected that Schiller would participate in a feeling so universal, and so accordant with his own wishes and prospects. The theatre of Mannheim was at that period one of the best in Germany; he felt proud of the share which he had in conducting it, and exerted himself with his usual alacrity in promoting its various objects. Connected with the duties of his office, was the more personal duty of improving his own faculties, and extending his knowledge of the art which he had engaged to cultivate. He read much, and studied more. The perusal of Corneille, Racine, Voltaire, and the other French classics, could not be without advantage to one whose exuberance of power, and defect of taste, were the only faults he had ever been reproached with; and the sounder ideas thus acquired, he was constantly busy in exemplifying by attempts of his own. His projected translations from Shakspeare and the French were postponed for the present: indeed, except in the instance of *Macbeth*, they were never finished: his *Conradin von Schwaben*, and a second part of the *Robbers*, were likewise abandoned: but a number of minor undertakings sufficiently evinced his diligence: and *Don Carlos*, which he had now seriously commenced, was occupying all his poetical faculties.

Another matter he had much at heart was the setting forth of a periodical work, devoted to the concerns of the stage. In this enterprise, Schiller had expected the patronage and coöperation of the German Society, of which he was a member. It did not strike him that any other motive than a genuine love of art, and zeal for its advancement, could have induced men to join such a body. But the zeal of the German Society was more according to knowledge than that of their new associate: they listened with approving ear to his vivid representations, and wide-spreading projects, but declined taking any part in the execution of them. Dalberg alone seemed willing to support him. Mortified, but not disheartened by their coldness, Schiller reckoned up his means of succeeding without them. The plan of his work was contracted within narrower limits; he determined to commence it on his own resources. After much delay, the first number of the *Rheinische Thalia*, enriched by three acts of *Don Carlos*, appeared in 1785. It was continued, with one short interruption, till 1794. The main purpose of the work being the furtherance of dramatic art, and the extension and improvement of the public taste for such entertainments, its chief contents are easy to be guessed at; theatrical criticisms, essays on the nature of the stage, its history in various countries, its moral and intellectual effects, and the best methods of producing them. A part of the publication was open to poetry and miscellaneous discussion.

Meditating so many subjects so assiduously, Schiller knew not what it was to be unemployed. Yet the task of composing dramatic varieties, of training players, and deliberating in the theatrical senate, or even of expressing philosophically his opinions on these points, could not wholly occupy such a mind as his. There were times when, notwithstanding his own prior habits, and all the vaunting of dramaturgists, he felt that their scenic glories were but an empty show, a lying refuge, where there was no abiding rest for the soul. His eager spirit turned away from their paltry world of pasteboard, to dwell among the deep and serious interests of the living world of men. The *Thalia*, besides its dramatic speculations and performances, contains several of his poems, which indicate that his attention, though officially directed elsewhither, was alive to all the common concerns of humanity; that he looked on life not more as a writer than as a man. The *Laura*, whom he celebrates, was not a vision of the mind; but a living fair one, whom he saw daily, and loved in the secrecy of his heart. His *Gruppe aus dem Tartarus* (Group from Tartarus), his *Kindesmörderinn* (Infanticide), are products of a mind brooding over dark and mysterious things. While improving in the art of poetry, in the capability of uttering his thoughts in the form best adapted to express them, he was likewise improving in the more valuable art of thought itself; and applying it not only to the business of the imagination, but also to those profound and solemn inquiries, which every reasonable mortal is called to engage with.

In particular, the *Philosophische Briefe*, written about this period, exhibits Schiller in a new, and to us more interesting point of view. Julius and Raphael are the emblems of his own fears and his own hopes; their *Philosophic Letters* unfold to us many a gloomy conflict that had passed in the secret chambers of their author's soul. Sceptical doubts on the most important of all subjects were natural to such an understanding as Schiller's; but his heart was not of a temper to rest satisfied with doubts; or to draw a sorry compensation for them from the pride of superior acuteness, or the vulgar pleasure of producing an effect on others by assailing their dearest and holiest persuasions. With him the question about the essence of our being was not a subject for shallow speculation, charitably named scientific; still less for vain jangling and polemical victories: it was a fearful mystery, which it concerned all the deepest sympathies and most sublime anticipations of his mind to have explained. It is no idle curiosity, but the shuddering voice of nature that asks: 'If our happiness depend on the harmonious play of the sensorium; if our conviction may waver with the beating of the pulse?' What Schiller's ultimate opinions on these points were, we are nowhere specially informed. That his heart was orthodox, that the whole universe was for him a temple, in which he offered up the continual sacrifice of devout adoration, his works and life bear noble testimony; yet, here and there, his fairest visions seem as if suddenly sicklied over with a pale cast of doubt; a withering shadow seems to flit across his soul, and chill it in his loftiest moods. The dark condition of the man who longs to believe and longs in vain, he can represent with a verisimilitude and touching beauty, which shows it to have been familiar to himself. Apart from their ingenuity, there is a certain severe pathos in some of these passages, which affects us with a peculiar emotion. The hero of another work is made to express himself in these terms:

'What went before and what will follow me, I regard as two black impenetrable curtains, which hang down at the two extremities of human life, and which no living man has yet drawn aside. Many hundreds of generations have already stood before them with their torches, guessing anxiously what lies behind. On the curtain of Futurity, many see their own shadows, the forms of their passions enlarged and put in motion; they shrink in terror at this image of themselves. Poets, philosophers, and founders of states, have painted this curtain with their dreams, more smiling or more dark, as the sky above them was cheerful or gloomy; and their pictures deceive the eye when viewed from a distance. Many jugglers too make profit of this our universal curiosity: by their strange mummeries, they have set the outstretched fancy in amazement. A deep silence reigns behind this curtain; no one once within it will answer those he has left without; all you can hear is a hollow echo of your question, as if you shouted into a chasm. To the other side of this curtain we are all bound: men grasp hold of it as they pass, trembling, uncertain who may stand within it to receive them, *quid sit id quod tantum morituri vident.* Some unbelieving people there have been, who have asserted that this curtain did but make a mockery of men, and that nothing could be seen because nothing *was* behind it: but to convince these people, the rest have seized them, and hastily pushed them in.'[11]

The *Philosophic Letters* paint the struggles of an ardent, enthusiastic, inquisitive spirit to deliver itself from the harassing uncertainties, to penetrate the dread obscurity, which overhangs the lot of man. The first faint scruples of the Doubter are settled by the maxim: 'Believe nothing but thy own reason; there is nothing holier than truth.' But Reason, employed in such an inquiry, can do but half the work: she is like the Conjuror that has pronounced the spell of invocation, but has forgot the counter-word; spectres and shadowy forms come crowding at his summons; in endless multitudes they press and hover round his magic circle, and the terror-struck Black-artist cannot lay them. Julius finds that on rejecting the primary dictates of feeling, the system of dogmatical belief, he is driven to the system of materialism. Recoiling in horror from this dead and cheerless creed, he toils and wanders in the labyrinths of pantheism, seeking comfort and rest, but finding none; till, baffled and tired, and sick at heart, he seems inclined, as far as we can judge, to renounce the dreary problem altogether, to shut the eyes of his too keen understanding, and take refuge under the shade of Revelation. The anxieties and errors of Julius are described in glowing terms; his intellectual subtleties are mingled with the eloquence of intense feeling. The answers of his friend are in a similar style; intended not more to convince than to persuade. The whole work is full of passion as well as acuteness; the impress of a philosophic and poetic mind striving with all its vast energies to make its poetry and its philosophy agree. Considered as exhibiting the state of Schiller's thoughts at this period, it possesses a peculiar interest. In other respects there is little in it to allure us. It is short and incomplete; there is little originality in the opinions it expresses, and none in the form of its composition. As an argument on either side, it is too rhetorical to be of much weight; it abandons the inquiry when its difficulties and its value are becoming greatest, and breaks off abruptly without arriving at any conclusion. Schiller has surveyed the dark Serbonian bog of Infidelity: but he has, made no causeway through it: the *Philosophic Letters* are a fragment.

Amid employments so varied, with health, and freedom from the coarser hardships of life, Schiller's feelings might be earnest, but could scarcely be unhappy. His mild and amiable manners, united to such goodness of heart, and such height of accomplishment, endeared him to all classes of society in Mannheim; Dalberg was still his warm friend; Schwann and Laura he conversed with daily. His genius was fast enlarging its empire, and fast acquiring more complete command of it; he was loved and admired, rich in the enjoyment of present activity and fame,

---

[11] *Der Geisterseher*, Schillers Werke, B. iv. p 350.

and richer in the hope of what was coming. Yet in proportion as his faculties and his prospects expanded, he began to view his actual situation with less and less contentment. For a season after his arrival, it was natural that Mannheim should appear to him as land does to the shipwrecked mariner, full of gladness and beauty, merely because it is land. It was equally natural that, after a time, this sentiment should abate and pass away; that his place of refuge should appear but as other places, only with its difficulties and discomforts aggravated by their nearness. His revenue was inconsiderable here, and dependent upon accidents for its continuance; a share in directing the concerns of a provincial theatre, a task not without its irritations, was little adequate to satisfy the wishes of a mind like his. Schiller longed for a wider sphere of action; the world was all before him; he lamented that he should still be lingering on the mere outskirts of its business; that he should waste so much time and effort in contending with the irascible vanity of players, or watching the ebbs and flows of public taste; in resisting small grievances, and realising a small result. He determined upon leaving Mannheim. If destitute of other holds, his prudence might still have taught him to smother this unrest, the never-failing inmate of every human breast, and patiently continue where he was: but various resources remained to him, and various hopes invited him from other quarters. The produce of his works, or even the exercise of his profession, would insure him a competence anywhere; the former had already gained him distinction and goodwill in every part of Germany. The first number of his *Thalia* had arrived at the court of Hessen-Darmstadt while the Duke of Sachsen-Weimar happened to be there: the perusal of the first acts of *Don Carlos* had introduced the author to that enlightened prince, who expressed his satisfaction and respect by transmitting him the title of Counsellor. A less splendid but not less truthful or pleasing testimonial had lately reached him from Leipzig.

'Some days ago,' he writes, 'I met with a very flattering and agreeable surprise. There came to me, out of Leipzig, from unknown hands, four parcels, and as many letters, written with the highest enthusiasm towards me, and overflowing with poetical devotion. They were accompanied by four miniature portraits, two of which are of very beautiful young ladies, and by a pocket-book sewed in the finest taste. Such a present, from people who can have no interest in it, but to let me know that they wish me well, and thank me for some cheerful hours, I prize extremely; the loudest applause of the world could scarcely have flattered me so agreeably.'

Perhaps this incident, trifling as it was, might not be without effect in deciding the choice of his future residence. Leipzig had the more substantial charm of being a centre of activity and commerce of all sorts, that of literature not excepted; and it contained some more effectual friends of Schiller than these his unseen admirers. He resolved on going thither. His wishes and intentions are minutely detailed to Huber, his chief intimate at Leipzig, in a letter written shortly before his removal. We translate it for the hints it gives us of Schiller's tastes and habits at that period of his history.

'This, then, is probably the last letter I shall write to you from Mannheim. The time from the fifteenth of March has hung upon my hands, like a trial for life; and, thank Heaven! I am now ten whole days nearer you. And now, my good friend, as you have already consented to take my entire confidence upon your shoulders, allow me the pleasure of leading you into the interior of my domestic wishes.

'In my new establishment at Leipzig, I purpose to avoid one error, which has plagued me a great deal here in Mannheim. It is this: No longer to conduct my own housekeeping, and also no longer to live alone. The former is not by any means a business I excel in. It costs me less to execute a whole conspiracy, in five acts, than to settle my domestic arrangements for a week; and poetry, you yourself know, is but a dangerous assistant in calculations of economy. My mind is drawn different ways; I fall headlong out of my ideal world, if a holed stocking remind me of the real world.

'As to the other point, I require for my private happiness to have a true warm friend that would be ever at my hand, like my better angel; to whom I could communicate my nascent ideas in the very act of conceiving them, not needing to transmit them, as at present, by letters or long visits. Nay, when this friend of mine lives beyond the four corners of my house, the trifling circumstance, that in order to reach him I must cross the street, dress myself, and so forth, will of itself destroy the enjoyment of the moment, and the train of my thoughts is torn in pieces before I see him.

'Observe you, my good fellow, these are petty matters; but petty matters often bear the weightiest result in the management of life. I know myself better than perhaps a thousand mothers' sons know themselves; I understand how much, and frequently how little, I require to be completely happy. The question therefore is: Can I get this wish of my heart fulfilled in Leipzig?

'If it were possible that I could make a lodgment with you, all my cares on that head would be removed. I am no bad neighbour, as perhaps you imagine; I have pliancy enough to suit myself to another, and here and there withal a certain knack, as Yorick says, at helping to make him merrier and better. Failing this, if you could find me any person that would undertake my small economy, everything would still be well.

'I want nothing but a bedroom, which might also be my working room; and another chamber for receiving visits. The house-gear necessary for me are a good chest of drawers, a desk, a bed and sofa, a table, and a few chairs. With these conveniences, my accommodation were sufficiently provided for.

'I cannot live on the ground-floor, nor close by the ridge-tile; also my windows positively must not look into the churchyard. I love men, and therefore like their bustle. If I cannot so arrange it that we (meaning the *quintuple alliance*[12]) shall mess together, I would engage at the *table d'hôte* of the inn; for I had rather fast than eat without company, large, or else particularly good.

'I write all this to you, my dearest friend, to forewarn you of my silly tastes; and, at all events, that I may put it in your power to take some preparatory steps, in one place or another, for my settlement. My demands are, in truth, confoundedly naïve, but your goodness has spoiled me.

[12] Who the other three were is nowhere particularly mentioned.

'The first part of the *Thalia* must already be in your possession; the doom of *Carlos* will ere now be pronounced. Yet I will take it from you orally. Had we five not been acquainted, who knows but we might have become so on occasion of this very *Carlos*?'

Schiller went accordingly to Leipzig; though whether Huber received him, or he found his humble necessaries elsewhere, we have not learned. He arrived in the end of March 1785, after eighteen months' residence at Mannheim. The reception he met with, his amusements, occupations, and prospects are described in a letter to the Kammerrath Schwann, a bookseller at Mannheim, alluded to above. Except Dalberg, Schwann had been his earliest friend; he was now endeared to him by subsequent familiarity, not of letters and writing, but of daily intercourse; and what was more than all, by the circumstance that *Laura* was his daughter. The letter, it will be seen, was written with a weightier object than the pleasure of describing Leipzig: it is dated 24th April 1785.

'You have an indubitable right to be angry at my long silence; yet I know your goodness too well to be in doubt that you will pardon me.

'When a man, unskilled as I am in the busy world, visits Leipzig for the first time, during the Fair, it is, if not excusable, at least intelligible, that among the multitude of strange things running through his head, he should for a few days lose recollection of himself. Such, my dearest friend, has till today been nearly my case; and even now I have to steal from many avocations the pleasing moments which, in idea, I mean to spend with you at Mannheim.

'Our journey hither, of which Herr Götz will give you a circumstantial description, was the most dismal you can well imagine; Bog, Snow and Rain were the three wicked foes that by turns assailed us; and though we used an additional pair of horses all the way from Vach, yet our travelling, which should have ended on Friday, was spun-out till Sunday. It is universally maintained that the Fair has visibly suffered by the shocking state of the roads; at all events, even in my eyes, the crowd of sellers and buyers is far *beneath* the description I used to get of it in the Empire.

'In the very first week of my residence here, I made innumerable new acquaintances; among whom, Weisse, Oeser, Hiller, Zollikofer, Professor Huber, Jünger, the famous actor Reinike, a few merchants' families of the place, and some Berlin people, are the most interesting. During Fair-time, as you know well, a person cannot get the *full* enjoyment of any one; our attention to the individual is dissipated in the noisy multitude.

'My most pleasant recreation hitherto has been to visit Richter's coffee-house, where I constantly find half the *world* of Leipzig assembled, and extend my acquaintance with foreigners and natives.

'From various quarters I have had some alluring invitations to Berlin and Dresden; which it will be difficult for me to withstand. It is quite a peculiar case, my friend, to have a literary name. The few men of worth and consideration who offer you their intimacy on that score, and whose regard is really worth coveting, are too disagreeably counterweighed by the baleful swarm of creatures who keep humming round you, like so many flesh-flies; gape at you as if you were a monster, and condescend moreover, on the strength of one or two blotted sheets, to present themselves as colleagues. Many people cannot understand how a man that wrote the *Robbers* should look like another son of Adam. Close-cut hair, at the very least, and postillion's boots, and a hunter's whip, were expected.

'Many families are in the habit here of spending the summer in some of the adjacent villages, and so enjoying the pleasures of the country. I mean to pass a few months in Gohlis, which lies only a quarter of a league from Leipzig, with a very pleasant walk leading to it, through the Rosenthal. Here I purpose being very diligent, working at *Carlos* and the *Thalia*; that so, which perhaps will please you more than anything, I may gradually and silently return to my medical profession. I long impatiently for that epoch of my life, when my prospects may be settled and determined, when I may follow my darling pursuits merely for my own pleasure. At one time I studied medicine *con amore*; could I not do it now with still greater keenness?

'This, my best friend, might of itself convince you of the truth and firmness of my purpose; but what should offer you the most complete security on that point, what must banish all your doubts about my steadfastness, I have yet kept secret. *Now or never* I must speak it out. Distance alone gives me courage to express the wish of my heart. Frequently enough, when I used to have the happiness of being near you, has this confession hovered on my tongue; but my confidence always forsook me, when I tried to utter it. My best friend! Your goodness, your affection, your generosity of heart, have encouraged me in a hope which I can justify by nothing but the friendship and respect you have always shown me. My free, unconstrained access to your house afforded me the opportunity of intimate acquaintance with your amiable daughter; and the frank, kind treatment with which both you and she honoured me, tempted my heart to entertain the bold wish of becoming your son. My prospects have hitherto been dim and vague; they now begin to alter in my favour. I will strive with more continuous vigour when the goal is clear; do you decide whether I can reach it, when the dearest wish of my heart supports my zeal.

'Yet two short years and my whole fortune will be determined. I feel how *much* I ask, how boldly, and with how little right I ask it. A year is past since this thought took possession of my soul; but my esteem for you and your excellent daughter was too high to allow room for a wish, which at that time I could found on no solid basis. I made it a duty with myself to visit your house less frequently, and to dissipate such feelings by absence; but this poor artifice did not avail me.

'The Duke of Weimar was the first person to whom I disclosed myself. His anticipating goodness, and the declaration that he took an interest in my happiness, induced me to confess that this happiness depended on a union with your noble daughter; and he expressed his satisfaction at my choice. I have reason to hope that he will do more, should it come to the point of completing my happiness by this union.

'I shall add nothing farther: I know well that hundreds of others might afford your daughter a more splendid fate than I at this moment can promise her; but that any other *heart* can be more worthy of her, I venture to deny. Your decision, which I look for with impatience and fearful expectation, will determine whether I may venture to write in person to your daughter. Fare you well, forever loved by—Your—

'FRIEDRICH SCHILLER.'

Concerning this proposal, we have no farther information to communicate; except that the parties did not marry, and did not cease being friends. That Schiller obtained the permission he concludes with requesting, appears from other sources. Three years afterwards, in writing to the same person, he alludes emphatically to his eldest daughter; and what is more ominous, *apologises* for his silence to her. Schiller's situation at this period was such as to preclude the idea of present marriage; perhaps, in the prospect of it, *Laura* and he commenced corresponding; and before the wished-for change of fortune had arrived, both of them, attracted to other objects, had lost one another in the vortex of life, and ceased to regard their finding one another as desirable.

Schiller's medical project, like many which he formed, never came to any issue. In moments of anxiety, amid the fluctuations of his lot, the thought of this profession floated through his mind, as of a distant stronghold, to which, in time of need, he might retire. But literature was too intimately interwoven with his dispositions and his habits to be seriously interfered with; it was only at brief intervals that the pleasure of pursuing it exclusively seemed overbalanced by its inconveniences. He needed a more certain income than poetry could yield him; but he wished to derive it from some pursuit less alien to his darling study. Medicine he never practised after leaving Stuttgard.

In the mean time, whatever he might afterwards resolve on, he determined to complete his *Carlos*, the half of which, composed a considerable time before, had lately been running the gauntlet of criticism in the *Thalia*.[13] With this for his chief occupation, Gohlis or Leipzig for his residence, and a circle of chosen friends for his entertainment, Schiller's days went happily along. His *Lied an die Freude* (Song to Joy), one of his most spirited and beautiful lyrical productions, was composed here: it bespeaks a mind impetuous even in its gladness, and overflowing with warm and earnest emotions.

But the love of change is grounded on the difference between anticipation and reality, and dwells with man till the age when habit becomes stronger than desire, or anticipation ceases to be hope. Schiller did not find that his establishment at Leipzig, though pleasant while it lasted, would realise his ulterior views: he yielded to some of his 'alluring invitations,' and went to Dresden in the end of summer. Dresden contained many persons who admired him, more who admired his fame, and a few who loved himself. Among the latter, the Appellationsrath Körner deserves especial mention.[14] Schiller found a true friend in Körner, and made his

---

[13] Wieland's rather harsh and not too judicious sentence on it may be seen at large in Gruber's *Wieland Geschildert*, B. ii. S. 571.

[14] The well-written life, prefixed to the Stuttgard and Tübingen edition of Schiller's

house a home. He parted his time between Dresden and Löschwitz, near it, where that gentleman resided: it was here that *Don Carlos*, the printing of which was meanwhile proceeding at Leipzig, received its completion and last corrections.[15] It was published in 1786.

The story of Don Carlos seems peculiarly adapted for dramatists. The spectacle of a royal youth condemned to death by his father, of which happily our European annals furnish but another example, is among the most tragical that can be figured; the character of that youth, the intermixture of bigotry and jealousy, and love, with the other strong passions, which brought on his fate, afford a combination of circumstances, affecting in themselves, and well calculated for the basis of deeply interesting fiction. Accordingly they have not been neglected: Carlos has often been the theme of poets; particularly since the time when his history, recorded by the Abbé St. Réal, was exposed in more brilliant colours to the inspection of every writer, and almost of every reader.

The Abbé St. Réal was a dexterous artist in that half-illicit species of composition, the historic novel: in the course of his operations, he lighted on these incidents; and, by filling-up according to his fancy, what historians had only sketched to him, by amplifying, beautifying, suppressing, and arranging, he worked the whole into a striking little narrative, distinguished by all the symmetry, the sparkling graces, the vigorous description, and keen thought, which characterise his other writings. This French Sallust, as his countrymen have named him, has been <u>of use to many dramatists. His *Conjuraison contre Venise* furnished</u> Otway with the works, is by this Körner. The Theodor Körner, whose *Lyre and Sword* became afterwards famous, was his son.

[15] In vol. x. of the Vienna edition of Schiller are some ludicrous verses, almost his sole attempt in the way of drollery, bearing a title equivalent to this: 'To the Right Honourable the Board of Washers, the most humble Memorial of a downcast Tragic Poet, at Löschwitz;' of which Doering gives the following account. 'The first part of *Don Carlos* being already printed, by Göschen, in Leipzig, the poet, pressed for the remainder, felt himself obliged to stay behind from an excursion which the Körner family were making, in a fine autumn day. Unluckily, the lady of the house, thinking Schiller was to go along with them, had locked all her cupboards and the cellar. Schiller found himself without meat or drink, or even wood for fuel; still farther exasperated by the dabbling of some washer-maids beneath his window, he produced these lines.' The poem is of the kind which cannot be translated; the first three stanzas are as follows:

> "Die Wäsche klatscht vor meiner Thür,
> Es plarrt die Küchenzofe,
> Und mich, mich fuhrt das Flügelthier
> Zu König Philips Hofe.
>
> Ich eile durch die Gallerie
> Mit schnellem Schritt, belausche
> Dort die Prinzessin Eboli
> Im süssen Liebesrausche.
>
> Schon ruft das schöne Weib: Triumph!
> Schon hör' ich—Tod und Hölle!
> Was hör' ich—einen nassen Strumpf
> Geworfen in die Welle."

outline of his best tragedy; *Epicaris* has more than once appeared upon the stage; and *Don Carlos* has been dramatised in almost all the languages of Europe. Besides Otway's *Carlos* so famous at its first appearance, many tragedies on this subject have been written: most of them are gathered to their final rest; some are fast going thither; two bid fair to last for ages. Schiller and Alfieri have both drawn their plot from St. Réal; the former has expanded and added; the latter has compressed and abbreviated.

Schiller's *Carlos* is the first of his plays that bears the stamp of anything like full maturity. The opportunities he had enjoyed for extending his knowledge of men and things, the sedulous practice of the art of composition, the study of purer models, had not been without their full effect. Increase of years had done something for him; diligence had done much more. The ebullience of youth is now chastened into the steadfast energy of manhood; the wild enthusiast, that spurned at the errors of the world, has now become the enlightened moralist, that laments their necessity, or endeavours to find out their remedy. A corresponding alteration is visible in the external form of the work, in its plot and diction. The plot is contrived with great ingenuity, embodying the result of much study, both dramatic and historical. The language is blank verse, not prose, as in the former works; it is more careful and regular, less ambitious in its object, but more certain of attaining it. Schiller's mind had now reached its full stature: he felt and thought more justly; he could better express what he felt and thought.

The merit we noticed in *Fiesco*, the fidelity with which the scene of action is brought before us, is observable to a still greater degree in *Don Carlos*. The Spanish court in the end of the sixteenth century; its rigid, cold formalities; its cruel, bigoted, but proud-spirited grandees; its inquisitors and priests; and Philip, its head, the epitome at once of its good and its bad qualities, in all his complex interests, are exhibited with wonderful distinctness and address. Nor is it at the surface or the outward movements alone that we look; we are taught the mechanism of their characters, as well as shown it in action. The stony-hearted Despot himself must have been an object of peculiar study to the author. Narrow in his understanding, dead in his affections, from his birth the lord of Europe, Philip has existed all his days above men, not among them. Locked up within himself, a stranger to every generous and kindly emotion, his gloomy spirit has had no employment but to strengthen or increase its own elevation, no pleasure but to gratify its own self-will. Superstition, harmonising with these native tendencies, has added to their force, but scarcely to their hatefulness: it lends them a sort of sacredness in his own eyes, and even a sort of horrid dignity in ours. Philip is not without a certain greatness, the greatness of unlimited external power, and of a will relentless in its dictates, guided by principles, false, but consistent and unalterable. The scene of his existence is haggard, stern and desolate; but it is all his own, and he seems fitted for it. We hate him and fear him; but the poet has taken care to secure him from contempt.

The contrast both of his father's fortune and character are those of Carlos. Few situations of a more affecting kind can be imagined, than the situation of this young, generous and ill-fated prince. From boyhood his heart had been bent on mighty things; he had looked upon the royal grandeur that awaited his maturer years, only as the means of realising those projects for the good of men, which his beneficent soul was ever busied with. His father's dispositions, and the temper of the court, which admitted no development of such ideas, had given the charm of concealment to his feelings; his life had been in prospect; and we are the more attached to him, that deserving to be glorious and happy, he had but expected to be either. Bright days, however, seemed approaching; shut out from the communion of the Albas and Domingos, among whom he lived a stranger, the communion of another and far dearer object was to be granted him; Elizabeth's love seemed to make him independent even of the future, which it painted with still richer hues. But in a moment she is taken from him by the most terrible of all visitations; his bride becomes his mother; and the stroke that deprives him of her, while it ruins him forever, is more deadly, because it cannot be complained of without sacrilege, and cannot be altered by the power of Fate itself. Carlos, as the poet represents him, calls forth our tenderest sympathies. His soul seems once to have been rich and glorious, like the garden of Eden; but the desert-wind has passed over it, and smitten it with perpetual blight. Despair has overshadowed all the fair visions of his youth; or if he hopes, it is but the gleam of delirium, which something sterner than even duty extinguishes in the cold darkness of death. His energy survives but to vent itself in wild gusts of reckless passion, or aimless indignation. There is a touching poignancy in his expression of the bitter melancholy that oppresses him, in the fixedness of misery with which he looks upon the faded dreams of former years, or the fierce ebullitions and dreary pauses of resolution, which now prompts him to retrieve what he has lost, now withers into powerlessness, as nature and reason tell him that it cannot, must not be retrieved.

Elizabeth, no less moving and attractive, is also depicted with masterly skill. If she returns the passion of her amiable and once betrothed lover, we but guess at the fact; for so horrible a thought has never once been whispered to her own gentle and spotless mind. Yet her heart bleeds for Carlos; and we see that did not the most sacred feelings of humanity forbid her, there is no sacrifice she would not make to restore his peace of mind. By her soothing influence she strives to calm the agony of his spirit; by her mild winning eloquence she would persuade him that for Don Carlos other objects must remain, when his hopes of personal felicity have been cut off; she would change his love for her into love for the millions of human beings whose destiny depends on his. A meek vestal, yet with the prudence of a queen, and the courage of a matron, with every graceful and generous quality of womanhood harmoniously blended in her nature, she lives in a scene that is foreign to her; the happiness she should have had is beside her, the misery she must endure is around her; yet she utters no regret, gives way to no complaint, but seeks to draw from duty itself a compensation for the cureless evil which duty has inflicted. Many tragic queens are more imposing and majestic than this Elizabeth of Schiller; but there is none who rules over us with a sway so soft and feminine, none whom we feel so much disposed to love as well as reverence.

The virtues of Elizabeth are heightened by comparison with the principles and actions of her attendant, the Princess Eboli. The character of Eboli is full of pomp and profession; magnanimity and devotedness are on her tongue, some shadow of them even floats in her imagination; but they are not rooted in her heart; pride, selfishness, unlawful passion are the only inmates there. Her lofty boastings of generosity are soon forgotten when the success of her attachment to Carlos becomes hopeless; the fervour of a selfish love once extinguished in her bosom, she regards the object of it with none but vulgar feelings. Virtue no longer according with interest, she ceases to be virtuous; from a rejected mistress the transition to a jealous spy is with her natural and easy. Yet we do not hate the Princess: there is a seductive warmth and grace about her character, which makes us lament her vices rather than condemn them. The poet has drawn her at once false and fair.

In delineating Eboli and Philip, Schiller seems as if struggling against the current of his nature; our feelings towards them are hardly so severe as he intended; their words and deeds, at least those of the latter, are wicked and repulsive enough; but we still have a kind of latent persuasion that they meant better than they spoke or acted. With the Marquis of Posa, he had a more genial task. This Posa, we can easily perceive, is the representative of Schiller himself. The ardent love of men, which forms his ruling passion, was likewise the constant feeling of his author; the glowing eloquence with which he advocates the cause of truth, and justice, and humanity, was such as Schiller too would have employed in similar circumstances. In some respects, Posa is the chief character of the piece; there is a preëminent magnificence in his object, and in the faculties and feelings with which he follows it. Of a splendid intellect, and a daring devoted heart, his powers are all combined upon a single purpose. Even his friendship for Carlos, grounded on the likeness of their minds, and faithful as it is, yet seems to merge in this paramount emotion, zeal for the universal interests of man. Aiming, with all his force of thought and action, to advance the happiness and best rights of his fellow-creatures; pursuing this noble aim with the skill and dignity which it deserves, his mind is at once unwearied, earnest and serene. He is another Carlos, but somewhat older, more experienced, and never crossed in hopeless love. There is a calm strength in Posa, which no accident of fortune can shake. Whether cheering the forlorn Carlos into new activity; whether lifting up his voice in the ear of tyrants and inquisitors, or taking leave of life amid his vast unexecuted schemes, there is the same sedate magnanimity, the same fearless composure: when the fatal bullet strikes him, he dies with the concerns of others, not his own, upon his lips. He is a reformer, the perfection of reformers; not a revolutionist, but a prudent though determined improver. His enthusiasm does not burst forth in violence, but in manly and enlightened energy; his eloquence is not more moving to the heart than his lofty philosophy is convincing to the head. There is a majestic vastness of thought in his precepts, which recommends them to the mind independently of the beauty of their dress. Few passages of poetry are more spirit-stirring than his last message to Carlos, through the Queen. The certainty of death seems to surround his spirit with a kind of martyr glory; he is kindled into transport, and speaks with a commanding power. The pathetic wisdom of the line, 'Tell him, that when he is a man, he must reverence the dreams of his youth,' has often been admired: that scene has many such.

The interview with Philip is not less excellent. There is something so striking in the idea of confronting the cold solitary tyrant with 'the only man in all his states that does not need him;' of raising the voice of true manhood for once within the gloomy chambers of thraldom and priestcraft, that we can forgive the stretch of poetic license by which it is effected. Philip and Posa are antipodes in all respects. Philip thinks his new instructor is 'a Protestant;' a charge which Posa rebuts with calm dignity, his object not being separation and contention, but union and peaceful gradual improvement. Posa seems to understand the character of Philip better; not attempting to awaken in his sterile heart any feeling for real glory, or the interests of his fellow-men, he attacks his selfishness and pride, represents to him the intrinsic meanness and misery of a throne, however decked with adventitious pomp, if built on servitude, and isolated from the sympathies and interests of others.

We translate the entire scene; though not by any means the best, it is among the fittest for extraction of any in the piece. Posa has been sent for by the King, and is waiting in a chamber of the palace to know what is required of him; the King enters, unperceived by Posa, whose attention is directed to a picture on the wall:

ACT III.
SCENE X.
THE KING AND MARQUIS DE POSA.

[*The latter, on noticing the King, advances towards him, and kneels, then rises, and waits without any symptom of embarrassment.*]

KING. [*looks at him with surprise*].
We have met before, then?

MAR. No.

KING. You did my crown
Some service: wherefore have you shunn'd my thanks?
Our memory is besieged by crowds of suitors;
Omniscient is none but He in Heaven.
You should have sought my looks: why did you not?

MAR. 'Tis scarcely yet two days, your Majesty,
Since I returned to Spain.

KING. I am not used
To be my servants' debtor; ask of me
Some favour.

MAR. I enjoy the laws.

KING. That right
The very murd'rer has.

MAR. And how much more
The honest citizen!—Sire, I'm content.

KING [*aside*]. Much self-respect indeed, and lofty daring!

But this was to be looked for: I would have
My Spaniards haughty; better that the cup
Should overflow than not be full. —I hear
You left my service, Marquis.

MAR. Making way
For men more worthy, I withdrew.

KING. 'Tis wrong:
When spirits such as yours play truant,
My state must suffer. You conceive, perhaps,
Some post unworthy of your merits
Might be offer'd you?

MAR. No, Sire, I cannot doubt
But that a judge so skilful, and experienced
In the gifts of men, has at a glance discover'd
Wherein I might do him service, wherein not.
I feel with humble gratitude the favour,
With which your Majesty is loading me
By thoughts so lofty: yet I can—[*He stops.*

KING. You pause?

MAR. Sire, at the moment I am scarce prepar'd
To speak, in phrases of a Spanish subject,
What as a citizen o' th' world I've thought.
Truth is, in parting from the Court forever,
I held myself discharged from all necessity
Of troubling it with reasons for my absence.

KING. Are your reasons bad, then? Dare you not risk
Disclosing them?

MAR. My life, and joyfully,
Were scope allow'd me to disclose them *all.*
'Tis not myself but Truth that I endanger,
Should the King refuse me a full hearing.
Your anger or contempt I fain would shun;
But forced to choose between them, I had rather
Seem to you a man deserving punishment
Than pity.

KING [*with a look of expectation*]. Well?

MAR. The servant of a prince
I cannot be. [*The King looks at him with astonishment.*
I will not cheat my merchant:
If you deign to take me as your servant,
You expect, you wish, my actions only;
You wish my arm in fight, my thought in counsel;
Nothing more you will accept of: not my actions,

Th' approval they might find at Court becomes
The object of my acting. Now for me
Right conduct has a value of its own:
The happiness my king might cause me plant
I would myself produce; and conscious joy,
And free selection, not the force of duty,
Should impel me. Is it thus your Majesty
Requires it? Could you suffer new creators
In your own creation? Or could I
Consent with patience to become the chisel,
When I hoped to be the statuary?
I love mankind; and in a monarchy,
Myself is all that I can love.

KING. This fire
Is laudable. You would do good to others;
How you do it, patriots, wise men think
Of little moment, so it be but done.
Seek for yourself the office in my kingdoms
That will give you scope to gratify
This noble zeal.

MAR. There is not such an office.

KING. How?

MAR. What the king desires to spread abroad
Through these weak hands, is it the good of men?
That good which my unfetter'd love would wish them?
Pale majesty would tremble to behold it!
No! Policy has fashioned in her courts
Another sort of human good; a sort
Which *she* is rich enough to give away,
Awakening with it in the hearts of men
New cravings, such as *it* can satisfy.
Truth she keeps coining in her mints, such truth
As she can tolerate; and every die
Except her own she breaks and casts away.
But is the royal bounty wide enough
For me to wish and work in? Must the love
I hear my brother pledge itself to be
My brother's jailor? Can I call him happy
When he dare not think? Sire, choose some other
To dispense the good which *you* have stamped for us.
With me it tallies not; a prince's servant
I cannot be.

KING [*rather quickly*].
You are a Protestant.

MAR. [*after some reflection*]
Sire, your creed is also mine. [*After a pause.*
I find
I am misunderstood: 'tis as I feared.
You see me draw the veil from majesty,
And view its mysteries with steadfast eye:
How should you know if I regard as holy
What I no more regard as terrible?
Dangerous I seem, for bearing thoughts too high:
My King, I am not dangerous: my wishes
Lie buried here. [*Laying his hand on his breast.*
The poor and purblind rage
Of innovation, that but aggravates
The weight o' th' fetters which it cannot break,
Will never heat *my* blood. The century
Admits not my ideas: I live a citizen
Of those that are to come. Sire, can a picture
Break your rest? Your breath obliterates it.

KING. No other knows you harbour such ideas?

MAR. Such, no one.

KING [*rises, walks a few steps, then stops opposite the Marquis.
—Aside*]. New at least, this dialect!
Flattery exhausts itself: a man of parts
Disdains to imitate. For once let's have
A trial of the opposite! Why not?
The strange is oft the lucky. —If so be
This is your principle, why let it pass!
I will conform; the crown shall have a servant
New in Spain,—a liberal!

MAR. Sire, I see
How very meanly you conceive of men;
How, in the language of the frank true spirit
You find but another deeper artifice
Of a more practis'd coz'ner: I can also
Partly see what causes this. 'Tis men;
'Tis men that force you to it: they themselves
Have cast away their own nobility,
Themselves have crouch'd to this degraded posture.
Man's innate greatness, like a spectre, frights them;
Their poverty seems safety; with base skill
They ornament their chains, and call it virtue
To wear them with an air of grace. Twas thus
You found the world; thus from your royal father
Came it to you: how in this distorted,
Mutilated image could you honour man?

KING. Some truth there is in this.

MAR. Pity, however,
That in taking man from the Creator,
And changing him into *your* handiwork,
And setting up yourself to be the god
Of this new-moulded creature, you should have
Forgotten one essential; you yourself
Remained a man, a very child of Adam!
You are still a suffering, longing mortal,
You call for sympathy, and to a god
We can but sacrifice, and pray, and tremble!
O unwise exchange! unbless'd perversion!
When you have sunk your brothers to be play'd
As harp-strings, who will join in harmony
With you the player?

KING [*aside*]. By Heaven, he touches me!

MAR. For you, however, this is unimportant;
It but makes you separate, peculiar;
'Tis the price you pay for being a god.
And frightful were it if you failed in this!
If for the desolated good of millions,
You the Desolator should gain—nothing!
If the very freedom you have blighted
And kill'd were that alone which could exalt
Yourself!—Sire, pardon me, I must not stay:
The matter makes me rash: my heart is full,
Too strong the charm of looking on the one
Of living men to whom I might unfold it.

[*The Count de Lerma enters, and whispers a few words to the King. The latter beckons to him to withdraw, and continues sitting in his former posture.*

KING [*to the Marquis, after Lerma is gone*].
Speak on!

MAR. [*after a pause*] I feel, Sire, all the worth—

KING. Speak on!
Y' had something more to say.

MAR. Not long since, Sire,
I chanced to pass through Flanders and Brabant.
So many rich and flourishing provinces;
A great, a mighty people, and still more,
An honest people!—And this people's Father!
That, thought I, must be divine: so thinking,
I stumbled on a heap of human bones.

[*He pauses; his eyes rest on the King, who endeavours to return his glance, but with an air of embarrassment is forced to look upon the ground.*

You are in the right, you *must* proceed so.
That you *could* do, what you saw you *must* do,
Fills me with a shuddering admiration.
Pity that the victim welt'ring in its blood
Should speak so feeble an eulogium
On the spirit of the priest! That mere men,
Not beings of a calmer essence, write
The annals of the world! Serener ages
Will displace the age of Philip; these will bring
A milder wisdom; the subject's good will then
Be reconcil'd to th' prince's greatness;
The thrifty State will learn to prize its children,
And necessity no more will be inhuman.

KING. And when, think you, would those blessed ages
Have come round, had I recoil'd before
The curse of this? Behold my Spain! Here blooms
The subject's good, in never-clouded peace:
Such peace will I bestow on Flanders.

MAR. Peace of a churchyard! And you hope to end
What you have entered on? Hope to withstand
The timeful change of Christendom; to stop
The universal Spring that shall make young
The countenance o' th' Earth? *You* purpose, single
In all Europe, alone, to fling yourself
Against the wheel of Destiny that rolls
For ever its appointed course; to clutch
Its spokes with mortal arm? You may not, Sire!
Already thousands have forsook your kingdoms,
Escaping glad though poor: the citizen
You lost for conscience' sake, he was your noblest.
With mother's arms Elizabeth receives
The fugitives, and rich by foreign skill,
In fertile strength her England blooms. Forsaken
Of its toilsome people, lies Grenada
Desolate; and Europe sees with glad surprise
Its enemy faint with self-inflicted wounds.

[*The King seems moved: the Marquis observes it, and advances some steps nearer.*

Plant for Eternity and death the seed?
Your harvest will be nothingness. The work
Will not survive the spirit of its former;
It will be in vain that you have labour'd;
That you have fought the fight with Nature;
And to plans of Ruin consecrated

A high and royal lifetime. Man is greater
Than you thought. The bondage of long slumber
He will break; his sacred rights he will reclaim.
With Nero and Busiris will he rank
The name of Philip, and—that grieves me, for
You once were good.

King. How know you that?

Mar. [*with warm energy*]You were;
Yes, by th' All-Merciful! Yes, I repeat it.
Restore to us what you have taken from us.
Generous as strong, let human happiness
Stream from your horn of plenty, let souls ripen
Round you. Restore us what you took from us.
Amid a thousand kings become a king.

[*He approaches him boldly, fixing on him firm and glowing looks.*

Oh, could the eloquence of all the millions,
Who participate in this great moment,
Hover on my lips, and raise into a flame
That gleam that kindles in your eyes!
Give up this false idolatry of self,
Which makes your brothers nothing! Be to us
A pattern of the Everlasting and the True!
Never, never, did a mortal hold so much,
To use it so divinely. All the kings
Of Europe reverence the name of Spain:
Go on in front of all the kings of Europe!
One movement of your pen, and new-created
Is the Earth. Say but, Let there be freedom!
[*Throwing himself at his feet.*

King [*surprised, turning his face away, then again towards Posa*].
Singular enthusiast! Yet—rise—I—

Mar. Look round and view God's lordly universe:
On Freedom it is founded, and how rich
Is it with Freedom! He, the great Creator,
Has giv'n the very worm its sev'ral dewdrop;
Ev'n in the mouldering spaces of Decay,
He leaves Free-will the pleasures of a choice.
This world of *yours*! how narrow and how poor!
The rustling of a leaf alarms the lord
Of Christendom. You quake at every virtue;
He, not to mar the glorious form of Freedom,
Suffers that the hideous hosts of Evil
Should run riot in his fair Creation.
Him the maker we behold not; calm

He veils himself in everlasting laws,
Which and not Him the sceptic seeing exclaims,
'Wherefore a God? The World itself is God. '
And never did a Christian's adoration
So praise him as this sceptic's blasphemy.

KING. And such a model you would undertake,
On Earth, in my domains to imitate?

MAR. You, you can: who else? To th' people's good
Devote the kingly power, which far too long
Has struggled for the greatness of the throne.
Restore the lost nobility of man.
Once more make of the subject what he was,
The purpose of the Crown; let no tie bind him,
Except his brethren's right, as sacred as
His own. And when, given back to self-dependence,
Man awakens to the feeling of his worth,
And freedom's proud and lofty virtues blossom,
Then, Sire, having made *your* realms the happiest
In the Earth, it may become your duty
To subdue the realms of others.

KING [*after a long pause*].
I have heard you to an end.
Not as in common heads, the world is painted
In that head of yours: nor will I mete you
By the common standard. I am the first
To whom your heart has been disclosed:
I know this, so believe it. For the sake
Of such forbearance; for your having kept
Ideas, embraced with such devotion, secret
Up to this present moment, for the sake
Of that reserve, young man, I will forget
That I have learned them, and how I learned them.
Arise. The headlong youth I will set right,
Not as his sovereign, but as his senior.
I will, because I will. So! bane itself,
I find, in generous natures may become
Ennobled into something better. But
Beware my Inquisition! It would grieve me
If you —

MAR. Would it? would it?

KING [*gazing at him, and lost in surprise*].
Such a mortal
Till this hour I never saw. No, Marquis!
No! You do me wrong. To you I will not

Be a Nero, not to you. *All* happiness
Shall not be blighted by me: you yourself
Shall be permitted to remain a man
Beside me.

MAR. [*quickly*] And my fellow-subjects, Sire?
Oh, not for *me*, not *my* cause was I pleading.
And your subjects, Sire?

KING. You see so clearly
How posterity will judge of me; yourself
Shall teach it how I treated men so soon
As I had found one.

MAR. O Sire! in being
The most just of kings, at the same instant
Be not the most unjust! In your Flanders
Are many thousands worthier than I.
'Tis but yourself,—shall I confess it, Sire?—
That under this mild form first truly see
What freedom is.

KING [*with softened earnestness*].
Young man, no more of this.
Far differently will you think of men,
When you have seen and studied them as I have.
Yet our first meeting must not be our last;
How shall I try to make you mine?

MAR. Sire, let me
Continue as I am. What good were it
To you, if I like others were corrupted?

KING. This pride I will not suffer. From this moment
You are in my service. No remonstrance!
I will have it so. * * * * *

Had the character of Posa been drawn ten years later, it would have been imputed, as all things are, to the 'French Revolution;' and Schiller himself perhaps
might have been called a Jacobin. Happily, as matters stand, there is room for no
such imputation. It is pleasing to behold in Posa the deliberate expression of a
great and good man's sentiments on these ever-agitated subjects: a noble monument, embodying the liberal ideas of his age, in a form beautified by his own
genius, and lasting as its other products.[16]

Connected with the superior excellence of Posa, critics have remarked a dramatic error, which the author himself was the first to acknowledge and account
for. The magnitude of Posa throws Carlos into the shade; the hero of the first three
acts is no longer the hero of the other two. The cause of this, we are informed, was

---

[16] Jean Paul nevertheless, not without some show of reason, has compared this Posa
to the tower of a lighthouse: 'high, far-shining,—empty!' (*Note of 1845.*)

that Schiller kept the work too long upon his own hands:

'In composing the piece,' he observes, 'many interruptions occurred; so that a considerable time elapsed between beginning and concluding it; and, in the mean while, much within myself had changed. The various alterations which, during this period, my way of thinking and feeling underwent, naturally told upon the work I was engaged with. What parts of it had at first attracted me, began to produce this effect in a weaker degree, and, in the end, scarcely at all. New ideas, springing up in the interim, displaced the former ones; Carlos himself had lost my favour, perhaps for no other reason than because I had become his senior; and, from the opposite cause, Posa had occupied his place. Thus I commenced the fourth and fifth acts with quite an altered heart. But the first three were already in the hands of the public; the plan of the whole could not now be re-formed; nothing therefore remained but to suppress the piece entirely, or to fit the second half to the first the best way I could.'

The imperfection alluded to is one of which the general reader will make no great account; the second half is fitted to the first with address enough for his purposes. Intent not upon applying the dramatic gauge, but on being moved and exalted, we may peruse the tragedy without noticing that any such defect exists in it. The pity and love we are first taught to feel for Carlos abide with us to the last; and though Posa rises in importance as the piece proceeds, our admiration of his transcendent virtues does not obstruct the gentler feelings with which we look upon the fate of his friend. A certain confusion and crowding together of events, about the end of the play, is the only fault in its plan that strikes us with any force. Even this is scarcely prominent enough to be offensive.

An intrinsic and weightier defect is the want of ease and lightness in the general composition of the piece; a defect which, all its other excellencies will not prevent us from observing. There is action enough in the plot, energy enough in the dialogue, and abundance of individual beauties in both; but there is throughout a certain air of stiffness and effort, which abstracts from the theatrical illusion. The language, in general impressive and magnificent, is now and then inflated into bombast. The characters do not, as it were, verify their human nature, by those thousand little touches and nameless turns, which distinguish the genius essentially dramatic from the genius merely poetical; the Proteus of the stage from the philosophic observer and trained imitator of life. We have not those careless felicities, those varyings from high to low, that air of living freedom which Shakspeare has accustomed us, like spoiled children, to look for in every perfect work of this species. Schiller is too elevated, too regular and sustained in his elevation, to be altogether natural.

Yet with all this, *Carlos* is a noble tragedy. There is a stately massiveness about the structure of it; the incidents are grand and affecting; the characters powerful, vividly conceived, and impressively if not completely delineated. Of wit and its kindred graces Schiller has but a slender share: nor among great poets is he much distinguished for depth or fineness of pathos. But what gives him a place of his own, and the loftiest of its kind, is the vastness and intense vigour of his mind; the splendour of his thoughts and imagery, and the bold vehemence of his passion for the true and the sublime, under all their various forms. He does not thrill, but he exalts us. His genius is impetuous, exuberant, majestic; and a heavenly fire gleams through all his creations. He transports us into a holier and higher world than our own; everything around us breathes of force and solemn beauty. The looks of his heroes may be more staid than those of men, the movements of their minds may be slower and more calculated; but we yield to the potency of their endowments, and the loveliness of the scene which they animate. The enchantments of the poet are strong enough to silence our scepticism; we forbear to inquire whether it is true or false.

The celebrity of Alfieri generally invites the reader of *Don Carlos* to compare it with *Filippo*. Both writers treat the same subject; both borrow their materials from the same source, the *nouvelle historique* of St. Réal: but it is impossible that two powerful minds could have handled one given idea in more diverse manners. Their excellencies are, in fact, so opposite, that they scarcely come in competition. Alfieri's play is short, and the characters are few. He describes no scene: his personages are not the King of Spain and his courtiers, but merely men; their place of action is not the Escurial or Madrid, but a vacant, objectless platform anywhere in space. In all this, Schiller has a manifest advantage. He paints manners and opinions, he sets before us a striking pageant, which interests us of itself, and gives a new interest to whatever is combined with it. The principles of the antique, or perhaps rather of the French drama, upon which Alfieri worked, permitted no such delineation. In the style there is the same diversity. A severe simplicity uniformly marks Alfieri's style; in his whole tragedy there is not a single figure. A hard emphatic brevity is all that distinguishes his language from that of prose. Schiller, we have seen, abounds with noble metaphors, and all the warm exciting eloquence of poetry. It is only in expressing the character of Philip that Alfieri has a clear superiority. Without the aid of superstition, which his rival, especially in the catastrophe, employs to such advantage, Alfieri has exhibited in his Filippo a picture of unequalled power. Obscurity is justly said to be essential to terror and sublimity; and Schiller has enfeebled the effect of his Tyrant, by letting us behold the most secret recesses of his spirit: we understand him better, but we fear him less. Alfieri does not show us the internal combination of Filippo: it is from its workings alone that we judge of his nature. Mystery, and the shadow of horrid cruelty, brood over his Filippo: it is only a transient word or act that gives us here and there a glimpse of his fierce, implacable, tremendous soul; a short and dubious glimmer that reveals to us the abysses of his being, dark, lurid, and terrific, 'as the throat of the infernal Pool.' Alfieri's Filippo is perhaps the most wicked man that human imagination has conceived.

Alfieri and Schiller were again unconscious competitors in the history of Mary Stuart. But the works before us give a truer specimen of their comparative merits. Schiller seems to have the greater genius; Alfieri the more commanding character. Alfieri's greatness rests on the stern concentration of fiery passion, under the dominion of an adamantine will: this was his own make of mind; and he represents it, with strokes in themselves devoid of charm, but in their union terrible as a prophetic scroll. Schiller's moral force is commensurate with his intellectual gifts, and nothing more. The mind of the one is like the ocean, beautiful in its strength, smiling in the radiance of summer, and washing luxuriant and romantic shores: that of the other is like some black unfathomable lake placed far amid the melancholy mountains; bleak, solitary, desolate; but girdled with grim sky-piercing cliffs, overshadowed with storms, and illuminated only by the red glare of the lightning. Schiller is magnificent in his expansion, Alfieri is overpowering in his condensed energy; the first inspires us with greater admiration, the last with greater awe.

This tragedy of *Carlos* was received with immediate and universal approbation. In the closet and on the stage, it excited the warmest applauses equally among the learned and unlearned. Schiller's expectations had not been so high: he knew both the excellencies and the faults of his work; but he had not anticipated that the former would be recognised so instantaneously. The pleasure of this new celebrity came upon him, therefore, heightened by surprise. Had dramatic eminence been his sole object, he might now have slackened his exertions; the public had already ranked him as the first of their writers in that favourite department. But this limited ambition was not his moving principle; nor was his mind of that sort for which rest is provided in this world. The primary disposition of his nature urged him to perpetual toil: the great aim of his life, the unfolding of his mental powers, was one of those which admit but a relative not an absolute progress. New ideas of perfection arise as the former have been reached; the student is always attaining, never has attained.

Schiller's worldly circumstances, too, were of a kind well calculated to prevent excess of quietism. He was still drifting at large on the tide of life; he was crowned with laurels, but without a home. His heart, warm and affectionate, fitted to enjoy the domestic blessings which it longed for, was allowed to form no permanent attachment: he felt that he was unconnected, solitary in the world; cut off from the exercise of his kindlier sympathies; or if tasting such pleasures, it was 'snatching them rather than partaking of them calmly.' The vulgar desire of wealth and station never entered his mind for an instant: but as years were added to his age, the delights of peace and continuous comfort were fast becoming more acceptable than any other; and he looked with anxiety to have a resting-place amid his wanderings, to be a man among his fellow-men.

For all these wishes, Schiller saw that the only chance of fulfilment depended on unwearied perseverance in his literary occupations. Yet though his activity was unabated, and the calls on it were increasing rather than diminished, its direction was gradually changing. The Drama had long been stationary, and of late been falling in his estimation: the difficulties of the art, as he viewed it at present, had been overcome, and new conquests invited him in other quarters. The latter part of *Carlos* he had written as a task rather than a pleasure; he contemplated no farther undertaking connected with the Stage. For a time, indeed, he seems to have wavered among a multiplicity of enterprises; now solicited to this, and now to that, without being able to fix decidedly on any. The restless ardour of his mind is evinced by the number and variety of his attempts; its fluctuation by the circumstance that all of them are either short in extent, or left in the state of fragments. Of the former kind are his lyrical productions, many of which were composed about this period, during intervals from more serious labours. The character of these performances is such as his former writings gave us reason to expect. With a deep insight into life, and a keen and comprehensive sympathy with its sorrows and enjoyments, there is combined that impetuosity of feeling, that pomp of thought and imagery which belong peculiarly to Schiller. If he had now left the Drama, it was clear that his mind was still overflowing with the elements of poetry; dwelling among the grandest conceptions, and the boldest or finest emotions; thinking intensely and profoundly, but decorating its thoughts with those graces, which other faculties than the understanding are required to afford them. With these smaller pieces, Schiller occupied himself at intervals of leisure throughout the remainder of his life. Some of them are to be classed among the most finished efforts of his genius. The *Walk*, the *Song of the Bell*, contain exquisite delineations of the fortunes and history of man; his *Ritter Toggenburg*, his *Cranes of Ibycus*, his *Hero and Leander*, are among the most poetical and moving ballads to be found in any language.

Of these poems, the most noted written about this time, the *Freethinking of Passion* (*Freigeisterei der Leidenschaft*), is said to have originated in a real attachment. The lady, whom some biographers of Schiller introduce to us by the mysterious designation of the 'Fräulein A ***', one of the first beauties in Dresden,' seems to have made a deep impression on the heart of the poet. They tell us that she sat for the picture of the princess Eboli, in his *Don Carlos*; that he paid his court to her with the most impassioned fervour, and the extreme of generosity. They add one or two anecdotes of dubious authenticity; which, as they illustrate nothing, but show us only that love could make Schiller crazy, as it is said to make all gods and men, we shall use the freedom to omit.

This enchanting and not inexorable spinster perhaps displaced the Mannheim *Laura* from her throne; but the gallant assiduities, which she required or allowed, seem not to have abated the zeal of her admirer in his more profitable undertakings. Her reign, we suppose, was brief and without abiding influence. Schiller never wrote or thought with greater diligence than while at Dresden. Partially occupied with conducting his *Thalia*, or with those more slight poetical performances, his mind was hovering among a multitude of weightier plans, and seizing with avidity any hint that might assist in directing its attempts. To this state of feeling we are probably indebted for the *Geisterseher*, a novel, naturalised in our circulating libraries by the title of the *Ghostseer*, two volumes of which were published about this time. The king of quacks, the renowned Cagliostro, was now playing his dextrous game at Paris; harrowing-up the souls of the curious and gullible of all ranks in that capital, by various thaumaturgic feats; raising the dead from their graves; and, what was more to the purpose, raising himself from the station of a poor Sicilian lacquey to that of a sumptuous and extravagant count. The noise of his exploits appears to have given rise to this work of Schiller's. It is an attempt to exemplify the process of hoodwinking an acute but too sensitive man; of working on the latent germ of superstition, which exists beneath his outward scepticism; harassing his mind by the terrors of magic,—the magic of chemistry and natural philosophy and natural cunning; till, racked by doubts and agonising fears, and plunging from one depth of dark uncertainty into another, he is driven at length to still his scruples in the bosom of the Infallible Church. The incidents are contrived with considerable address, displaying a familiar acquaintance, not only with several branches of science, but also with some curious forms of life and human nature. One or two characters are forcibly drawn; particularly that of the amiable but feeble Count, the victim of the operation. The strange Foreigner, with the visage of stone, who conducts the business of mystification, strikes us also, though we see but little of him. The work contains some vivid description, some passages of deep tragical effect: it has a vein of keen observation; in general, a certain rugged power, which might excite regret that it was never finished. But Schiller found that his views had been mistaken: it was thought that he meant only to electrify his readers, by an accumulation of surprising horrors, in a novel of the Mrs. Radcliffe fashion. He felt, in consequence, discouraged to proceed; and finally abandoned it.

Schiller was, in fact, growing tired of fictitious writing. Imagination was with him a strong, not an exclusive, perhaps not even a predominating faculty: in the sublimest flights of his genius, intellect is a quality as conspicuous as any other; we are frequently not more delighted with the grandeur of the drapery in which he clothes his thoughts, than with the grandeur of the thoughts themselves. To a mind so restless, the cultivation of all its powers was a peremptory want; in one so earnest, the love of truth was sure to be among its strongest passions. Even while revelling, with unworn ardour, in the dreamy scenes of the Imagination, he had often cast a longing look, and sometimes made a hurried inroad, into the calmer provinces of reason: but the first effervescence of youth was past, and now more than ever, the love of contemplating or painting things as they should be, began to yield to the love of knowing things as they are. The tendency of his mind was gradually changing; he was about to enter on a new field of enterprise, where new triumphs awaited him.

For a time he had hesitated what to choose; at length he began to think of History. As a leading object of pursuit, this promised him peculiar advantages. It was new to him; and fitted to employ some of his most valuable gifts. It was grounded on reality, for which, as we have said, his taste was now becoming stronger; its mighty revolutions and events, and the commanding characters that figure in it, would likewise present him with things great and moving, for which his taste had always been strong. As recording the past transactions, and indicating the prospects of nations, it could not fail to be delightful to one, for whom not only human nature was a matter of most fascinating speculation, but who looked on all mankind with the sentiments of a brother, feeling truly what he often said, that 'he had no dearer wish than to see every living mortal happy and contented with his lot.' To all these advantages another of a humbler sort was added, but which the nature of his situation forbade him to lose sight of. The study of History, while it afforded him a subject of continuous and regular exertion, would also afford him, what was even more essential, the necessary competence of income for which he felt reluctant any longer to depend on the resources of poetry, but which the produce of his pen was now the only means he had of realising.

For these reasons, he decided on commencing the business of historian. The composition of *Don Carlos* had already led him to investigate the state of Spain under Philip II.; and, being little satisfied with Watson's clear but shallow Work on that reign, he had turned to the original sources of information, the writings of Grotius, Strada, De Thou, and many others. Investigating these with his usual fidelity and eagerness, the Revolt of the Netherlands had, by degrees, become familiar to his thoughts; distinct in many parts where it was previously obscure; and attractive, as it naturally must be to a temper such as his. He now determined that his first historical performance should be a narrative of that event. He resolved to explore the minutest circumstance of its rise and progress; to arrange the materials he might collect, in a more philosophical order; to interweave with them the general opinions he had formed, or was forming, on many points of polity, and national or individual character; and, if possible, to animate the whole with that warm sympathy, which, in a lover of Freedom, this most glorious of her triumphs naturally called forth.

In the filling-up of such an outline, there was scope enough for diligence. But it was not in Schiller's nature to content himself with ordinary efforts; no sooner did a project take hold of his mind, than, rallying round it all his accomplishments and capabilities, he stretched it out into something so magnificent and comprehensive, that little less than a lifetime would have been sufficient to effect it. This History of the Revolt of the Netherlands, which formed his chief study, he looked upon but as one branch of the great subject he was yet destined to engage with. History at large, in all its bearings, was now his final aim; and his mind was continually occupied with plans for acquiring, improving, and diffusing the knowledge of it.

Of these plans many never reached a describable shape; very few reached even partial execution. One of the latter sort was an intended *History of the most remarkable Conspiracies and Revolutions in the Middle and Later Ages*. A first volume of the work was published in 1787. Schiller's part in it was trifling; scarcely more than that of a translator and editor. St. Réal's *Conspiracy of Bedmar against Venice*, here furnished with an extended introduction, is the best piece in the book. Indeed, St. Réal seems first to have set him on this task: the Abbé had already signified his predilection for plots and revolutions, and given a fine sample of his powers in treating such matters. What Schiller did was to expand this idea, and communicate a systematic form to it. His work might have been curious and valuable, had it been completed; but the pressure of other engagements, the necessity of limiting his views to the Netherlands, prevented this for the present; it was afterwards forgotten, and never carried farther.

Such were Schiller's occupations while at Dresden; their extent and variety are proof enough that idleness was not among his vices. It was, in truth, the opposite extreme in which he erred. He wrote and thought with an impetuosity beyond what nature always could endure. His intolerance of interruptions first put him on the plan of studying by night; an alluring but pernicious practice, which began at Dresden, and was never afterwards forsaken. His recreations breathed a similar spirit; he loved to be much alone, and strongly moved. The banks of the Elbe were the favourite resort of his mornings: here wandering in solitude amid groves and lawns, and green and beautiful places, he abandoned his mind to delicious musings; watched the fitful current of his thoughts, as they came sweeping through his soul in their vague, fantastic, gorgeous forms; pleased himself with the transient images of memory and hope; or meditated on the cares and studies which had lately been employing, and were again soon to employ him. At times, he might be seen floating on the river in a gondola, feasting himself with the loveliness of earth and sky. He delighted most to be there when tempests were abroad; his unquiet spirit found a solace in the expression of his own unrest on the face of Nature; danger lent a charm to his situation; he felt in harmony with the scene, when the rack was sweeping stormfully across the heavens, and the forests were sounding in the breeze, and the river was rolling its chafed waters into wild eddying heaps.

Yet before the darkness summoned him exclusively to his tasks, Schiller commonly devoted a portion of his day to the pleasures of society. Could he have found enjoyment in the flatteries of admiring hospitality, his present fame would have procured them for him in abundance. But these things were not to Schiller's taste. His opinion of the 'flesh-flies' of Leipzig we have already seen: he retained the same sentiments throughout all his life. The idea of being what we call a *lion* is offensive enough to any man, of not more than common vanity, or less than common understanding; it was doubly offensive to him. His pride and his modesty alike forbade it. The delicacy of his nature, aggravated into shyness by his education and his habits, rendered situations of display more than usually painful to him; the *digito prætereuntium* was a sort of celebration he was far from coveting. In the circles of fashion he appeared unwillingly, and seldom to advantage: their glitter and parade were foreign to his disposition; their strict ceremonial cramped the play of his mind. Hemmed in, as by invisible fences, among the intricate barriers of etiquette, so feeble, so inviolable, he felt constrained and helpless; alternately chagrined and indignant. It was the giant among pigmies; Gulliver, in Lilliput, tied down by a thousand packthreads. But there were more congenial minds, with whom he could associate; more familiar scenes, in which he found the pleasures he was seeking. Here Schiller was himself; frank, unembarrassed, pliant to the humour of the hour. His conversation was delightful, abounding at once in rare and simple charms. Besides the intellectual riches which it carried with it, there was that flow of kindliness and unaffected good humour, which can render dulness itself agreeable. Schiller had many friends in Dresden, who loved him as a man, while they admired him as a writer. Their intercourse was of the kind he liked, sober, as well as free and mirthful. It was the careless, calm, honest effusion of his feelings that he wanted, not the noisy tumults and coarse delirium of dissipation. For this, under any of its forms, he at no time showed the smallest relish.

A visit to Weimar had long been one of Schiller's projects: he now first accomplished it in 1787. Saxony had been, for ages, the Attica of Germany; and Weimar had, of late, become its Athens. In this literary city, Schiller found what he expected, sympathy and brotherhood with men of kindred minds. To Goethe he was not introduced;[17] but Herder and Wieland received him with a cordial welcome; with the latter he soon formed a most friendly intimacy. Wieland, the Nestor of German letters, was grown gray in the service: Schiller reverenced him

---

[17] Doering says, 'Goethe was at this time absent in Italy;' an error, as will by and by appear.

as a father, and he was treated by him as a son. 'We shall have bright hours,' he said; 'Wieland is still young, when he loves.' Wieland had long edited the *Deutsche Mercur*: in consequence of their connexion, Schiller now took part in contributing to that work. Some of his smaller poems, one or two fragments of the History of the Netherlands, and the *Letters on Don Carlos*, first appeared here. His own *Thalia* still continued to come out at Leipzig. With these for his incidental employments, with the Belgian Revolt for his chief study, and the best society in Germany for his leisure, Schiller felt no wish to leave Weimar. The place and what it held contented him so much, that he thought of selecting it for his permanent abode. 'You know the men,' he writes, 'of whom Germany is proud; a Herder, a Wieland, with their brethren; and one wall now encloses me and them. What excellencies are in Weimar! In this city, at least in this territory, I mean to settle for life, and at length once more to get a country.'

So occupied and so intentioned, he continued to reside at Weimar. Some months after his arrival, he received an invitation from his early patroness and kind protectress, Madam von Wolzogen, to come and visit her at Bauerbach. Schiller went accordingly to this his ancient city of refuge; he again found all the warm hospitality, which he had of old experienced when its character could less be mistaken; but his excursion thither produced more lasting effects than this. At Rudolstadt, where he stayed for a time on occasion of this journey, he met with a new friend. It was here that he first saw the Fräulein Lengefeld, a lady whose attractions made him loth to leave Rudolstadt, and eager to return.

Next year he did return; he lived from May till November there or in the neighbourhood. He was busy as usual, and he visited the Lengefeld family almost every day. Schiller's views on marriage, his longing for 'a civic and domestic existence,' we already know. 'To be united with a person,' he had said, 'that shares our sorrows and our joys, that responds to our feelings, that moulds herself so pliantly, so closely to our humours; reposing on her calm and warm affection, to relax our spirit from a thousand distractions, a thousand wild wishes and tumultuous passions; to dream away all the bitterness of fortune, in the bosom of domestic enjoyment; this the true delight of life.' Some years had elapsed since he expressed these sentiments, which time had confirmed, not weakened: the presence of the Fräulein Lengefeld awoke them into fresh activity. He loved this lady; the return of love, with which she honoured him, diffused a sunshine over all his troubled world; and, if the wish of being hers excited more impatient thoughts about the settlement of his condition, it also gave him fresh strength to attain it. He was full of occupation, while in Rudolstadt; ardent, serious, but not unhappy. His literary projects were proceeding as before; and, besides the enjoyment of virtuous love, he had that of intercourse with many worthy and some kindred minds.

Among these, the chief in all respects was Goethe. It was during his present visit, that Schiller first met with this illustrious person; concerning whom, both by reading and report, his expectations had been raised so high. No two men, both of exalted genius, could be possessed of more different sorts of excellence, than the two that were now brought together, in a large company of their mutual friends. The English reader may form some approximate conception of the contrast, by figuring an interview between Shakspeare and Milton. How gifted, how diverse in their gifts! The mind of the one plays calmly, in its capricious and inimitable graces, over all the provinces of human interest; the other concentrates powers as vast, but far less various, on a few subjects; the one is catholic, the other is sectarian. The first is endowed with an all-comprehending spirit; skilled, as if by personal experience, in all the modes of human passion and opinion; therefore, tolerant of all; peaceful, collected; fighting for no class of men or principles; rather looking on the world, and the various battles waging in it, with the quiet eye of one already reconciled to the futility of their issues; but pouring over all the forms of many-coloured life the light of a deep and subtle intellect, and the decorations of an overflowing fancy; and allowing men and things of every shape and hue to have their own free scope in his conception, as they have it in the world where Providence has placed them. The other is earnest, devoted; struggling with a thousand mighty projects of improvement; feeling more intensely as he feels more narrowly; rejecting vehemently, choosing vehemently; at war with the one half of things, in love with the other half; hence dissatisfied, impetuous, without internal rest, and scarcely conceiving the possibility of such a state. Apart from the difference of their opinions and mental culture, Shakspeare and Milton seem to have stood in some such relation as this to each other, in regard to the primary structure of their minds. So likewise, in many points, was it with Goethe and Schiller. The external circumstances of the two were, moreover, such as to augment their several peculiarities. Goethe was in his thirty-ninth year; and had long since found his proper rank and settlement in life. Schiller was ten years younger, and still without a fixed destiny; on both of which accounts, his fundamental scheme of thought, the principles by which he judged and acted, and maintained his individuality, although they might be settled, were less likely to be sobered and matured. In these circumstances we can hardly wonder that on Schiller's part the first impression was not very pleasant. Goethe sat talking of Italy, and art, and travelling, and a thousand other subjects, with that flow of brilliant and deep sense, sarcastic humour, knowledge, fancy and good nature, which is said to render him the best talker now alive.[18] Schiller looked at him in quite a different mood; he felt his natural constraint increased under the influence of a man so opposite in character, so potent in resources, so singular and so expert in using them; a man whom he could not agree with, and knew not how to contradict. Soon after their interview, he thus writes:

'On the whole, this personal meeting has not at all diminished the idea, great as it was, which I had previously formed of Goethe; but I doubt whether we shall ever come into any close communication with each other. Much that still interests me has already had its epoch with him. His whole nature is, from its very origin, otherwise constructed than mine; his world is not my world; our modes of conceiving things appear to be essentially different. From such a combination, no secure, substantial intimacy can result. Time will try.'

The aid of time was not, in fact, unnecessary. On the part of Goethe there existed prepossessions no less hostile; and derived from sources older and deeper than the present transitory meeting, to the discontents of which they probably

---

[18] 1825.

contributed. He himself has lately stated them with his accustomed frankness and good humour, in a paper, part of which some readers may peruse with an interest more than merely biographical.

'On my return from Italy,' he says, 'where I had been endeavouring to train myself to greater purity and precision in all departments of art, not heeding what meanwhile was going on in Germany, I found here some older and some more recent works of poetry, enjoying high esteem and wide circulation, while unhappily their character to me was utterly offensive. I shall only mention Heinse's *Ardinghello* and Schiller's *Robbers*. The first I hated for its having undertaken to exhibit sensuality and mystical abstruseness, ennobled and supported by creative art: the last, because in it, the very paradoxes moral and dramatic, from which I was struggling to get liberated, had been laid hold of by a powerful though an immature genius, and poured in a boundless rushing flood over all our country.

'Neither of these gifted individuals did I blame for what he had performed or purposed: it is the nature and the privilege of every mortal to attempt working in his own peculiar way; he attempts it first without culture, scarcely with the consciousness of what he is about; and continues it with consciousness increasing as his culture increases; whereby it happens that so many exquisite and so many paltry things are to be found circulating in the world, and one perplexity is seen to rise from the ashes of another.

'But the rumour which these strange productions had excited over Germany, the approbation paid to them by every class of persons, from the wild student to the polished court-lady, frightened me; for I now thought all my labour was to prove in vain; the objects, and the way of handling them, to which I had been exercising all my powers, appeared as if defaced and set aside. And what grieved me still more was, that all the friends connected with me, Heinrich Meyer and Moritz, as well as their fellow-artists Tischbein and Bury, seemed in danger of the like contagion. I was much hurt. Had it been possible, I would have abandoned the study of creative art, and the practice of poetry altogether; for where was the prospect of surpassing those performances of genial worth and wild form, in the qualities which recommended them? Conceive my situation. It had been my object and my task to cherish and impart the purest exhibitions of poetic art; and here was I hemmed in between Ardinghello and Franz von Moor!

'It happened also about this time that Moritz returned from Italy, and stayed with me awhile; during which, he violently confirmed himself and me in these persuasions. I avoided Schiller, who was now at Weimar, in my neighbourhood. The appearance of *Don Carlos* was not calculated to approximate us; the attempts of our common friends I resisted; and thus we still continued to go on our way apart.'

By degrees, however, both parties found that they had been mistaken. The course of accidents brought many things to light, which had been hidden; the true character of each became unfolded more and more completely to the other; and the cold, measured tribute of respect was on both sides animated and exalted by feelings of kindness, and ultimately of affection. Ere long, Schiller had by gratifying proofs discovered that 'this Goethe was a very worthy man;' and Goethe, in his love of genius, and zeal for the interests of literature, was performing for Schiller the essential duties of a friend, even while his personal repugnance continued unabated.

A strict similarity of characters is not necessary, or perhaps very favourable, to friendship. To render it complete, each party must no doubt be competent to understand the other; both must be possessed of dispositions kindred in their great lineaments: but the pleasure of comparing our ideas and emotions is heightened, when there is 'likeness in unlikeness.' *The same sentiments, different opinions*, Rousseau conceives to be the best material of friendship: reciprocity of kind words and actions is more effectual than all. Luther loved Melancthon; Johnson was not more the friend of Edmund Burke than of poor old Dr. Levitt. Goethe and Schiller met again; as they ultimately came to live together, and to see each other oftener, they liked each other better; they became associates, friends; and the harmony of their intercourse, strengthened by many subsequent communities of object, was never interrupted, till death put an end to it. Goethe, in his time, has done many glorious things; but few on which he should look back with greater pleasure than his treatment of Schiller. Literary friendships are said to be precarious, and of rare occurrence: the rivalry of interest disturbs their continuance; a rivalry greater, where the subject of competition is one so vague, impalpable and fluctuating, as the favour of the public; where the feeling to be gratified is one so nearly allied to vanity, the most irritable, arid and selfish feeling of the human heart. Had Goethe's prime motive been the love of fame, he must have viewed with repugnance, not the misdirection but the talents of the rising genius, advancing with such rapid strides to dispute with him the palm of intellectual primacy, nay as the million thought, already in possession of it; and if a sense of his own dignity had withheld him from offering obstructions, or uttering any whisper of discontent, there is none but a truly patrician spirit that would cordially have offered aid. To being secretly hostile and openly indifferent, the next resource was to enact the patron; to solace vanity, by helping the rival whom he could not hinder, and who could do without his help. Goethe adopted neither of these plans. It reflects much credit on him that he acted as he did. Eager to forward Schiller's views by exerting all the influence within his power, he succeeded in effecting this; and what was still more difficult, in suffering the character of benefactor to merge in that of equal. They became not friends only, but fellow-labourers: a connection productive of important consequences in the history of both, particularly of the younger and more undirected of the two.

Meanwhile the *History of the Revolt of the United Netherlands* was in part before the world; the first volume came out in 1788. Schiller's former writings had given proofs of powers so great and various, such an extent of general intellectual strength, and so deep an acquaintance, both practical and scientific, with the art of composition, that in a subject like history, no ordinary work was to be looked for from his hands. With diligence in accumulating materials, and patient care in elaborating them, he could scarcely fail to attain distinguished excellence. The present volume was well calculated to fulfil such expectations. The *Revolt of the Netherlands* possesses all the common requisites of a good history, and many which are in some degree peculiar to itself. The information it conveys is minute and copious; we have all the circumstances of the case, remote and near, set distinctly before us. Yet, such is the skill of the arrangement, these are at once briefly and impressively presented. The work is not stretched out into a continuous narrative; but gathered up into masses, which are successively exhibited to view, the minor facts being grouped around some leading one, to which, as to the central object, our attention is chiefly directed. This method of combining the details of events, of proceeding as it were, *per saltum*, from eminence to eminence, and thence surveying the surrounding scene, is undoubtedly the most philosophical of any: but few men are equal to the task of effecting it rightly. It must be executed by a mind able to look on all its facts at once; to disentangle their perplexities, referring each to its proper head; and to choose, often with extreme address, the station from which the reader is to view them. Without this, or with this inadequately done, a work on such a plan would be intolerable. Schiller has accomplished it in great perfection; the whole scene of affairs was evidently clear before his own eye, and he did not want expertness to discriminate and seize its distinctive features. The bond of cause and consequence he never loses sight of; and over each successive portion of his narrative he pours that flood of intellectual and imaginative brilliancy, which all his prior writings had displayed. His reflections, expressed or implied, are the fruit of strong, comprehensive, penetrating thought. His descriptions are vivid; his characters are studied with a keen sagacity, and set before us in their most striking points of view; those of Egmont and Orange occur to every reader as a rare union of perspicacity and eloquence. The work has a look of order; of beauty joined to calm reposing force. Had it been completed, it might have ranked as the very best of Schiller's prose compositions. But no second volume ever came to light; and the first concludes at the entrance of Alba into Brussels. Two fragments alone, the *Siege of Antwerp*, and the *Passage of Alba's Army*, both living pictures, show us still farther what he might have done had he proceeded. The surpassing and often highly-picturesque movements of this War, the devotedness of the Dutch, their heroic achievement of liberty, were not destined to be painted by the glowing pen of Schiller, whose heart and mind were alike so qualified to do them justice.[19]

The accession of reputation, which this work procured its author, was not the only or the principal advantage he derived from it. Eichhorn, Professor of History, was at this time about to leave the University of Jena: Goethe had already introduced his new acquaintance Schiller to the special notice of Amelia, the accomplished Regent of Sachsen-Weimar; he now joined with Voigt, the head Chaplain of the Court, in soliciting the vacant chair for him. Seconded by the general voice, and the persuasion of the Princess herself, he succeeded. Schiller was appointed Professor at Jena; he went thither in 1789.

With Schiller's removal to Jena begins a new epoch in his public and private

[19] If we mistake not, Madame de Staël, in her *Révolution Française*, had this performance of Schiller's in her eye. Her work is constructed on a similar though a rather looser plan of arrangement: the execution of it bears the same relation to that of Schiller; it is less irregular; more ambitious in its rhetoric; inferior in precision, though often not in force of thought and imagery.

life. His connexion with Goethe here first ripened into friendship, and became secured and cemented by frequency of intercourse.[20] Jena is but a few miles distant from Weimar; and the two friends, both settled in public offices belonging to the same Government, had daily opportunities of interchanging visits. Schiller's wanderings were now concluded: with a heart tired of so fluctuating an existence, but not despoiled of its capacity for relishing a calmer one; with a mind experienced by much and varied intercourse with men; full of knowledge and of plans to turn it to account, he could now repose himself in the haven of domestic comforts, and look forward to days of more unbroken exertion, and more wholesome and permanent enjoyment than hitherto had fallen to his lot. In the February following his settlement at Jena, he obtained the hand of Fräulein Lengefeld; a happiness, with the prospect of which he had long associated all the pleasures which he hoped for from the future. A few months after this event, he thus expresses himself, in writing to a friend:

'Life is quite a different thing by the side of a beloved wife, than so forsaken and alone; even in Summer. Beautiful Nature! I now for the first time fully enjoy it, live in it. The world again clothes itself around me in poetic forms; old feelings are again awakening in my breast. What a life I am leading here! I look with a glad mind around me; my heart finds a perennial contentment without it; my spirit so fine, so refreshing a nourishment. My existence is settled in harmonious composure; not strained and impassioned, but peaceful and clear. I look to my future destiny with a cheerful heart; now when standing at the wished-for goal, I wonder with myself how it all has happened, so far beyond my expectations. Fate has conquered the difficulties for me; it has, I may say, forced me to the mark. From the future I expect everything. A few years, and I shall live in the full enjoyment of my spirit; nay, I think my very youth will be renewed; an inward poetic life will give it me again.'

To what extent these smiling hopes were realised will be seen in the next and concluding Part of this Biography.

---

[20] The obstacles to their union have already been described in the words of Goethe; the steps by which these were surmounted, are described by him in the same paper with equal minuteness and effect. It is interesting, but cannot be inserted here. See Appendix I., No. 3.

PART III.

FROM HIS SETTLEMENT AT JENA TO HIS DEATH. (1790-1805.)

THE duties of his new office naturally called upon Schiller to devote himself with double zeal to History: a subject, which from choice he had already entered on with so much eagerness. In the study of it, we have seen above how his strongest faculties and tastes were exercised and gratified: and new opportunities were now combined with new motives for persisting in his efforts. Concerning the plan or the success of his academical prelections, we have scarcely any notice: in his class, it is said, he used most frequently to speak extempore; and his delivery was not distinguished by fluency or grace, a circumstance to be imputed to the agitation of a public appearance; for, as Woltmann assures us, 'the beauty, the elegance, ease, and true instructiveness with which he could continuously express himself in private, were acknowledged and admired by all his friends.' His matter, we suppose, would make amends for these deficiencies of manner: to judge from his introductory lecture, preserved in his works, with the title, *What is Universal History, and with what views should it be studied*, there perhaps has never been in Europe another course of history sketched out on principles so magnificent and philosophical.[21] But college exercises were far from being his ultimate object, nor did he rest satisfied with mere visions of perfection: the compass of the outline he had traced, for a proper Historian, was scarcely greater than the assiduity with which he strove to fill it up. His letters breathe a spirit not only of diligence but of ardour; he seems intent with all his strength upon this fresh pursuit; and delighted with the vast prospects of untouched and attractive speculation, which were opening around him on every side. He professed himself to be 'exceedingly contented with his business;' his ideas on the nature of it were acquiring both extension and distinctness; and every moment of his leisure was employed in reducing them to practice. He was now busied with the *History of the Thirty-Years War*.

This work, which appeared in 1791, is considered by the German critics as his chief performance in this department of literature: *The Revolt of the Netherlands*, the only one which could have vied with it, never was completed; otherwise, in our opinion, it might have been superior. Either of the two would have sufficed to se-

---

[21] The paper entitled *Hints on the Origin of Human Society, as indicated in the Mosaic Records*, the *Mission of Moses*, the *Laws of Solon and Lycurgus*, are pieces of the very highest order; full of strength and beauty; delicious to the lovers of that plastic philosophy, which employs itself in giving form and life to the 'dry bones' of those antique events, that lie before us so inexplicable in the brief and enigmatic pages of their chroniclers. The *Glance over Europe at the period of the first Crusade*; the *Times of the Emperor Frederick I.*; the *Troubles in France*, are also masterly sketches, in a simpler and more common style.

cure for Schiller a distinguished rank among historians, of the class denominated philosophical; though even both together, they afford but a feeble exemplification of the ideas which he entertained on the manner of composing history. In his view, the business of history is not merely to record, but to interpret; it involves not only a clear conception and a lively exposition of events and characters, but a sound, enlightened theory of individual and national morality, a general philosophy of human life, whereby to judge of them, and measure their effects. The historian now stands on higher ground, takes in a wider range than those that went before him; he can now survey vast tracts of human action, and deduce its laws from an experience extending over many climes and ages. With his ideas, moreover, his feelings ought to be enlarged: he should regard the interests not of any sect or state, but of mankind; the progress not of any class of arts or opinions, but of universal happiness and refinement. His narrative, in short, should be moulded according to the science, and impregnated with the liberal spirit of his time.

Voltaire is generally conceived to have invented and introduced a new method of composing history; the chief historians that have followed him have been by way of eminence denominated philosophical. This is hardly correct. Voltaire wrote history with greater talent, but scarcely with a new species of talent: he applied the ideas of the eighteenth century to the subject; but in this there was nothing radically new. In the hands of a thinking writer history has always been 'philosophy teaching by experience;' that is, such philosophy as the age of the historian has afforded. For a Greek or Roman, it was natural to look upon events with an eye to their effect on his own city or country; and to try them by a code of principles, in which the prosperity or extension of this formed a leading object. For a monkish chronicler, it was natural to estimate the progress of affairs by the number of abbeys founded; the virtue of men by the sum-total of donations to the clergy. And for a thinker of the present day, it is equally natural to measure the occurrences of history by quite a different standard: by their influence upon the general destiny of man, their tendency to obstruct or to forward him in his advancement towards liberty, knowledge, true religion and dignity of mind. Each of these narrators simply measures by the scale which is considered for the time as expressing the great concerns and duties of humanity.

Schiller's views on this matter were, as might have been expected, of the most enlarged kind. 'It seems to me,' said he in one of his letters, 'that in writing history for the moderns, we should try to communicate to it such an interest as the History of the Peloponnesian War had for the Greeks. Now this is the problem: to choose and arrange your materials so that, to interest, they shall not need the aid of decoration. We moderns have a source of interest at our disposal, which no Greek or Roman was acquainted with, and which the *patriotic* interest does not nearly equal. This last, in general, is chiefly of importance for unripe nations, for the youth of the world. But we may excite a very different sort of interest if we represent each remarkable occurrence that happened to *men* as of importance to *man*. It is a poor and little aim to write for one nation; a philosophic spirit cannot tolerate such limits, cannot bound its views to a form of human nature so arbitrary, fluctuating, accidental. The most powerful nation is but a fragment; and thinking minds will not grow warm on its account, except in so far as this nation or its fortunes have been influential on the progress of the species.'

That there is not some excess in this comprehensive cosmopolitan philosophy, may perhaps be liable to question. Nature herself has, wisely no doubt, partitioned us into 'kindreds, and nations, and tongues:' it is among our instincts to grow warm in behalf of our country, simply for its own sake; and the business of Reason seems to be to chasten and direct our instincts, never to destroy them. We require individuality in our attachments: the sympathy which is expanded over all men will commonly be found so much attenuated by the process, that it cannot be effective on any. And as it is in nature, so it is in art, which ought to be the image of it. Universal philanthropy forms but a precarious and very powerless rule of conduct; and the 'progress of the species' will turn out equally unfitted for deeply exciting the imagination. It is not with freedom that we can sympathise, but with free men. There ought, indeed, to be in history a spirit superior to petty distinctions and vulgar partialities; our particular affections ought to be enlightened and purified; but they should not be abandoned, or, such is the condition of humanity, our feelings must evaporate and fade away in that extreme diffusion. Perhaps, in a certain sense, the surest mode of pleasing and instructing all nations *is* to write for one.

This too Schiller was aware of, and had in part attended to. Besides, the Thirty-Years War is a subject in which nationality of feeling may be even wholly spared, better than in almost any other. It is not a German but a European subject; it forms the concluding portion of the Reformation, and this is an event belonging not to any country in particular, but to the human race. Yet, if we mistake not, this over-tendency to generalisation, both in thought and sentiment, has rather hurt the present work. The philosophy, with which it is embued, now and then grows vague from its abstractness, ineffectual from its refinement: the enthusiasm which pervades it, elevated, strong, enlightened, would have told better on our hearts, had it been confined within a narrower space, and directed to a more specific class of objects. In his extreme attention to the philosophical aspects of the period, Schiller has neglected to take advantage of many interesting circumstances, which it offered under other points of view. The Thirty-Years War abounds with what may be called picturesqueness in its events, and still more in the condition of the people who carried it on. Harte's *History of Gustavus*, a wilderness which mere human patience seems unable to explore, is yet enlivened here and there with a cheerful spot, when he tells us of some scalade or camisado, or speculates on troopers rendered bullet-proof by art-magic. His chaotic records have, in fact, afforded to our Novelist the raw materials of Dugald Dalgetty, a cavalier of the most singular equipment, of character and manners which, for many reasons, merit study and description. To much of this, though, as he afterwards proved, it was well known to him, Schiller paid comparatively small attention; his work has lost in liveliness by the omission, more than it has gained in dignity or instructiveness.

Yet, with all its imperfections, this is no ordinary history. The speculation, it is true, is not always of the kind we wish; it excludes more moving or enlivening topics, and sometimes savours of the inexperienced theorist who had passed his days remote from practical statesmen; the subject has not sufficient unity; in spite of every effort, it breaks into fragments towards the conclusion: but still there is an energy, a vigorous beauty in the work, which far more than redeems its failings. Great thoughts at every turn arrest our attention, and make us pause to confirm or contradict them; happy metaphors,[22] some vivid descriptions of events and men, remind us of the author of *Fiesco* and *Don Carlos*. The characters of Gustavus and Wallenstein are finely developed in the course of the narrative. Tilly's passage of the Lech, the battles of Leipzig and Lützen figure in our recollection, as if our eyes had witnessed them: the death of Gustavus is described in terms which might draw 'iron tears' from the eyes of veterans.[23] If Schiller had inclined to dwell upon the mere visual or imaginative department of his subject, no man could have painted it more graphically, or better called forth our emotions, sympathetic or romantic. But this, we have seen, was not by any means his leading aim.

On the whole, the present work is still the best historical performance which Germany can boast of. Müller's histories are distinguished by merits of another sort; by condensing, in a given space, and frequently in lucid order, a quantity of information, copious and authentic beyond example: but as intellectual productions, they cannot rank with Schiller's. Woltmann of Berlin has added to the *Thirty-Years War* another work of equal size, by way of continuation, entitled *History of the Peace of Munster*; with the first negotiations of which treaty the former concludes. Woltmann is a person of ability; but we dare not say of him, what Wieland said of Schiller, that by his first historical attempt he 'has discovered a decided capability of rising to a level with Hume, Robertson and Gibbon.' He will rather rise to a level with Belsham or Smollett.

This first complete specimen of Schiller's art in the historical department, though but a small fraction of what he meant to do, and could have done, proved in fact to be the last he ever undertook. At present very different cares awaited him: in 1791, a fit of sickness overtook him; he had to exchange the inspiring labours of literature for the disgusts and disquietudes of physical disease. His disorder, which had its seat in the chest, was violent and threatening; and though nature overcame it in the present instance, the blessing of entire health never more returned to him. The cause of this severe affliction seemed to be the unceasing toil and anxiety of mind, in which his days had hitherto been passed: his frame, which, though tall, had never been robust, was too weak for the vehement and sleepless soul that dwelt within it; and the habit of nocturnal study had, no doubt, aggravated all the other mischiefs. Ever since his residence at Dresden, his constitution had been weakened: but this rude shock at once shattered its remaining strength; for a time the strictest precautions were required barely to preserve existence. A total cessation from every intellectual effort was one of the most peremptory laws prescribed to him. Schiller's habits and domestic circumstances equally rebelled

[22] Yet we scarcely meet with one so happy as that in the *Revolt of the Netherlands*, where he finishes his picture of the gloomy silence and dismay that reigned in Brussels on the first entrance of Alba, by this striking simile: 'Now that the City had received the Spanish General within its walls, it had the air as of a man that has drunk a cup of poison, and with shuddering expectation watches, every moment, for its deadly agency.'

[23] See Appendix I., No. 4.

against this measure; with a beloved wife depending on him for support, inaction itself could have procured him little rest. His case seemed hard; his prospects of innocent felicity had been too banefully obscured. Yet in this painful and difficult position, he did not yield to despondency; and at length, assistance, and partial deliverance, reached him from a very unexpected quarter. Schiller had not long been sick, when the hereditary Prince, now reigning Duke of Holstein-Augustenburg, jointly with the Count Von Schimmelmann, conferred on him a pension of a thousand crowns for three years.[24] No stipulation was added, but merely that he should be careful of his health, and use every attention to recover. This speedy and generous aid, moreover, was presented with a delicate politeness, which, as Schiller said, touched him more than even the gift itself. We should remember this Count and this Duke; they deserve some admiration and some envy.

This disorder introduced a melancholy change into Schiller's circumstances: he had now another enemy to strive with, a secret and fearful impediment to vanquish, in which much resolute effort must be sunk without producing any positive result. Pain is not entirely synonymous with Evil; but bodily pain seems less redeemed by good than almost any other kind of it. From the loss of fortune, of fame, or even of friends, Philosophy pretends to draw a certain compensating benefit; but in general the permanent loss of health will bid defiance to her alchymy. It is a universal diminution; the diminution equally of our resources and of our capacity to guide them; a penalty unmitigated, save by love of friends, which then first becomes truly dear and precious to us; or by comforts brought from beyond this earthly sphere, from that serene Fountain of peace and hope, to which our weak Philosophy cannot raise her wing. For all men, in itself, disease is misery; but chiefly for men of finer feelings and endowments, to whom, in return for such superiorities, it seems to be sent most frequently and in its most distressing forms. It is a cruel fate for the poet to have the sunny land of his imagination, often the sole territory he is lord of, disfigured and darkened by the shades of pain; for one whose highest happiness is the exertion of his mental faculties, to have them chained and paralysed in the imprisonment of a distempered frame. With external activity, with palpable pursuits, above all, with a suitable placidity of nature, much even in certain states of sickness may be performed and enjoyed. But for him whose heart is already over-keen, whose world is of the mind, ideal, internal; when the mildew of lingering disease has struck that world, and begun to blacken and consume its beauty, nothing seems to remain but despondency and bitterness and desolate sorrow, felt and anticipated, to the end.

Woe to him if his will likewise falter, if his resolution fail, and his spirit bend its neck to the yoke of this new enemy! Idleness and a disturbed imagination will gain the mastery of him, and let loose their thousand fiends to harass him, to torment him into madness. Alas! the bondage of Algiers is freedom compared with this of the sick man of genius, whose heart has fainted and sunk beneath its load. His clay dwelling is changed into a gloomy prison; every nerve is become an avenue of disgust or anguish; and the soul sits within, in her melancholy loneliness, a

---

[24] It was to Denmark likewise that Klopstock owed the means of completing his *Messias*.

prey to the spectres of despair, or stupefied with excess of suffering, doomed as it were to a 'life in death,' to a consciousness of agonised existence, without the consciousness of power which should accompany it. Happily, death, or entire fatuity, at length puts an end to such scenes of ignoble misery; which, however, ignoble as they are, we ought to view with pity rather than contempt.

Such are frequently the fruits of protracted sickness, in men otherwise of estimable qualities and gifts, but whose sensibility exceeds their strength of mind. In Schiller, its worst effects were resisted by the only availing antidote, a strenuous determination to neglect them. His spirit was too vigorous and ardent to yield even in this emergency: he disdained to dwindle into a pining valetudinarian; in the midst of his infirmities, he persevered with unabated zeal in the great business of his life. As he partially recovered, he returned as strenuously as ever to his intellectual occupations; and often, in the glow of poetical conception, he almost forgot his maladies. By such resolute and manly conduct, he disarmed sickness of its cruelest power to wound; his frame might be in pain, but his spirit retained its force, unextinguished, almost unimpeded; he did not lose his relish for the beautiful, the grand, or the good, in any of their shapes; he loved his friends as formerly, and wrote his finest and sublimest works when his health was gone. Perhaps no period of his life displayed more heroism than the present one.

After this severe attack, and the kind provision which he had received from Denmark, Schiller seems to have relaxed his connexion with the University of Jena: the weightiest duties of his class appear to have been discharged by proxy, and his historical studies to have been forsaken. Yet this was but a change, not an abatement, in the activity of his mind. Once partially free from pain, all his former diligence awoke; and being also free from the more pressing calls of duty and economy, he was now allowed to turn his attention to objects which attracted it more. Among these one of the most alluring was the Philosophy of Kant.

The transcendental system of the Königsberg Professor had, for the last ten years, been spreading over Germany, which it had now filled with the most violent contentions. The powers and accomplishments of Kant were universally acknowledged; the high pretensions of his system, pretensions, it is true, such as had been a thousand times put forth, a thousand times found wanting, still excited notice, when so backed by ability and reputation. The air of mysticism connected with these doctrines was attractive to the German mind, with which the vague and the vast are always pleasing qualities; the dreadful array of first principles, the forest huge of terminology and definitions, where the panting intellect of weaker men wanders as in pathless thickets, and at length sinks powerless to the earth, oppressed with fatigue, and suffocated with scholastic miasma, seemed sublime rather than appalling to the Germans; men who shrink not at toil, and to whom a certain degree of darkness appears a native element, essential for giving play to that deep meditative enthusiasm which forms so important a feature in their character. Kant's Philosophy, accordingly, found numerous disciples, and possessed them with a zeal unexampled since the days of Pythagoras. This, in fact, resembled spiritual fanaticism rather than a calm ardour in the cause of science; Kant's warmest admirers seemed to regard him more in the light of a prophet than of a mere earthly sage. Such admiration was of course opposed by corresponding censure; the transcendental neophytes had to encounter sceptical gainsayers as determined as themselves. Of this latter class the most remarkable were Herder and Wieland. Herder, then a clergyman of Weimar, seems never to have comprehended what he fought against so keenly: he denounced and condemned the Kantean metaphysics, because he found them heterodox. The young divines came back from the University of Jena with their minds well nigh delirious; full of strange doctrines, which they explained to the examinators of the Weimar Consistorium in phrases that excited no idea in the heads of these reverend persons, but much horror in their hearts.[25] Hence reprimands, and objurgations, and excessive bitterness between the applicants for ordination and those appointed to confer it: one young clergyman at Weimar shot himself on this account; heresy, and jarring, and unprofitable logic, were universal. Hence Herder's vehement attacks on this 'pernicious quackery;' this delusive and destructive 'system of words.'[26] Wieland strove against it for another reason. He had, all his life, been labouring to give currency among his countrymen to a species of diluted epicurism; to erect a certain smooth, and elegant, and very slender scheme of taste and morals, borrowed from our Shaftesbury and the French. All this feeble edifice the new doctrine was sweeping before it to utter ruin, with the violence of a tornado. It grieved Wieland to see the work of half a century destroyed: he fondly imagined that but for Kant's philosophy it might have been perennial. With scepticism quickened into action by such motives, Herder and he went forth as brother champions against the transcendental metaphysics; they were not long without a multitude of hot assailants. The uproar produced among thinking men by the conflict, has scarcely been equalled in Germany since the days of Luther. Fields were fought, and victories lost and won; nearly all the minds of the nation were, in secret or openly, arrayed on this side or on that. Goethe alone seemed altogether to retain his wonted composure; he was clear for allowing the Kantean scheme to 'have its day, as all things have.' Goethe has already lived to see the wisdom of this sentiment, so characteristic of his genius and turn of thought.

In these controversies, soon pushed beyond the bounds of temperate or wholesome discussion, Schiller took no part: but the noise they made afforded him a fresh inducement to investigate a set of doctrines, so important in the general estimation. A system which promised, even with a very little plausibility, to accomplish all that Kant asserted his complete performance of; to explain the difference between Matter and Spirit, to unravel the perplexities of Necessity and Free-will; to show us the true grounds of our belief in God, and what hope nature gives us of the soul's immortality; and thus at length, after a thousand failures, to interpret the enigma of our being,—hardly needed that additional inducement

[25] Schelling has a book on the 'Soul of the World:' Fichte's expression to his students, "Tomorrow, gentlemen, I shall create God," is known to most readers.

[26] See *Herder's Leben*, by his Widow. That Herder was not usually troubled with any unphilosophical scepticism, or aversion to novelty, may be inferred from his patronising Dr. Gall's system of Phrenology, or 'Skull-doctrine' as they call it in Germany. But Gall had referred with acknowledgment and admiration to the *Philosophie der Geschichte der Menschheit*. Here lay a difference.

to make such a man as Schiller grasp at it with eager curiosity. His progress also was facilitated by his present circumstances; Jena had now become the chief well-spring of Kantean doctrine, a distinction or disgrace it has ever since continued to deserve. Reinhold, one of Kant's ablest followers, was at this time Schiller's fellow-teacher and daily companion: he did not fail to encourage and assist his friend in a path of study, which, as he believed, conducted to such glorious results. Under this tuition, Schiller was not long in discovering, that at least the 'new philosophy was more poetical than that of Leibnitz, and had a grander character;' persuasions which of course confirmed him in his resolution to examine it.

How far Schiller penetrated into the arcana of transcendentalism it is impossible for us to say. The metaphysical and logical branches of it seem to have afforded him no solid satisfaction, or taken no firm hold of his thoughts; their influence is scarcely to be traced in any of his subsequent writings. The only department to which he attached himself with his ordinary zeal was that which relates to the principles of the imitative arts, with their moral influences, and which in the Kantean nomenclature has been designated by the term *Æsthetics*,[27] or the doctrine of sentiments and emotions. On these subjects he had already amassed a multitude of thoughts; to see which expressed by new symbols, and arranged in systematic form, and held together by some common theory, would necessarily yield enjoyment to his intellect, and inspire him with fresh alacrity in prosecuting such researches. The new light which dawned, or seemed to dawn, upon him, in the course of these investigations, is reflected, in various treatises, evincing, at least, the honest diligence with which he studied, and the fertility with which he could produce. Of these the largest and most elaborate are the essays on *Grace and Dignity*; on *Naïve and Sentimental Poetry*; and the *Letters on the Æsthetic Culture of Man*: the other pieces are on *Tragic Art*; on the *Pathetic*; on the *Cause of our Delight in Tragic Objects*; on *Employing the Low and Common in Art*.

Being cast in the mould of Kantism, or at least clothed in its garments, these productions, to readers unacquainted with that system, are encumbered here and there with difficulties greater than belong intrinsically to the subject. In perusing them, the uninitiated student is mortified at seeing so much powerful thought distorted, as he thinks, into such fantastic forms: the principles of reasoning, on which they rest, are apparently not those of common logic; a dimness and doubt overhangs their conclusions; scarcely anything is proved in a convincing manner. But this is no strange quality in such writings. To an exoteric reader the philosophy of Kant almost always appears to invert the common maxim; its end and aim seem not to be 'to make abstruse things simple, but to make simple things abstruse.' Often a proposition of inscrutable and dread aspect, when resolutely grappled with, and torn from its shady den, and its bristling entrenchments of uncouth terminology, and dragged forth into the open light of day, to be seen by the natural eye, and tried by merely human understanding, proves to be a very harmless truth, familiar to us from of old, sometimes so familiar as to be a truism. Too frequently, the anxious novice is reminded of Dryden in the *Battle of the Books*: there is a helmet of rusty iron, dark, grim, gigantic; and within it, at the farthest

---

[27] From the verb αισθάνομαι, *to feel.*—The term is Baumgarten's; prior to Kant (1845).

corner, is a head no bigger than a walnut. These are the general errors of Kantean criticism; in the present works, they are by no means of the worst or most pervading kind; and there is a fundamental merit which does more than counterbalance them. By the aid of study, the doctrine set before us can, in general, at length be comprehended; and Schiller's fine intellect, recognisable even in its masquerade, is ever and anon peering forth in its native form, which all may understand, which all must relish, and presenting us with passages that show like bright verdant islands in the misty sea of metaphysics.

We have been compelled to offer these remarks on Kant's Philosophy; but it is right to add that they are the result of only very limited acquaintance with the subject. We cannot wish that any influence of ours should add a note, however feeble, to the loud and not at all melodious cry which has been raised against it in this country. When a class of doctrines so involved in difficulties, yet so sanctioned by illustrious names, is set before us, curiosity must have a theory respecting them, and indolence and other humbler feelings are too ready to afford her one. To call Kant's system a laborious dream, and its adherents crazy mystics, is a brief method, brief but false. The critic, whose philosophy includes the *craziness* of men like these, so easily and smoothly in its formulas, should render thanks to Heaven for having gifted him with science and acumen, as few in any age or country have been gifted. Meaner men, however, ought to recollect that where we do not understand, we should postpone deciding, or, at least, keep our decision for our own exclusive benefit. We of England may reject this Kantean system, perhaps with reason; but it ought to be on other grounds than are yet before us. Philosophy is science, and science, as Schiller has observed, cannot always be explained in 'conversations by the parlour fire,' or in written treatises that resemble such. The *cui bono* of these doctrines may not, it is true, be expressible by arithmetical computations: the subject also is perplexed with obscurities, and probably with manifold delusions; and too often its interpreters with us have been like 'tenebrific stars,' that 'did ray out darkness' on a matter itself sufficiently dark. But what then? Is the jewel always to be found among the common dust of the highway, and always to be estimated by its value in the common judgment? It lies embosomed in the depths of the mine; rocks must be rent before it can be reached; skilful eyes and hands must separate it from the rubbish where it lies concealed, and kingly purchasers alone can prize it and buy it. This law of *ostracism* is as dangerous in science as it was of old in politics. Let us not forget that many things are true which cannot be demonstrated by the rules of *Watts's Logic*; that many truths are valuable, for which no price is given in Paternoster Row, and no preferment offered at St. Stephen's! Whoever reads these treatises of Schiller with attention, will perceive that they depend on principles of an immensely higher and more complex character than our 'Essays on Taste,' and our 'Inquiries concerning the Freedom of the Will.' The laws of criticism, which it is their purpose to establish, are derived from the inmost nature of man; the scheme of morality, which they inculcate, soars into a brighter region, very far beyond the ken of our 'Utilities' and 'Reflex-senses.' They do not teach us 'to judge of poetry and art as we judge of dinner,' merely by observing the impressions it produced in us; and they *do* derive the duties and chief end of man from other grounds than the philosophy of Profit and

Loss. These *Letters on Æsthetic Culture*, without the aid of anything which the most sceptical could designate as superstition, trace out and attempt to sanction for us a system of morality, in which the sublimest feelings of the Stoic and the Christian are represented but as stages in our progress to the pinnacle of true human grandeur; and man, isolated on this fragment of the universe, encompassed with the boundless desolate Unknown, at war with Fate, without help or the hope of help, is confidently called upon to rise into a calm cloudless height of internal activity and peace, and *be*, what he has fondly named himself, the god of this lower world. When such are the results, who would not make an effort for the steps by which they are attained? In Schiller's treatises, it must be owned, the reader, after all exertions, will be fortunate if he can find them. Yet a second perusal will satisfy him better than the first; and among the shapeless immensities which fill the Night of Kantism, and the meteoric coruscations, which perplex him rather than enlighten, he will fancy he descries some streaks of a serener radiance, which he will pray devoutly that time may purify and ripen into perfect day. The Philosophy of Kant is probably combined with errors to its very core; but perhaps also, this ponderous unmanageable dross may bear in it the everlasting gold of truth! Mighty spirits have already laboured in refining it: is it wise in us to take up with the base pewter of Utility, and renounce such projects altogether? We trust, not.[28]

That Schiller's *genius* profited by this laborious and ardent study of Æsthetic Metaphysics, has frequently been doubted, and sometimes denied. That, after such investigations, the process of composition would become more difficult, might be inferred from the nature of the case. That also the principles of this critical theory were in part erroneous, in still greater part too far-fetched and fine-spun for application to the business of writing, we may farther venture to assert. But excellence, not ease of composition, is the thing to be desired; and in a mind like Schiller's, so full of energy, of images and thoughts and creative power, the more sedulous practice of selection was little likely to be detrimental. And though considerable errors might mingle with the rules by which he judged himself, the habit of judging carelessly, or not at all, is far worse than that of sometimes judging wrong. Besides, once accustomed to attend strictly to the operations of his genius, and rigorously to try its products, such a man as Schiller could not fail in time to discover what was false in the principles by which he tried them, and consequently, in the end, to retain the benefits of this procedure without its evils. There is doubtless a purism in taste, a rigid fantastical demand of perfection, a horror at approaching the limits of impropriety, which obstructs the free impulse of the faculties, and if excessive, would altogether deaden them. But the excess on the other side is much more frequent, and, for high endowments, infinitely more pernicious. After the strongest efforts, there may be little realised; without strong efforts, there must be little. That too much care does hurt in any of our tasks is a doctrine so flattering to indolence, that we ought to receive it with extreme caution. In works impressed with the stamp of true genius, their quality, not their extent, is what we value: a dull man may spend his lifetime writing little; better so than writing much; but

---

[28] Are our hopes from Mr. Coleridge always to be fruitless? Sneers at the common-sense philosophy of the Scotch are of little use: it is a poor philosophy, perhaps; but not so poor as none at all, which seems to be the state of matters here at present.

a man of powerful mind is liable to no such danger. Of all our authors, Gray is perhaps the only one that from fastidiousness of taste has written less than he should have done: there are thousands that have erred the other way. What would a Spanish reader give, had Lope de Vega composed a hundred times as little, and that little a hundred times as well!

Schiller's own ideas on these points appear to be sufficiently sound: they are sketched in the following extract of a letter, interesting also as a record of his purposes and intellectual condition at this period:

'Criticism must now make good to me the damage she herself has done. And damaged me she most certainly has; for the boldness, the living glow which I felt before a rule was known to me, have for several years been wanting. I now *see* myself *create* and *form*: I watch the play of inspiration; and my fancy, knowing she is not without witnesses of her movements, no longer moves with equal freedom. I hope, however, ultimately to advance so far that *art* shall become a second *nature*, as polished manners are to well-bred men; then Imagination will regain her former freedom, and submit to none but voluntary limitations.'

Schiller's subsequent writings are the best proof that in these expectations he had not miscalculated.

The historical and critical studies, in which he had been so extensively and seriously engaged, could not remain without effect on Schiller's general intellectual character. He had spent five active years in studies directed almost solely to the understanding, or the faculties connected with it; and such industry united to such ardour had produced an immense accession of ideas. History had furnished him with pictures of manners and events, of strange conjunctures and conditions of existence; it had given him more minute and truer conceptions of human nature in its many forms, new and more accurate opinions on the character and end of man. The domain of his mind was both enlarged and enlightened; a multitude of images and detached facts and perceptions had been laid up in his memory; and his intellect was at once enriched by acquired thoughts, and strengthened by increased exercise on a wider circle of knowledge.

But to understand was not enough for Schiller; there were in him faculties which this could not employ, and therefore could not satisfy. The primary vocation of his nature was poetry: the acquisitions of his other faculties served but as the materials for his poetic faculty to act upon, and seemed imperfect till they had been sublimated into the pure and perfect forms of beauty, which it is the business of this to elicit from them. New thoughts gave birth to new feelings: and both of these he was now called upon to body forth, to represent by visible types, to animate and adorn with the magic of creative genius. The first youthful blaze of poetic ardour had long since passed away; but this large increase of knowledge awakened it anew, refined by years and experience into a steadier and clearer flame. Vague shadows of unaccomplished excellence, gleams of ideal beauty, were now hovering fitfully across his mind: he longed to turn them into shape, and give them a local habitation and a name. Criticism, likewise, had exalted his notions of art: the modern writers on subjects of taste, Aristotle, the ancient poets, he had lately studied; he had carefully endeavoured to extract the truth from each, and to amalgamate their principles with his own; in choosing, he was now more difficult to satisfy. Minor poems had all along been partly occupying his attention; but they yielded no space for the intensity of his impulses, and the magnificent ideas that were rising in his fancy. Conscious of his strength, he dreaded not engaging with the highest species of his art: the perusal of the Greek tragedians had given rise to some late translations;[29] the perusal of Homer seems now to have suggested the idea of an epic poem. The hero whom he first contemplated was Gustavus Adolphus; he afterwards changed to Frederick the Great of Prussia.

Epic poems, since the time of the *Epigoniad*, and *Leonidas*, and especially since that of some more recent attempts, have with us become a mighty dull affair. That Schiller aimed at something infinitely higher than these faint and superannuated imitations, far higher than even Klopstock has attained, will appear by the following extract from one of his letters:

'An epic poem in the eighteenth century should be quite a different thing from such a poem in the childhood of the world. And it is that very circumstance which attracts me so much towards this project. Our manners, the finest essence of our philosophies, our politics, economy, arts, in short, of all we know and do, would require to be introduced without constraint, and interwoven in such a composition, to live there in beautiful harmonious freedom, as all the branches of Greek culture live and are made visible in Homer's *Iliad*. Nor am I disinclined to invent a species of machinery for this purpose; being anxious to fulfil, with hairsbreadth accuracy, all the requisitions that are made of epic poets, even on the side of form. Besides, this machinery, which, in a subject so modern, in an age so prosaic, appears to present the greatest difficulty, might exalt the interest in a high degree, were it suitably adapted to this same modern spirit. Crowds of confused ideas on this matter are rolling to and fro within my head; something distinct will come out of them at last.

'As for the sort of metre I would choose, this I think you will hardly guess: no other than *ottave rime*. All the rest, except iambic, are become insufferable to me. And how beautifully might the earnest and the lofty be made to play in these light fetters! What attractions might the epic *substance* gain by the soft yielding *form* of this fine rhyme! For, the poem must, not in name only, but in very deed, be capable of being *sung*; as the *Iliad* was sung by the peasants of Greece, as the stanzas of *Jerusalem Delivered* are still sung by the Venetian gondoliers.

'The epoch of Frederick's life that would fit me best, I have considered also. I should wish to select some unhappy situation; it would allow me to unfold his mind far more poetically. The chief action should, if possible, be very simple, perplexed with no complicated circumstances, that the whole might easily be comprehended at a glance, though the episodes were never so numerous. In this respect there is no better model than the *Iliad*.'

Schiller did not execute, or even commence, the project he has here so philo-

---

[29] These were a fine version, of Euripides' *Iphigenia in Aulide*, and a few scenes of his *Phœnissæ*.

sophically sketched: the constraints of his present situation, the greatness of the enterprise compared with the uncertainty of its success, were sufficient to deter him. Besides, he felt that after all his wide excursions, the true home of his genius was the Drama, the department where its powers had first been tried, and were now by habit or nature best qualified to act. To the Drama he accordingly returned. The *History of the Thirty-Years War* had once suggested the idea of Gustavus Adolphus as the hero of an epic poem; the same work afforded him a subject for a tragedy: he now decided on beginning *Wallenstein*. In this undertaking it was no easy task that he contemplated; a common play did not now comprise his aim; he required some magnificent and comprehensive object, in which he could expend to advantage the new poetical and intellectual treasures which he had for years been amassing; something that should at once exemplify his enlarged ideas of art, and give room and shape to his fresh stores of knowledge and sentiment. As he studied the history of Wallenstein, and viewed its capabilities on every side, new ideas gathered round it: the subject grew in magnitude, and often changed in form. His progress in actual composition was, of course, irregular and small. Yet the difficulties of the subject, increasing with his own wider, more ambitious conceptions, did not abate his diligence: *Wallenstein*, with many interruptions and many alterations, sometimes stationary, sometimes retrograde, continued on the whole, though slowly, to advance.

This was for several years his chosen occupation, the task to which he consecrated his brightest hours, and the finest part of his faculties. For humbler employments, demanding rather industry than inspiration, there still remained abundant leisure, of which it was inconsistent with his habits to waste a single hour. His occasional labours, accordingly, were numerous, varied, and sometimes of considerable extent. In the end of 1792, a new object seemed to call for his attention; he once about this time seriously meditated mingling in politics. The French Revolution had from the first affected him with no ordinary hopes; which, however, the course of events, particularly the imprisonment of Louis, were now fast converting into fears. For the ill-fated monarch, and the cause of freedom, which seemed threatened with disgrace in the treatment he was likely to receive, Schiller felt so deeply interested, that he had determined, in his case a determination not without its risks, to address an appeal on these subjects to the French people and the world at large. The voice of reason advocating liberty as well as order might still, he conceived, make a salutary impression in this period of terror and delusion; the voice of a distinguished man would at first sound like the voice of the nation, which he seemed to represent. Schiller was inquiring for a proper French translator, and revolving in his mind the various arguments that might be used, and the comparative propriety of using or forbearing to use them; but the progress of things superseded the necessity of such deliberation. In a few months, Louis perished on the scaffold; the Bourbon family were murdered, or scattered over Europe; and the French government was changed into a frightful chaos, amid the tumultuous and bloody horrors of which, calm truth had no longer a chance to be heard. Schiller turned away from these repulsive and appalling scenes, into other regions where his heart was more familiar, and his powers more likely to produce effect. The French Revolution had distressed and shocked him; but it did not lessen his attachment to liberty, the name of which had been so desecrated in its wild convulsions. Perhaps in his subsequent writings we can trace a more respectful feeling towards old establishments; more reverence for the majesty of Custom; and with an equal zeal, a weaker faith in human perfectibility: changes indeed which are the common fruit of years themselves, in whatever age or climate of the world our experience may be gathered.

Among the number of fluctuating engagements, one, which for ten years had been constant with him, was the editing of the *Thalia*. The principles and performances of that work he had long looked upon as insufficient: in particular, ever since his settlement at Jena, it had been among his favourite projects to exchange it for some other, conducted on a more liberal scheme, uniting more ability in its support, and embracing a much wider compass of literary interests. Many of the most distinguished persons in Germany had agreed to assist him in executing such a plan; Goethe, himself a host, undertook to go hand in hand with him. The *Thalia* was in consequence relinquished at the end of 1793: and the first number of the *Horen* came out early in the following year. This publication was enriched with many valuable pieces on points of philosophy and criticism; some of Schiller's finest essays first appeared here: even without the foreign aids which had been promised him, it already bade fair to outdo, as he had meant it should, every previous work of that description.

The *Musen-Almanach*, of which he likewise undertook the superintendence, did not aim so high: like other works of the same title, which are numerous in Germany, it was intended for preserving and annually delivering to the world, a series of short poetical effusions, or other fugitive compositions, collected from various quarters, and often having no connexion but their juxtaposition. In this work, as well as in the *Horen*, some of Schiller's finest smaller poems made their first appearance; many of these pieces being written about this period, especially the greater part of his ballads, the idea of attempting which took its rise in a friend-ly rivalry with Goethe. But the most noted composition sent forth in the pages of the *Musen-Almanach*, was the *Xenien*;[30] a collection of epigrams which originated partly, as it seems, in the mean or irritating conduct of various contemporary authors. In spite of the most flattering promises, and of its own intrinsic character, the *Horen*, at its first appearance, instead of being hailed with welcome by the leading minds of the country, for whom it was intended as a rallying point, met in many quarters with no sentiment but coldness or hostility. The controversies of the day had sown discord among literary men; Schiller and Goethe, associating together, had provoked ill-will from a host of persons, who felt the justice of such mutual preference, but liked not the inferences to be drawn from it; and eyed this intellectual duumvirate, however meek in the discharge of its functions and the wearing of its honours, with jealousy and discontent.

The cavilling of these people, awkwardly contrasted with their personal absurdity and insipidity, at length provoked the serious notice of the two illustrious associates: the result was this German Dunciad; a production of which the plan

---

[30] So called from ξένιον, *munus hospitale*; a title borrowed from Martial, who has thus designated a series of personal epigrams in his Thirteenth Book.

was, that it should comprise an immense multitude of detached couplets, each conveying a complete thought within itself, and furnished by one of the joint operators. The subjects were of unlimited variety; 'the most,' as Schiller says, 'were wild satire, glancing at writers and writings, intermixed with here and there a flash of poetical or philosophic thought.' It was at first intended to provide about a thousand of these pointed monodistichs; unity in such a work appearing to consist in a certain boundlessness of size, which should hide the heterogeneous nature of the individual parts: the whole were then to be arranged and elaborated, till they had acquired the proper degree of consistency and symmetry; each sacrificing something of its own peculiar spirit to preserve the spirit of the rest. This number never was completed: and, Goethe being now busy with his *Wilhelm Meister*, the project of completing it was at length renounced; and the *Xenien* were published as unconnected particles, not pretending to constitute a whole. Enough appeared to create unbounded commotion among the parties implicated: the *Xenien* were exclaimed against, abused, and replied to, on all hands; but as they declared war not on persons but on actions; not against Gleim, Nicolai, Manso, but against bad taste, dulness, and affectation, nothing criminal could be sufficiently made out against them.[31] The *Musen-Almanach*, where they appeared in 1797, continued to be published till the time of Schiller's leaving Jena: the *Horen* ceased some months before.

The coöperation of Goethe, which Schiller had obtained so readily in these pursuits, was of singular use to him in many others. Both possessing minds of the first order, yet constructed and trained in the most opposite modes, each had much that was valuable to learn of the other, and suggest to him. Cultivating different kinds of excellence, they could joyfully admit each other's merit; connected by mutual services, and now by community of literary interests, few unkindly feelings could have place between them. For a man of high equalities, it is rare to find a meet companion; painful and injurious to want one. Solitude exasperates or deadens the heart, perverts or enervates the faculties; association with inferiors leads to dogmatism in thought, and self-will even in affections. Rousseau never should have lived in the Val de Montmorenci; it had been good for Warburton that Hurd had not existed; for Johnson never to have known Boswell or Davies. From such evils Schiller and Goethe were delivered; their intimacy seems to have been equal, frank and cordial; from the contrasts and the endowments of their minds, it must have had peculiar charms. In his critical theories, Schiller had derived much profit from communicating with an intellect as excursive as his own, but far cooler and more sceptical: as he lopped off from his creed the excrescences of Kantism, Goethe and he, on comparing their ideas, often found in them a striking similarity; more striking and more gratifying, when it was considered from what diverse premises these harmonious conclusions had been drawn. On such subjects they often corresponded when absent, and conversed when together. They were in the habit of paying long visits to each other's houses; frequently they used to travel in company between Jena and Weimar. 'At Triesnitz, a couple of English miles from

---

[31] This is but a lame account of the far-famed *Xenien* and their results. See more of the matter in Franz Horn's *Poesie und Beredtsamkeit*; in Carlyle's *Miscellanies* (i. 67); &c. (*Note of 1845.*)

Jena, Goethe and he,' we are told, 'might sometimes be observed sitting at table, beneath the shade of a spreading tree; talking, and looking at the current of passengers.'—There are some who would have 'travelled fifty miles on foot' to join the party!

Besides this intercourse with Goethe, he was happy in a kindly connexion with many other estimable men, both in literary and in active life. Dalberg, at a distance, was to the last his friend and warmest admirer. At Jena, he had Schütz, Paul, Hufland, Reinhold. Wilhelm von Humboldt, also, brother of the celebrated traveller, had come thither about this time, and was now among his closest associates. At Weimar, excluding less important persons, there were still Herder and Wieland, to divide his attention with Goethe. And what to his affectionate heart must have been the most grateful circumstance of all, his aged parents were yet living to participate in the splendid fortune of the son whom they had once lamented and despaired of, but never ceased to love. In 1793 he paid them a visit in Swabia, and passed nine cheerful months among the scenes dearest to his recollection: enjoying the kindness of those unalterable friends whom Nature had given him; and the admiring deference of those by whom it was most delightful to be honoured,—those who had known him in adverse and humbler circumstances, whether they might have respected or contemned him. By the Grand Duke, his ancient censor and patron, he was not interfered with; that prince, in answer to a previous application on the subject, having indirectly engaged to take no notice of this journey. The Grand Duke had already interfered too much with him, and bitterly repented of his interference. Next year he died; an event which Schiller, who had long forgotten past ill-treatment, did not learn without true sorrow, and grateful recollections of bygone kindness. The new sovereign, anxious to repair the injustice of his predecessor, almost instantly made offer of a vacant Tübingen professorship to Schiller; a proposal flattering to the latter, but which, by the persuasion of the Duke of Weimar, he respectfully declined.

Amid labours and amusements so multiplied, amid such variety of intellectual exertion and of intercourse with men, Schiller, it was clear, had not suffered the encroachments of bodily disease to undermine the vigour of his mental or moral powers. No period of his life displayed in stronger colours the lofty and determined zeal of his character. He had already written much; his fame stood upon a firm basis; domestic wants no longer called upon him for incessant effort; and his frame was pining under the slow canker of an incurable malady. Yet he never loitered, never rested; his fervid spirit, which had vanquished opposition and oppression in his youth; which had struggled against harassing uncertainties, and passed unsullied through many temptations, in his earlier manhood, did not now yield to this last and most fatal enemy. The present was the busiest, most productive season of his literary life; and with all its drawbacks, it was probably the happiest. Violent attacks from his disorder were of rare occurrence; and its constant influence, the dark vapours with which it would have overshadowed the faculties of his head and heart, were repelled by diligence and a courageous exertion of his will. In other points, he had little to complain of, and much to rejoice in. He was happy in his family, the chosen scene of his sweetest, most lasting satisfaction; by the world he was honoured and admired; his wants were provided for; he had tasks which inspired and occupied him; friends who loved him, and whom he loved. Schiller had much to enjoy, and most of it he owed to himself.

In his mode of life at Jena, simplicity and uniformity were the most conspicuous qualities; the single excess which he admitted being that of zeal in the pursuits of literature, the sin which all his life had most easily beset him. His health had suffered much, and principally, it was thought, from the practice of composing by night: yet the charms of this practice were still too great for his self-denial; and, except in severe fits of sickness, he could not discontinue it. The highest, proudest pleasure of his mind was that glow of intellectual production, that 'fine frenzy,' which makes the poet, while it lasts, a new and nobler creature; exalting him into brighter regions, adorned by visions of magnificence and beauty, and delighting all his faculties by the intense consciousness of their exerted power. To enjoy this pleasure in perfection, the solitary stillness of night, diffusing its solemn influence over thought as well as earth and air, had at length in Schiller's case grown indispensable. For this purpose, accordingly, he was accustomed, in the present, as in former periods, to invert the common order of things: by day he read, refreshed himself with the aspect of nature, conversed or corresponded with his friends; but he wrote and studied in the night. And as his bodily feelings were too often those of languor and exhaustion, he adopted, in impatience of such mean impediments, the pernicious expedient of stimulants, which yield a momentary strength, only to waste our remaining fund of it more speedily and surely.

'During summer, his place of study was in a garden, which at length he purchased, in the suburbs of Jena, not far from the Weselhöfts' house, where at that time was the office of the *Allgemeine Litteratur-Zeitung*. Reckoning from the market-place of Jena, it lies on the south-west border of the town, between the Engelgatter and the Neuthor, in a hollow defile, through which a part of the Leutrabach flows round the city. On the top of the acclivity, from which there is a beautiful prospect into the valley of the Saal, and the fir mountains of the neighbouring forest, Schiller built himself a small house, with a single chamber.[32] It was his favourite abode during hours of composition; a great part of the works he then wrote were written here. In winter he likewise dwelt apart from the noise of men; in the Griesbachs' house, on the outside of the city-trench. *** On sitting down to his desk at night, he was wont to keep some strong coffee, or wine-chocolate, but more frequently a flask of old Rhenish, or Champagne, standing by him, that he might from time to time repair the exhaustion of nature. Often the neighbours used to hear him earnestly declaiming, in the silence of the night: and whoever had an opportunity of watching him on such occasions, a thing very easy to be done from the heights lying opposite his little garden-house, on the other side of the dell, might see him now speaking aloud and walking swiftly to and fro in his chamber, then suddenly throwing himself down into his chair and writing; and drinking the while, sometimes more than once, from the glass standing near him. In winter he was to be found at his desk till four, or even five o'clock in the morn-

---

[32] 'The street leading from Schiller's dwelling-house to this, was by some wags named the *Xenien-gasse*; a name not yet entirely disused.'

ing; in summer, till towards three. He then went to bed, from which he seldom rose till nine or ten.'[33]

Had prudence been the dominant quality in Schiller's character, this practice would undoubtedly have been abandoned, or rather never taken up. It was an error so to waste his strength; but one of those which increase rather than diminish our respect; originating, as it did, in generous ardour for what was best and grandest, they must be cold censurers that can condemn it harshly. For ourselves, we but lament and honour this excess of zeal; its effects were mournful, but its origin was noble. Who can picture Schiller's feelings in this solitude, without participating in some faint reflection of their grandeur! The toil-worn but devoted soul, alone, under the silent starry canopy of Night, offering up the troubled moments of existence on the altar of Eternity! For here the splendour that gleamed across the spirit of a mortal, transient as one of us, was made to be perpetual; these images and thoughts were to pass into other ages and distant lands; to glow in human hearts, when the heart that conceived them had long been mouldered into common dust. To the lovers of genius, this little garden-house might have been a place to visit as a chosen shrine; nor will they learn without regret that the walls of it, yielding to the hand of time, have already crumbled into ruin, and are now no longer to be traced. The piece of ground that it stood on is itself hallowed with a glory that is bright, pure and abiding; but the literary pilgrim could not have surveyed, without peculiar emotion, the simple chamber, in which Schiller wrote the *Reich der Schatten*, the *Spaziergang*, the *Ideal*, and the immortal scenes of *Wallenstein*.

The last-named work had cost him many an anxious, given him many a pleasant, hour. For seven years it had continued in a state of irregular, and oft-suspended progress; sometimes 'lying endless and formless' before him; sometimes on the point of being given up altogether. The multitude of ideas, which he wished to incorporate in the structure of the piece, retarded him; and the difficulty of contenting his taste, respecting the manner of effecting this, retarded him still more. In *Wallenstein* he wished to embody the more enlarged notions which experience had given him of men, especially which history had given him of generals and statesmen; and while putting such characters in action, to represent whatever was, or could be made, poetical, in the stormy period of the Thirty-Years War. As he meditated on the subject, it continued to expand; in his fancy, it assumed successively a thousand forms; and after all due strictness of selection, such was still the extent of materials remaining on his hands, that he found it necessary to divide the play into three parts, distinct in their arrangements, but in truth forming a continuous drama of eleven acts. In this shape it was sent forth to the world, in 1799; a work of labour and persevering anxiety, but of anxiety and labour, as it then appeared, which had not been bestowed in vain. *Wallenstein* is by far the best performance he had yet produced; it merits a long chapter of criticism by itself; and a few hurried pages are all that we can spend on it.

As a porch to the great edifice stands Part first, entitled *Wallenstein's Camp*, a piece in one act. It paints, with much humour and graphical felicity, the manners of that rude tumultuous host which Wallenstein presided over, and had made the

[33] Doering, pp. 118-131.

engine of his ambitious schemes. Schiller's early experience of a military life seems now to have stood him in good stead; his soldiers are delineated with the distinctness of actual observation; in rugged sharpness of feature, they sometimes remind us of Smollett's seamen. Here are all the wild lawless spirits of Europe assembled within the circuit of a single trench. Violent, tempestuous, unstable is the life they lead. Ishmaelites, their hands against every man, and every man's hand against them; the instruments of rapine; tarnished with almost every vice, and knowing scarcely any virtue but those of reckless bravery and uncalculating obedience to their leader, their situation still presents some aspects which affect or amuse us; and these the poet has seized with his accustomed skill. Much of the cruelty and repulsive harshness of these soldiers, we are taught to forget in contemplating their forlorn houseless wanderings, and the practical magnanimity, with which even they contrive to wring from Fortune a tolerable scantling of enjoyment. Their manner of existence Wallenstein has, at an after period of the action, rather movingly expressed:

> 'Our life was but a battle and a march,
> And, like the wind's blast, never-resting, homeless,
> We storm'd across the war-convulsed Earth.'

Still farther to soften the asperities of the scene, the dialogue is cast into a rude Hudibrastic metre, full of forced rhymes, and strange double-endings, with a rhythm ever changing, ever rough and lively, which might almost be compared to the hard, irregular, fluctuating sound of the regimental drum. In this ludicrous doggrel, with phrases and figures of a correspondent cast, homely, ridiculous, graphic, these men of service paint their hopes and doings. There are ranks and kinds among them; representatives of all the constituent parts of the motley multitude, which followed this prince of *Condottieri*. The solemn pedantry of the ancient Wachtmeister is faithfully given; no less so are the jocund ferocity and heedless daring of Holky's Jägers, or the iron courage and stern camp-philosophy of Pappenheim's Cuirassiers. Of the Jäger the sole principle is military obedience; he does not reflect or calculate; his business is to do whatever he is ordered, and to enjoy whatever he can reach. 'Free wished I to live,' he says,

> 'Free wished I to live, and easy and gay,
> And see something new on each new day;
> In the joys of the moment lustily sharing,
> 'Bout the past or the future not thinking or caring:
> To the Kaiser, therefore, I sold my bacon,
> And by him good charge of the whole is taken.
> Order me on 'mid the whistling fiery shot,
> Over the Rhine-stream rapid and roaring wide,
> A third of the troop must go to pot, —
> Without loss of time, I mount and ride;
> But farther, I beg very much, do you see,
> That in all things else you would leave me free.'

The Pappenheimer is an older man, more sedate and more indomitable; he has wandered over Europe, and gathered settled maxims of soldierly principle and soldierly privilege: he is not without a *rationale* of life; the various professions of men have passed in review before him, but no coat that he has seen has pleased him like his own 'steel doublet,' cased in which, it is his wish,

> 'Looking down on the world's poor restless scramble,
> Careless, through it, astride of his nag to ramble.'

Yet at times with this military stoicism there is blended a dash of homely pathos; he admits,

> 'This sword of ours is no plough or spade,
> You cannot delve or reap with the iron blade;
> For us there falls no seed, no corn-field grows,
> Neither home nor kindred the soldier knows:
> Wandering over the face of the earth,
> Warming his hands at another's hearth:
> From the pomp of towns he must onward roam;
> In the village-green with its cheerful game,
> In the mirth of the vintage or harvest-home,
> No part or lot can the soldier claim.
> Tell me then, in the place of goods or pelf,
> What has he unless to honour himself?
> Leave not even *this* his own, what wonder
> The man should burn and kill and plunder?

But the camp of Wallenstein is fall of bustle as well as speculation; there are gamblers, peasants, sutlers, soldiers, recruits, capuchin friars, moving to and fro in restless pursuit of their several purposes. The sermon of the Capuchin is an unparalleled composition;[34] a medley of texts, puns, nicknames, and verbal logic, conglutinated by a stupid judgment, and a fiery catholic zeal. It seems to be delivered with great unction, and to find fit audience in the camp: towards the conclusion they rush upon him, and he narrowly escapes killing or ducking, for having ventured to glance a censure at the General. The soldiers themselves are jeering, wrangling, jostling; discussing their wishes and expectations; and, at last, they combine in a profound deliberation on the state of their affairs. A vague exaggerated outline of the coming events and personages is imaged to us in their coarse conceptions. We dimly discover the precarious position of Wallenstein; the plots which threaten him, which he is meditating: we trace the leading qualities of the principal officers; and form a high estimate of the potent spirit which, binds this fierce discordant mass together, and seems to be the object of universal reverence where nothing else is revered.

In the *Two Piccolomini*, the next division of the work, the generals for whom we have thus been prepared appear in person on the scene, and spread out before us their plots and counterplots; Wallenstein, through personal ambition and evil

[34] Said to be by Goethe; the materials faithfully extracted from a real sermon (by the Jesuit Santa Clara) of the period it refers to. — There were various Jesuits Santa Clara, of that period: this is the *German* one, Abraham by name; specimens of whose Sermons, a fervent kind of preaching-run-mad, have been reprinted in late years, for dilettante purposes, (*Note of 1845.*)

counsel, slowly resolving to revolt; and Octavio Piccolomini, in secret, undermining his influence among the leaders, and preparing for him that pit of ruin, into which, in the third Part, *Wallenstein's Death*, we see him sink with all his fortunes. The military spirit which pervades the former piece is here well sustained. The ruling motives of these captains and colonels are a little more refined, or more disguised, than those of the Cuirassiers and Jägers; but they are the same in substance; the love of present or future pleasure, of action, reputation, money, power; selfishness, but selfishness distinguished by a superficial external propriety, and gilded over with the splendour of military honour, of courage inflexible, yet light, cool and unassuming. These are not imaginary heroes, but genuine hired men of war: we do not love them; yet there is a pomp about their operations, which agreeably fills up the scene. This din of war, this clash of tumultuous conflicting interests, is felt as a suitable accompaniment to the affecting or commanding movements of the chief characters whom it envelops or obeys.

Of the individuals that figure in this world of war, Wallenstein himself, the strong Atlas which supports it all, is by far the most imposing. Wallenstein is the model of a high-souled, great, accomplished man, whose ruling passion is ambition. He is daring to the utmost pitch of manhood; he is enthusiastic and vehement; but the fire of his soul burns hid beneath a deep stratum of prudence, guiding itself by calculations which extend to the extreme limits of his most minute concerns. This prudence, sometimes almost bordering on irresolution, forms the outward rind of his character, and for a while is the only quality which we discover in it. The immense influence which his genius appears to exert on every individual of his many followers, prepares us to expect a great man; and, when Wallenstein, after long delay and much forewarning, is in fine presented to us, we at first experience something like a disappointment. We find him, indeed, possessed of a staid grandeur; yet involved in mystery; wavering between two opinions; and, as it seems, with all his wisdom, blindly credulous in matters of the highest import. It is only when events have forced decision on him, that he rises in his native might, that his giant spirit stands unfolded in its strength before us;

'Night must it be, ere Friedland's star will beam:'

amid difficulties, darkness and impending ruin, at which the boldest of his followers grow pale, he himself is calm, and first in this awful crisis feels the serenity and conscious strength of his soul return. Wallenstein, in fact, though pre-eminent in power, both external and internal, of high intellect and commanding will, skilled in war and statesmanship beyond the best in Europe, the idol of sixty thousand fearless hearts, is not yet removed above our sympathy. We are united with him by feelings, which he reckons weak, though they belong to the most generous parts of his nature. His indecision partly takes its rise in the sensibilities of his heart, as well as in the caution of his judgment: his belief in astrology, which gives force and confirmation to this tendency, originates in some soft kindly emotions, and adds a new interest to the spirit of the warrior; it humbles him, to whom the earth is subject, before those mysterious Powers which weigh the destinies of man in their balance, in whose eyes the greatest and the least of mortals scarcely differ in littleness. Wallenstein's confidence in the friendship of Octavio, his disinterested love for Max Piccolomini, his paternal and brotherly kindness, are feelings which cast an affecting lustre over the harsher, more heroic qualities wherewith they are combined. His treason to the Emperor is a crime, for which, provoked and tempted as he was, we do not greatly blame him; it is forgotten in our admiration of his nobleness, or recollected only as a venial trespass. Schiller has succeeded well with Wallenstein, where it was not easy to succeed. The truth of history has been but little violated; yet we are compelled to feel that Wallenstein, whose actions individually are trifling, unsuccessful, and unlawful, is a strong, sublime, commanding character; we look at him with interest, our concern at his fate is tinged with a shade of kindly pity.

In Octavio Piccolomini, his war-companion, we can find less fault, yet we take less pleasure. Octavio's qualities are chiefly negative: he rather walks by the letter of the moral law, than by its spirit; his conduct is externally correct, but there is no touch of generosity within. He is more of the courtier than of the soldier: his weapon is intrigue, not force. Believing firmly that 'whatever is, is best,' he distrusts all new and extraordinary things; he has no faith in human nature, and seems to be virtuous himself more by calculation than by impulse. We scarcely thank him for his loyalty; serving his Emperor, he ruins and betrays his friend: and, besides, though he does not own it, personal ambition is among his leading motives; he wishes to be general and prince, and Wallenstein is not only a traitor to his sovereign, but a bar to this advancement. It is true, Octavio does not personally tempt him towards his destruction; but neither does he warn him from it; and perhaps he knew that fresh temptation was superfluous. Wallenstein did not deserve such treatment from a man whom he had trusted as a brother, even though such confidence was blind, and guided by visions and starry omens. Octavio is a skilful, prudent, managing statesman; of the kind praised loudly, if not sincerely, by their friends, and detested deeply by their enemies. His object may be lawful or even laudable; but his ways are crooked; we dislike him but the more that we know not positively how to blame him.

Octavio Piccolomini and Wallenstein are, as it were, the two opposing forces by which this whole universe of military politics is kept in motion. The struggle of magnanimity and strength combined with treason, against cunning and apparent virtue, aided by law, gives rise to a series of great actions, which are here vividly presented to our view. We mingle in the clashing interests of these men of war; we see them at their gorgeous festivals and stormy consultations, and participate in the hopes or fears that agitate them. The subject had many capabilities; and Schiller has turned them all to profit. Our minds are kept alert by a constant succession of animating scenes of spectacle, dialogue, incident: the plot thickens and darkens as we advance; the interest deepens and deepens to the very end.

But among the tumults of this busy multitude, there are two forms of celestial beauty that solicit our attention, and whose destiny, involved with that of those around them, gives it an importance in our eyes which it could not otherwise have had. Max Piccolomini, Octavio's son, and Thekla, the daughter of Wallenstein, diffuse an ethereal radiance over all this tragedy; they call forth the finest feelings of the heart, where other feelings had already been aroused; they superadd to the stirring pomp of scenes, which had already kindled our imaginations, the enthusiasm of bright unworn humanity, 'the bloom of young desire, the purple light of love.' The history of Max and Thekla is not a rare one in poetry; but Schiller has treated it with a skill which is extremely rare. Both of them are represented as combining every excellence; their affection is instantaneous and unbounded; yet the coolest, most sceptical reader is forced to admire them, and believe in them.

Of Max we are taught from the first to form the highest expectations: the common soldiers and their captains speak of him as of a perfect hero; the Cuirassiers had, at Pappenheim's death, on the field of Lützen, appointed him their colonel by unanimous election. His appearance answers these ideas: Max is the very spirit of honour, and integrity, and young ardour, personified. Though but passing into maturer age, he has already seen and suffered much; but the experience of the man has not yet deadened or dulled the enthusiasm of the boy. He has lived, since his very childhood, constantly amid the clang of war, and with few ideas but those of camps; yet here, by a native instinct, his heart has attracted to it all that was noble and graceful in the trade of arms, rejecting all that was repulsive or ferocious. He loves Wallenstein his patron, his gallant and majestic leader: he loves his present way of life, because it is one of peril and excitement, because he knows no other, but chiefly because his young unsullied spirit can shed a resplendent beauty over even the wastest region in the destiny of man. Yet though a soldier, and the bravest of soldiers, he is not this alone. He feels that there are fairer scenes in life, which these scenes of havoc and distress but deform or destroy; his first acquaintance with the Princess Thekla unveils to him another world, which till then he had not dreamed of; a land of peace and serene elysian felicity, the charms of which he paints with simple and unrivalled eloquence. Max is not more daring than affectionate; he is merciful and gentle, though his training has been under tents; modest and altogether unpretending, though young and universally admired. We conceive his aspect to be thoughtful but fervid, dauntless but mild: he is the very poetry of war, the essence of a youthful hero. We should have loved him anywhere; but here, amid barren scenes of strife and danger, he is doubly dear to us.

His first appearance wins our favour; his eloquence in sentiment prepares us to expect no common magnanimity in action. It is as follows: *Octavio* and *Questenberg* are consulting on affairs of state; *Max* enters: he is just returned from convoying the *Princess Thekla* and her mother, the daughter and the wife of *Friedland*, to the camp at Pilsen.

ACT I.
SCENE IV.
MAX PICCOLOMINI, OCTAVIO PICCOLOMINI, QUESTENBERG.

Max. 'Tis he himself! My father, welcome, welcome!

[*He embraces him: on turning round, he observes Questenberg, and draws coldly back.*

Busied, I perceive? I will not interrupt you.

Oct. How now, Max? View this stranger better!
An old friend deserves regard and kindness;
The Kaiser's messenger should be rever'd!

Max. [*drily*] Von Questenberg! If it is good that brings you
To our head-quarters, welcome!

Quest. [*has taken his hand*] Nay, draw not
Your hand away, Count Piccolomini!
Not on mine own account alone I grasp it,
And nothing common will I say therewith.
Octavio, Max, Piccolomini![*Taking both their hands.*
Names of benignant solemn import! Never
Can Austria's fortune fail while two such stars,
To guide and guard her, gleam above our hosts.

Max. You play it wrong, Sir Minister! To praise,
I wot, you come not hither; to blame and censure
You are come. Let me be no exception.

Oct. [*to Max.*] He comes from Court, where every one is not
So well contented with the Duke as here.

Max. And what new fault have they to charge him with?
That he alone decides what he alone
Can understand? Well! Should it not be so?
It should and must! This man was never made
To ply and mould himself like wax to others:
It goes against his heart; he cannot do it,
He has the spirit of a ruler, and
The station of a ruler. Well for us
It is so! Few can rule themselves, can use
Their wisdom wisely: happy for the whole
Where there is one among them that can be
A centre and a hold for many thousands;
That can plant himself like a firm column,
For the whole to lean on safely! Such a one
Is Wallenstein; some other man might better
Serve the Court, none else could serve the Army.

Quest. The Army, truly!

Max.And it is a pleasure
To behold how all awakes and strengthens
And revives around him; how men's faculties
Come forth; their gifts grow plainer to themselves!
From each he can elicit his endowment,
His peculiar power; and does it wisely;
Leaving each to be the man he found him,
Watching only that he always be so.
I' th' proper place: and thus he makes the talents

Of all mankind his own.

Quest.No one denies him
Skill in men, and skill to use them. His fault is
That in the ruler he forgets the servant,
As if he had been born to be commander.

Max. And is he not? By birth he is invested
With all gifts for it, and with the farther gift
Of finding scope to use them; of acquiring
For the ruler's faculties the ruler's office.

Quest. So that how far the rest of us have rights
Or influence, if any, lies with Friedland?

Max. He is no common person; he requires
No common confidence: allow him space;
The proper limit he himself will set.

Quest. The trial shows it!

Max.Ay! Thus it is with them!
Still so! All frights them that has any depth;
Nowhere are they at ease but in the shallows.

Oct. [*to Quest.*] Let him have his way, my friend! The argument
Will not avail us.

Max.They invoke the spirit
I' th' hour of need, and shudder when he rises.
The great, the wonderful, must be accomplished
Like a thing of course!—In war, in battle,
A moment is decisive; on the spot
Must be determin'd, in the instant done.
With ev'ry noble quality of nature
The leader must be gifted: let him live, then,
In their noble sphere! The oracle within him,
The living spirit, not dead books, old forms,
Not mould'ring parchments must he take to counsel.

Oct. My Son! despise not these old narrow forms!
They are as barriers, precious walls and fences,
Which oppressed mortals have erected
To mod'rate the rash will of their oppressors.
For the uncontrolled has ever been destructive.
The way of Order, though it lead through windings,
Is the best. Right forward goes the lightning
And the cannon-ball: quick, by the nearest path,
They come, op'ning with murderous crash their way,
To blast and ruin! My Son! the quiet road
Which men frequent, where peace and blessings travel,
Follows the river's course, the valley's bendings;

Modest skirts the cornfield and the vineyard,
Revering property's appointed bounds;
And leading safe though slower to the mark.

QUEST. O, hear your Father! him who is at once
A hero and a man!

OCT.It is the child
O' th' camp that speaks in thee, my Son: a war
Of fifteen years has nursed and taught thee; peace
Thou hast never seen. My Son, there is a worth
Beyond the worth of warriors: ev'n in war itself
The object is not war. The rapid deeds
Of power, th' astounding wonders of the moment—
It is not these that minister to man
Aught useful, aught benignant or enduring.
In haste the wandering soldier comes, and builds
With canvas his light town: here in a moment
Is a rushing concourse; markets open;
Roads and rivers crowd with merchandise
And people; Traffic stirs his hundred arms.
Ere long, some morning, look,—and it is gone!
The tents are struck, the host has marched away;
Dead as a churchyard lies the trampled seed-field,
And wasted is the harvest of the year.

MAX. O Father! that the Kaiser *would* make peace!
The bloody laurel I would gladly change
For the first violet Spring should offer us,
The tiny pledge that Earth again was young!

OCT. How's this? What is it that affects thee so?

MAX. Peace I have never seen? Yes, I have seen it!
Ev'n now I come from it: my journey led me
Through lands as yet unvisited by war.
O Father! life has charms, of which we know not:
We have but seen the barren coasts of life;
Like some wild roving crew of lawless pirates,
Who, crowded in their narrow noisome ship,
Upon the rude sea, with rude manners dwell;
Naught of the fair land knowing but the bays,
Where they may risk their hurried thievish landing.
Of the loveliness that, in its peaceful dales,
The land conceals—O Father!—O, of this,
In our wild voyage we have seen no glimpse.

OCT. [*gives increased attention*]
And did this journey show thee much of it?

MAX. 'Twas the first holiday of my existence.

Tell me, where's the end of all this labour,
This grinding labour that has stolen my youth,
And left my heart uncheer'd and void, my spirit
Uncultivated as a wilderness?
This camp's unceasing din; the neighing steeds;
The trumpet's clang; the never-changing round
Of service, discipline, parade, give nothing
To the heart, the heart that longs for nourishment.
There is no soul in this insipid bus'ness;
Life has another fate and other joys.

OCT. Much hast thou learn'd, my Son, in this short journey!

MAX. O blessed bright day, when at last the soldier
Shall turn back to life, and be again a man!
Through th' merry lines the colours are unfurl'd,
And homeward beats the thrilling soft peace-march;
All hats and helmets deck'd with leafy sprays,
The last spoil of the fields! The city's gates
Fly up; now needs not the petard to burst them:
The walls are crowded with rejoicing people;
Their shouts ring through the air: from every tower
Blithe bells are pealing forth the merry vesper
Of that bloody day. From town and hamlet
Flow the jocund thousands; with their hearty
Kind impetuosity our march impeding.
The old man, weeping that he sees this day,
Embraces his long-lost son: a stranger
He revisits his old home; with spreading boughs
The tree o'ershadows him at his return,
Which waver'd as a twig when he departed;
And modest blushing comes a maid to meet him,
Whom on her nurse's breast he left. O happy,
For whom some kindly door like this, for whom
Soft arms to clasp him shall be open'd! —

QUEST. [*with emotion*]O that
The times you speak of should be so far distant!
Should not be tomorrow, be today!

MAX. And who's to blame for it but you at Court?
I will deal plainly with you, Questenberg:
When I observ'd you here, a twinge of spleen
And bitterness went through me. It is you
That hinder peace; yes, you. The General
Must force it, and you ever keep tormenting him,
Obstructing all his steps, abusing him;
For what? Because the good of Europe lies
Nearer his heart, than whether certain acres

More or less of dirty land be Austria's!
You call him traitor, rebel, God knows what,
Because he spares the Saxons; as if that
Were not the only way to peace; for how
If during war, war end not, *can* peace follow?
Go to! go to! As I love goodness, so I hate
This paltry work of yours: and here I vow to God,
For him, this rebel, traitor Wallenstein,
To shed my blood, my heart's blood, drop by drop,
Ere I will see you triumph in his fall!

The Princess Thekla is perhaps still dearer to us. Thekla, just entering on life, with 'timid steps,' with the brilliant visions of a cloister yet undisturbed by the contradictions of reality, beholds in Max, not merely her protector and escort to her father's camp, but the living emblem of her shapeless yet glowing dreams. She knows not deception, she trusts and is trusted: their spirits meet and mingle, and 'clasp each other firmly and forever.' All this is described by the poet with a quiet inspiration, which finds its way into our deepest sympathies. Such beautiful simplicity is irresistible. 'How long,' the Countess Terzky asks,

How long is it since you disclosed your heart?
MAX. This morning first I risked a word of it.
COUN. Not till this morning during twenty days?
MAX. 'Twas at the castle where you met us, 'twixt this
And Nepomuk, the last stage of the journey.
On a balcony she and I were standing, our looks
In silence turn'd upon the vacant landscape;
And before us the dragoons were riding,
Whom the Duke had sent to be her escort.
Heavy on my heart lay thoughts of parting,
And with a faltering voice at last I said:
All this reminds me, Fräulein, that today
I must be parted from my happiness;
In few hours you will find a father,
Will see yourself encircled by new friends;
And I shall be to you nought but a stranger,
Forgotten in the crowd—"Speak with Aunt Terzky!"
Quick she interrupted me; I noticed
A quiv'ring in her voice; a glowing blush
Spread o'er her cheeks; slow rising from the ground,
Her eyes met mine: I could control myself
No longer—

[*The Princess appears at the door, and stops; the Countess, but not Piccolomini, observing her.*

—I clasp'd her wildly in my arms,
My lips were join'd with hers. Some footsteps stirring
I' th' next room parted us; 'twas you; what then

Took place, you know.

Coun.And can you be so modest,
Or incurious, as not once to ask me
For *my* secret, in return?

Max.Your secret?

Coun. Yes, sure! On coming in the moment after,
How my niece receiv'd me, what i' th' instant
Of her first surprise she—

Max.Ha?

Thekla [*enters hastily*].Spare yourself
The trouble, Aunt! That he can learn from me.

We rejoice in the ardent, pure and confiding affection of these two angelic beings: but our feeling is changed and made more poignant, when we think that the inexorable hand of Destiny is already lifted to smite their world with blackness and desolation. Thekla has enjoyed 'two little hours of heavenly beauty;' but her native gaiety gives place to serious anticipations and alarms; she feels that the camp of Wallenstein is not a place for hope to dwell in. The instructions and explanations of her aunt disclose the secret: she is not to love Max; a higher, it may be a royal, fate awaits her; but she is to tempt him from his duty, and make him lend his influence to her father, whose daring projects she now for the first time discovers. From that moment her hopes of happiness have vanished, never more to return. Yet her own sorrows touch her less than the ruin which she sees about to overwhelm her tender and affectionate mother. For herself, she waits with gloomy patience the stroke that is to crush her. She is meek, and soft, and maiden-like; but she is Friedland's daughter, and does not shrink from what is unavoidable. There is often a rectitude, and quick inflexibility of resolution about Thekla, which contrasts beautifully with her inexperience and timorous acuteness of feeling: on discovering her father's treason, she herself decides that Max 'shall obey his first impulse,' and forsake her.

There are few scenes in poetry more sublimely pathetic than this. We behold the sinking but still fiery glory of Wallenstein, opposed to the impetuous despair of Max Piccolomini, torn asunder by the claims of duty and of love; the calm but broken-hearted Thekla, beside her broken-hearted mother, and surrounded by the blank faces of Wallenstein's desponding followers. There is a physical pomp corresponding to the moral grandeur of the action; the successive revolt and departure of the troops is heard without the walls of the Palace; the trumpets of the Pappenheimers reëcho the wild feelings of their leader. What follows too is equally affecting. Max being forced away by his soldiers from the side of Thekla, rides forth at their head in a state bordering on frenzy. Next day come tidings of his fate, which no heart is hard enough to hear unmoved. The effect it produces upon Thekla displays all the hidden energies of her soul. The first accidental hearing of the news had almost overwhelmed her; but she summons up her strength: she sends for the messenger, that she may question him more closely, and listen to his stern details with the heroism of a Spartan virgin.

ACT IV.
SCENE X.
THEKLA; THE SWEDISH CAPTAIN; FRÄULEIN NEUBRUNN.

CAPT. [*approaches respectfully*]
Princess—I—must pray you to forgive me
My most rash unthinking words: I could not—

THEKLA [*with noble dignity*].
You saw me in my grief; a sad chance made you
At once my confidant, who were a stranger.

CAPT. I fear the sight of me is hateful to you:
They were mournful tidings I brought hither.

THEKLA. The blame was mine! 'Twas I that forced them from you;
Your voice was but the voice of Destiny.
My terror interrupted your recital:
Finish it, I pray you.

CAPT.'Twill renew your grief!

THEKLA. I am prepared for't, I will be prepared.
Proceed! How went the action? Let me hear.

CAPT. At Neustadt, dreading no surprise, we lay
Slightly entrench'd; when towards night a cloud
Of dust rose from the forest, and our outposts
Rush'd into the camp, and cried: The foe was there!
Scarce had we time to spring on horseback, when
The Pappenheimers, coming at full gallop,
Dash'd o'er the palisado, and next moment
These fierce troopers pass'd our camp-trench also.
But thoughtlessly their courage had impelled them
To advance without support; their infantry
Was far behind; only the Pappenheimers
Boldly following their bold leader—

[*Thekla makes a movement. The Captain pauses for a moment, till she beckons
him to proceed.*

On front and flank with all our horse we charged them;
And ere long forc'd them back upon the trench,
Where rank'd in haste our infantry presented
An iron hedge of pikes to stop their passage.
Advance they could not, nor retreat a step,
Wedg'd in this narrow prison, death on all sides.
Then the Rheingraf call'd upon their leader,
In fair battle, fairly to surrender:
But Colonel Piccolomini—[*Thekla, tottering, catches by a seat.*
—We knew him

By's helmet-plume and his long flowing hair,
The rapid ride had loosen'd it: to th' trench
He points; leaps first himself his gallant steed
Clean over it; the troop plunge after him:
But—in a twinkle it was done!—his horse
Run through the body by a partisan,
Rears in its agony, and pitches far
Its rider; and fierce o'er him tramp the steeds
O' th' rest, now heeding neither bit nor bridle.

[*Thekla, who has listened to the last words with increasing anguish, falls into a violent tremor; she is sinking to the ground; Fräulein Neubrunn hastens to her, and receives her in her arms.*

NEU. Lady, dearest mistress—

CAPT. [*moved*]Let me begone.

THEKLA. 'Tis past; conclude it.

CAPT.Seeing their leader fall,
A grim inexorable desperation
Seiz'd the troops: their own escape forgotten,
Like wild tigers they attack us; their fury
Provokes our soldiers, and the battle ends not
Till the last man of the Pappenheimers falls.

THEKLA [*with a quivering voice*].
And where—where is—You have not told me all.

CAPT. [*after a pause*]
This morning we interr'd him. He was borne
By twelve youths of the noblest families,
And all our host accompanied the bier.
A laurel deck'd his coffin; and upon it
The Rheingraf laid his own victorious sword.
Nor were tears wanting to his fate: for many
Of us had known his noble-mindedness,
And gentleness of manners; and all hearts
Were mov'd at his sad end. Fain would the Rheingraf
Have sav'd him; but himself prevented it;
'Tis said he wish'd to die.

NEU. [*with emotion, to Thekla, who hides her face*]
O! dearest mistress,
Look up! O, why would you insist on this?

THEKLA. Where is his grave?

CAPT.I' th' chapel of a cloister
At Neustadt is he laid, till we receive
Directions from his father.

THEKLA.What is its name?

CAPT. St. Catharine's.

THEKLA.Is't far from this?

CAPT.Seven leagues.

THEKLA. How goes the way?

CAPT.You come by Tirschenreit
And Falkenberg, and through our farthest outposts.

THEKLA. Who commands them?

CAPT.Colonel Seckendorf.

THEKLA [*steps to a table, and takes a ring from her jewel-box*].
You have seen me in my grief, and shown me
A sympathising heart: accept a small
Memorial of this hour [*giving him the ring*].Now leave me.

CAPT. [*overpowered*]Princess!

[*Thekla silently makes him a sign to go, and turns from him. He lingers, and attempts to speak; Neubrunn repeats the sign; he goes.*

SCENE XI.
NEUBRUNN; THEKLA.

THEKLA [*falls on Neubrunn's neck*].
Now, good Neubrunn, is the time to show the love
Which thou hast always vow'd me. Prove thyself
A true friend and attendant! We must go,
This very night.

NEU.Go! This very night! And whither?

THEKLA. Whither? There is but one place in the world,
The place where he lies buried: to his grave.

NEU. Alas, what would you there, my dearest mistress?

THEKLA. What there? Unhappy girl! Thou wouldst not ask
If thou hadst ever lov'd. There, there, is all
That yet remains of him; that one small spot
Is all the earth to me. Do not detain me!
O, come! Prepare, think how we may escape.

NEU. Have you reflected on your father's anger?

THEKLA. I dread no mortal's anger now.

NEU.The mockery
Of the world, the wicked tongue of slander!

THEKLA. I go to seek one that is cold and low:
Am I, then, hast'ning to my lover's arms?

O God! I am but hast'ning to his grave!

Neu. And we alone? Two feeble, helpless women?

Thekla. We will arm ourselves; my hand shall guard thee.

Neu. In the gloomy night-time?

Thekla.Night will hide us.

Neu. In this rude storm?

Thekla.Was *his* bed made of down,
When the horses' hoofs went o'er him?

Neu.O Heaven!
And then the many Swedish posts! They will not
Let us pass.

Thekla. Are they not men? Misfortune
Passes free through all the earth.

Neu.So far! So—

Thekla. Does the pilgrim count the miles, when journeying
To the distant shrine of grace?

Neu.How shall we
Even get out of Eger?

Thekla.Gold opens gates.
Go! Do go!

Neu.If they should recognise us?

Thekla. In a fugitive despairing woman
No one will look to meet with Friedland's daughter.

Neu. And where shall we get horses for our flight?

Thekla. My Equerry will find them. Go and call him.

Neu. Will he venture without his master's knowledge?

Thekla. He will, I tell thee. Go! O, linger not!

Neu. Ah! And what will your mother do when you
Are vanish'd?

Thekla [*recollecting this, and gazing with a look of anguish*].
O my mother!

Neu. Your good mother!
She has already had so much to suffer.
Must this last heaviest stroke too fall on her?

Thekla. I cannot help it. Go, I prithee, go!

Neu. Think well what you are doing.

Thekla.All is thought
That can be thought, already.

Neu.*Were* we there,
What would you do?

Thekla.God will direct me, there.

Neu. Your heart is full of trouble: O my lady!
This way leads *not* to peace.

Thekla.To that deep peace
Which he has found. O, hasten! Go! No words!
There is some force, I know not what to call it,
Pulls me irresistibly, and drags me
On to his grave: there I shall find some solace
Instantly; the strangling band of sorrow
Will be loosen'd; tears will flow. O, hasten!
Long time ago we might have been o' th' road.
No rest for me till I have fled these walls:
They fall upon me, some dark power repels me
From them—Ha! What's this? The chamber's filling
With pale gaunt shapes! No room is left for me!
More! more! The crowding spectres press on me,
And push me forth from this accursed house.

Neu. You frighten me, my lady: I dare stay
No longer; quickly I'll call Rosenberg.

SCENE XII.
THEKLA.

It is his spirit calls me! 'Tis the host
Of faithful souls that sacrificed themselves
In fiery vengeance for him. They upbraid me
For this loit'ring: *they* in death forsook him not,
Who in their life had led them; their rude hearts
Were capable of this: and *I* can live?

No! No! That laurel-garland which they laid
Upon his bier was twined for both of us!
What is this life without the light of love?
I cast it from me, since its worth is gone.
Yes, when we found and lov'd each other, life
Was something! Glittering lay before me
The golden morn: I had two hours of Heaven.

Thou stoodest at the threshold of the scene
Of busy life; with timid steps I cross'd it:
How fair it lay in solemn shade and sheen!
And thou beside me, like some angel, posted
To lead me out of childhood's fairy land
On to life's glancing summit, hand in hand!

My first thought was of joy no tongue can tell,
My first look on *thy* spotless spirit fell.
[*She sinks into a reverie, then with signs of horror proceeds.*
And Fate put forth his hand: inexorable, cold,
My friend it grasp'd and clutch'd with iron hold,
And—under th' hoofs of their wild horses hurl'd:
Such is the lot of loveliness i' th' world!

Thekla has yet another pang to encounter; the parting with her mother: but she persists in her determination, and goes forth, to die beside her lover's grave. The heart-rending emotions, which this amiable creature has to undergo, are described with an almost painful effect: the fate of Max and Thekla might draw tears from the eyes of a stoic.

Less tender, but not less sublimely poetical, is the fate of Wallenstein himself. We do not pity Wallenstein; even in ruin he seems too great for pity. His daughter having vanished like a fair vision from the scene, we look forward to Wallenstein's inevitable fate with little feeling save expectant awe:

This kingly Wallenstein, whene'er he falls,
Will drag a world to ruin down with him;
And as a ship that in the midst of ocean
Catches fire, and shiv'ring springs into the air,
And in a moment scatters between sea and sky
The crew it bore, so will he hurry to destruction
Ev'ry one whose fate was join'd with his.

Yet still there is some touch of pathos in his gloomy fall; some visitings of nature in the austere grandeur of his slowly-coming, but inevitable and annihilating doom. The last scene of his life is among the finest which poetry can boast of. Thekla's death is still unknown to him; but he thinks of Max, and almost weeps. He looks at the stars: dim shadows of superstitious dread pass fitfully across his spirit, as he views these fountains of light, and compares their glorious and enduring existence with the fleeting troubled life of man. The strong spirit of his sister is subdued by dark forebodings; omens are against him; his astrologer entreats, one of the relenting conspirators entreats, his own feelings call upon him, to watch and beware. But he refuses to let the resolution of his mind be overmastered; he casts away these warnings, and goes cheerfully to sleep, with dreams of hope about his pillow, unconscious that the javelins are already grasped which will send him to his long and dreamless sleep. The death of Wallenstein does not cause tears; but it is perhaps the most high-wrought scene of the play. A shade of horror, of fateful dreariness, hangs over it, and gives additional effect to the fire of that brilliant poetry, which glows in every line of it. Except in *Macbeth* or the conclusion of *Othello*, we know not where to match it. Schiller's genius is of a kind much narrower than Shakspeare's; but in his own peculiar province, the exciting of lofty, earnest, strong emotion, he admits of no superior. Others are finer, more piercing, varied, thrilling, in their influence: Schiller, in his finest mood, is overwhelming.

This tragedy of *Wallenstein*, published at the close of the eighteenth century, may safely be rated as the greatest dramatic work of which that century can boast. France never rose into the sphere of Schiller, even in the days of her Corneille: nor can our own country, since the times of Elizabeth, name any dramatist to be compared with him in general strength of mind, and feeling, and acquired accomplishment. About the time of *Wallenstein's* appearance, we of this gifted land were shuddering at *The Castle Spectre*! Germany, indeed, boasts of Goethe: and on some rare occasions, it must be owned that Goethe has shown talents of a higher order than are here manifested; but he has made no equally regular or powerful exertion of them: *Faust* is but a careless effusion compared with *Wallenstein*. The latter is in truth a vast and magnificent work. What an assemblage of images, ideas, emotions, disposed in the most felicitous and impressive order! We have conquerors, statesmen, ambitious generals, marauding soldiers, heroes, and heroines, all acting and feeling as they would in nature, all faithfully depicted, yet all embellished by the spirit of poetry, and all made conducive to heighten one paramount impression, our sympathy with the three chief characters of the piece.[35]

Soon after the publication of *Wallenstein*, Schiller once more changed his abode. The 'mountain air of Jena' was conceived by his physicians to be prejudicial in disorders of the lungs; and partly in consequence of this opinion, he determined henceforth to spend his winters in Weimar. Perhaps a weightier reason in favour of this new arrangement was the opportunity it gave him of being near the theatre, a constant attendance on which, now that he had once more become a dramatist, seemed highly useful for his farther improvement. The summer he, for several years, continued still to spend in Jena; to which, especially its beautiful environs, he declared himself particularly attached. His little garden-house was still his place of study during summer; till at last he settled constantly at Weimar. Even then he used frequently to visit Jena; to which there was a fresh attraction in later years, when Goethe chose it for his residence, which, we understand, it still occasionally is. With Goethe he often stayed for months.

This change of place produced little change in Schiller's habits or employment: he was now as formerly in the pay of the Duke of Weimar; now as formerly engaged in dramatic composition as the great object of his life. What the amount of his pension was, we know not: that the Prince behaved to him in a princely manner, we have proof sufficient. Four years before, when invited to the University of Tübingen, Schiller had received a promise, that, in case of sickness or any other cause preventing the continuance of his literary labour, his salary should be doubled. It was actually increased on occasion of the present removal; and again still farther in 1804, some advantageous offers being made to him from Berlin. Schiller seems to have been, what he might have wished to be, neither poor nor rich: his simple unostentatious economy went on without embarrassment: and this was

[35] *Wallenstein* has been translated into French by M. Benjamin Constant; and the last two parts of it have been faithfully rendered into English by Mr. Coleridge. As to the French version, we know nothing, save that it is an *improved* one; but that little is enough: Schiller, as a dramatist, improved by M. Constant, is a spectacle we feel no wish to witness. Mr. Coleridge's translation is also, as a whole, unknown to us: but judging from many large specimens, we should pronounce it, excepting Sotheby's *Oberon*, to be the best, indeed the only sufferable, translation from the German with which our literature has yet been enriched.

all that he required. To avoid pecuniary perplexities was constantly among his aims: to amass wealth, never. We ought also to add that, in 1802, by the voluntary solicitation of the Duke, he was ennobled; a fact which we mention, for his sake by whose kindness this honour was procured; not for the sake of Schiller, who accepted it with gratitude, but had neither needed nor desired it.

The official services expected of him in return for so much kindness seem to have been slight, if any. Chiefly or altogether of his own accord, he appears to have applied himself to a close inspection of the theatre, and to have shared with Goethe the task of superintending its concerns. The rehearsals of new pieces commonly took place at the house of one of these friends; they consulted together on all such subjects, frankly and copiously. Schiller was not slow to profit by the means of improvement thus afforded him; in the mechanical details of his art he grew more skilful: by a constant observation of the stage, he became more acquainted with its capabilities and its laws. It was not long till, with his characteristic expansiveness of enterprise, he set about turning this new knowledge to account. In conjunction with Goethe, he remodelled his own *Don Carlos* and his friend's *Count Egmont*, altering both according to his latest views of scenic propriety. It was farther intended to treat, in the same manner, the whole series of leading German plays, and thus to produce a national stock of dramatic pieces, formed according to the best rules; a vast project, in which some progress continued to be made, though other labours often interrupted it. For the present, Schiller was engaged with his *Maria Stuart*: it appeared in 1800.

This tragedy will not detain us long. It is upon a subject, the incidents of which are now getting trite, and the moral of which has little that can peculiarly recommend it. To exhibit the repentance of a lovely but erring woman, to show us how her soul may be restored to its primitive nobleness, by sufferings, devotion and death, is the object of *Maria Stuart*. It is a tragedy of sombre and mournful feelings; with an air of melancholy and obstruction pervading it; a looking backward on objects of remorse, around on imprisonment, and forward on the grave. Its object is undoubtedly attained. We are forced to pardon and to love the heroine; she is beautiful, and miserable, and lofty-minded; and her crimes, however dark, have been expiated by long years of weeping and woe. Considering also that they were the fruit not of calculation, but of passion acting on a heart not dead, though blinded for a time, to their enormity, they seem less hateful than the cold premeditated villany of which she is the victim. Elizabeth is selfish, heartless, envious; she violates no law, but she has no virtue, and she lives triumphant: her arid, artificial character serves by contrast to heighten our sympathy with her warm-hearted, forlorn, ill-fated rival. These two Queens, particularly Mary, are well delineated: their respective qualities are vividly brought out, and the feelings they were meant to excite arise within us. There is also Mortimer, a fierce, impetuous, impassioned lover; driven onward chiefly by the heat of his blood, but still interesting by his vehemence and unbounded daring. The dialogue, moreover, has many beauties; there are scenes which have merited peculiar commendation. Of this kind is the interview between the Queens; and more especially the first entrance of Mary, when, after long seclusion, she is once more permitted to behold the cheerful sky. In the joy of a momentary freedom, she forgets that she is still a captive; she addresses the clouds, the 'sailors of the air, who 'are not subjects of Elizabeth,' and bids them carry tidings of her to the hearts that love her in other lands. Without doubt, in all that he intended, Schiller has succeeded; *Maria Stuart* is a beautiful tragedy; it would have formed the glory of a meaner man, but it cannot materially alter his. Compared with *Wallenstein*, its purpose is narrow, and its result is common. We have no manners or true historical delineation. The figure of the English court is not given; and Elizabeth is depicted more like one of the French Medici, than like our own politic, capricious, coquettish, imperious, yet on the whole true-hearted, 'good Queen Bess.' With abundant proofs of genius, this tragedy produces a comparatively small effect, especially on English readers. We have already wept enough for Mary Stuart, both over prose and verse; and the persons likely to be deeply touched with the moral or the interest of her story, as it is recorded here, are rather a separate class than men in general. Madame de Staël, we observe, is her principal admirer.

Next year, Schiller took possession of a province more peculiarly his own: in 1801, appeared his *Maid of Orleans (Jungfrau von Orleans)*; the first hint of which was suggested to him by a series of documents, relating to the sentence of Jeanne d'Arc, and its reversal, first published about this time by De l'Averdy of the *Académie des Inscriptions*. Schiller had been moved in perusing them: this tragedy gave voice to his feelings.

Considered as an object of poetry or history, Jeanne d'Arc, the most singular personage of modern times, presents a character capable of being viewed under a great variety of aspects, and with a corresponding variety of emotions. To the English of her own age, bigoted in their creed, and baffled by her prowess, she appeared inspired by the Devil, and was naturally burnt as a sorceress. In this light, too, she is painted in the poems of Shakspeare. To Voltaire, again, whose trade it was to war with every kind of superstition, this child of fanatic ardour seemed no better than a moonstruck zealot; and the people who followed her, and believed in her, something worse than lunatics. The glory of what she had achieved was forgotten, when the means of achieving it were recollected; and the Maid of Orleans was deemed the fit subject of a poem, the wittiest and most profligate for which literature has to blush. Our illustrious *Don Juan* hides his head when contrasted with Voltaire's *Pucelle*: Juan's biographer, with all his zeal, is but an innocent, and a novice, by the side of this arch-scorner.

Such a manner of considering the Maid of Orleans is evidently not the right one. Feelings so deep and earnest as hers can never be an object of ridicule: whoever pursues a purpose of any sort with such fervid devotedness, is entitled to awaken emotions, at least of a serious kind, in the hearts of others. Enthusiasm puts on a different shape in every different age: always in some degree sublime, often it is dangerous; its very essence is a tendency to error and exaggeration; yet it is the fundamental quality of strong souls; the true nobility of blood, in which all greatness of thought or action has its rise. *Quicquid vult valdè vult* is ever the first and surest test of mental capability. This peasant girl, who felt within her such fiery vehemence of resolution, that she could subdue the minds of kings and captains to her will, and lead armies on to battle, conquering, till her country was cleared of its invaders, must evidently have possessed the elements of a majestic character. Benevolent feelings, sublime ideas, and above all an overpowering will, are here indubitably marked. Nor does the form, which her activity assumed, seem less adapted for displaying these qualities, than many other forms in which we praise them. The gorgeous inspirations of the Catholic religion are as real as the phantom of posthumous renown; the love of our native soil is as laudable as ambition, or the principle of military honour. Jeanne d'Arc must have been a creature of shadowy yet far-glancing dreams, of unutterable feelings, of 'thoughts that wandered through Eternity.' Who can tell the trials and the triumphs, the splendours and the terrors, of which her simple spirit was the scene! 'Heartless, sneering, god-forgetting French!' as old Suwarrow called them,—they are not worthy of this noble maiden. Hers were errors, but errors which a generous soul alone could have committed, and which generous souls would have done more than pardon. Her darkness and delusions were of the understanding only; they but make the radiance of her heart more touching and apparent; as clouds are gilded by the orient light into something more beautiful than azure itself.

It is under this aspect that Schiller has contemplated the Maid of Orleans, and endeavoured to make us contemplate her. For the latter purpose, it appears that more than one plan had occurred to him. His first idea was, to represent Joanna, and the times she lived in, as they actually were: to exhibit the superstition, ferocity, and wretchedness of the period, in all their aggravation; and to show us this patriotic and religious enthusiast beautifying the tempestuous scene by her presence; swaying the fierce passions of her countrymen; directing their fury against the invaders of France; till at length, forsaken and condemned to die, she perished at the stake, retaining the same steadfast and lofty faith, which had ennobled and redeemed the errors of her life, and was now to glorify the ignominy of her death. This project, after much deliberation, he relinquished, as too difficult. By a new mode of management, much of the homeliness and rude horror, that defaced and encumbered the reality, is thrown away. The Dauphin is not here a voluptuous weakling, nor is his court the centre of vice and cruelty and imbecility: the misery of the time is touched but lightly, and the Maid of Arc herself is invested with a certain faint degree of mysterious dignity, ultimately represented as being in truth a preternatural gift; though whether preternatural, and if so, whether sent from above or from below, neither we nor she, except by faith, are absolutely sure, till the conclusion.

The propriety of this arrangement is liable to question; indeed, it has been more than questioned. But external blemishes are lost in the intrinsic grandeur of the piece: the spirit of Joanna is presented to us with an exalting and pathetic force sufficient to make us blind to far greater improprieties. Joanna is a pure creation, of half-celestial origin, combining the mild charms of female loveliness with the awful majesty of a prophetess, and a sacrifice doomed to perish for her country. She resembled, in Schiller's view, the Iphigenia of the Greeks; and as such, in some respects, he has treated her.

The woes and desolation of the land have kindled in Joanna's keen and fervent heart a fire, which the loneliness of her life, and her deep feelings of religion, have nourished and fanned into a holy flame. She sits in solitude with her flocks, beside the mountain chapel of the Virgin, under the ancient Druid oak, a wizard spot, the haunt of evil spirits as well as of good; and visions are revealed to her such as human eyes behold not. It seems the force of her own spirit, expressing its feelings in forms which react upon itself. The strength of her impulses persuades her that she is called from on high to deliver her native France; the intensity of her own faith persuades others; she goes forth on her mission; all bends to the fiery vehemence of her will; she is inspired because she thinks herself so. There is something beautiful and moving in the aspect of a noble enthusiasm, fostered in the secret soul, amid obstructions and depressions, and at length bursting forth with an overwhelming force to accomplish its appointed end: the impediments which long hid it are now become testimonies of its power; the very ignorance, and meanness, and error, which still in part adhere to it, increase our sympathy without diminishing our admiration; it seems the triumph, hardly contested, and not wholly carried, but still the triumph, of Mind over Fate, of human volition over material necessity.

All this Schiller felt, and has presented with even more than his usual skill. The secret mechanism of Joanna's mind is concealed from us in a dim religious obscurity; but its active movements are distinct; we behold the lofty heroism of her feelings; she affects us to the very heart. The quiet, devout innocence of her early years, when she lived silent, shrouded in herself, meek and kindly though not communing with others, makes us love her: the celestial splendour which illuminates her after-life adds reverence to our love. Her words and actions combine an overpowering force with a calm unpretending dignity: we seem to understand how they must have carried in their favour the universal conviction. Joanna is the most noble being in tragedy. We figure her with her slender lovely form, her mild but spirit-speaking countenance; 'beautiful and terrible;' bearing the banner of the Virgin before the hosts of her country; travelling in the strength of a rapt soul; irresistible by faith; 'the lowly herdsmaid,' greater in the grandeur of her simple spirit than the kings and queens of this world. Yet her breast is not entirely insensible to human feeling, nor her faith never liable to waver. When that inexorable vengeance, which had shut her ear against the voice of mercy to the enemies of France, is suspended at the sight of Lionel, and her heart experiences the first touch of mortal affection, a baleful cloud overspreads the serene of her mind; it seems as if Heaven had forsaken her, or from the beginning permitted demons or earthly dreams to deceive her. The agony of her spirit, involved in endless and horrid labyrinths of doubt, is powerfully portrayed. She has crowned the king at Rheims; and all is joy, and pomp, and jubilee, and almost adoration of Joanna: but Joanna's thoughts are not of joy. The sight of her poor but kind and true-hearted sisters in the crowd, moves her to the soul. Amid the tumult and magnificence of this royal pageant, she sinks into a reverie; her small native dale of Arc, between its quiet hills, rises on her mind's eye, with its straw-roofed huts, and its clear greensward; where the sun is even then shining so brightly, and the sky is so blue, and all is so calm and motherly and safe. She sighs for the peace of that sequestered home; then shudders to think that she shall never see it more. Accused of witchcraft, by her own ascetic melancholic father, she utters no word of denial to the charge; for her heart is dark, it is tarnished by earthly love, she dare not raise her thoughts to Heaven. Parted from her sisters; cast out with horror by the people she had lately saved from despair, she wanders forth, desolate, forlorn, not knowing whither. Yet she does not sink under this sore trial: as she suffers from without, and is forsaken of men, her mind grows clear and strong, her confidence returns. She is now more firmly fixed in our admiration than before; tenderness is united to our other feelings; and her faith has been proved by sharp vicissitudes. Her countrymen recognise their error; Joanna closes her career by a glorious death; we take farewell of her in a solemn mood of heroic pity.

Joanna is the animating principle of this tragedy; the scenes employed in developing her character and feelings constitute its great charm. Yet there are other personages in it, that leave a distinct and pleasing impression of themselves in our memory. Agnes Sorel, the soft, languishing, generous mistress of the Dauphin, relieves and heightens by comparison the sterner beauty of the Maid. Dunois, the Bastard of Orleans, the lover of Joanna, is a blunt, frank, sagacious soldier, and well described. And Talbot, the gray veteran, delineates his dark, unbelieving, indomitable soul, by a few slight but expressive touches: he sternly passes down to the land, as he thinks, of utter nothingness, contemptuous even of the fate that destroys him, and

> 'On the soil of France he sleeps, as does
> A hero on the shield he would not quit.'

A few scattered extracts may in part exhibit some of these inferior personages to our readers, though they can afford us no impression of the Maid herself. Joanna's character, like every finished piece of art, to be judged of must be seen in all its bearings. It is not in parts, but as a whole, that the delineation moves us; by light and manifold touches, it works upon our hearts, till they melt before it into that mild rapture, free alike from the violence and the impurities of Nature, which it is the highest triumph of the Artist to communicate.

ACT III.
SCENE IV.

[*The* DAUPHIN CHARLES, *with his suite: afterwards* JOANNA. *She is in armour, but without her helmet; and wears a garland in her hair.*

DUNOIS [*steps forward*].
My heart made choice of her while she was lowly;
This new honour raises not her merit
Or my love. Here, in the presence of my King
And of this holy Archbishop, I offer her
My hand and princely rank, if she regard me
As worthy to be hers.

CHARLES.Resistless Maid,
Thou addest miracle to miracle!
Henceforward I believe that nothing is
Impossible to thee. Thou hast subdued

This haughty spirit, that till now defied
Th' omnipotence of Love.

LA HIRE [*steps forward*]. If I mistake not
Joanna's form of mind, what most adorns her
Is her modest heart. The rev'rence of the great
She merits; but her thoughts will never rise
So high. She strives not after giddy splendours:
The true affection of a faithful soul
Contents her, and the still, sequester'd lot
Which with this hand I offer her.

CHARLES.Thou too,
La Hire? Two valiant suitors, equal in
Heroic virtue and renown of war!
—Wilt thou, that hast united my dominions,
Soften'd my opposers, part my firmest friends?
Both may not gain thee, each deserving thee:
Speak, then! Thy heart must here be arbiter.

AGNES SOREL [*approaches*].
Joanna is embarrass'd and surprised;
I see the bashful crimson tinge her cheeks.
Let her have time to ask her heart, to open
Her clos'd bosom in trustful confidence
With me. The moment is arriv'd when I
In sisterly communion also may
Approach the rigorous Maid, and offer her
The solace of my faithful, silent breast.
First let us women sit in secret judgment
On this matter that concerns us; then expect
What we shall have decided.

CHARLES [*about to go*].Be it so, then!

JOANNA. Not so, Sire! 'Twas not the embarrassment
Of virgin shame that dy'd my cheeks in crimson:
To this lady I have nothing to confide,
Which I need blush to speak of before men.
Much am I honour'd by the preference
Of these two noble Knights; but it was not
To chase vain worldly grandeurs, that I left
The shepherd moors; not in my hair to bind
The bridal garland, that I girt myself
With warlike armour. To far other work
Am I appointed: and the spotless virgin
Alone can do it. I am the soldier
Of the God of Battles; to no living man
Can I be wife.

ARCHBISHOP. As kindly help to man
Was woman born; and in obeying Nature
She best obeys and reverences Heaven.
When the command of God who summon'd thee
To battle is fulfull'd, thou wilt lay down
Thy weapons, and return to that soft sex
Which thou deny'st, which is not call'd to do
The bloody work of war.

JOANNA.Father, as yet
I know not how the Spirit will direct me:
When the needful time comes round, His voice
Will not be silent, and I will obey it.
For the present, I am bid complete the task.
He gave me. My sov'reign's brow is yet uncrown'd,
His head unwetted by the holy oil,
He is not yet a King.

CHARLES.We are journeying
Towards Rheims.

JOANNA.Let us not linger by the way.
Our foes are busy round us, shutting up
Thy passage: I will lead thee through them all.

DUNOIS. And when the work shall be fulfill'd, when we
Have marched in triumph into Rheims,
Will not Joanna then—

JOANNA.If God see meet
That I return with life and vict'ry from
These broils, my task is ended, and the herdsmaid
Has nothing more to do in her King's palace.

CHARLES [*taking her hand*].
It is the Spirit's voice impels thee now,
And Love is mute in thy inspired bosom.
Believe me, it will not be always mute!
Our swords will rest; and Victory will lead
Meek Peace by th' hand, and Joy will come again
To ev'ry breast, and softer feelings waken
In every heart: in thy heart also waken;
And tears of sweetest longing wilt thou weep,
Such as thine eyes have never shed. This heart,
Now fill'd by Heav'n, will softly open
To some terrestrial heart. Thou hast begun
By blessing thousands; but thou wilt conclude
By blessing one.

JOANNA.Dauphin! Art thou weary
Of the heavenly vision, that thou seekest

To deface its chosen vessel, wouldst degrade
To common dust the Maid whom God has sent thee?
Ye blind of heart! O ye of little faith!
Heaven's brightness is about you, before your eyes
Unveils its wonders; and ye see in me
Nought but a woman. Dare a woman, think ye,
Clothe herself in iron harness, and mingle
In the wreck of battle? Woe, woe to me,
If bearing in my hand th' avenging sword
Of God, I bore in my vain heart a love
To earthly man! Woe to me! It were better
That I never had been born. No more,
No more of this! Unless ye would awake the wrath
Of HIM that dwells in me! The eye of man
Desiring me is an abomination
And a horror.

CHARLES.Cease! 'Tis vain to urge her.

JOANNA. Bid the trumpets sound! This loit'ring grieves
And harasses me. Something chases me
From sloth, and drives me forth to do my mission,
Stern beck'ning me to my appointed doom.

SCENE V.
A KNIGHT [IN HASTE].

CHARLES. How now?

KNIGHT.The enemy has pass'd the Marne;
Is forming as for battle.

JOANNA [*as if inspired*]. Arms and battle!
My soul has cast away its bonds! To arms!
Prepare yourselves, while I prepare the rest![*She hastens out*

[*Trumpets sound with a piercing tone, and while the scene is changing pass into a wild tumultuous sound of battle.*]

SCENE VI.

[*The scene changes to an open space encircled with trees. During the music, soldiers are seen hastily retreating across the background.*]

TALBOT, *leaning upon* FASTOLF, *and accompanied by* Soldiers. *Soon after,* LIONEL.

TALBOT. Here set me down beneath this tree, and you
Betake yourselves again to battle: quick!
I need no help to die.

FASTOLF.O day of woe![*Lionel enters.*

Look, what a sight awaits you, Lionel!
Our General expiring of his wounds!

LIONEL. Now God forbid! Rise, noble Talbot! This
Is not a time for you to faint and sink.
Yield not to Death; force faltering Nature
By your strength of soul, that life depart not!

TALBOT. In vain! The day of Destiny is come
That prostrates with the dust our power in France.
In vain, in the fierce clash of desp'rate battle,
Have I risk'd our utmost to withstand it:
The bolt has smote and crush'd me, and I lie
To rise no more forever. Rheims is lost;
Make haste to rescue Paris.

LIONEL.Paris has surrender'd
To the Dauphin: an express is just arriv'd
With tidings.

TALBOT [*tears away his bandages*].
Then flow out, ye life-streams;
I am grown to loathe this Sun.

LIONEL.They want me!
Fastolf, bear him to a place of safety:
We can hold this post few instants longer,
The coward knaves are giving way on all sides,
Irresistible the Witch is pressing on.

TALBOT. Madness, thou conquerest, and I must yield:
Stupidity can baffle the very gods.
High Reason, radiant Daughter of God's Head,
Wise Foundress of the system of the Universe,
Conductress of the stars, who art thou, then,
If, tied to th' tail o' th' wild horse Superstition,
Thou must plunge, eyes open, vainly shrieking,
Sheer down with that drunk Beast to the Abyss?
Cursed who sets his life upon the great
And dignified; and with forecasting spirit
Forms wise projects! The Fool-king rules this world.

LIONEL. O, Death is near you! Think of your Creator!

TALBOT. Had we as brave men been defeated
By brave men, we might have consoled ourselves
With common thoughts of Fortune's fickleness:
But that a sorry farce should be our ruin! —
Did our earnest toilsome struggle merit
No graver end than this?

LIONEL [*grasps his hand*]. Talbot, farewell!

The meed of bitter tears I'll duly pay you,
When the fight is done, should I outlive it.
Now Fate calls me to the field, where yet
She wav'ring sits, and shakes her doubtful urn.
Farewell! we meet beyond the unseen shore.
Brief parting for long friendship! God be with you![*Exit.*

TALBOT. Soon it is over, and to th' Earth I render,
To the everlasting Sun, the atoms,
Which for pain and pleasure join'd to form me;
And of the mighty Talbot, whose renown
Once fill'd the world, remains nought but a handful
Of light dust. Thus man comes to his end;
And our one conquest in this fight of life
Is the conviction of life's nothingness,
And deep disdain of all that sorry stuff
We once thought lofty and desirable.

SCENE VII.

Enter CHARLES; BURGUNDY; DUNOIS; DU CHATEL; *and* Soldiers.

BURGUN. The trench is storm'd.

DUNOIS.The victory is ours.

CHARLES [*observing Talbot*].
Ha! who is this that to the light of day
Is bidding his constrained and sad farewell?
His bearing speaks no common man: go, haste,
Assist him, if assistance yet avail.

[*Soldiers from the Dauphin's suite step forward.*

FASTOLF. Back! Keep away! Approach not the Departing,
Whom in life ye never wish'd too near you.

BURGUN. What do I see? Lord Talbot in his blood!

[*He goes towards him. Talbot gazes fixedly at him, and dies.*

FASTOLF. Off, Burgundy! With th' aspect of a traitor
Poison not the last look of a hero.

DUNOIS. Dreaded Talbot! stern, unconquerable!
Dost thou content thee with a space so narrow,
And the wide domains of France once could not
Stay the striving of thy giant spirit?—
Now for the first time, Sire, I call you King:
The crown but totter'd on your head, so long
As in this body dwelt a soul.

CHARLES [*after looking at the dead in silence*]. It was
A higher hand that conquer'd him, not we.

Here on the soil of France he sleeps, as does
A hero on the shield he would not quit.
Bring him away.[*Soldiers lift the corpse, and carry it off.*
And peace be with his dust!
A fair memorial shall arise to him
I' th' midst of France: here, where the hero's course
And life were finished, let his bones repose.
Thus far no other foe has e'er advanced.
His epitaph shall be the place he fell on.

SCENE IX.

Another empty space in the field of battle. In the distance are seen the towers of Rheims illuminated by the sun.

A Knight, cased in black armour, with his visor shut. JOANNA *follows him to the front of the scene, where he stops and awaits her.*

JOANNA. Deceiver! Now I see thy craft. Thou hast,
By seeming flight, enticed me from the battle,
And warded death and destiny from off the head
Of many a Briton. Now they reach thy own.

KNIGHT. Why dost thou follow me, and track my stops
With murd'rous fury? I am not appointed
To die by thee.

JOANNA.Deep in my lowest soul
I hate thee as the Night, which is thy colour.
To sweep thee from the face of Earth, I feel
Some irresistible desire impelling me.
Who art thou? Lift thy visor: had not I
Seen Talbot fall, I should have named thee Talbot.

KNIGHT. Speaks not the prophesying Spirit in thee?

JOANNA. It tells me loudly, in my inmost bosom,
That Misfortune is at hand.

KNIGHT.Joanna d'Arc!
Up to the gates of Rheims hast thou advanced,
Led on by victory. Let the renown
Already gain'd suffice thee! As a slave
Has Fortune serv'd thee: emancipate her,
Ere in wrath she free herself; fidelity
She hates; no one obeys she to the end.

JOANNA. How say'st thou, in the middle of my course,
That I should pause and leave my work unfinish'd?
I will conclude it, and fulfil my vow.

KNIGHT. Nothing can withstand thee; thou art most strong;

In ev'ry battle thou prevailest. But go
Into no other battle. Hear my warning!

JOANNA. This sword I quit not, till the English yield.

KNIGHT. Look! Yonder rise the towers of Rheims, the goal
And purpose of thy march; thou seest the dome
Of the cathedral glittering in the sun:
There wouldst thou enter in triumphal pomp,
To crown thy sov'reign and fulfil thy vow.
Enter not there. Turn homewards. Hear my warning!

JOANNA. Who art thou, false, double-tongued betrayer,
That wouldst frighten and perplex me? Dar'st thou
Utter lying oracles to me?

[*The Black Knight attempts to go; she steps in his way.*

No!
Thou shalt answer me, or perish by me!
[*She lifts her arm to strike him.*

KNIGHT [*touches her with his hand: she stands immovable*].
Kill what is mortal!

[*Darkness, lightning and thunder. The Knight sinks.*

JOANNA [*stands at first amazed: but soon recovers herself*].
It was nothing earthly.
Some delusive form of Hell, some spirit
Of Falsehood, sent from th' everlasting Pool
To tempt and terrify my fervent soul!
Bearing the sword of God, what do I fear?
Victorious will I end my fated course;
Though Hell itself with all its fiends assail me,
My heart and faith shall never faint or fail me.[*She is going.*

SCENE X.
LIONEL, JOANNA.

LIONEL. Accursed Sorceress, prepare for battle:
Not both of us shall leave the place alive.
Thou hast destroyed the chosen of my host;
Brave Talbot has breath'd out his mighty spirit
In my bosom. I will avenge the Dead,
Or share his fate. And wouldst thou know the man
Who brings thee glory, let him die or conquer,
I am Lionel, the last survivor
Of our chiefs; and still unvanquish'd is this arm.

[*He rushes towards her; after a short contest, she strikes the sword from his hand.*

Faithless fortune![*He struggles with her.*

JOANNA [*seizes him by the plume from behind, and tears his helmet
violently down, so that his face is exposed: at
the same time she lifts her sword with the right
hand*].
Suffer what thou soughtest!
The Virgin sacrifices thee through me!

[*At this moment she looks in his face; his aspect touches her; she stands immovable, and then slowly drops her arm.*

LIONEL. Why lingerest thou, and stayest the stroke of death?
My honour thou hast taken, take my life:
'Tis in thy hands to take it; I want not mercy.
[*She gives him a sign with her hand to depart.*
Fly from *thee*? Owe *thee* my life? Die rather!

JOANNA [*her face turned away*].
I will not remember that thou owedst
Thy life to me.

LIONEL.I hate thee and thy gift.
I want not mercy. Kill thy enemy,
Who meant to kill thee, who abhors thee!

JOANNA. Kill me, and fly!

LIONEL.Ha! How is this?

JOANNA [*hides her face*].Woe's me!

LIONEL [*approaches her*].
Thou killest every Briton, I have heard,
Whom thou subdu'st in battle: why spare me?

JOANNA [*lifts her sword with a rapid movement against him,
but quickly lets it sink again, when she observes his
face*]. O Holy Virgin!

LIONEL.Wherefore namest thou
The Virgin? *She* knows nothing of thee; Heaven
Has nought to say to thee.

JOANNA [*in violent anguish*]. What have I done!
My vow, my vow is broke![*Wrings her hands in despair.*

LIONEL [*looks at her with sympathy, and comes nearer*].
Unhappy girl!
I pity thee; thou touchest me; thou showedst
Mercy to me alone. My hate is going:
I am constrain'd to feel for thee. Who art thou?
Whence comest thou?

JOANNA.Away! Begone!

LIONEL.Thy youth,
Thy beauty melt and sadden me; thy look
Goes to my heart: I could wish much to save thee;
Tell me how I may! Come, come with me! Forsake
This horrid business; cast away those arms!

JOANNA. I no more deserve to bear them!

LIONEL.Cast them
Away, then, and come with me!

JOANNA [*with horror*].Come with thee!

LIONEL. Thou mayst be sav'd: come with me! I will save thee.
But delay not. A strange sorrow for thee
Seizes me, and an unspeakable desire
To save thee.[*Seizes her arm.*

JOANNA.Ha! Dunois! 'Tis they!
If they should find thee! —

LIONEL.Fear not; I will guard thee.

JOANNA. I should die, were they to kill thee.

LIONEL.Am I
Dear to thee?

JOANNA.Saints of Heaven!

LIONEL.Shall I ever
See thee, hear of thee, again?

JOANNA.Never! Never!

LIONEL. This sword for pledge that I will see thee!
[*He wrests the sword from her.*

JOANNA.Madman!
Thou dar'st?

LIONEL. I yield to force; again I'll see thee.[*Exit.*

The introduction of supernatural agency in this play, and the final aberration
from the truth of history, have been considerably censured by the German critics:
Schlegel, we recollect, calls Joanna's end a 'rosy death.' In this dramaturgic discussion, the mere reader need take no great interest. To require our belief in appari-
tions and miracles, things which we cannot now believe, no doubt for a moment
disturbs our submission to the poet's illusions: but the miracles in this story are
rare and transient, and of small account in the general result: they give our reason
little trouble, and perhaps contribute to exalt the heroine in our imaginations. It is
still the mere human grandeur of Joanna's spirit that we love and reverence; the
lofty devotedness with which she is transported, the generous benevolence, the
irresistible determination. The heavenly mandate is but the means of unfolding
these qualities, and furnishing them with a proper passport to the minds of her
age. To have produced, without the aid of fictions like these, a Joanna so beautified

and exalted, would undoubtedly have yielded greater satisfaction: but it may be questioned whether the difficulty would not have increased in a still higher ratio. The sentiments, the characters, are not only accurate, but exquisitely beautiful; the incidents, excepting the very last, are possible, or even probable: what remains is but a very slender evil.

After all objections have been urged, and this among others has certainly a little weight, the *Maid of Orleans* will remain one of the very finest of modern dramas. Perhaps, among all Schiller's plays, it is the one which evinces most of that quality denominated *genius* in the strictest meaning of the word. *Wallenstein* embodies more thought, more knowledge, more conception; but it is only in parts illuminated by that ethereal brightness, which shines over every part of this. The spirit of the romantic ages is here imaged forth; but the whole is exalted, embellished, ennobled. It is what the critics call idealised. The heart must be cold, the imagination dull, which the *Jungfrau von Orleans* will not move.

In Germany this case did not occur: the reception of the work was beyond example flattering. The leading idea suited the German mind; the execution of it inflamed the hearts and imaginations of the people; they felt proud of their great poet, and delighted to enthusiasm with his poetry. At the first exhibition of the play in Leipzig, Schiller being in the theatre, though not among the audience, this feeling was displayed in a rather singular manner. When the curtain dropped at the end of the first act, there arose on all sides a shout of *"Es lebe Friedrich Schiller!"* accompanied by the sound of trumpets and other military music: at the conclusion of the piece, the whole assembly left their places, went out, and crowded round the door through which the poet was expected to come; and no sooner did he show himself, than his admiring spectators, uncovering their heads, made an avenue for him to pass; and as he waited along, many, we are told, held up their children, and exclaimed, *"That is he!"* [36]

This must have been a proud moment for Schiller; but also an agitating, painful one; and perhaps on the whole, the latter feeling, for the time, prevailed. Such noisy, formal, and tumultuous plaudits were little to his taste: the triumph they confer, though plentiful, is coarse; and Schiller's modest nature made him shun the public gaze, not seek it. He loved men, and did not affect to despise their approbation; but neither did this form his leading motive. To him art, like virtue, was its own reward; he delighted in his tasks for the sake of the fascinating feelings which they yielded him in their performance. Poetry was the chosen gift of his mind, which his pleasure lay in cultivating: in other things he wished not that his habits or enjoyments should be different from those of other men.

---

[36] Doering (p. 176);—who adds as follows: 'Another testimony of approval, very different in its nature, he received at the first production of the play in Weimar. Knowing and valuing, as he did, the public of that city, it could not but surprise him greatly, when a certain young Doctor S— — called out to him, *"Bravo, Schiller!"* from the gallery, in a very loud tone of voice. Offended at such impertinence, the poet hissed strongly, in which the audience joined him. He likewise expressed in words his displeasure at this conduct; and the youthful sprig of medicine was, by direction of the Court, farther punished for his indiscreet applause, by some admonitions from the police.'

At Weimar his present way of life was like his former one at Jena: his business was to study and compose; his recreations were in the circle of his family, where he could abandon himself to affections, grave or trifling, and in frank and cheerful intercourse with a few friends. Of the latter he had lately formed a social club, the meetings of which afforded him a regular and innocent amusement. He still loved solitary walks: in the Park at Weimar he might frequently be seen wandering among the groves and remote avenues, with a note-book in his hand; now loitering slowly along, now standing still, now moving rapidly on; if any one appeared in sight, he would dart into another alley, that his dream might not be broken.[37] 'One of his favourite resorts,' we are told, 'was the thickly-overshadowed rocky path which leads to the *Römische Haus*, a pleasure-house of the Duke's, built under the direction of Goethe. There he would often sit in the gloom of the crags, overgrown with cypresses and boxwood; shady hedges before him; not far from the murmur of a little brook, which there gushes in a smooth slaty channel, and where some verses of Goethe are cut upon a brown plate of stone, and fixed in the rock.' He still continued to study in the night: the morning was spent with his children and his wife, or in pastimes such as we have noticed; in the afternoon he revised what had been last composed, wrote letters, or visited his friends. His evenings were often passed in the theatre; it was the only public place of amusement which he ever visited; nor was it for the purpose of amusement that he visited this: it was his observatory, where he watched the effect of scenes and situations; devised new schemes of art, or corrected old ones. To the players he was kind, friendly: on nights when any of his pieces had been acted successfully or for the first time, he used to invite the leaders of the company to a supper in the Stadthaus, where the time was spent in mirthful diversions, one of which was frequently a recitation, by Genast, of the Capuchin's sermon in *Wallenstein's Camp*. Except on such rare occasions, he returned home directly from the theatre, to light his midnight lamp, and commence the most earnest of his labours.

The assiduity, with which he struggled for improvement in dramatic composition, had now produced its natural result: the requisitions of his taste no longer hindered the operation of his genius; art had at length become a second nature. A new proof at once of his fertility, and of his solicitude for farther improvement, appeared in 1803. The *Braut von Messina* was an experiment; an attempt to exhibit a modern subject and modern sentiments in an antique garb. The principle on which the interest of this play rests is the Fatalism of the ancients: the plot is of extreme simplicity; a Chorus also is introduced, an elaborate discussion of the nature and uses of that accompaniment being prefixed by way of preface. The experiment was not successful: with a multitude of individual beauties this *Bride of Messina* is found to be ineffectual as a whole: it does not move us; the great object of every tragedy is not attained. The Chorus, which Schiller, swerving from the Greek models, has divided into two contending parts, and made to enter and depart with the principals to whom they are attached, has in his hands become the medium

---

[37] 'Whatever he intended to write, he first composed in his head, before putting down a line of it on paper. He used to call a work *ready* so soon as its existence in his spirit was complete: hence in the public there often were reports that such and such a piece of his was finished, when, in the common sense, it was not even begun.'—*Jördens Lexicon*, § Schiller.

of conveying many beautiful effusions of poetry; but it retards the progress of the plot; it dissipates and diffuses our sympathies; the interest we should take in the fate and prospects of Manuel and Cæsar, is expended on the fate and prospects of man. For beautiful and touching delineations of life; for pensive and pathetic reflections, sentiments, and images, conveyed in language simple but nervous and emphatic, this tragedy stands high in the rank of modern compositions. There is in it a breath of young tenderness and ardour, mingled impressively with the feelings of gray-haired experience, whose recollections are darkened with melancholy, whose very hopes are chequered and solemn. The implacable Destiny which consigns the brothers to mutual enmity and mutual destruction, for the guilt of a past generation, involving a Mother and a Sister in their ruin, spreads a sombre hue over all the poem; we are not unmoved by the characters of the hostile Brothers, and we pity the hapless and amiable Beatrice, the victim of their feud. Still there is too little action in the play; the incidents are too abundantly diluted with reflection; the interest pauses, flags, and fails to produce its full effect. For its specimens of lyrical poetry, tender, affecting, sometimes exquisitely beautiful, the *Bride of Messina* will long deserve a careful perusal; but as exemplifying a new form of the drama, it has found no imitators, and is likely to find none.

The slight degree of failure or miscalculation which occurred in the present instance, was next year abundantly redeemed. *Wilhelm Tell*, sent out in 1804, is one of Schiller's very finest dramas; it exhibits some of the highest triumphs which his genius, combined with his art, ever realised. The first descent of Freedom to our modern world, the first unfurling of her standard on the rocky pinnacle of Europe, is here celebrated in the style which it deserved. There is no false timsel-decoration about *Tell*, no sickly refinement, no declamatory sentimentality. All is downright, simple, and agreeable to Nature; yet all is adorned and purified and rendered beautiful, without losing its resemblance. An air of freshness and wholesomeness breathes over it; we are among honest, inoffensive, yet fearless peasants, untainted by the vices, undazzled by the theories, of more complex and perverted conditions of society. The opening of the first scene sets us down among the Alps. It is 'a high rocky shore of the Luzern Lake, opposite to Schwytz. The lake makes a little bight in the land, a hut stands at a short distance from the bank, the fisher-boy is rowing himself about in his boat. Beyond the lake, on the other side, we see the green meadows, the hamlets and farms of Schwytz, lying in the clear sunshine. On our left are observed the peaks of the Hacken surrounded with clouds: to the right, and far in the distance, appear the glaciers. We hear the *rance des vaches* and the tinkling of cattle-bells.' This first impression never leaves us; we are in a scene where all is grand and lovely; but it is the loveliness and grandeur of unpretending, unadulterated Nature. These Switzers are not Arcadian shepherds or speculative patriots; there is not one crook or beechen bowl among them, and they never mention the Social Contract, or the Rights of Man. They are honest people, driven by oppression to assert their privileges; and they go to work like men in earnest, bent on the despatch of business, not on the display of sentiment. They are not philosophers or tribunes; but frank, stalwart landmen: even in the field of Rütli, they do not forget their common feelings; the party that arrive first indulge in a harmless little ebullition of parish vanity: "*We* are first here!" they say, "we Unterwaldeners!"

They have not charters or written laws to which they can appeal; but they have the traditionary rights of their fathers, and bold hearts and strong arms to make them good. The rules by which they steer are not deduced from remote premises, by a fine process of thought; they are the accumulated result of experience, transmitted from peasant sire to peasant son. There is something singularly pleasing in this exhibition of genuine humanity; of wisdom, embodied in old adages and practical maxims of prudence; of magnanimity, displayed in the quiet unpretending discharge of the humblest every-day duties. Truth is superior to Fiction: we feel at home among these brave good people; their fortune interests us more than that of all the brawling, vapid, sentimental heroes in creation. Yet to make them interest us was the very highest problem of art; it was to copy lowly Nature, to give us a copy of it embellished and refined by the agency of genius, yet preserving the likeness in every lineament. The highest quality of art is to conceal itself: these peasants of Schiller's are what every one imagines he could imitate successfully; yet in the hands of any but a true and strong-minded poet they dwindle into repulsive coarseness or mawkish insipidity. Among our own writers, who have tried such subjects, we remember none that has succeeded equally with Schiller. One potent but ill-fated genius has, in far different circumstances and with far other means, shown that he could have equalled him: the *Cotter's Saturday Night* of Burns is, in its own humble way, as quietly beautiful, as *simplex munditiis*, as the scenes of *Tell*. No other has even approached them; though some gifted persons have attempted it. Mr. Wordsworth is no ordinary man; nor are his pedlars, and leech-gatherers, and dalesmen, without their attractions and their moral; but they sink into whining drivellers beside *Rösselmann the Priest*, *Ulric the Smith*, *Hans of the Wall*, and the other sturdy confederates of Rütli.

The skill with which the events are concatenated in this play corresponds to the truth of its delineation of character. The incidents of the Swiss Revolution, as detailed in Tschudi or Müller, are here faithfully preserved, even to their minutest branches. The beauty of Schiller's descriptions all can relish; their fidelity is what surprises every reader who has been in Switzerland. Schiller never saw the scene of his play; but his diligence, his quickness and intensity of conception, supplied this defect. Mountain and mountaineer, conspiracy and action, are all brought before us in their true forms, all glowing in the mild sunshine of the poet's fancy. The tyranny of Gessler, and the misery to which it has reduced the land; the exasperation, yet patient courage of the people; their characters, and those of their leaders, Fürst, Stauffacher, and Melchthal; their exertions and ultimate success, described as they are here, keep up a constant interest in the piece. It abounds in action, as much as the *Bride of Messina* is defective in that point.

But the finest delineation is undoubtedly the character of Wilhelm Tell, the hero of the Swiss Revolt, and of the present drama. In Tell are combined all the attributes of a great man, without the help of education or of great occasions to develop them. His knowledge has been gathered chiefly from his own experience, and this is bounded by his native mountains: he has had no lessons or examples of splendid virtue, no wish or opportunity to earn renown: he has grown up to manhood, a simple yeoman of the Alps, among simple yeomen; and has never aimed at being more. Yet we trace in him a deep, reflective, earnest spirit, thirsting for activity, yet bound in by the wholesome dictates of prudence; a heart benevolent, generous, unconscious alike of boasting or of fear. It is this salubrious air of rustic, unpretending honesty that forms the great beauty in Tell's character: all is native, all is genuine; he does not declaim: he dislikes to talk of noble conduct, he exhibits it. He speaks little of his freedom, because he has always enjoyed it, and feels that he can always defend it. His reasons for destroying Gessler are not drawn from jurisconsults and writers on morality, but from the everlasting instincts of Nature: the Austrian Vogt must die; because if not, the wife and children of Tell will be destroyed by him. The scene, where the peaceful but indomitable archer sits waiting for Gessler in the hollow way among the rocks of Küssnacht, presents him in a striking light. Former scenes had shown us Tell under many amiable and attractive aspects; we knew that he was tender as well as brave, that he loved to haunt the mountain tops, and inhale in silent dreams the influence of their wild and magnificent beauty: we had seen him the most manly and warm-hearted of fathers and husbands; intrepid, modest, and decisive in the midst of peril, and venturing his life to bring help to the oppressed. But here his mind is exalted into stern solemnity; its principles of action come before us with greater clearness, in this its fiery contest. The name of murder strikes a damp across his frank and fearless spirit; while the recollection of his children and their mother proclaims emphatically that there is no remedy. Gessler must perish: Tell swore it darkly in his secret soul, when the monster forced him to aim at the head of his boy; and he will keep his oath. His thoughts wander to and fro, but his volition is unalterable; the free and peaceful mountaineer is to become a shedder of blood: woe to them that have made him so!

Travellers come along the pass; the unconcern of their every-day existence is strikingly contrasted with the dark and fateful purposes of Tell. The shallow innocent garrulity of Stüssi the Forester, the maternal vehemence of Armgart's Wife, the hard-hearted haughtiness of Gessler, successively presented to us, give an air of truth to the delineation, and deepen the impressiveness of the result.

ACT IV.
SCENE III.

The hollow way at Küssnacht. You descend from behind amid rocks; and travellers, before appearing on the scene, are seen from the height above. Rocks encircle the whole space; on one of the foremost is a projecting crag overgrown with brushwood.

TELL [*enters with his bow*].
Here through the hollow way he'll pass; there is
No other road to Küssnacht: here I'll do it!
The opportunity is good; the bushes
Of alder there will hide me; from that point
My arrow hits him; the strait pass prevents
Pursuit. Now, Gessler, balance thy account
With Heaven! Thou must be gone: thy sand is run.

Remote and harmless I have liv'd; my bow
Ne'er bent save on the wild beast of the forest;
My thoughts were free of murder. Thou hast scar'd me
From my peace; to fell asp-poison hast thou
Changed the milk of kindly temper in me;
Thou hast accustom'd me to horrors. Gessler!
The archer who could aim at his boy's head
Can send an arrow to his enemy's heart.

Poor little boys! My kind true wife! I will
Protect them from thee, Landvogt! When I drew
That bowstring, and my hand was quiv'ring,
And with devilish joy thou mad'st me point it
At the child, and I in fainting anguish
Entreated thee in vain; then with a grim
Irrevocable oath, deep in my soul,
I vow'd to God in Heav'n, that the *next* aim
I took should be thy heart. The vow I made
In that despairing moment's agony
Became a holy debt; and I will pay it.

Thou art my master, and my Kaiser's Vogt;
Yet would the Kaiser not have suffer'd thee
To do as thou hast done. He sent thee hither
To judge us; rigorously, for he is angry;
But not to glut thy savage appetite
With murder, and thyself be safe, among us:
There is a God to punish them that wrong us.

Come forth, thou bringer once of bitter sorrow,
My precious jewel now, my trusty yew!
A mark I'll set thee, which the cry of woe
Could never penetrate: to *thee* it shall not
Be impenetrable. And, good bowstring!
Which so oft in sport hast serv'd me truly,
Forsake me not in this last awful earnest;
Yet once hold fast, thou faithful cord; thou oft
For me hast wing'd the biting arrow;
Now send it sure and piercing, now or never!
Fail this, there is no second in my quiver.
[*Travellers cross the scene.*

Here let me sit on this stone bench, set up
For brief rest to the wayfarer; for here
There is no home. Each pushes on quick, transient,
Regarding not the other or his sorrows.
Here goes the anxious merchant, and the light
Unmoneyed pilgrim; the pale pious monk,
The gloomy robber, and the mirthful showman;

The carrier with his heavy-laden horse,
Who comes from far-off lands; for every road
Will lead one to the end o' th' World.
They pass; each hastening forward on his path,
Pursuing his own business: mine is death![*Sits down.*

Erewhile, my children, were your father out,
There was a merriment at his return;
For still, on coming home, he brought you somewhat,
Might be an Alpine flower, rare bird, or elf-bolt,
Such as the wand'rer finds upon the mountains:
Now he is gone in quest of other spoil
On the wild way he sits with thoughts of murder:
'Tis for his enemy's life he lies in wait
And yet on you, dear children, you alone
He thinks as then: for your sake is he here;
To guard you from the Tyrant's vengeful mood,
He bends his peaceful bow for work of blood.[*Rises.*

No common game I watch for. Does the hunter
Think it nought to roam the livelong day,
In winter's cold; to risk the desp'rate leap
From crag to crag, to climb the slipp'ry face
O' th' dizzy steep, glueing his steps in's blood;
And all to catch a pitiful chamois?
Here is a richer prize afield: the heart
Of my sworn enemy, that would destroy me.
[*A sound of gay music is heard in the distance; it approaches.*

All my days, the bow has been my comrade,
I have trained myself to archery; oft
Have I took the bull's-eye, many a prize
Brought home from merry shooting; but today
I will perform my master-feat, and win me
The best prize in the circuit of the hills.

[*A wedding company crosses the scene, and mounts up through the Pass. Tell
looks at them, leaning on his bow; Stüssi the Forester joins him.*

Stüssi. 'Tis Klostermey'r of Morlischachen holds
His bridal feast today: a wealthy man;
Has half a score of glens i' th' Alps. They're going
To fetch the bride from Imisee; tonight
There will be mirth and wassail down at Küssnacht.
Come you! All honest people are invited.

Tell. A serious guest befits not bridal feasts.

Stüssi. If sorrow press you, dash it from your heart!
Seize what you can: the times are hard; one needs
To snatch enjoyment nimbly while it passes.

Here 'tis a bridal, there 'twill be a burial.

Tell. And oftentimes the one leads to the other.

Stüssi. The way o' th' world at present! There is nought
But mischief everywhere: an avalanche
Has come away in Glarus; and, they tell me,
A side o' th' Glarnish has sunk under ground.

Tell. Do, then, the very hills give way! On earth
Is nothing that endures.

Stüssi. In foreign parts, too,
Are strange wonders. I was speaking with a man
From Baden: a Knight, it seems, was riding
To the King; a swarm of hornets met him
By the way, and fell on's horse, and stung it
Till it dropt down dead of very torment,
And the poor Knight was forced to go afoot.

Tell. Weak creatures too have stings.

[*Armgart's Wife enters with several children, and places herself at the entrance of the Pass.*

Stüssi. 'Tis thought to bode
Some great misfortune to the land; some black
Unnatural action.

Tell. Ev'ry day such actions
Occur in plenty: needs no sign or wonder
To foreshow them.

Stüssi. Ay, truly! Well for him
That tills his field in peace, and undisturb'd
Sits by his own fireside!

Tell. The peacefulest
Dwells not in peace, if wicked neighbours hinder.

[*Tell looks often, with restless expectation, towards the top of the Pass.*

Stüssi. Too true. — Good b'ye! — You're waiting here for some one?

Tell. That am I.

Stüssi. Glad meeting with your friends!
You are from Uri? His Grace the Landvogt
Is expected thence today.

Traveller [*enters*]. Expect not
The Landvogt now. The waters, from the rain,
Are flooded, and have swept down all the bridges. [*Tell stands up.*

Armgart [*coming forward*].
The Vogt not come!

STÜSSI.Did you want aught with him?

ARMGART. Ah! yes, indeed!

STÜSSI.Why have you placed yourself
In this strait pass to meet him?

ARMGART.In the pass
He cannot turn aside from me, must hear me.

FRIESSHARDT [*comes hastily down the Pass, and calls into the Scene*].
Make way! make way! My lord the Landvogt
Is riding close at hand.

ARMGART.The Landvogt coming!

[*She goes with her children to the front of the Scene. Gessler and Rudolph der
Harras appear on horseback at the top of the Pass.*

STÜSSI [*to Friesshardt*].
How got you through the water, when the flood
Had carried down the bridges?

FRIESS.We have battled
With the billows, friend; we heed no Alp-flood.

STÜSSI. Were you o' board i' th' storm?

FRIESS.That were we;
While I live, I shall remember 't.

STÜSSI.Stay, stay!
O, tell me!

FRIESS. Cannot; must run on t' announce
His lordship in the Castle. [*Exit.*

STÜSSI.Had these fellows
I' th' boat been honest people, 't would have sunk
With ev'ry soul of them. But for such rakehells,
Neither fire nor flood will kill them. [*He looks round.*] Whither
Went the Mountain-man was talking with me?[*Exit.*

GESSLER *and* RUDOLPH DER HARRAS *on horseback.*

GESSLER. Say what you like, I am the Kaiser's servant,
And must think of pleasing him. He sent me
Not to caress these hinds, to soothe or nurse them:
Obedience is the word! The point at issue is
Shall Boor or Kaiser here be lord o' th' land.

ARMGART. Now is the moment! Now for my petition!
[*Approaches timidly.*

GESSLER. This Hat at Aldorf, mark you, I set up
Not for the joke's sake, or to try the hearts
O' th' people; these I know of old: but that

They might be taught to bend their necks to me,
Which are too straight and stiff: and in the way
Where they are hourly passing, I have planted
This offence, that so their eyes may fall on't,
And remind them of their lord, whom they forget.

RUDOLPH. But yet the people have some rights—

GESSLER.Which now
Is not a time for settling or admitting.
Mighty things are on the anvil. The house
Of Hapsburg must wax powerful; what the Father
Gloriously began, the Son must forward:
This people is a stone of stumbling, which
One way or t'other must be put aside.

[*They are about to pass along. The Woman throws herself before the Landvogt.*

ARMGART. Mercy, gracious Landvogt! Justice! Justice!

GESSLER. Why do you plague me here, and stop my way,
I' th' open road? Off! Let me pass!

ARMGART.My husband
Is in prison; these orphans cry for bread.
Have pity, good your Grace, have pity on us!

RUDOLPH. Who or what are you, then? Who is your husband?

ARMGART. A poor wild-hay-man of the Rigiberg,
Whose trade is, on the brow of the abyss,
To mow the common grass from craggy shelves
And nooks to which the cattle dare not climb.

RUDOLPH [*to Gessler*]. By Heaven, a wild and miserable life!
Do now! do let the poor drudge free, I pray you!
Whatever be his crime, that horrid trade
Is punishment enough.
[*To the Woman*] You shall have justice:
In the Castle there, make your petition;
This is not the place.

ARMGART.No, no! I stir not
From the spot till you give up my husband!
'Tis the sixth month he has lain i' th' dungeon,
Waiting for the sentence of some judge, in vain.

GESSLER. Woman! Wouldst' lay hands on me? Begone!

ARMGART. Justice, Landvogt! thou art judge o' th' land here,
I' th' Kaiser's stead and God's. Perform thy duty!
As thou expectest justice from above,
Show it to us.

GESSLER. Off! Take the mutinous rabble
From my sight.

ARMGART [*catches the bridle of the horse*].
No, no! I now have nothing
More to lose. Thou shalt not move a step, Vogt,
Till thou hast done me right. Ay, knit thy brows,
And roll thy eyes as sternly as thou wilt;
We are so wretched, wretched now, we care not
Aught more for thy anger.

GESSLER.Woman, make way!
Or else my horse shall crush thee.

ARMGART.Let it! there—

[*She pulls her children to the ground, and throws herself along with them in his way.*

Here am I with my children: let the orphans
Be trodden underneath thy horse's hoofs!
'Tis not the worst that thou hast done.

RUDOLPH. Woman! Art' mad?

ARMGART [*with still greater violence*].
'Tis long that thou hast trodden.
The Kaiser's people under foot. Too long!
O, I am but a woman; were I a man,
I should find something else to do than lie
Here crying in the dust.

[*The music of the Wedding is heard again, at the top of the Pass, but softened by distance.*

GESSLER.Where are my servants?
Quick! Take her hence! I may forget myself,
And do the thing I shall repent.

RUDOLPH.My lord,
The servants cannot pass; the place above
Is crowded by a bridal company.

GESSLER. I've been too mild a ruler to this people;
They are not tamed as they should be; their tongues
Are still at liberty. This shall be alter'd!
I will break that stubborn humour; Freedom
With its pert vauntings shall no more be heard of:
I will enforce a new law in these lands;
There shall not—

[*An arrow pierces him; he claps his hand upon his heart, and is about to sink. With a faint voice*

God be merciful to me!

RUDOLPH. Herr Landvogt—God! What is it? Whence came it?

ARMGART [*springing up*].
Dead! dead! He totters, sinks! 'T has hit him!

RUDOLPH [*springs from his horse*].
Horrible!—O God of Heaven!—Herr Ritter,
Cry to God for mercy! You are dying.

GESSLER. 'Tis Tell's arrow.

[*Has slid down from his horse into Rudolph's arms, who sets him on the stone bench.*

TELL [*appears above, on the point of the rock*].
Thou hast found the archer;
Seek no other. Free are the cottages,
Secure is innocence from thee; thou wilt
Torment the land no more.
[*Disappears from the height. The people rush in.*

STÜSSI [*foremost*].What? What has happen'd?

ARMGART. The Landvogt shot, kill'd by an arrow.

PEOPLE [*rushing in*].Who?
Who is shot?

[*Whilst the foremost of the wedding company enter on the Scene, the hindmost are still on the height, and the music continues.*

RUDOLPH. He's bleeding, bleeding to death.
Away! Seek help; pursue the murderer!
Lost man! Must it so end with thee? Thou wouldst not
Hear my warning!

STÜSSI.Sure enough! There lies he
Pale and going fast.

MANY VOICES.Who was it killed him?

RUDOLPH. Are the people mad, that they make music
Over murder? Stop it, I say!

[*The music ceases suddenly; more people come crowding round.*

Herr Landvogt,
Can you not speak to me? Is there nothing
You would entrust me with?

[*Gessler makes signs with his hand, and vehemently repeats them, as they are not understood.*

Where shall I run?
To Küssnacht! I cannot understand you:
O, grow not angry! Leave the things of Earth,

And think how you shall make your peace with Heaven!

[*The whole bridal company surround the dying man with an expression of unsympathising horror.*

STÜSSI. Look there! How pale he grows! Now! Death is coming
Round his heart: his eyes grow dim and fixed.

ARMGART [*lifts up one of her children*].
See, children, how a miscreant departs!

RUDOLPH. Out on you, crazy hags! Have ye no touch
Of feeling in you, that ye feast your eyes
On such an object? Help me, lend your hands!
Will no one help to pull the tort'ring arrow
From his breast?

WOMEN [*start back*]. *We* touch him whom God has smote!

RUDOLPH. My curse upon you![*Draws his sword.*

STÜSSI [*lays his hand on Rudolph's arm*].
Softly, my good Sir!
Your government is at an end. The Tyrant
Is fallen: we will endure no farther violence:
We are free.

ALL [*tumultuously*]. The land is free!

RUDOLPH.Ha! runs it so?
Are rev'rence and obedience gone already?
[*To the armed Attendants, who press in.*
You see the murd'rous deed that has been done.
Our help is vain, vain to pursue the murd'rer;
Other cares demand us. On! To Küssnacht!
To save the Kaiser's fortress! For at present
All bonds of order, duty, are unloosed,
No man's fidelity is to be trusted.

[*Whilst he departs with the Attendants, appear six Fratres Misericordiæ.*

ARMGART. Room! Room! Here come the Friars of Mercy.

STÜSSI. The victim slain, the ravens are assembling!

FRATRES MISERICORDIÆ [*form a half-circle round the dead body, and sing in a deep tone*].
With noiseless tread death comes on man,
No plea, no prayer delivers him;
From midst of busy life's unfinished plan,
With sudden hand, it severs him:
And ready or not ready,—no delay,
Forth to his Judge's bar he must away!

The death of Gessler, which forms the leading object of the plot, happens at the end of the fourth act; the fifth, occupied with representing the expulsion of his satellites, and the final triumph and liberation of the Swiss, though diversified with occurrences and spectacles, moves on with inferior animation. A certain want of unity is, indeed, distinctly felt throughout all the piece; the incidents do not point one way; there is no connexion, or a very slight one, between the enterprise of Tell and that of the men of Rütli. This is the principal, or rather sole, deficiency of the present work; a deficiency inseparable from the faithful display of the historical event, and far more than compensated by the deeper interest and the wider range of action and delineation, which a strict adherence to the facts allows. By the present mode of management, Alpine life in all its length and breadth is placed before us: from the feudal halls of Attinghausen to Ruodi the Fisher of the Luzern Lake, and Armgart, —

> The poor wild-hay-man of the Rigiberg,
> Whose trade is, on the brow of the abyss,
> To mow the common grass from craggy shelves
> And nooks to which the cattle dare not climb, —

we stand as if in presence of the Swiss, beholding the achievement of their freedom in its minutest circumstances, with all its simplicity and unaffected greatness. The light of the poet's genius is upon the Four Forest Cantons, at the opening of the Fourteenth Century: the whole time and scene shine as with the brightness, the truth, and more than the beauty, of reality.

The tragedy of *Tell* wants unity of interest and of action; but in spite of this, it may justly claim the high dignity of ranking with the very best of Schiller's plays. Less comprehensive and ambitious than *Wallenstein*, less ethereal than the *Jungfrau*, it has a look of nature and substantial truth, which neither of its rivals can boast of. The feelings it inculcates and appeals to are those of universal human nature, and presented in their purest, most unpretending form. There is no high-wrought sentiment, no poetic love. Tell loves his wife as honest men love their wives; and the episode of Bertha and Rudenz, though beautiful, is very brief, and without effect on the general result. It is delightful and salutary to the heart to wander among the scenes of *Tell*: all is lovely, yet all is real. Physical and moral grandeur are united; yet both are the unadorned grandeur of Nature. There are the lakes and green valleys beside us, the Schreckhorn, the Jungfrau, and their sister peaks, with their avalanches and their palaces of ice, all glowing in the southern sun; and dwelling among them are a race of manly husbandmen, heroic without ceasing to be homely, poetical without ceasing to be genuine.

We have dwelt the longer on this play, not only on account of its peculiar fascinations, but also — as it is our last! Schiller's faculties had never been more brilliant than at present: strong in mature age, in rare and varied accomplishments, he was now reaping the full fruit of his studious vigils; the rapidity with which he wrote such noble poems, at once betokened the exuberant riches of his mind and the prompt command which he enjoyed of them. Still all that he had done seemed but a fraction of his appointed task: a bold imagination was carrying him forward into distant untouched fields of thought and poetry, where triumphs yet more glorious were to be gained. Schemes of new writings, new kinds of writing, were budding in his fancy; he was yet, as he had ever been, surrounded by a multitude of projects, and full of ardour to labour in fulfilling them. But Schiller's labours and triumphs were drawing to a close. The invisible Messenger was already near, which overtakes alike the busy and the idle, which arrests man in the midst of his pleasures or his occupations, *and changes his countenance and sends him away*.

In 1804, having been at Berlin witnessing the exhibition of his *Wilhelm Tell*, he was seized, while returning, with a paroxysm of that malady which for many years had never wholly left him. The attack was fierce and violent; it brought him to the verge of the grave; but he escaped once more; was considered out of danger, and again resumed his poetical employments. Besides various translations from the French and Italian, he had sketched a tragedy on the history of Perkin Warbeck, and finished two acts of one on that of a kindred but more fortunate impostor, Dimitri of Russia. His mind, it would appear, was also frequently engaged with more solemn and sublime ideas. The universe of human thought he had now explored and enjoyed; but he seems to have found no permanent contentment in any of its provinces. Many of his later poems indicate an incessant and increasing longing for some solution of the mystery of life; at times it is a gloomy resignation to the want and the despair of any. His ardent spirit could not satisfy itself with things seen, though gilded with all the glories of intellect and imagination; it soared away in search of other lands, looking with unutterable desire for some surer and brighter home beyond the horizon of this world. Death he had no reason to regard as probably a near event; but we easily perceive that the awful secrets connected with it had long been familiar to his contemplation. The veil which hid them from his eyes was now shortly, when he looked not for it, to be rent asunder.

The spring of 1805, which Schiller had anticipated with no ordinary hopes of enjoyment and activity, came on in its course, cold, bleak, and stormy; and along with it his sickness returned. The help of physicians was vain; the unwearied services of trembling affection were vain: his disorder kept increasing; on the 9th of May it reached a crisis. Early in the morning of that day, he grew insensible, and by degrees delirious. Among his expressions, the word *Lichtenberg* was frequently noticed; a word of no import; indicating, as some thought, the writer of that name, whose works he had lately been reading; according to others, the castle of Leuchtenberg, which, a few days before his sickness, he had been proposing to visit. The poet and the sage was soon to lie low; but his friends were spared the farther pain of seeing him depart in madness. The fiery canopy of physical suffering, which had bewildered and blinded his thinking faculties, was drawn aside; and the spirit of Schiller looked forth in its wonted serenity, once again before it passed away forever. After noon his delirium abated; about four o'clock he fell into a soft sleep, from which he ere long awoke in full possession of his senses. Restored to consciousness in that hour, when the soul is cut off from human help, and man must front the King of Terrors on his own strength, Schiller did not faint or fail in this his last and sharpest trial. Feeling that his end was come, he addressed himself to meet it as became him; not with affected carelessness or superstitious fear, but with the quiet unpretending manliness which had marked the tenor of his life. Of his friends and family he took a touching but a tranquil farewell: he ordered that his funeral should be private, without pomp or parade. Some one inquiring how he felt, he said *"Calmer and calmer;"* simple but memorable words, expressive of the mild heroism of the man. About six he sank into a deep sleep; once for a moment he looked up with a lively air, and said, *"Many things were growing plain and clear to him!"* Again he closed his eyes; and his sleep deepened and deepened, till it changed into the sleep from which there is no awakening; and all that remained of Schiller was a lifeless form, soon to be mingled with the clods of the valley.

The news of Schiller's death fell cold on many a heart: not in Germany alone, but over Europe, it was regarded as a public loss, by all who understood its meaning. In Weimar especially, the scene of his noblest efforts, the abode of his chosen friends, the sensation it produced was deep and universal. The public places of amusement were shut; all ranks made haste to testify their feelings, to honour themselves and the deceased by tributes to his memory. It was Friday when Schiller died; his funeral was meant to be on Sunday; but the state of his remains made it necessary to proceed before. Doering thus describes the ceremony:

'According to his own directions, the bier was to be borne by private burghers of the city; but several young artists and students, out of reverence for the deceased, took it from them. It was between midnight and one in the morning, when they approached the churchyard. The overclouded heaven threatened rain. But as the bier was set down beside the grave, the clouds suddenly split asunder, and the moon, coming forth in peaceful clearness, threw her first rays on the coffin of the Departed. They lowered him into the grave; and the moon again retired behind her clouds. A fierce tempest of wind began to howl, as if it were reminding the bystanders of their great, irreparable loss. At this moment who could have applied without emotion the poet's own words:

> Alas, the ruddy morning tinges
> A silent, cold, sepulchral stone;
> And evening throws her crimson fringes
> But round his slumber dark and lone!'

So lived and so died Friedrich Schiller; a man on whose history other men will long dwell with a mingled feeling of reverence and love. Our humble record of his life and writings is drawing to an end: yet we still linger, loth to part with a spirit so dear to us. From the scanty and too much neglected field of his biography, a few slight facts and indications may still be gleaned; slight, but distinctive of him as an individual, and not to be despised in a penury so great and so unmerited.

Schiller's age was forty-five years and a few months when he died.[38] Sickness had long wasted his form, which at no time could boast of faultless symmetry. He was tall and strongly boned; but unmuscular and lean: his body, it might be perceived, was wasting under the energy of a spirit too keen for it. His face was pale, the cheeks and temples rather hollow, the chin somewhat deep and slightly projecting, the nose irregularly aquiline, his hair inclined to auburn. Withal his

[38] 'He left a widow, two sons, and two daughters,' of whom we regret to say that we have learned nothing. 'Of his three sisters, the youngest died before him; the eldest is married to the Hofrath Reinwald, in Meinungen; the second to Herr Frankh, the clergyman of Meckmuhl, in Würtemberg.' *Doering.*

countenance was attractive, and had a certain manly beauty. The lips were curved together in a line, expressing delicate and honest sensibility; a silent enthusiasm, impetuosity not unchecked by melancholy, gleamed in his softly kindled eyes and pale cheeks, and the brow was high and thoughtful. To judge from his portraits, Schiller's face expressed well the features of his mind: it is mildness tempering strength; fiery ardour shining through the clouds of suffering and disappointment, deep but patiently endured. Pale was its proper tint; the cheeks and temples were best hollow. There are few faces that affect us more than Schiller's; it is at once meek, tender, unpretending, and heroic.

In his dress and manner, as in all things, he was plain and unaffected. Among strangers, something shy and retiring might occasionally be observed in him: in his own family, or among his select friends, he was kind-hearted, free, and gay as a little child. In public, his external appearance had nothing in it to strike or attract. Of an unpresuming aspect, wearing plain apparel, his looks as he walked were constantly bent on the ground; so that frequently, as we are told, 'he failed to notice the salutation of a passing acquaintance; but if he heard it, he would catch hastily at his hat, and give his cordial *"Guten Tag."'* Modesty, simplicity, a total want of all parade or affectation were conspicuous in him. These are the usual concomitants of true greatness, and serve to mitigate its splendour. Common things he did as a common man. His conduct in such matters was uncalculated, spontaneous; and therefore natural and pleasing.

Concerning his mental character, the greater part of what we had to say has been already said, in speaking of his works. The most cursory perusal of these will satisfy us that he had a mind of the highest order; grand by nature, and cultivated by the assiduous study of a lifetime. It is not the predominating force of any one faculty that impresses us in Schiller; but the general force of all. Every page of his writings bears the stamp of internal vigour; new truths, new aspects of known truth, bold thought, happy imagery, lofty emotion. Schiller would have been no common man, though he had altogether wanted the qualities peculiar to poets. His intellect is clear, deep, and comprehensive; its deductions, frequently elicited from numerous and distant premises, are presented under a magnificent aspect, in the shape of theorems, embracing an immense multitude of minor propositions. Yet it seems powerful and vast, rather than quick or keen; for Schiller is not notable for wit, though his fancy is ever prompt with its metaphors, illustrations, comparisons, to decorate and point the perceptions of his reason. The earnestness of his temper farther disqualified him for this: his tendency was rather to adore the grand and the lofty than to despise the little and the mean. Perhaps his greatest faculty was a half-poetical, half-philosophical imagination: a faculty teeming with magnificence and brilliancy; now adorning, or aiding to erect, a stately pyramid of scientific speculation; now brooding over the abysses of thought and feeling, till thoughts and feelings, else unutterable, were embodied in expressive forms, and palaces and landscapes glowing in ethereal beauty rose like exhalations from the bosom of the deep.

Combined and partly of kindred with these intellectual faculties was that vehemence of temperament which is necessary for their full development. Schiller's heart was at once fiery and tender; impetuous, soft, affectionate, his enthusiasm clothed the universe with grandeur, and sent his spirit forth to explore its secrets and mingle warmly in its interests. Thus poetry in Schiller was not one but many gifts. It was not the 'lean and flashy song' of an ear apt for harmony, combined with a maudlin sensibility, or a mere animal ferocity of passion, and an imagination creative chiefly because unbridled: it was, what true poetry is always, the quintessence of general mental riches, the purified result of strong thought and conception, and of refined as well as powerful emotion. In his writings, we behold him a moralist, a philosopher, a man of universal knowledge: in each of these capacities he is great, but also in more; for all that he achieves in these is brightened and gilded with the touch of another quality; his maxims, his feelings, his opinions are transformed from the lifeless shape of didactic truths, into living shapes that address faculties far finer than the understanding.

The gifts by which such transformation is effected, the gift of pure, ardent, tender sensibility, joined to those of fancy and imagination, are perhaps not wholly denied to any man endowed with the power of reason; possessed in various degrees of strength, they add to the products of mere intellect corresponding tints of new attractiveness; in a degree great enough to be remarkable they constitute a poet. Of this peculiar faculty how much had fallen to Schiller's lot, we need not attempt too minutely to explain. Without injuring his reputation, it may be admitted that, in general, his works exhibit rather extraordinary strength than extraordinary fineness or versatility. His power of dramatic imitation is perhaps never of the very highest, the Shakspearean kind; and in its best state, it is farther limited to a certain range of characters. It is with the grave, the earnest, the exalted, the affectionate, the mournful, that he succeeds: he is not destitute of humour, as his *Wallenstein's Camp* will show, but neither is he rich in it; and for sprightly ridicule in any of its forms he has seldom shown either taste or talent. Chance principally made the drama his department; he might have shone equally in many others. The vigorous and copious invention, the knowledge of life, of men and things, displayed in his theatrical pieces, might have been available in very different pursuits; frequently the charm of his works has little to distinguish it from the charm of intellectual and moral force in general; it is often the capacious thought, the vivid imagery, the impetuous feeling of the orator, rather than the wild pathos and capricious enchantment of the poet. Yet that he was capable of rising to the loftiest regions of poetry, no reader of his *Maid of Orleans*, his character of Thekla, or many other of his pieces, will hesitate to grant. Sometimes we suspect that it is the very grandeur of his general powers which prevents us from exclusively admiring his poetic genius. We are not lulled by the syren song of poetry, because her melodies are blended with the clearer, manlier tones of serious reason, and of honest though exalted feeling.

Much laborious discussion has been wasted in defining genius, particularly by the countrymen of Schiller, some of whom have narrowed the conditions of the term so far, as to find but three *men of genius* since the world was created: Homer, Shakspeare, and Goethe! From such rigid precision, applied to a matter in itself indefinite, there may be an apparent, but there is no real, increase of accuracy. The creative power, the faculty not only of imitating given forms of being, but of imagining and representing new ones, which is here attributed with such distinctness and so sparingly, has been given by nature in complete perfection to no man, nor entirely denied to any. The shades of it cannot be distinguished by so loose a scale as language. A definition of genius which excludes such a mind as Schiller's will scarcely be agreeable to philosophical correctness, and it will tend rather to lower than to exalt the dignity of the word. Possessing all the general mental faculties in their highest degree of strength, an intellect ever active, vast, powerful, far-sighted; an imagination never weary of producing grand or beautiful forms; a heart of the noblest temper, sympathies comprehensive yet ardent, feelings vehement, impetuous, yet full of love and kindliness and tender pity; conscious of the rapid and fervid exercise of all these powers within him, and able farther to present their products refined and harmonised, and 'married to immortal verse,' Schiller may or may not be called a man of genius by his critics; but his mind in either case will remain one of the most enviable which can fall to the share of a mortal.

In a poet worthy of that name, the powers of the intellect are indissolubly interwoven with the moral feelings, and the exercise of his art depends not more on the perfection of the one than of the other. The poet, who does not feel nobly and justly, as well as passionately, will never permanently succeed in making others feel: the forms of error and falseness, infinite in number, are transitory in duration; truth, of thought and sentiment, but chiefly of sentiment, truth alone is eternal and unchangeable. But, happily, a delight in the products of reason and imagination can scarcely ever be divided from, at least, a love for virtue and genuine greatness. Our feelings are in favour of heroism; we *wish* to be pure and perfect. Happy he whose resolutions are so strong, or whose temptations are so weak, that he can convert these feelings into action! The severest pang, of which a proud and sensitive nature can be conscious, is the perception of its own debasement. The sources of misery in life are many: vice is one of the surest. Any human creature, tarnished with guilt, will in general be wretched; a man of genius in that case will be doubly so, for his ideas of excellence are higher, his sense of failure is more keen. In such miseries, Schiller had no share. The sentiments, which animated his poetry, were converted into principles of conduct; his actions were as blameless as his writings were pure. With his simple and high predilections, with his strong devotedness to a noble cause, he contrived to steer through life, unsullied by its meanness, unsubdued by any of its difficulties or allurements. With the world, in fact, he had not much to do; without effort, he dwelt apart from it; its prizes were not the wealth which could enrich him. His great, almost his single aim, was to unfold his spiritual faculties, to study and contemplate and improve their intellectual creations. Bent upon this, with the steadfastness of an apostle, the more sordid temptations of the world passed harmlessly over him. Wishing not to seem, but to be, envy was a feeling of which he knew but little, even before he rose above its level. Wealth or rank he regarded as a means, not an end; his own humble fortune supplying him with all the essential conveniences of life, the world had nothing more that he chose to covet, nothing more that it could give him. He was not rich; but his habits were simple, and, except by reason of his sickness and its consequences, unexpensive. At all times he was far above the meanness of self-interest, particularly in its meanest shape, a love of money. Doering tells us, that a bookseller having travelled from a distance expressly to offer him a higher price for the copyright of *Wallenstein*, at that time in the press, and for which he was on terms with Cotta of Tübingen, Schiller answering, "Cotta deals steadily with me, and I with him," sent away this new merchant, without even the hope of a future bargain. The anecdote is small; but it seems to paint the integrity of the man, careless of pecuniary concerns in comparison with the strictest uprightness in his conduct. In fact, his real wealth lay in being able to pursue his darling studies, and to live in the sunshine of friendship and domestic love. This he had always longed for; this he at last enjoyed. And though sickness and many vexations annoyed him, the intrinsic excellence of his nature chequered the darkest portions of their gloom with an effulgence derived from himself. The ardour of his feelings, tempered by benevolence, was equable and placid: his temper, though overflowing with generous warmth, seems almost never to have shown any hastiness or anger. To all men he was humane and sympathising; among his friends, open-hearted, generous, helpful; in the circle of his family, kind, tender, sportive. And what gave an especial charm to all this was, the unobtrusiveness with which it was attended: there was no parade, no display, no particle of affectation; rating and conducting himself simply as an honest man and citizen, he became greater by forgetting that he was great.

Such were the prevailing habits of Schiller. That in the mild and beautiful brilliancy of their aspect there must have been some specks and imperfections, the common lot of poor humanity, who knows not? That these were small and transient, we judge from the circumstance that scarcely any hint of them has reached us: nor are we anxious to obtain a full description of them. For practical uses, we can sufficiently conjecture what they were; and the heart desires not to dwell upon them. This man is passed away from our dim and tarnished world: let him have the benefit of departed friends; let him be transfigured in our thoughts, and shine there without the little blemishes that clung to him in life.

Schiller gives a fine example of the German character: he has all its good qualities in a high degree, with very few of its defects. We trace in him all that downrightness and simplicity, that sincerity of heart and mind, for which the Germans are remarked; their enthusiasm, their patient, long-continuing, earnest devotedness; their imagination, delighting in the lofty and magnificent; their intellect, rising into refined abstractions, stretching itself into comprehensive generalisations. But the excesses to which such a character is liable are, in him, prevented by a firm and watchful sense of propriety. His simplicity never degenerates into ineptitude or insipidity; his enthusiasm must be based on reason; he rarely suffers his love of the vast to betray him into toleration of the vague. The boy Schiller was extravagant; but the man admits no bombast in his style, no inflation in his thoughts or actions. He is the poet of truth; our understandings and consciences are satisfied, while our hearts and imaginations are moved. His fictions are emphatically nature copied and embellished; his sentiments are refined and touchingly beautiful, but they are likewise manly and correct; they exalt and inspire, but they do not mislead. Above all, he has no cant; in any of its thousand branches, ridiculous or hateful, none. He does not distort his character or genius into shapes, which he thinks more becoming than their natural one: he does not hang out principles which are not his, or harbour beloved persuasions which he half or wholly knows to be false. He did not often speak of wholesome prejudices; he did not 'embrace the Roman Catholic religion because it was the grandest and most comfortable.' Truth with Schiller, or what seemed such, was an indispensable requisite: if he but suspected an opinion to be false, however dear it may have been, he seems to have examined it with rigid scrutiny, and if he found it guilty, to have plucked it out, and resolutely cast it forth. The sacrifice might cause him pain, permanent pain; real damage, he imagined, it could hardly cause him. It is irksome and dangerous to travel in the dark; but better so, than with an *Ignis-fatuus* to guide us. Considering the warmth of his sensibilities, Schiller's merit on this point is greater than we might at first suppose. For a man with whom intellect is the ruling or exclusive faculty, whose sympathies, loves, hatreds, are comparatively coarse and dull, it may be easy to avoid this half-wilful entertainment of error, and this cant which is the consequence and sign of it. But for a man of keen tastes, a large fund of innate probity is necessary to prevent his aping the excellence which he loves so much, yet is unable to attain. Among persons of the latter sort, it is extremely rare to meet with one completely unaffected. Schiller's other noble qualities would not have justice, did we neglect to notice this, the truest proof of their nobility. Honest, unpretending, manly simplicity pervades all parts of his character and genius and habits of life. We not only admire him, we trust him and love him.

'The character of child-like simplicity,' he has himself observed,[39] 'which genius impresses on its works, it shows also in its private life and manners. It is bashful, for nature is ever so; but it is not prudish, for only corruption is prudish. It is clear-sighted, for nature can never be the contrary; but it is not cunning, for this only art can be. It is faithful to its character and inclinations; but not so much because it is directed by principles, as because after all vibrations nature constantly reverts to her original position, constantly renews her primitive demand. It is modest, nay timid, for genius is always a secret to itself; but it is not anxious, for it knows not the dangers of the way which it travels. Of the private habits of the persons who have been peculiarly distinguished by their genius, our information is small; but the little that has been recorded for us of the chief of them, —of Sophocles, Archimedes, Hippocrates; and in modern times, of Dante and Tasso, of Rafaelle, Albrecht Dürer, Cervantes, Shakspeare, Fielding, and others, —confirms this observation.' Schiller himself confirms it; perhaps more strongly than most of the examples here adduced. No man ever wore his faculties more meekly, or performed great works with less consciousness of their greatness. Abstracted from the contemplation of himself, his eye was turned upon the objects of his labour, and he pursued them with the eagerness, the entireness, the spontaneous sincerity, of a boy pursuing sport. Hence this 'child-like simplicity,' the last perfection of his other excellencies. His was a mighty spirit unheedful of its might. He walked the earth in calm power: 'the staff of his spear was like a weaver's beam;' but he wielded it like a wand.

Such, so far as we can represent it, is the form in which Schiller's life and

---

[39] *Naive und sentimentalische Dichtung.*

works have gradually painted their character in the mind of a secluded individual, whose solitude he has often charmed, whom he has instructed, and cheered, and moved. The original impression, we know, was faint and inadequate, the present copy of it is still more so; yet we have sketched it as we could: the figure of Schiller, and of the figures he conceived and drew are there; himself, 'and in his hand a glass which shows us many more.' To those who look on him as we have wished to make them, Schiller will not need a farther panegyric. For the sake of Literature, it may still be remarked, that his merit was peculiarly due to her. Literature was his creed, the dictate of his conscience; he was an Apostle of the Sublime and Beautiful, and this his calling made a hero of him. For it was in the spirit of a true man that he viewed it, and undertook to cultivate it; and its inspirations constantly maintained the noblest temper in his soul. The end of Literature was not, in Schiller's judgment, to amuse the idle, or to recreate the busy, by showy spectacles for the imagination, or quaint paradoxes and epigrammatic disquisitions for the understanding: least of all was it to gratify in any shape the selfishness of its professors, to minister to their malignity, their love of money, or even of fame. For persons who degrade it to such purposes, the deepest contempt of which his kindly nature could admit was at all times in store. 'Unhappy mortal!' says he to the literary tradesman, the man who writes for gain, 'Unhappy mortal, who with science and art, the noblest of all instruments, effectest and attemptest nothing more than the day-drudge with the meanest; who, in the domain of perfect Freedom, bearest about in thee the spirit of Slave!' As Schiller viewed it, genuine Literature includes the essence of philosophy, religion, art; whatever speaks to the immortal part of man. The daughter, she is likewise the nurse of all that is spiritual and exalted in our character. The boon she bestows is truth; truth not merely physical, political, economical, such as the sensual man in us is perpetually demanding, ever ready to reward, and likely in general to find; but truth of moral feeling, truth of taste, that inward truth in its thousand modifications, which only the most ethereal portion of our nature can discern, but without which that portion of it languishes and dies, and we are left divested of our birthright, thenceforward 'of the earth earthy,' machines for earning and enjoying, no longer worthy to be called the Sons of Heaven. The treasures of Literature are thus celestial, imperishable, beyond all price: with her is the shrine of our best hopes, the palladium of pure manhood; to be among the guardians and servants of this is the noblest function that can be intrusted to a mortal. Genius, even in its faintest scintillations, is 'the inspired gift of God;' a solemn mandate to its owner to go forth and labour in his sphere, to keep alive 'the sacred fire' among his brethren, which the heavy and polluted atmosphere of this world is forever threatening to extinguish. Woe to him if he neglect this mandate, if he hear not its small still voice! Woe to him if he turn this inspired gift into the servant of his evil or ignoble passions; if he offer it on the altar of vanity, if he sell it for a piece of money!

'The Artist, it is true,' says Schiller, 'is the son of his age; but pity for him if he is its pupil, or even its favourite! Let some beneficent Divinity snatch him when a suckling from the breast of his mother, and nurse him with the milk of a better time; that he may ripen to his full stature beneath a distant Grecian sky. And having grown to manhood, let him return, a foreign shape, into his century; not, however, to delight it by his presence; but terrible, like the Son of Agamemnon, to purify it. The Matter of his works he will take from the present; but their Form he will derive from a nobler time, nay from beyond all time, from the absolute unchanging unity of his nature. Here from the pure æther of his spiritual essence, flows down the Fountain of Beauty, uncontaminated by the pollutions of ages and generations, which roll to and fro in their turbid vortex far beneath it. His Matter caprice can dishonour as she has ennobled it; but the chaste Form is withdrawn from her mutations. The Roman of the first century had long bent the knee before his Cæsars, when the statues of Rome were still standing erect; the temples continued holy to the eye, when their gods had long been a laughing-stock; and the abominations of a Nero and a Commodus were silently rebuked by the style of the edifice which lent them its concealment. Man has lost his dignity, but Art has saved it, and preserved it for him in expressive marbles. Truth still lives in fiction, and from the copy the original will be restored.

'But how is the Artist to guard himself from the corruptions of his time, which on every side assail him? By despising its decisions. Let him look upwards to his dignity and his mission, not downwards to his happiness and his wants. Free alike from the vain activity, that longs to impress its traces on the fleeting instant; and from the discontented spirit of enthusiasm, that measures by the scale of perfection the meagre product of reality, let him leave to *common sense*, which is here at home, the province of the actual; while *he* strives from the union of the possible with the necessary to bring out the ideal. This let him imprint and express in fiction and truth, imprint it in the sport of his imagination and the earnest of his actions, imprint it in all sensible and spiritual forms, and cast it silently into everlasting Time.'[40]

Nor were these sentiments, be it remembered, the mere boasting manifesto of a hot-brained inexperienced youth, entering on literature with feelings of heroic ardour, which its difficulties and temptations would soon deaden or pervert: they are the calm principles of a man, expressed with honest manfulness, at a period when the world could compare them with a long course of conduct. In this just and lofty spirit, Schiller undertook the business of literature; in the same spirit he pursued it with unflinching energy all the days of his life. The common, and some uncommon, difficulties of a fluctuating and dependent existence could not quench or abate his zeal: sickness itself seemed hardly to affect him. During his last fifteen years, he wrote his noblest works; yet, as it has been proved too well, no day of that period could have passed without its load of pain.[41] Pain could not turn him from his purpose, or shake his equanimity: in death itself he was *calmer and calmer*. Nor has he gone without his recompense. To the credit of the world it can be recorded, that their suffrages, which he never courted, were liberally bestowed on him: happier than the mighty Milton, he found 'fit hearers,' even in his lifetime,

---

[40] *Über die æsthetische Erziehung des Menschen.*

[41] On a surgical inspection of his body after death, the most vital organs were found totally deranged. 'The structure of the lungs was in great part destroyed, the cavities of the heart were nearly grown up, the liver had become hard, and the gall-bladder was extended to an extraordinary size.' *Doering.*

and they were not 'few.' His effect on the mind of his own country has been deep and universal, and bids fair to be abiding: his effect on other countries must in time be equally decided; for such nobleness of heart and soul shadowed forth in beautiful imperishable emblems, is a treasure which belongs not to one nation, but to all. In another age, this Schiller will stand forth in the foremost rank among the master-spirits of his century; and be admitted to a place among the chosen of all centuries. His works, the memory of what he did and was, will rise afar off like a towering landmark in the solitude of the Past, when distance shall have dwarfed into invisibility the lesser people that encompassed him, and hid him from the near beholder.

On the whole, we may pronounce him happy. His days passed in the contemplation of ideal grandeurs, he lived among the glories and solemnities of universal Nature; his thoughts were of sages and heroes, and scenes of elysian beauty. It is true, he had no rest, no peace; but he enjoyed the fiery consciousness of his own activity, which stands in place of it for men like him. It is true, he was long sickly; but did he not even then conceive and body-forth Max Piccolomini, and Thekla, and the Maid of Orleans, and the scenes of *Wilhelm Tell*? It is true, he died early; but the student will exclaim with Charles XII. in another case, "Was it not enough of life when he had conquered kingdoms?" These kingdoms which Schiller conquered were not for one nation at the expense of suffering to another; they were soiled by no patriot's blood, no widow's, no orphan's tear: they are kingdoms conquered from the barren realms of Darkness, to increase the happiness, and dignity, and power, of all men; new forms of Truth, new maxims of Wisdom, new images and scenes of Beauty, won from the 'void and formless Infinite;' a κτημα ες αιει, 'a possession forever,' to all the generations of the Earth.

SUPPLEMENT.

SCHILLER'S PARENTAGE, BOYHOOD, AND YOUTH

HERR SAUPE'S BOOK. [NOTE IN PEOPLE'S EDITION.]

In the end of Autumn last a considerately kind old Friend of mine brought home to me, from his Tour in Germany, a small Book by a Herr Saupe, one of the Head-masters of Gera High-School,—Book entitled 'Schiller and His Father's Household,'[42]—of which, though it has been before the world these twenty years and more, I had not heard till then. The good little Book,—an altogether modest, lucid, exact and amiable, though not very lively performance, offering new little facts about the Schiller world, or elucidations and once or twice a slight correction of the old,—proved really interesting and instructive; awoke, in me especially, multifarious reflections, mournfully beautiful old memories;—and led to farther readings in other Books touching on the same subject, particularly in these three mentioned below,[43]—the first two of them earlier than Saupe's, the third later and slightly corrective of him once or twice;—all which agreeably employed me for some weeks, and continued to be rather a pious recreation than any labour.

To this accident of Saupe's little Book there was, meanwhile, added another not less unexpected: a message, namely, from Bibliopolic Head-quarters that my own poor old Book on Schiller was to be reprinted, and that in this *"People's Edition"* it would want (on deduction of the German Piece by Goethe, which had gone into the *"Library Edition,"* but which had no fitness here) some sixty or seventy pages for the proper size of the volume. *Saupe*, which I was still reading, or idly reading-about, offered the ready expedient:—and here accordingly *Saupe* is. I have had him faithfully translated, and with some small omissions or abridgments, slight transposals here and there for clearness' sake, and one or two elucidative patches, gathered from the three subsidiary Books already named, all duly distinguished from Saupe's text;—whereby the gap or deficit of pages is well filled up, almost of its own accord. And thus I can now certify that, in all essential respects, the authentic *Saupe* is here made accessible to English readers as to German; and

[42] *Schiller und sein Väterliches Haus.* Von Ernst Julius Saupe, Subconrector am Gymnasium zu Gera. Leipzig: Verlagsbuchhandlung von J.J. Weber, 1851.

[43] *Schiller's Leben von Gustav Schwab* (Stuttgart, 1841).

Schiller's Leben, verfasst aus, &c. By Caroline von Wolzogen, *born* von Lengefeld (Schiller's Sister-in-law): Stuttgart und Tübingen, 1845.

Schiller's Beziehungen zu Eltern, Geschwistern und der Familie von Wolzogen, aus den Familien-Papieren. By Baroness von Gleichen (Schiller's youngest Daughter) and Baron von Wolzogen (her Cousin): Stuttgart, 1859.

hope that to many lovers of Schiller among us, who are likely to be lovers also of humbly beautiful Human Worth, and of such an unconsciously noble scene of Poverty made *richer* than any California, as that of the elder Schiller Household here manifests, it may be a welcome and even profitable bit of reading.

T.C.

Chelsea, Nov. 1872.

SAUPE'S
"SCHILLER AND HIS FATHER'S HOUSEHOLD."

I. THE FATHER.

'SCHILLER's Father, Johann Caspar Schiller, was born at Bittenfeld, a parish hamlet in the ancient part of Würtemberg, a little north of Waiblingen, on the 27th October 1723. He had not yet completed his tenth year when his Father, Johannes Schiller, *Schultheiss*, "Petty Magistrate," of the Village, and by trade a Baker, died, at the age of fifty-one. Soon after which the fatherless Boy, hardly fitted out with the most essential elements of education, had to quit school, and was apprenticed to a Surgeon; with whom, according to the then custom, he was to learn the art of "Surgery;" but in reality had little more to do than follow the common employment of a Barber.

'After completing his apprenticeship and proof-time, the pushing young lad, eager to get forward in the world, went, during the Austrian-Succession War, in the year 1745, with a Bavarian Hussar Regiment, as "Army-Doctor," into the Netherlands. Here, as his active mind found no full employment in the practice of his Art, he willingly undertook, withal, the duties of a sub-officer in small military enterprises. On the Peace of Aix-la-Chapelle, 1748, when a part of this Regiment was disbanded, and Schiller with them, he returned to his homeland; and set himself down in Marbach, a pleasant little country town on the Neckar, as practical Surgeon there. Here, in 1749, he married the Poet's Mother; then a young girl of sixteen: Elisabetha Dorothea, born at Marbach in the year 1733, the daughter of a respectable townsman, Georg Friedrich Kodweis, who, to his trade of Baker adding that of Innkeeper and Woodmeasurer, had gathered a little fortune, and was at this time counted well-off, though afterwards, by some great inundation of the Neckar,' date not given, 'he was again reduced to poverty. The brave man by this unavoidable mischance came, by degrees, so low that he had to give-up his house in the Market-Place, and in the end to dwell in a poor hut, as Porter at one of the Toll-Gates of Marbach. Elisabetha was a comely girl to look upon; slender, well-formed, without quite being tall; the neck long, hair high-blond, almost red, brow broad, eyes as if a little sorish, face covered with freckles; but with all these features enlivened by a soft expression of kindliness and good-nature.

'This marriage, for the first eight years, was childless; after that, they gradually had six children, two of whom died soon after birth; the Poet Schiller was the second of these six, and the only Boy. The young couple had to live in a very narrow, almost needy condition, as neither of them had any fortune; and the Husband's business could hardly support a household. There is still in existence a legal Marriage Record and Inventory, such as is usual in these cases, which estimates the money and money's worth brought together by the young people at a little over 700 gulden (70*l.*). Out of the same Inventory, one sees, by the small value put upon the surgical instruments, and the outstanding debts of patients, distinctly enough, that Caspar Schiller's practice, at that point of time, did not much exceed that of a third-class Surgeon, and was scarcely adequate, as above stated, to support the thriftiest household. And therefore it is not surprising that Schiller, intent on improving so bare a position, should, at the breaking-out of the Seven-Years War, have anew sought a military appointment, as withal more fit for employing his young strength and ambitions.

'In the beginning of the year 1757 he went, accordingly, as Ensign and Adjutant, into the Würtemberg Regiment Prince Louis; which in several of the campaigns in the Seven-Years War belonged to an auxiliary corps of the Austrian Army.'—Was he at the *Ball of Fulda*, one wonders? Yes, for certain! He was at the Ball of Fulda (tragi-comical Explosion of a Ball, *not* yet got to the dancing-point); and had to run for life, as his Duke, in a highly-ridiculous manner, had already done. And, again, tragically, it is certain that he stood on the fated Austrian left-wing at the *Battle of Leuthen*; had his horse shot under him there, and was himself nearly drowned in a quagmire, struggling towards Breslau that night.[44]

'In Bohemia this Corps was visited by an infectious fever, and suffered by the almost pestilential disorder a good deal of loss. In this bad time, Schiller, who by his temperance and frequent movement in the open air had managed to retain perfect health, showed himself very active and helpful; and cheerfully undertook every kind of business in which he could be of use. He attended the sick, there being a scarcity of Doctors; and served at the same time as Chaplain to the Regiment, so far as to lead the Psalmody, and read the Prayers. When, after this, he was changed into another Würtemberg Regiment, which served in Hessen and Thüringen, he employed every free hour in filling up, by his own industrious study, the many deeply-felt defects in his young schooling; and was earnestly studious. By his perseverant zeal and diligence, he succeeded in the course of these war-years in acquiring not only many medical, military and agricultural branches of knowledge, but also, as his Letters prove, in amassing a considerable amount of general culture. Nor did his praiseworthy efforts remain without recognition and external reward. At the end of the Seven-Years War, he had risen to be a Captain, and had even saved a little money.

'His Wife, who, during these War-times, lived, on money sent by him, in her Father's house at Marbach, he could only visit seldom, and for short periods in winter-quarters, much as he longed for his faithful Wife; who, after the birth of a Daughter, in September 1757, was dearer to him than ever. But never had the rigid fetters of War-discipline appeared more oppressive than when, two years later, in November 1759, a Son, the Poet, was born. With joyful thanks to God, he saluted

---

[44] See *Life of Friedrich* (Book xix. chap. 8; Book xviii. chap. 10), and Schiller Senior's rough bit of Autobiography, called '*Meine Lebensgeschichte*,' in *Schiller's Beziehungen zu Eltern, Geschwistern und der Familie von Wolzogen* (mentioned above), p. 1 et seqq.

this dear Gift of Heaven; in daily prayer commended Mother and Child to "the Being of all Beings;" and waited now with impatience the time when he should revisit his home, and those that were his there. Yet there still passed four years before Father Schiller, on conclusion of the Hubertsburg Peace, 1763, could return home from the War, and again take up his permanent residence in his home-country. Where, on his return, his first Garrison quarters were, whether at Ludwigsburg, Cannstadt or what other place, is not known. On the other hand, all likelihoods are, that, so soon as he could find it possible, he carried over his Wife and his two Children, the little Daughter Christophine six, and the little Friedrich now four, out of Marbach to his own quarters, wherever these were.'

There is no date to the Neckar Inundation above mentioned; but we have elsewhere evidence that the worthy Father Kodweis with his Wife, at this time, still dwelt in their comfortable house in the Market-Place. We know also, though it is not mentioned in the text, that their pious Daughter struggled zealously to the last to alleviate their sore poverty; and the small effect, so far as money goes, may testify how poor and straitened the Schiller Family itself then was.

'With the Father's return out of War, there came a new element into the Family, which had so long been deprived of its natural Guardian and Counsellor. To be House-Father in the full sense of the word was now all the more Captain Schiller's need and duty, the longer his War-service had kept him excluded from the sacred vocation of Husband and Father. For he was throughout a rational and just man, simple, strong, expert, active for practical life, if also somewhat quick and rough. This announced itself even in the outward make and look of him; for he was of short stout stature and powerful make of limbs; the brow high-arched, eyes sharp and keen. Withal, his erect carriage, his firm step, his neat clothing, as well as his clear and decisive mode of speech, all testified of strict military training; which also extended itself over his whole domestic life, and even over the daily devotions of the Family. For although the shallow Illuminationism of that period had produced some influence on his religious convictions, he held fast by the pious principles of his forebears; read regularly to his household out of the Bible; and pronounced aloud, each day, the Morning and Evening Prayer. And this was, in his case, not merely an outward decorous bit of discipline, but in fact the faithful expression of his Christian conviction, that man's true worth and true happiness can alone be found in the fear of the Lord, and the moral purity of his heart and conduct. He himself had even, in the manner of those days, composed a long Prayer, which he in later years addressed to God every morning, and which began with the following lines:

> True Watcher of Israel!
> To Thee be praise, thanks and honour.
> Praying aloud I praise Thee,
> That earth and Heaven may hear.[45]

---

[45] 'Treuer Wächter Israels!
     Dir sei Preis und Dank und Ehren;
     Laut betend lob' ich Dich,
     Dass es Erd' und Himmel hören' &c.

'If, therefore, a certain otherwise accredited Witness calls him a kind of crotchety, fantastic person, mostly brooding over strange thoughts and enterprises, this can only have meant that Caspar Schiller in earlier years appeared such, namely at the time when, as incipient Surgeon at Marbach, he saw himself forced into a circle of activity which corresponded neither to his inclination, strength nor necessities.

'On the spiritual development of his Son this conscientious Father employed his warmest interest and activities; and appears to have been for some time assisted herein by a near relation, a certain Johann Friedrich Schiller from Bittenfeld; the same who, as *Studiosus Philosophiæ*, was, in 1759, Godfather to the Boy. He is said to have given the little Godson Fritz his first lessons in Writing, Natural-History and Geography. A more effective assistance in this matter the Father soon after met with on removing to Lorch.

'In the year 1765, the reigning Duke, Karl of Würtemberg, sent Captain Schiller as Recruiting Officer to the Imperial Free-Town Schwäbish-Gmünd; with permission to live with his Family in the nearest Würtemberg place, the Village and Cloister of Lorch. Lorch lies in a green meadow-ground, surrounded by beech-woods, at the foot of a hill, which is crowned by the weird buildings of the Cloister, where the Hohenstaufen graves are; opposite the Cloister and Hamlet, rise the venerable ruins of Hohenstaufen itself, with a series of hills; at the bottom winds the Rems,' a branch of the Neckar, 'towards still fruitfuler regions. In this attractive rural spot the Schiller Family resided for several years; and found from the pious and kindly people of the Hamlet, and especially from a friend of the house, Moser, the worthy Parish-Parson there, the kindliest reception. The Schiller children soon felt themselves at home and happy in Lorch, especially Fritz did, who, in the Parson's Son, Christoph Ferdinand Moser, a soft gentle child, met with his first boy-friend. In this worthy Parson's house he also received, along with the Parson's own Sons, the first regular and accurate instruction in reading and writing, as also in the elements of Latin and Greek. This arrangement pleased and comforted Captain Schiller not a little: for the more distinctly he, with his clear and candid character, recognised the insufficiency of his own instruction and stock of knowledge, the more impressively it lay on him that his Son should early acquire a good foundation in Languages and Science, and learn something solid and effective. What he could himself do in that particular he faithfully did; bringing out, with this purpose, partly the grand historical memorials of that neighbourhood, partly his own life-experiences, in instructive and exciting dialogues with his children. He would point out to the listening little pair the venerable remains of the Hohenstaufen Ancestral Castle, or tell them of his own soldier-career. He took the Boy with him into the Exercise Camp, to the Woodmen in the Forest, and even into the farther-distant pleasure-castle of Hohenheim; and thereby led their youthful imagination into many changeful imaginings of life.[46]

'Externally little Fritz and his Sister were not like; Christophine more resembling the Father, whilst Friedrich was the image of the Mother. On the other hand, they had internally very much in common; both possessed a lively apprehension for whatever was true, beautiful or good. Both had a temper capable of enthusi-

---

[46] *Saupe*, p. 11.

asm, which early and chiefly turned towards the sublime and grand: in short, the strings of their souls were tuned on a cognate tone. Add to this, that both, in the beautifulest, happiest period of their life, had been under the sole care and direction of the pious genial Mother; and that Fritz, at least till his sixth year, was exclusively limited to Christophine's society, and had no other companion. They two had to be, and were, all to each other. Christophine on this account stood nearer to her Brother throughout all his life than the Sisters who were born later.

'In rural stillness, and in almost uninterrupted converse with out-door nature, flowed by for Fritz and her the greatest part of their childhood and youth. Especially dear to them was their abode in this romantic region. Every hour that was free from teaching or other task, they employed in roaming about in the neighbourhood; and they knew no higher joy than a ramble into the neighbouring hills. In particular they liked to make pilgrimages together to a chapel on the Calvary Hill at Gmünd, a few miles off, to which the way was still through the old monkish grief-stations, on to the Cloister of Lorch noticed above. Often they would sit with closely-grasped hands, under the thousand-years-old Linden, which stood on a projection before the Cloister-walls, and seemed to whisper to them long-silent tales of past ages. On these walks the hearts of the two clasped each other ever closer and more firmly, and they faithfully shared their little childish joys and sorrows. Christophine would bitterly weep when her vivacious Brother had committed some small misdeed and was punished for it. In such cases, she often enough confessed Fritz's faults as her own, and was punished when she had in reality had no complicity in them. It was with great sorrow that they two parted from their little Paradise; and both of them always retained a great affection for Lorch and its neighbourhood. Christophine, who lived to be ninety, often even in her latter days looked back with tender affection to their abode there.[47]

'In his family-circle, the otherwise hard-mannered Father showed always to Mother and Daughters the tenderest respect and the affectionate tone which the heart suggests. Thus, if at table a dish had chanced to be especially prepared for him, he would never eat of it without first inviting the Daughters to be helped. As little could he ever, in the long-run, withstand the requests of his gentle Wife; so that not seldom she managed to soften his rough severity. The Children learned to make use of this feature in his character; and would thereby save themselves from the first outburst of his anger. They confessed beforehand to the Mother their bits of misdoings, and begged her to inflict the punishment, and prevent their falling into the heavier paternal hand. Towards the Son again, whose moral development his Father anxiously watched over, his wrath was at times disarmed by touches of courage and fearlessness on the Boy's part. Thus little Fritz, once on a visit at Hohenheim, in the house where his Father was calling, and which formed part of the side-buildings of the Castle, whilst his Father followed his business within doors, had, unobserved, clambered out of a saloon-window, and undertaken a voyage of discovery over the roofs. The Boy, who had been missed and painfully sought after, was discovered just on the point of trying to have a nearer view of the Lion's Head, by which one of the roof-gutters discharges itself, when the terrified Father

---

[47] *Saupe*, pp. 106-108.

got eye on him, and called out aloud. Cunning Fritz, however, stood motionless where he was on the roof, till his Father's anger had stilled itself, and pardon was promised him.' — Here farther is a vague anecdote made authentic: 'Another time the little fellow was not to be found at the evening meal, while, withal, there was a heavy thunderstorm in the sky, and fiery bolts were blazing through the black clouds. He was searched for in vain, all over the house; and at every new thunder-clap the misery of his Parents increased. At last they found him, not far from the house, on the top of the highest lime-tree, which he was just preparing to descend, under the crashing of a very loud peal. "In God's name, what hast thou been doing there?" cried the agitated Father. "I wanted to know," answered Fritz, "where all that fire in the sky was coming from!"

'Three full years the Schiller Family lived at Lorch; and this in rather narrow circumstances, as the Father, though in the service of his Prince, could not, during the whole of this time, receive the smallest part of his pay, but had to live on the little savings he had made during War-time. Not till 1768, after the most impressive petitioning to the Duke, was he at last called away from his post of Recruiting Officer, and transferred to the Garrison of Ludwigsburg, where he, by little and little, squeezed out the pay owing him.

'Upon his removal, the Father's first care was to establish his little Boy, now nine years old, — who, stirred-on probably by the impressions he had got in the Parsonage at Lorch, and the visible wish of his Parents, had decided for the Clerical Profession, — in the Latin school at Ludwigsburg. This done, he made it his chief care that his Son's progress should be swift and satisfying there. But on that side, Fritz could never come up to his expectations, though the Teachers were well enough contented. But out of school-time, Fritz was not so zealous and diligent as could be wished; liked rather to spring about and sport in the garden. The arid, stony, philological instruction of his teacher, Johann Friedrich Jahn, who was a solid Latiner, and nothing more, was not calculated to make a specially alluring impression on the clever and lively Boy; thus it was nothing but the reverence and awe of his Father that could drive him on to diligence.

'To this time belongs the oldest completely preserved Poem of Schiller's; it is in the form of a little Hymn, in which, on New-year's day 1769, the Boy, now hardly over nine years old, presents to his Parents the wishes of the season. It may stand here by way of glimpse into the position of the Son towards his Parents, especially towards his Father.

MUCH-LOVED PARENTS.[48]

----

[48]   HERZGELIEBTE ELTERN.

> *Eltern, die ich zärtlich ehre,*
> *Mein Herz ist heut' voll Dankbarkeit!*
> *Der treue Gott dies Jahr vermehre*
> *Was Sie erquickt zu jeder Zeit!*
>
> *Der Herr, die Quelle aller Freude,*
> *Verbleibe stets Ihr Trost und Theil;*
> *Sein Wort sei Ihres Herzens Weide,*
> *Und Jesus Ihr erwunschtes Heil.*

Parents, whom I lovingly honour,
Today my heart is full of thankfulness!
This Year may a gracious God increase
What is at all times your support!

The Lord, the Fountain of all joy,
Remain always your comfort and portion;
His Word be the nourishment of your heart,
And Jesus your wished-for salvation.

I thank you for all your proofs of love,
For all your care and patience;
My heart shall praise all your goodness,
And ever comfort itself in your favour.

Obedience, diligence and tender love
I promise you for this Year.
God send me only good inclinations,
And make true all my wishes! Amen.

1 January 1769.

Johann Friedrich Schiller.

'According to the pious wish of their Son, this year, 1769, did bring somewhat which "comforted" them. Captain Schiller, from of old a lover of rural occupations, and skilful in gardening and nursery affairs, had, at Ludwigsburg, laid-out for himself a little Nursery. It was managed on the same principles which he afterwards made public in his Book, *Die Baumzucht im Grossen* (Neustrelitz, 1795, and second edition, Giessen, 1806); and was prospering beautifully. The Duke, who had noticed this, signified satisfaction in the thing; and he appointed him, in 1770, to shift to his beautiful Forest-Castle, Die Solitüde, near Stuttgart, as overseer of all his Forest operations there. Hereby to the active man was one of his dearest wishes fulfilled; and a sphere of activity opened, corresponding to his acquirements and his inclination. At Solitüde, by the Duke's order, he laid-out a Model Nursery for all Würtemberg, which he managed with perfect care and fidelity; and in this post he so completely satisfied the expectations entertained of him, that his Prince by and by raised him to the rank of Major.' He is reckoned to have raised from seeds, and successfully planted, 60,000 trees, in discharge of this function, which continued for the rest of his life.

Ich dank' von alle Liebes-Proben,
Von alle Sorgfalt und Geduld,

Mein Herz soll alle Güte loben,
Und trösten sich stets Ihrer Huld.

Gehorsam, Fleiss und zarte Liebe
Verspreche ich auf dieses Jahr.
Der Herr schenk' mir nur gute Treibe,
Und mache all' mein Wunschen wahr. Amen.

Johann Christoph Friedrich Schiller.

Den 1 Januarii Anno 1769.

'His Family, which already at Lorch, in 1766, had been increased by the birth of a Daughter, Luise, waited but a short time in Ludwigsburg till the Father brought them over to the new dwelling at Solitüde. Fritz, on the removal of his Parents, was given over as boarder to his actual Teacher, the rigorous pedant Jahn; and remained yet two years at the Latin school in Ludwigsburg. During this time, the lively, and perhaps also sometimes mischievous Boy, was kept in the strictest fetters; and, by the continual admonitions, exhortations, and manually practical corrections of Father and of Teacher, not a little held down and kept in fear. The fact, for instance, that he liked more the potent Bible-words and pious songs of a Luther, a Paul Gerhard, and Gellert, than he did the frozen lifeless catechism-drill of the Ludwigsburg Institute, gave surly strait-laced Jahn occasion to lament from time to time to the alarmed Parents, that "their Son had no feeling whatever for religion." In this respect, however, the otherwise so irritable Father easily satisfied himself, not only by his own observations of an opposite tendency, but chiefly by stricter investigation of one little incident that was reported to him. The teacher of religion in the Latin school, Superintendent Zilling, whose name is yet scornful-ly remembered, had once, in his dull awkwardness, introduced even Solomon's Song as an element of nurture for his class; and was droning out, in an old-fash-ioned way, his interpretation of it as symbolical of the Christian Church and its Bridegroom Christ, when he was, on the sudden, to his no small surprise and an-ger, interrupted by the audible inquiry of little Schiller, "But was this Song, then, actually sung to the Church?" Schiller Senior took the little heretic to task for this rash act; and got as justification the innocent question, "Has the Church really got teeth of ivory?" The Father was enlightened enough to take the Boy's opposition for a natural expression of sound human sense; nay, he could scarcely forbear a laugh; whirled swiftly round, and murmured to himself, "Occasionally she has Wolf's teeth." And so the thing was finished.[49]

'At Ludwigsburg Schiller and Christophine first saw a Theatre; where at that time, in the sumptuous Duke's love of splendour, only pompous operas and bal-lets were given. The first effect of this new enjoyment, which Fritz and his Sister strove to repeat as often as they could, was that at home, with little clipped and twisted paper dolls, they set about representing scenes; and on Christophine's part it had the more important result of awakening and nourishing, at an early age, her æsthetic taste. Schiller considered her, ever after these youthful sports, as a true and faithful companion in his poetic dreams and attempts; and constantly not only told his Sister, whose silence on such points could be perfect, of all that he secretly did in the way of verse-making in the Karl's School, — which, as we shall see, he entered in 1773, — but if possible brought it upon the scene with her. Scenes from the lyrical operetta of *Semele* were acted by Schiller and Christophine, on those terms; which appears in a complete shape for the first time in Schiller's *Anthology*, printed 1782.[50]

'So soon as Friedrich had gone through the Latin school at Ludwigsburg, which was in 1772, he was, according to the standing regulation, to enter one of the

---

[49] *Saupe*, p. 18.
[50] Ibid. p. 109.

four Lower Cloister-schools; and go through the farther curriculum for a Würtemberg clergyman. But now there came suddenly from the Duke to Captain Schiller an offer to take his Son, who had been represented to him as a clever boy, into the new Military Training-School, founded by his Highness at Solitüde, in 1771; where he would be brought up, and taken charge of, free of cost.

'In the Schiller Family this offer caused great consternation and painful embarrassment. The Father was grieved to be obliged to sacrifice a long-cherished paternal plan to the whim of an arbitrary ruler; and the Son felt himself cruelly hurt to be torn away so rudely from his hope and inclination. Accordingly, how dangerous soever for the position of the Family a declining of the Ducal grace might seem, the straightforward Father ventured nevertheless to lay open to the Duke, in a clear and distinct statement, how his purpose had always been to devote his Son, in respect both of his inclination and his hitherto studies, to the Clerical Profession; for which in the new Training-School he could not be prepared. The Duke showed no anger at this step of the elder Schiller's; but was just as little of intention to let a capable and hopeful scholar, who was also the Son of one of his Officers and Dependents, escape him. He simply, with brevity, repeated his wish, and required the choice of another study, in which the Boy would have a better career and outlook than in the Theological Department. Nill they, will they, there was nothing for the Parents but compliance with the so plainly intimated will of this Duke, on whom their Family's welfare so much depended.

'Accordingly, 17th January 1773, Friedrich Schiller, then in his fourteenth year, stept over to the Military Training-School at Solitüde.

'In September of the following year, Schiller's Parents had, conformably to a fundamental law of the Institution, to acknowledge and engage by a written Bond, "That their Son, in virtue of his entrance into this Ducal Institution, did wholly devote himself to the service of the Würtemberg Ducal House; that he, without special Ducal permission, was not empowered to go out of it; and that he had, with his best care, to observe not only this, but all other regulations of the Institute." By this time, indeed directly upon signature of this strict Bond, young Schiller had begun to study Jurisprudence;—which, however, when next year, 1775, the Training-School, raised now to be a "Military Academy," had been transferred to Stuttgart, he either of his own accord, or in consequence of a discourse and interview of the Duke with his Father, exchanged for the Study of Medicine.

'From the time when Schiller entered this "Karl's School"' (Military Academy, in official style), 'he was nearly altogether withdrawn from any tutelage of his Father; for it was only to Mothers, and to Sisters still under age, that the privilege of visiting their Sons and Brothers, and this on the Sunday only, was granted: beyond this, the Karl's Scholars, within their monastic cells, were cut off from family and the world, by iron-doors and sentries guarding them. This rigorous seclusion from actual life and all its friendly impressions, still more the spiritual constraint of the Institution, excluding every free activity, and all will of your own, appeared to the Son in a more hateful light than to the Father, who, himself an old soldier, found it quite according to order that the young people should be kept in strict military discipline and subordination. What filled the Son with bitter discontent and indignation, and at length brought him to a kind of poetic outburst of revolution in the *Robbers*, therein the Father saw only a wholesome regularity, and indispensable substitute for paternal discipline. Transient complaints of individual teachers and superiors little disturbed the Father's mind; for, on the whole, the official testimonies concerning his Son were steadily favourable. The Duke too treated young Schiller, whose talents had not escaped his sharpness of insight, with particular goodwill, nay distinction. To this Prince, used to the accurate discernment of spiritual gifts, the complaints of certain Teachers, that Schiller's slow progress in Jurisprudence proceeded from want of head, were of no weight whatever; and he answered expressly, "Leave me that one alone; he will come to something yet!" But that Schiller gave his main strength to what in the Karl's School was a strictly forbidden object, to poetry namely, this I believe was entirely hidden from his Father, or appeared to him, on occasional small indications, the less questionable, as he saw that, in spite of this, the Marketable-Sciences were not neglected.

'At the same age, viz. about twenty-two, at which Captain Schiller had made his first military sally into the Netherlands and the Austrian-Succession War, his Son issued from the Karl's School, 15th December 1780; and was immediately appointed Regimental-Doctor at Stuttgart; with a monthly pay of twenty-three gulden' (*2l. 6s.=11s.* and a fraction per week). 'With this appointment, Schiller had, as it were, openly altogether outgrown all special paternal guardianship or guidance; and was, from this time, treated by his Father as come to majority, and standing on his own feet. If he came out, as frequently happened, with a comrade to Solitüde, he was heartily welcome there, and the Father's looks often dwelt on him with visible satisfaction. If in the conscientious and rigorous old man, with his instructive and serious experiences of life, there might yet various anxieties and doubts arise when he heard of the exuberantly genial ways of his hopeful Son at Stuttgart, he still looked upon him with joyful pride, in remarking how those so promising Karl's Scholars, who had entered into the world along with him, recognised his superiority of mind, and willingly ranked themselves under him. Nor could it be otherwise than highly gratifying to his old heart to remark always with what deep love the gifted Son constantly regarded his Parents and Sisters.'[51]—Of Schiller's first procedures in Stuttgart, after his emancipation from the Karl's School, and appointment as Regimental-Surgeon, or rather of his general behaviour and way of life there, which are said to have been somewhat wild, genially, or even *un*genially extravagant, and to have involved him in many paltry entanglements of debts, as one bad consequence,—there will be some notice in the next Section, headed "*The Mother*." His Regimental Doctorship, and stay in Stuttgart altogether, lasted twenty-two months.

This is Schiller's bodily appearance, as it first presented itself to an old School-fellow, who, after an interval of eighteen months, saw him again on Parade, as Doctor of the Regiment Augé,—more to his astonishment than admiration.

'Crushed into the stiff tasteless Old-Prussian Uniform; on each of his temples three stiff rolls as if done with gypsum; the tiny three-cocked hat scarcely covering his crown; so much the thicker the long pigtail, with the slender neck crammed

---

[51] *Saupe*, p. 25.

into a very narrow horsehair stock; the felt put under the white spatterdashes, smirched by traces of shoe-blacking, giving to the legs a bigger diameter than the thighs, squeezed into their tight-fitting breeches, could boast of. Hardly, or not at all, able to bend his knees, the whole man moved like a stork.'

'The Poet's form,' says this Witness elsewhere, a bit of a dilettante artist it seems, 'had somewhat the following appearance: Long straight stature; long in the legs, long in the arms; pigeon-breasted; his neck very long; something rigorously stiff; in gait and carriage not the smallest elegance. His brow was broad; the nose thin, cartilaginous, white of colour, springing out at a notably sharp angle, much bent,—a parrot-nose, and very sharp in the point (according to Dannecker the Sculptor, Schiller, who took snuff, had pulled it out so with his hand). The red eyebrows, over the deep-lying dark-gray eyes, were bent too close together at the nose, which gave him a pathetic expression. The lips were thin, energetic; the under-lip protruding, as if pushed forward by the inspiration of his feelings; the chin strong; cheeks pale, rather hollow than full, freckly; the eyelids a little inflamed; the bushy hair of the head dark red; the whole head rather ghostlike than manlike, but impressive even in repose, and all expression when Schiller declaimed. Neither the features nor the somewhat shrieky voice could he subdue. Dannecker,' adds the satirical Witness, 'has unsurpassably cut this head in marble for us.'[52]

'The publication of the *Robbers*' (Autumn 1781),—'which Schiller, driven on by rage and desperation, had composed in the fetters of the Karl's School,—raised him on the sudden to a phenomenon on which all eyes in Stuttgart were turned. What, with careless exaggeration, he had said to a friend some months before, on setting forth his *Elegy on the Death of a Young Man,* "The thing has made my name hereabouts more famous than twenty years of practice would have done; but it is a name like that of him who burnt the Temple of Ephesus: God be merciful to me a sinner!" might now with all seriousness be said of the impression his *Robbers* made on the harmless townsfolk of Stuttgart. But how did Father Schiller at first take up this eccentric product of his Son, which openly declared war on all existing order? Astonishment and terror, anger and detestation, boundless anxiety, with touches of admiration and pride, stormed alternately through the solid honest man's paternal breast, as he saw the frank picture of a Prodigal Son rolled out before him; and had to gaze into the most revolting deeps of the passions and vices. Yet he felt himself irresistibly dragged along by the uncommon vivacity of action in this wild Drama; and at the same time powerfully attracted by the depth, the tenderness and fulness of true feeling manifested in it: so that, at last, out of those contradictory emotions of his, a clear admiration and pride for his Son's bold and rich spirit maintained the upper hand. By Schiller's friends and closer connections, especially by his Mother and Sisters, all pains were of course taken to keep up this favourable humour in the Father, and carefully to hide from him all disadvantageous or disquieting tidings about the Piece and its consequences and practical effects. Thus he heard sufficiently of the huge excitement and noise which the *Robbers* was making all over Germany, and of the seductive approval which came streaming-in on the youthful Poet, even out of distant provinces; but

[52] Schwab, *Schiller's Leben* (Stuttgart, 1841), p. 68.

heard nothing either of the Duke's offended and angry feelings over the *Robbers*, a production horrible to him; nor of the Son's secret journeys to Mannheim, and the next consequences of these' (his brief arrest, namely), 'nor of the rumour circulating in spiteful quarters, that this young Doctor was neglecting his own province of medicine, and meaning to become a play-actor. How could the old man, in these circumstances, have a thought that the *Robbers* would be the loss of Family and Country to his poor Fritz! And yet so it proved.

'Excited by all kinds of messagings, informings and insinuations, the imperious Prince, in spite of his secret pleasure in this sudden renown of his Pupil, could in no wise be persuaded to revoke or soften his harsh Order, which "forbade the Poet henceforth, under pain of military imprisonment, either to write anything poetic or to communicate the same to foreign persons"' (non-Würtembergers). In vain were all attempts of Schiller to obtain his discharge from Military Service and his "Entschwäbung" (Un-Swabian-ing); such petitions had only for result new sharper rebukes and hard threatening expressions, to which the mournful fate of Schubart in the Castle of Hohenasperg[53] formed a too questionable background.

'Thus by degrees there ripened in the strong soul of this young man the determination to burst these laming fetters of his genius, by flight from despotic Würtemberg altogether; and, in some friendlier country, gain for himself the freedom without which his spiritual development was impossible. Only to one friend, who clung to him with almost enthusiastic devotion, did he impart his secret. This was Johann Andreas Streicher of Stuttgart, who intended to go next year to Hamburg, and there, under Bach's guidance, study music; but declared himself ready to accompany Schiller even now, since it had become urgent. Except to this trustworthy friend, Schiller had imparted his plan to his elder Sister Christophine alone; and she had not only approved of the sad measure, but had undertaken also to prepare their Mother for it. The Father naturally had to be kept dark on the subject; all the more that, if need were, he might pledge his word as an Officer that he had known nothing of his Son's intention.

'Schiller went out, in company of Madam Meier, Wife of the *Regisseur* (Theatre-manager) at Mannheim, a native of Stuttgart, and of this Streicher, one last time to Solitüde, to have one more look of it and of his dear ones there; especially to soothe and calm his Mother. On the way, which they travelled on foot, Schiller kept up a continual discourse about the Mannheim Theatre and its interests, without betraying his secret to Madam Meier. The Father received these welcome guests with frank joy; and gave to the conversation, which at first hung rather embarrassed, a happy turn by getting into talk, with cheery circumstantiality, of the grand Pleasure-Hunt, of the Play and of the Illumination, which were to take place, in honour of the Russian Grand-Prince, afterwards Czar Paul, and his Bride, the Duke of Würtemberg's Niece, on the 17th September instant, at Solitüde. Far other was the poor Mother's mood; she was on the edge of betraying herself, in seeing the sad eyes of her Son; and she could not speak for emotion. The presence of Streicher and a Stranger with whom the elder Schiller was carrying on a, to him, attractive conversation, permitted Mother and Son to withdraw speedily and un-

[53] See Appendix II. *infrà*.

remarked. Not till after an hour did Schiller reappear, alone now, to the company; neither this circumstance, nor Schiller's expression of face, yet striking the preoccupied Father. Though to the observant Streicher, his wet red eyes betrayed how painful the parting must have been. Gradually on the way back to Stuttgart, amid general talk of the three, Schiller regained some composure and cheerfulness.

'The bitter sorrow of this hour of parting renewed itself yet once in Schiller's soul, when on the flight itself, about midnight of the 17th. In effect it was these same festivities that had decided the young men's time and scheme of journey; and under the sheltering noise of which their plan was luckily executed. Towards midnight of the above-said day, when the Castle of Solitüde, with all its surroundings, was beaming in full splendour of illumination, there rolled past, almost rubbing elbows with it, the humble Schiller Vehicle from Stuttgart, which bore the fugitive Poet with his true Friend on their way. Schiller pointed out to his Friend the spot where his Parents lived, and, with a half-suppressed sigh and a woe-begone exclamation, "Oh, my Mother!" sank back upon his seat.'

Mannheim, the goal of their flight, is in Baden-Baden, under another Sovereign; lies about 80 miles to N.W. of Stuttgart. Their dreary journey lasted two days,—arrival not till deep in the night of the second. Their united stock of money amounted to 51 gulden,—Schiller 23, Streicher 28,—5*l.* 6*s.* in all. Streicher subsequently squeezed out from home 3*l.* more; and that appears to have been their sum-total.[54]

'Great was the astonishment and great the wrath of the Father, when at length he understood that his Son had broken the paternal, written Bond, and withdrawn himself by flight from the Ducal Service. He dreaded, not without reason, the heavy consequences of so rash an action; and a thousand gnawing anxieties bestormed the heart of the worthy man. Might not the Duke, in the first outburst of his indignation, overwhelm forever the happiness of their Family, which there was nothing but the income of his post that supported in humble competence? And what a lot stood before the Son himself, if he were caught in flight, or if, what was nowise improbable, his delivery back was required and obtained? Sure enough, there had risen on the otherwise serene heaven of the Schiller Family a threatening thundercloud; which, any day, might discharge itself, bringing destruction on their heads.

'The thing, however, passed away in merciful peace. Whatever may have been the Duke's motives or inducements to let the matter, in spite of his embitterment, silently drop,—whether his bright festal humour in presence of those high kinsfolk, or the noble frankness with which the Runaway first of all, to save his Family, had in a respectful missive, dated from Mannheim, explained to his Princely Educator the necessity of his flight; or the expectation, flattering to the Ducal pride, that the future greatness of his Pupil might be a source of glory to him and his Karl's-School: enough, on his part, there took place no kind of hostile step against the Poet, and still less against his Family. Captain Schiller again breathed freer when he saw himself delivered from his most crushing anxiety on this side; but there remained still a sharp sting in his wounded heart. His military feeling of

[54] Schwab, *Schiller's Leben.*

honour was painfully hurt by the thought that they might now look upon his Son as a deserter; and withal the future of this voluntary Exile appeared so uncertain and wavering, that it did not offer the smallest justification of so great a risk. By degrees, however, instead of anger and blame there rose in him the most sympathetic anxiety for the poor Son's fate; to whom, from want of a free, firm and assuring position in life, all manner of contradictions and difficulties must needs arise.

'And Schiller did actually, at Mannheim, find himself in a bad and difficult position. The Superintendent of the celebrated Mannheim Theatre, the greatly powerful Imperial Baron von Dalberg, with whom Schiller, since the bringing out of his *Robbers*, had stood in lively correspondence, drew back when Schiller himself was here; and kept the Poet at a distance as a political Fugitive; leaving him to shift as he could. In vain had Schiller explained to him, in manly open words, his economic straits, and begged from him a loan of 300 gulden' (30*l.*) 'to pay therewith a pressing debt in Stuttgart, and drag himself along, and try to get started in the world. Dalberg returned the *Fiesco*, Schiller's new republican Tragedy, which had been sent him, with the declaration that he could advance no money on the *Fiesco* in its present form; the Piece must first be remodelled to suit the stage. During this remodelling, which the otherwise so passionately vivid and hopeful Poet began without murmur, he lived entirely on the journey-money that had been saved up by the faithful Streicher, who would on no account leave him.'

What became of this good Streicher afterwards, I have inquired considerably, but with very little success. On the total exhaustion of their finance, Schiller and he had to part company,—Schiller for refuge at Bauerbach, as will soon be seen. Streicher continued about Mannheim, not as Schiller's fellow-lodger any longer, but always at his hand, passionately eager to serve him with all his faculties by night or by day; and they did not part finally till Schiller quitted Mannheim, two years hence, for Leipzig. After which they never met again. Streicher, in Mannheim, seems to have subsisted by his musical talent; and to have had some connection with the theatre in that capacity. In similar dim positions, with what shiftings, adventures and vicissitudes is quite unknown to me, he long survived Schiller, and, at least fifty years after these Mannheim struggles, wrote some Book of bright and loving Reminiscences concerning him, the exact *title* of which I can nowhere find,—though passages from it are copied by Biographer Schwab here and there. His affection for Schiller is of the nature of worship rather, of constant adoration; and probably formed the sunshine to poor Streicher's life. Schiller nowhere mentions him in his writings or correspondences, after that final parting at Mannheim, 1784.

'The necessities of the two Friends reached by and by such a height that Schiller had to sell his Watch, although they had already for several weeks been subsisting on loans. To all which now came Dalberg's overwhelming message, that even this Remodelling of *Fiesco* could not be serviceable; and of course could not have money paid for it. Schiller thereupon, at once resolute what to do, walked off to the worthy Bookseller Schwann,' with whom he was already on a trustful, even grateful footing; 'and sold him his MS. at one louis-d'or the sheet. At the same time, too, he recognised the necessity of quitting Mannheim, and finding a new asylum in

Saxony; seeing, withal, his farther continuance here might be as dangerous for him as it was a matter of apprehension to his Friends. For although the Duke of Würtemberg undertook nothing that was hostile to him, and his Family at Solitüde experienced no annoyance, yet the impetuous Prince might, any day, take it into his head to have him put in prison. In the ever livelier desire after a securely-hidden place of abode, where he might execute in peace his poetic plans and enterprises, Schiller suddenly took up an earlier purpose, which had been laid aside.

'In the Stuttgart time he had known Wilhelm von Wolzogen, by and by his Brother-in-law' (they married two sisters), 'who, with three Brothers, had been bred in the Karl's School. The two had, indeed, during the academic time, Wolzogen being some years younger, had few points of contact, and were not intimate. But now on the appearance of the *Robbers*, Wolzogen took a cordial affection and enthusiasm for the widely-celebrated Poet, and on closer acquaintance with Schiller, also affected his Mother,—who, as Widow, for her three Sons' sake, lived frequently at Stuttgart,—with a deep and zealous sympathy in Schiller's fate. Schiller had, with a truly childlike trust, confided himself to this excellent Lady, and after his Arrest,—a bitter consequence of his secret visit to Mannheim,—had confessed to her his purpose to run away. Frau von Wolzogen, who feared no sacrifice when the question was of the fortune of her friends, had then offered him her family mansion, Bauerbach, near Meiningen, as a place of refuge. Schiller's notion had also been to fly thither; though, deceived by false hopes, he changed that purpose. He now wrote at once to Stuttgart, and announced to Frau von Wolzogen his wish to withdraw for 'some time to Bauerbach.' To which, as is well known, the assent was ready and zealous.

'Before quitting Mannheim, Schiller could not resist the longing wish, to see his Parents yet one time; and wrote to them accordingly, 19 Nov. 1782, in visible haste and excitement:

> "Best Parents,—As I am at present in Mannheim, and am to go away forever in five days, I wished to prepare for myself and you the one remaining satisfaction of seeing one another once more. Today is the 19th, on the 21st you receive this Letter;—if you therefore, without the least delay (that is indispensable), leave Stuttgart, you might on the 22d be at the Post-house in Bretten, which is about half way from Mannheim, and where you would find me. I think it would be best if Mamma and Christophine, under the pretext of going to Ludwigsburg to Wolzogen, should make this journey. Take the Frau Vischerin" (a Captain's Widow, sung of under the name of "Laura," with whom he had last lodged in Stuttgart) "and also Wolzogen with you, as I wish to speak with both of them, perhaps for the last time, Wolzogen excepted. I will give you a Karolin as journey-money; but not till I see you at Bretten. By the prompt fulfilment of my Prayer, I will perceive whether is still dear to you,
>
> Your ever-grateful Son,
> Schiller."'

From Mannheim, Bauerbach or Meiningen lies about 120 miles N.E.; and from Stuttgart almost as far straight North. Bretten, 'a little town on a hill, celebrated as Melancthon's Birthplace, his Father's house still standing there,' is some 35 miles S.E. of Mannheim, and as far N.W. from Stuttgart. From Mannheim, in this wise, it is not at all on the road to Meiningen, though only a few miles more remote in direct distance. Schiller's purpose had been, after this affectionate interview, to turn at once leftward and make for Meiningen, by what road or roads there were from Bretten thither. Schiller's poor guinea (Karolin) was not needed on this occasion; the rendezvous at Bretten being found impossible or inexpedient at the Stuttgart end of it. Our Author continues:

'Although this meeting, on which the loving Son and Brother wished to spend his last penny, did not take effect; yet this mournful longing of his, evident from the Letter, and from the purpose itself, must have touched the Father's heart with somewhat of a reconciliatory feeling. Schiller Senior writes accordingly, 8 December 1782, the very day after his Son's arrival at Bauerbach, to Bookseller Schwan in Mannheim: "I have not noticed here the smallest symptom that his Ducal Durchlaucht has any thought of having my Son searched for and prosecuted; and indeed his post here has long since been filled up; a circumstance which visibly indicates that they can do without him." This Letter to Schwan concludes in the following words, which are characteristic: "He (my Son) has, by his untimely withdrawal, against the advice of his true friends, plunged himself into this difficult position; and it will profit him in soul and body that he feel the pain of it, and thereby become wiser for the future. I am not afraid, however, that want of actual necessaries should come upon him, for in such case I should feel myself obliged to lend a hand."

'And in effect Schiller, during his abode in Bauerbach, did once or twice receive little subventions of money from his Father, although never without earnest and not superfluous admonition to become more frugal, and take better heed in laying-out his money. For economics were, by Schiller's own confession, "not at all his talent; it cost him less," he says, "to execute a whole conspiracy and tragedy-plot than to adjust his scheme of housekeeping." —At this time it was never the Father himself who wrote to Schiller, but always Christophine, by his commission; and on the other hand, Schiller too never risked writing directly to his Father, as he felt but too well how little on his part had been done to justify the flight in his Father's eyes. He writes accordingly, likewise on that 8th December 1782, to his Publisher Schwan: "If you can accelerate the printing of my *Fiesco*, you will very much oblige me by doing so. You know that nothing but the prohibition to become an Author drove me out of the Würtemberg service. If I now, on this side, don't soon let my native country hear of me, they will say the step I took was useless and without real motive."

'In Bauerbach Schiller lived about eight months, under the name of Doctor Ritter, unknown to everybody; and only the Court-Librarian, Reinwald, in Meiningen, afterwards his Brother-in-law,' as we shall see, 'in whom he found a solid friend, had been trusted by Frau von Wolzogen with the name and true situation of the mysterious stranger. The most of Schiller's time here was spent in dramatic labours, enterprises and dreams. The outcome of all these were his third civic Tragedy, *Louise Miller*, or *Kabale und Liebe*, which was finished in February 1783, and the settling on *Don Carlos* as a new tragic subject. Many reasons, meanwhile, in the last eight months, had been pushing Schiller into the determination to leave his asylum, and anew turn towards Mannheim. A passionate, though unreturned attachment to Charlotte von Wolzogen at that time filled Schiller's soul; and his removal therefore must both to Frau von Wolzogen for her own and her Daughter's sake, and to Schiller himself, have appeared desirable. It was Frau von Wolzogen's own advice to him to go for a short time to Mannheim, there to get into clear terms with Dalberg, who had again begun corresponding with him: so, in July 1783, Schiller bade his solitary, and, by this time dear and loved, abode a hasty adieu; and, much contrary to fond hope, never saw it again.

'In September 1783, his bargainings with Dalberg had come to this result, That for a fixed salary of 500 gulden,' 50*l*. a year, 'he was appointed Theatre-Poet here. By this means, to use his own words, the way was open to him gradually to pay-off a considerable portion of his debts, and so escape from the drowning whirlpool, and remain an honest man. Now, furthermore, he thought it permissible to show himself to his Family with a certain composure of attitude; and opened straightway a regular correspondence with his Parents again. And Captain Schiller volunteers a stiff-starched but true and earnest Letter to the Baron Dalberg himself; most humbly thanking that gracious nobleman for such beneficent favour shown my poor Son; and begs withal the far stranger favour that Dalberg would have the extreme goodness to appoint the then inexperienced young man some true friend who might help him to arrange his housekeeping, and in moral things might be his Mentor!

'Soon after this, an intermittent fever threw the Poet on a sick-bed; and lamed him above five weeks from all capacity of mental labour. Not even in June of the following year was the disease quite overcome. Visits, acquaintanceships, all kinds of amusements, and more than anything else, over-hasty attempts at work, delayed his cure;—so that his Father had a perfect right to bring before him his, Schiller's, own blame in the matter: "That thou"' (*Er*, He; the then usual tone towards servants and children) '"for eight whole months hast weltered about with intermittent fever, surely that does little honour to thy study of medicine; and thou wouldst, with great justice, have poured the bitterest reproaches on any Patient who, in a case like thine, had not held himself to the diet and regimen that were prescribed to him!" —

'In Autumn 1783, there seized Schiller so irresistible a longing to see his kindred again, that he repeatedly expressed to his Father the great wish he had for a meeting, either at Mannheim or some other place outside the Würtemberg borders. To the fulfilment of this scheme there were, however, in the sickness which his Mother had fallen into, in the fettered position of the Father, and in the rigorously frugal economies of the Family, insuperable obstacles. Whereupon his Father made him the proposal, that he, Friedrich, either himself or by him, the Captain, should apply to the Duke Karl's Serene Highness; and petition him for permission to return to his country and kindred. As Schiller to this answered nothing, Christophine time after time pressingly repeated to him the Father's proposal. At the risk of again angering his Father, Schiller gave, in his answer to Christophine, of 1st January 1784, the decisive declaration that his honour would frightfully suffer if he, without connection with any other Prince, without character and lasting means of support, after his forceful withdrawal from Würtemberg, should again show face there. "That my Father," adds he, as ground of this refusal, "give his name to such a petition can help me little; for every one will at once, so long as I cannot make it plain that I no longer need the Duke of Würtemberg, suspect in a return, obtained on petition (by myself or by another is all one), a desire to get settled in Würtemberg again. Sister, consider with serious attention these circumstances; for the happiness of thy Brother may, by rash haste in this matter, suffer an incurable wound. Great part of Germany knows of my relations to your Duke and of the way I left him. People have interested themselves for me at the expense of this Duke; how horribly would the respect of the public (and on this depends my whole future fortune), how miserably would my own honour sink by the suspicion that I had sought this return; that my circumstances had forced me to repent my former step; that the support which I had sought in the wide world had misgone, and I was seeking it anew in my Birthland! The open manlike boldness, which I showed in my forceful withdrawal, would get the name of a childish outburst of mutiny, a stupid bit of impotent bluster, if I do not make it good. Love for my dear ones, longing for my Fatherland might perhaps excuse me in the heart of this or the other candid man; but the world makes no account of all that.

"For the rest, if my Father is determined to do it, I cannot hinder him; only this I say to thee, Sister, that in case even the Duke would permit it, I will not show myself on Würtemberg ground till I have at least a character (for which object I shall zealously labour); and that in case the Duke refuses, I shall not be able to restrain myself from avenging the affront thereby put upon me by open fooleries (*sottisen*) and expressions of myself in print."

'The intended Petition to the Duke was not drawn out, — and Father Schiller overcame his anger on the matter; as, on closer consideration of the Son's aversion to this step, he could not wholly disapprove him. Yet he did not hide from Schiller Junior the steadfast wish that he would in some way or other try to draw near to the Duke; at any rate he, Father Schiller, "hoped to God that their parting would not last forever; and that, in fine, he might still live to see his only Son near him again."

'In Mannheim Schiller's financial position, in spite of his earnest purpose to manage wisely, grew by degrees worse rather than better. Owing to the many little expenses laid upon him by his connections in society, his income would not suffice; and the cash-box was not seldom run so low that he had not wherewithal to support himself next day. Of assistance from home, with the rigorous income of his Father, which scarcely amounted to 40*l.* a year, there could nothing be expected; and over and above, the Father himself had, in this respect, very clearly spoken his mind. "Parents and Sisters," said Schiller Senior, "have as just a right as they have a confidence, in cases of necessity, to expect help and support from a Son." To fill to overflowing the measure of the Poet's economical distress, there now stept forth suddenly some secret creditors of his in Stuttgart, demanding immediate payment. Whereupon, in quick succession, there came to Captain Schiller, to his great terror, two drafts from the Son, requiring of him, the one 10*l.*, the other 5*l.* The Captain, after stern reflection, determined at last to be good for both demands; but wrote to the Son that he only did so in order that his, the Son's, labour might not be disturbed; and in the confident anticipation that the Son, regardful of his poor Sisters and their bit of portion, would not leave him in the lurch.

'But Schiller, whom still other debts in Stuttgart, unknown to his Father, were pressing hard, could only repay the smaller of these drafts; and thus the worthy Father saw himself compelled to pay the larger, the 10*l.*, out of the savings he had made for outfit of his Daughters. Whereupon, as was not undeserved, he took his Son tightly to task, and wrote to him: "As long as thou, my Son, shalt make thy reckoning on resources that are still to come, and therefore are still subject to chance and mischance, so long wilt thou continue in thy mess of embarrassments. Furthermore, as long as thou thinkest, This gulden or batzen (shilling or farthing) can't help me to get over it; so long will thy debts become never the smaller: and, what were a sorrow to me, thou wilt not be able, after a heavy labour of head got done, to recreate thyself in the society of other good men. But, withal, to make recreation-days of that kind more numerous than work-days, that surely will not turn out well. Best Son, thy abode in Bauerbach has been of that latter kind. *Hinc illæ lacrymæ!* For these thou art now suffering, and that not by accident. The embarrassment thou now art in is verily a work of Higher Providence, to lead thee off from too great trust in thy own force; to make thee soft and contrite; that, laying aside all self-will, thou mayest follow more the counsel of thy Father and other true friends; must meet every one with due respectful courtesy and readiness to oblige; and become ever more convinced that our most gracious Duke, in his restrictive plans, meant well with thee; and that altogether thy position and outlooks had now been better, hadst thou complied, and continued in thy country. Many a time I find thou hast wayward humours, that make thee to thy truest friend scarcely endurable; stiff ways which repel the best-wishing man;—for example, when I sent thee my excellent old friend Herr Amtmann Cramer from Altdorf near Speier, who had come to Herr Hofrath Schwan's in the end of last year, thy reception of him was altogether dry and stingy, though by my Letter I had given thee so good an opportunity to seek the friendship of this honourable, rational and influential man (who has no children of his own), and to try whether he might not have been of help to thee. Thou wilt do well, I think, to try and make good this fault on another opportunity."

'At the same time the old man repeatedly pressed him to return to Medicine, and graduate in Heidelberg: "a theatre-poet in Germany," he signified, "was but a small light; and as he, the Son, with all his Three Pieces, had not made any footing for himself, what was to be expected of the future ones, which might not be of equal strength! Doctorship, on the other hand, would give him a sure income and reputation as well."—Schiller himself was actually determined to follow his Father's advice as to Medicine; but this project and others of the same, which were sometimes taken up, went to nothing, now and always, for want of money to begin with.

'Amid these old tormenting hindrances, affronts and embarrassments, Schiller had also many joyful experiences, to which even his Father was not wholly indifferent. To these belong, besides many others, his reception into the *Kurpfälzische Deutsche Gesellschaft*', German Society of the Electoral Palatinate, 'of this year; which he himself calls a great step for his establishment; as well as the stormy applause with which his third Piece, *Kabale und Liebe*, came upon the boards, in March following. His Father acknowledged receipt of this latter Work with the words, "That I possess a copy of thy new Tragedy I tell nobody; for I dare not, on account of certain passages, let any one notice that it has pleased me." Nevertheless the Piece, as already the *Robbers* had done, came in Stuttgart also to the acting point; and was received with loud approval. Schiller now, with new pleasure and inspiration, laid hands on his *Don Carlos*; and with the happy progress of this Work, there began for him a more confident temper of mind, and a clearing-up of horizon and outlook; which henceforth only transiently yielded to embarrassments in his outer life.

'Soon after this, however, there came upon him an unexpected event so suddenly and painfully that, in his extremest excitement and misery, he fairly hurt the feelings of his Father by unreasonable requirements of him, and reproaches on their being refused. A principal Stuttgart Cautioner of his, incessantly pressed upon by the stringent measures of the creditors there, had fairly run off, saved himself by flight, from Stuttgart, and been seized in Mannheim, and there put in jail. Were not this Prisoner at once got out, Schiller's honour and peace of conscience were at stake. And so, before his (properly Streicher's) Landlord, the Architect Hölzel, could get together the required 300 gulden, and save this unlucky friend, the half-desperate Poet had written home, and begged from his Father that indispensable sum. And on the Father's clear refusal, had answered him with a very unfilial Letter. Not till after the lapse of seven weeks, did the Father reply; in a Letter, which, as a luminous memorial of his faithful honest father-heart and of his considerate just character as a man, deserves insertion here:

"Very unwilling," writes he, "am I to proceed to the answering of thy last Letter, 21st November of the past year; which I could rather wish never to have read than now to taste again the bitterness contained there. Not enough that thou, in the beginning of the said Letter, very undeservedly reproachest me, as if I could and should have raised the 300 gulden for thee,—thou continuest to blame me, in a very painful way, for my inquiries about thee on this occasion. Dear Son, the relation between a good Father and his Son fallen into such a strait, who, although gifted with many faculties of mind, is still, in all that belongs to true greatness and contentment, much mistaken and astray, can never justify the Son in taking up as an injury what the Father has said out of love, out of consideration and experience of his own, and meant only for his Son's good. As to what concerns those 300 gulden, every one, alas, who knows my position here, knows that it cannot be possible for me to have even 50 gulden, not to speak of 300, before me in store; and that I should borrow such a sum, to the still farther disadvantage of my other children, for a Son, who of the much that he has promised me has been able to perform so little,—there, for certain, were I an unjust Father." Farther on, the old man takes him up on another side, a private family affair. Schiller had, directly and through others, in reference to the prospect of a marriage between his elder Sister Christophine and his friend Reinwald the Court Librarian of Meiningen, expressed himself in a doubting manner, and thereby delayed the settlement of this affair. In regard to which his Father tells him:

"And now I have something to remark in respect of thy Sister. As thou, my Son, partly straight out, and partly through Frau von Kalb, hast pictured Reinwald in a way to deter both me and thy Sister in counselling and negotiating in the way we intended, the affair seems to have become quite retrograde: for Reinwald, these two months past, has not written a word more. Whether thou, my Son, didst well to hinder a match not unsuitable for the age, and the narrow pecuniary circumstances of thy Sister, God, who sees into futurity, knows. As I am now sixty-one years of age, and can leave little fortune when I die; and as thou, my Son, how happily soever thy hopes be fulfilled, wilt yet have to struggle, years long, to get out of these present embarrassments, and arrange thyself suitably; and as, after that, thy own probable marriage will always require thee to have more thy own advantages in view, than to be able to trouble thyself much about those of thy Sisters;—it would not, all things considered, have been ill if Christophine had got a settlement. She would quite certainly, with her apparent regard for Reinwald, have been able to fit herself into his ways and him; all the better as she, God be thanked, is not yet smit with ambition, and the wish for great things, and can suit herself to all conditions."

The Reinwald marriage did take place by and by, in spite of Schiller Junior's doubts; and had not Christophine been the paragon of Wives, might have ended very ill for all parties.

'After these incidents, Schiller bent his whole strength to disengage himself from the crushing burden of his debts, and to attain the goal marked out for him by his Parents' wishes,—an enduring settlement and steady way of life. Two things essentially contributed to enliven his activity, and brighten his prospects into the future. One was, the original beginning, which falls in next June 1784, of his friendly intimacy with the excellent Körner; in whom he was to find not only the first founder of his outer fortune in life, but also a kindred spirit, and cordial friend such as he had never before had. The second was, that he made, what shaped his future lot, acquaintance with Duke Karl August of Weimar; who, after hearing him read the first act of *Don Carlos* at the Court of Darmstadt, had a long conversation with the Poet, and officially, in consequence of the same, bestowed on him the title of Rath. This new relation to a noble German Prince gave him a certain standing-ground for the future; and at the same time improved his present condition, by completely securing him in respect of any risk from Würtemberg. The now Schiller, as Court-Counsellor (*Hofrath*) to the Duke of Weimar; distinguished in this way by a Prince, who was acquainted with the Muses, and accustomed only to what was excellent,—stept forth in much freer attitude, secure of his position and himself, than the poor fugitive under ban of law had done.

'Out of this, however, and the fact resulting from it, that he now assumed a more decisive form of speech in the Periodical "*Thalia*" founded by him, and therein spared the players as little as the public, there grew for him so many and such irritating brabbles and annoyances that he determined to quit his connection with the Theatre, leave Mannheim altogether; and, at Leipzig with his new title of Rath, to begin a new honourable career. So soon as the necessary moneys and advices from his friend' (Körner) had arrived, he repaired thither, end of March 1785; and remained there all the summer. In October of the same year, he followed his friend Körner to Dresden; and found in the family of this just-minded, clear-seeing man the purest and warmest sympathy for himself and his fortunes. The year 1787 led him at last to Weimar. But here too he had still long to struggle, under the pressure of poverty and want of many things, while the world, in ever-increasing admiration, was resounding with his name, till, in 1789, his longing for a civic existence, and therewith the intensest wish of his Parents, was fulfilled.

'Inexpressible was the joy of the now elderly Father to see his deeply-beloved Son, after so many roamings, mischances and battles, at last settled as Professor in Jena; and soon thereafter, at the side of an excellent Wife, happy at a hearth of his own. The economic circumstances of the Son were now also shaped to the Father's satisfaction. If his College salary was small, his literary labours, added thereto, yielded him a sufficient income; his Wife moreover had come to him quite fitted out, and her Mother had given all that belongs to a household. "Our economical adjustment," writes Schiller to his Father, some weeks after their marriage, "has fallen out, beyond all my wishes, well; and the order, the dignity which I see around me here serves greatly to exhilarate my mind. Could you but for a moment get to me, you would rejoice at the happiness of your Son."

'Well satisfied and joyful of heart, from this time, the Father's eye followed his Son's career of greatness and renown upon which the admired Poet every year stepped onwards, powerfuler, and richer in results, without ever, even transiently, becoming strange to his Father's house and his kindred there. Quite otherwise, all letters of the Son to Father and Mother bear the evident stamp of true-hearted, grateful and pious filial love. He took, throughout, the heartiest share in all, even the smallest, events that befell in his Father's house; and in return communicated to his loved ones all of his own history that could soothe and gratify them. Of this the following Letter, written by him, 26th October 1791, on receipt of a case of wine sent from home, furnishes a convincing proof:

> "Dearest Father,—I have just returned with my dear Lotte from Rudolstadt" (her native place), "where I was passing part of my holidays; and find your Letter. Thousand thanks for the thrice-welcome news you give me there, of the improving health of our dear Mother, and of the general welfare of you all. The conviction that it goes well with you, and that none of my dear loved ones is suffering, heightens for me the happiness which I enjoy here at the side of my dear Lotte.
>
> You are careful, even at this great distance, for your children, and gladden our little household with gifts. Heartiest thanks from us both for the Wine you have sent; and with the earliest

carriage-post the Reinwalds shall have their share. Day after to-morrow we will celebrate your Birthday as if you were present, and with our whole heart drink your health.

Here I send you a little production of my pen, which may perhaps give pleasure to my dear Mother and Sisters; for it should be at least written for ladies. In the year 1790 Wieland edited the *Historical Calendar*, and in this of 1791 and in the 1792 that will follow, I have undertaken the task. Insignificant as a *Calendar* seems to be, it is that kind of book which the Publishers can circulate the most extensively, and which accordingly brings them the best payment. To the Authors also they can, accordingly, offer much more. For this Essay on the *Thirty-Years War* they have given me 80 Louis-d'or, and I have in the middle of my Lectures written it in four weeks. Print, copperplates, binding, Author's honorarium cost the Publisher 4,500 *reichsthaler* (675*l.*), and he counts on a sale of 7,000 copies or more.

"*28th.* Today," so he continues, after some remarks on a good old friend of his Father's, written after interruption,—"Today is your Birthday, dearest Father, which we both celebrate with a pious joy that Heaven has still preserved you sound and happy for us thus far. May Heaven still watch over your dear life and your health, and preserve your days to the latest age, that so your grateful Son may be able to spread, with all the power he has, joy and contentment over the evening of your life, and pay the debts of filial duty to you!

"Farewell, my dearest Father; loving kisses to our dearest Mother and my dear Sisters. We will soon write again.

"The Wine has arrived in good condition; once more receive our hearty thanks.—Your grateful and obedient Son

"FRIEDRICH."

'In the beginning of this year (1791) the Poet had been seized with a violent and dangerous affection of the chest. The immediate danger was now over; but his bodily health was, for the rest of his life, shattered to ruin, and required, for the time coming, especially for the time just come, all manner of soft treatment and repose. The worst, therefore, was to be feared if his friends and he could not manage to place him, for the next few years, in a position freer from economic cares than now. Unexpectedly, in this difficulty, help appeared out of Denmark. Two warm admirers of Schiller's genius, the then hereditary Prince of Holstein-Augustenburg' (Grandfather of the Prince Christian now, 1872, conspicuous in our English Court), 'and Count von Schimmelmann, offered the Poet a pension of 1,000 thalers' (150*l.*) 'for three years; and this with a fineness and delicacy of manner, which touched the recipient more even than the offer itself did, and moved him to immediate assent. The Pension was to remain a secret; but how could Schiller prevail on himself to be silent of it to his Parents? With tears of thankfulness the Parents received this glad message; in their pious minds they gathered out of this the beneficent conviction that their Son's heavy sorrows, and the danger in which his life hung, had only been decreed by Providence to set in its right light the love and veneration which he far and near enjoyed. Schiller himself this altogether unexpected proof of tenderest sympathy in his fate visibly cheered, and strengthened even in health; at lowest, the strength of his spirit, which now felt itself free from outward embarrassments, subdued under it the weakness of his body.

'In the middle of the year 1793, the love of his native country, and the longing after his kindred, became so lively in him that he determined, with his Wife, to visit Swabia. He writes to Körner: "The Swabian, whom I thought I had altogether got done with, stirs himself strongly in me; but indeed I have been eleven years parted from Swabia; and Thüringen is not the country in which I can forget it." In August he set out, and halted first in the then *Reichstadt*' (Imperial Free-town) 'Heilbronn, where he found the friendliest reception; and enjoyed the first indescribable emotion in seeing again his Parents, Sisters and early friends. "My dear ones," writes he to Körner, 27th August, from Heilbronn, "I found well to do, and, as thou canst suppose, greatly rejoiced to meet me again. My Father, in his seventieth year, is the image of a healthy old age; and any one who did not know his years would not count them above sixty. He is in continual activity, and this it is which keeps him healthy and youthful." In large draughts the robust old man enjoyed the pleasure, long forborne, of gazing into the eyes of his Son, who now stood before him a completed man. He knew not whether more to admire than love him; for, in his whole appearance, and all his speeches and doings, there stamped itself a powerful lofty spirit, a tender loving heart, and a pure noble character. His youthful fire was softened, a mild seriousness and a friendly dignity did not leave him even in jest; instead of his old neglect in dress, there had come a dignified elegance; and his lean figure and his pale face completed the interest of his look. To this was yet added the almost wonderful gift of conversation upon the objects that were dear to him, whenever he was not borne down by attacks of illness.

'From Heilbronn, soon after his arrival, Schiller wrote to Duke Karl, in the style of a grateful former Pupil, whom contradictory circumstances had pushed away from his native country. He got no answer from the Duke; but from Stuttgart friends he did get sure tidings that the Duke, on receipt of this Letter, had publicly said, if Schiller came into Würtemberg Territory, he, the Duke, would take no notice. To Schiller Senior, too, he had at the same time granted the humble petition that he might have leave to visit his Son in Heilbronn now and then.

'Under these circumstances, Schiller, perfectly secure, visited Ludwigsburg and even Solitüde, without, as he himself expressed it, asking permission of the "Schwabenkönig." And, in September, in the near prospect of his Wife's confinement, he went altogether to Ludwigsburg, where he was a good deal nearer to his kindred; and moreover, in the clever Court-Doctor von Hoven, a friend of his youth, hoped to find counsel, help and enjoyment. Soon after his removal, Schiller had, in the birth of his eldest Son, Karl, the sweet happiness of first paternal joy; and with delight saw fulfilled what he had written to a friend shortly before his departure from Jena: "I shall taste the joys of a Son and of a Father, and it will, between these two feelings of Nature, go right well with me."

'The Duke, ill of gout, and perhaps feeling that death was nigh, seemed to make a point of strictly ignoring Schiller; and laid not the least hindrance in his way. On the contrary, he granted Schiller Senior, on petition, the permission to make use of a certain Bath as long as he liked; and this Bath lay so near Ludwigsburg that he could not but think the meaning merely was, that the Father wished to be nearer his Son. Absence was at once granted by the Duke, useful and necessary as the elder Schiller always was to him at home. For the old man, now Major Schiller, still carried on his overseeing of the Ducal Gardens and Nurseries at Solitüde, and his punctual diligence, fidelity, intelligence and other excellences in that function had long been recognised.

'In a few weeks after, 24th October 1793, Duke Karl died; and was, by his illustrious Pupil, regarded as in some sort a paternal friend. Schiller thought only of the great qualities of the deceased, and of the good he had done him; not of the great faults which as Sovereign, and as man, he had manifested. Only to his most familiar friend did he write: "The death of old Herod has had no influence either on me or my Family,—except indeed that all men who had immediately to do with that Sovereign Herr, as my Father had, are glad now to have the prospect of a man before them. That the new Duke is, in every good, and also in every bad meaning of the word." Withal, however, his Father, to whom naturally the favour of the new Duke, Ludwig Eugen, was of importance, could not persuade Schiller to welcome him to the Sovereignty with a poem. To Schiller's feelings it was unendurable to awaken, for the sake of an external advantage from the new Lord, any suspicions as if he welcomed the death of the old.'[55]

Christophine, Schiller's eldest Sister, whom he always loved the most, was not here in Swabia;—long hundred miles away, poor Christophine, with her sickly and gloomy Husband at Meiningen, these ten years past!—but the younger two, Luise and Nanette, were with him, the former daily at his hand. Luise was then twenty-seven, and is described as an excellent domestic creature, amiable affectionate, even enthusiastic; yet who at an early period though full of admiration about her Brother and his affairs, had turned all her faculties and tendencies upon domestic practicality, and the satisfaction of being useful to her loved ones in their daily life and wants.[56] 'Her element was altogether house-management; the aim of her endeavour to attain the virtues by which she saw her pious Mother made happy herself, in making others happy in the narrow in-door kingdom. This quiet household vocation with its manifold labours and its simple joys, was Luise's world; beyond which she needed nothing and demanded nothing. From her Father she had inherited this feeling for the practical, and this restless activity; from the Mother her piety, compassion and kindliness; from both, the love of order, regularity and contentment. Luise, in the weak state of Schiller's Wife's health, was right glad to take charge of her Brother's housekeeping; and, first at Heilbronn and then at Ludwigsburg, did it to the complete satisfaction both of Brother and Sister-in-law. Schiller himself gives to Körner the grateful testimony, that she "very well

[55] *Saupe*, p. 60.
[56] *Saupe*, p. 136 et seqq.

understands household management."

'In this daily relation with her delicate and loving Brother, to whom Luise looked up with a sort of timid adoration, he became ever dearer to her; with a silent delight, she would often look into the soft eyes of the great and wonderful man; from whose powerful spirit she stood so distant, and to whose rich heart so near. All-too rapidly for her flew-by the bright days of his abode in his homeland, and long she looked after the vanished one with sad longing; and Schiller also felt himself drawn closer to his Sister than before; by whose silent faithful working his abode in Swabia had been made so smooth and agreeable.'

Nanette he had, as will by and by appear, seen at Jena, on her Mother's visit there, the year before;—with admiration and surprise he then saw the little creature whom he had left a pretty child of five years old, now become a blooming maiden, beautiful to eye and heart, and had often thought of her since. She too was often in his house, at present; a loved and interesting object always. She had been a great success in the foreign Jena circle, last year; and had left bright memories there. This is what Saupe says afterwards, of her appearance at Jena, and now in Schiller's temporary Swabian home:

'She evinced the finest faculties of mind, and an uncommon receptivity and docility, and soon became to all that got acquainted with her a dear and precious object. To declaim passages from her Brother's Poems was her greatest joy; she did her recitation well; and her Swabian accent and naïvety of manner gave her an additional charm for her new relatives, and even exercised a beneficent influence on the Poet's own feelings. With hearty pleasure his beaming eyes rested often on the dear Swabian girl, who understood how to awaken in his heart the sweet tones of childhood and home. "She is good," writes he of her to his friend Körner, "and it seems as if something could be made of her. She is yet much the child of nature, and that is still the best she could be, never having been able to acquire any reasonable culture." With Schiller's abode in Swabia, from August 1793 till May 1794, Nanette grew still closer to his heart, and in his enlivening and inspiring neighbourhood her spirit and character shot out so many rich blossoms, that Schiller on quitting his Father's house felt justified in the fairest hopes for the future.' Just before her visit to Jena, Schiller Senior writes to his Son: "It is a great pity for Nanette that I cannot give her a better education. She has sense and talent and the best of hearts; much too of my dear Fritz's turn of mind, as he will himself see, and be able to judge."[57]

'For the rest, on what childlike confidential terms Schiller lived with his Parents at this time, one may see by the following Letter, of 8th November 1793, from Ludwigsburg:

> "Right sorry am I, dearest Parents, that I shall not be able to
> celebrate my Birthday, 11th November, along with you. But I see
> well that good Papa cannot rightly risk just now to leave Solitüde
> at all,—a visit from the Duke being expected there every day. On
> the whole, it does not altogether depend on the day on which one

---

[57] *Saupe,* pp. 149-50.

is to be merry with loved souls; and every day on which I can be where my dear Parents are shall be festal and welcome to me like a Birthday.

"About the precious little one here Mamma is not to be uneasy." (Here follow some more precise details about the health of this little Gold Son; omitted.) "Of watching and nursing he has no lack; that you may believe; and he is indeed, a little leanness excepted, very lively and has a good appetite.

"I have been, since I made an excursion to Stuttgart, tolerably well; and have employed this favourable time to get a little forward in my various employments which have been lying waste so long. For this whole week, I have been very diligent, and getting on briskly. This is also the cause that I have not written to you. I am always supremely happy when I am busy and my labour speeds.

"For your so precious Portrait I thank you a thousand times, dearest Father: yet glad as I am to possess this memorial of you, much gladder still am I that Providence has granted me to have you yourself, and to live in your neighbourhood. But we must profit better by this good time, and no longer make such pauses before coming together again. If you once had seen the Duke at Solitüde and known how you stand with him, there would be, I think, no difficulty in a short absence of a few days, especially at this season of the year. I will send up the carriage" (hired at Jena for the visit thither and back) "at the very first opportunity, and leave it with you, to be ready always when you can come.

"My and all our hearty and childlike salutations to you both, and to the good Nane" (Nanette) "my brotherly salutation.

"Hoping soon for a joyful meeting, — Your obedient Son,

"FRIEDRICH SCHILLER."

'In the new-year time 1794, Schiller spent several agreeable weeks in Stuttgart; whither he had gone primarily on account of some family matter which had required settling there. At least he informs his friend Körner, on the 17th March, from Stuttgart, "I hope to be not quite useless to my Father here, though, from the connections in which I stand, I can expect nothing for myself."

'By degrees, however, the sickly, often-ailing Poet began to long again for a quiet, uniform way of life; and this feeling, daily strengthened by the want of intellectual conversation, which had become a necessary for him, grew at length so strong, that he, with an alleviated heart, thought of departure from his Birth-land, and of quitting his loved ones; glad that Providence had granted him again to possess his Parents and Sisters for months long and to live in their neighbourhood. He gathered himself into readiness for the journey back; and returned, first to his original quarters at Heilbronn, and, in May 1794, with Wife and Child, to Jena.

'Major Schiller, whom the joy to see his Son and Grandson seemed to have made young again, lived with fresh pleasure in his idyllic calling; and in free hours busied himself with writing down his twenty-years experiences in the domain of garden- and tree-culture, — in a Work, the printing and publication of which were got managed for him by his renowned Son. In November 1794 he was informed that the young Publisher of the first *Musen-Almanach* had accepted his MS. for an honorarium of twenty-four Karolins; and that the same was already gone to press. Along with this, the good old Major was valued by his Prince, and by all who knew him. His subordinates loved him as a just impartial man; feared him, too, however, in his stringent love of order. Wife and children showed him the most reverent regard and tender love; but the Son was the ornament of his old age. He lived to see the full renown of the Poet, and his close connection with Goethe, through which he was to attain complete mastership and lasting composure. With hands quivering for joy the old man grasped the MSS. of his dear Son; which from Jena, *viâ* Cotta's Stuttgart Warehouses, were before all things transmitted to him. In a paper from his hand, which is still in existence, there is found a touching expression of thanks, That God had given him such a joy in his Son. "And Thou Being of all beings," says he in the same, "to Thee did I pray, at the birth of my one Son, that Thou wouldst supply to him in strength of intellect and faculty what I, from want of learning, could not furnish; and Thou hast heard me. Thanks to Thee, most merciful Being, that Thou hast heard the prayer of a mortal!"

'Schiller had left his loved ones at Solitüde whole and well; and with the firm hope that he would see them all again. And the next-following years did pass untroubled over the prosperous Family. But "ill-luck," as the proverb says, "comes with a long stride." In the Spring of 1796, when the French, under Jourdan and Moreau, had overrun South Germany, there reached Schiller, on a sudden, alarming tidings from Solitüde. In the Austrian chief Hospital, which had been established in the Castle there, an epidemic fever had broken out; and had visited the Schiller Family among others. The youngest Daughter Nanette had sunk under this pestilence, in the flower of her years; and whilst the second Daughter Luise lay like to die of the same, the Father also was laid bedrid with gout. For fear of infection, nobody except the Doctors would risk himself at Solitüde; and so the poor weakly Mother stood forsaken there, and had, for months long, to bear alone the whole burden of the household distress. Schiller felt it painfully that he was unable to help his loved ones, in so terrible a posture of affairs; and it cost him great effort to hide these feelings from his friends. In his pain and anxiety, he turned himself at last to his eldest Sister Christophine, Wife of Hofrath Reinwald in Meiningen; and persuaded her to go to Solitüde to comfort and support her people there. Had not the true Sister-heart at once acceded to her Brother's wishes, he had himself taken the firm determination to go in person to Swabia, in the middle of May, and bring his Family away from Solitüde, and make arrangements for their nursing and accommodation. The news of his Sister's setting-out relieved him of a great and continual anxiety. "Heaven bless thee," writes he to her on the 6th May, "for this proof of thy filial love." He earnestly entreats her to prevent his dear Parents from delaying, out of thrift, any wholesome means of improvement to their health; and declares himself ready, with joy, to bear all costs, those of travelling included:

she is to draw on Cotta in Tübingen for whatever money she needs. Her Husband also he thanks, in a cordial Letter, for his consent to this journey of his Wife.

'July 11, 1796, was born to the Poet, who had been in much trouble about his own household for some time, his second Son, Ernst. Great fears had been entertained for the Mother; which proving groundless, the happy event lifted a heavy burden from his heart; and he again took courage and hope. But soon after, on the 15th August, he writes again to the faithful Körner about his kinsfolk in Swabia: "From the War we have not suffered so much; but all the more from the condition of my Father, who, broken-down under an obstinate and painful disease, is slowly wending towards death. How sad this fact is, thou mayest think."

'Within few weeks after, 7th September 1796, the Father died; in his seventy-third year, after a sick-bed of eight months. Though his departure could not be reckoned other than a blessing, yet the good Son was deeply shattered by the news of it. What his filially faithful soul suffered, in these painful days, is touchingly imaged in two Letters, which may here make a fitting close to this Life-sketch of Schiller's Father. It was twelve days after his Father's death when he wrote to his Brother-in-law, Reinwald, in Meiningen:

> "Thou hast here news, dear Brother, of the release of our good Father; which, much as it had to be expected, nay wished, has deeply affected us all. The conclusion of so long and withal so active a life is, even for bystanders, a touching object: what must it be to those whom it so nearly concerns? I have to tear myself away from thinking of this painful loss, since it is my part to help the dear remaining ones. It is a great comfort to thy Wife that she has been able to continue and fulfil her daughterly duty till her Father's last release. She would never have consoled herself, had he died a few days after her departure home.

> "Thou understandest how in the first days of this fatal breach among us, while so many painful things storm-in upon our good Mother, thy Christophine could not have left, even had the Post been in free course. But this still remains stopped, and we must wait the War-events on the Franconian, Swabian and Palatinate borders. How much this absence of thy Wife must afflict, I feel along with thee; but who can fight against such a chain of inevitable destinies? Alas, public and universal disorder rolls up into itself our private events too, in the fatalest way.

> "Thy Wife longs from her heart for home; and she only the more deserves our regard that she, against her inclination and her interest, resolved to be led only by the thought of her filial duties. Now, however, she certainly will not delay an hour longer with her return, the instant it can be entered upon without danger and impossibility. Comfort her too when thou writest to her; it grieves her to know thee forsaken, and to have no power to help thee.

> "Fare right well, dear Brother. — Thine,

SCHILLER."

'Nearly at the same time he wrote to his Mother:

"Grieved to the heart, I take up the pen to lament with you and my dear Sisters the loss we have just sustained. In truth, for a good while past I have expected nothing else: but when the inevitable actually comes, it is always a sad and overwhelming stroke. To think that one who was so dear to us, whom we hung upon with the feelings of early childhood, and also in later years were bound to by respect and love, that such an object is gone from the world, that with all our striving we cannot bring it back, — to think of this is always something frightful. And when, like you, my dearest best Mother, one has shared with the lost Friend and Husband joy and sorrow for so many long years, the parting is all the painfuler. Even when I look away from what the good Father that is gone was to myself and to us all, I cannot without mournful emotion contemplate the close of so steadfast and active a life, which God continued to him so long, in such soundness of body and mind, and which he managed so honourably and well. Yes truly, it is not a small thing to hold out so faithfully upon so long and toilsome a course; and like him, in his seventy-third year, to part from the world in so childlike and pure a mood. Might I but, if it cost me all his sorrows, pass away from my life as innocently as he from his! Life is so severe a trial; and the advantages which Providence, in some respects, may have granted me compared with him, are joined with so many dangers for the heart and for its true peace!

"I will not attempt to comfort you and my dear Sisters. You all feel, like me, how much we have lost; but you feel also that Death alone could end these long sorrows. With our dear Father it is now well; and we shall all follow him ere long. Never shall the image of him fade from our hearts; and our grief for him can only unite us still closer together.

"Five or six years ago it did not seem likely that you, my dear ones, should, after such a loss, find a Friend in your Brother, — that I should survive our dear Father. God has ordered it otherwise; and He grants me the joy to feel that I may still be something to you. How ready I am thereto, I need not assure you. We all of us know one another in this respect, and are our dear Father's not unworthy children."

This earnest and manful lamentation, which contains also a just recognition of the object lamented, may serve to prove, think Saupe and others, what is very evident, that Caspar Schiller, with his stiff, military regulations, spirit of discipline and rugged, angular ways, was, after all, the proper Father for a wide-flowing, sensitive, enthusiastic, somewhat lawless Friedrich Schiller; and did beneficently compress him into something of the shape necessary for his task in this world.

II. THE MOTHER.

Of Schiller's Mother, Elisabetha Dorothea Kodweis, born at Marbach 1733, the preliminary particulars have been given above: That she was the daughter of an Innkeeper, Woodmeasurer and Baker; prosperous in the place when Schiller Senior first arrived there. We should have added, what Saupe omits, that the young

Surgeon boarded in their house; and that by the term Woodmeasurer (*Holzmesser,* Measurer of Wood) is signified an Official Person appointed not only to measure and divide into portions the wood supplied as fuel from the Ducal or Royal Forests, but to be responsible also for payment of the same. In which latter capacity, Kodweis, as Father Schiller insinuates, was rash, imprudent and unlucky, and at one time had like to have involved that prudent, parsimonious Son-in-law in his disastrous economics. We have also said what Elisabetha's comely looks were, and particular features; pleasing and hopeful, more and more, to the strict young Surgeon, daily observant of her and them.

'In her circle,' Saupe continues, 'she was thought by her early playmates a kind of enthusiast; because she, with average faculties of understanding combined deep feeling, true piety and love of Nature, a talent for Music, nay even for Poetry. But perhaps it was the very reverse qualities in her, the fact namely that what she wanted in culture, and it may be also in clearness and sharpness of understanding, was so richly compensated by warmth and lovingness of character,—perhaps it was this which most attracted to her the heart of her deeply-reasonable Husband. And never had he cause to repent his choice. For she was, and remained, as is unanimously testified of her by trustworthy witnesses, an unpretending, soft and dutiful Wife; and, as all her Letters testify, had the tenderest mother-heart. She read a good deal, even after her marriage, little as she had of time for reading. Favourite Books with her were those on Natural History; but she liked best of all to study the Biographies of famous men, or to dwell in the spiritual poetising of an Utz, a Gellert and Klopstock. She also liked, and in some measure had the power, to express her own feelings in verses; which, with all their simplicity, show a sense for rhythm and some expertness in diction. Here is one instance; her salutation to the Husband who was her First-love, on New-year's day 1757, the ninth year of their as yet childless marriage:

> O could I but have found forget-me-not in the Valley,
> And roses beside it! Then had I plaited thee
> In fragrant blossoms the garland for this New Year,
> Which is still brighter to me than that of our Marriage was.
>
> I grumble, in truth, that the cold North now governs us,
> And every flowret's bud is freezing in the cold earth!
> Yet one thing does not freeze, I mean my loving heart;
> Thine that is, and shares with thee its joys and sorrows.[58]

'The Seven-Years War threw the young Wife into manifold anxiety and agitation; especially since she had become a Mother, and in fear for the life of her

---

[58] *'O hätt ich doch im Thal Vergissmeinnicht gefunden*
Und Rosen nebenbei! Dann hat' ich Dir gewunden
In Blüthenduft den Kranz zu diesem neuen Jahr,
Der schöner noch als der am Hochzeittage war.

Ich zürne, traun, dass itzt der kalte Nord regieret,
Und jedes Blümchens Keim in kalter Erde frieret!
Doch eines frieret nicht, es ist mein liebend Herz;
Dein ist es, theilt mit Dir die Freuden und den Schmerz.'

tenderly-loved Husband, had to tremble for the Father of her children too. To this circumstance Christophine ascribes, certainly with some ground, the world-important fact that her Brother had a much weaker constitution than herself. He had in fact been almost born in a camp. In late Autumn 1759, the Infantry Regiment of Major-General Romann, in which Caspar Schiller was then a Lieutenant, had, for sake of the Autumn Manœuvres of the Würtemberg Soldiery, taken Camp in its native region. The Mother had thereupon set out from Marbach to visit her long-absent Husband in the Camp; and it was in his tent that she felt the first symptoms of her travail. She rapidly hastened back to Marbach; and by good luck still reached her Father's house in the Market-Place there, near by the great Fountain; where she, on the 11th November, was delivered of a Boy. For almost four years the little Friedrich with Christophine and Mother continued in the house of the well-contented Grandparents (who had not yet fallen poor), under her exclusive care. With self-sacrificing love and careful fidelity, she nursed her little Boy; whose tender body had to suffer not only from the common ailments of children, but was heavily visited with fits of cramp. In a beautiful region, on the bosom of a tender Mother, and in these first years far from the oversight of a rigorous Father, the Child grew up, and unfolded himself under cheerful and harmonious impressions.

'On the return of his Father from the War, little Fritz, now four years old, was quite the image of his Mother; long-necked, freckled and reddish-haired like her. It was the pious Mother's work, too, that a feeling of religion, early and vivid, displayed itself in him. The easily-receptive Boy was indeed keenly attentive to all that his Father, in their Family-circle, read to them, and inexhaustible in questions till he had rightly caught the meaning of it: but he listened with most eagerness when his Father read passages from the Bible, or vocally uttered them in prayer. "It was a touching sight," says his eldest Sister, "the expression of devotion on the dear little Child's countenance. With its blue eyes directed towards Heaven, its high-blond hair about the clear brow, and its fast-clasped little hands. It was like an angel's head to look upon."

'With Father's return, the happy Mother conscientiously shared with him the difficult and important business of bringing up their Son; and both in union worked highly beneficially for his spiritual development. The practical and rigorous Father directed his chief aim to developing the Boy's intellect and character; the mild, pious, poetic-minded Mother, on the other hand, strove for the ennobling nurture of his temper and his imagination. It was almost exclusively owing to her that his religious feeling, his tender sense of all that was good and beautiful, his love of mankind, tolerance, and capability of self-sacrifice, in the circle of his Sisters and playmates, distinguished the Boy.

'On Sunday afternoons, when she went to walk with both the Children, she was wont to explain to them the Church-Gospel of the day. "Once," so stands it in Christophine's Memorials, "when we two, as children, had set out walking with dear Mamma to see our Grandparents, she took the way from Ludwigsburg to Marbach, which leads straight over the Hill, a walk of some four miles. It was a beautiful Easter Monday, and our Mother related to us the history of the two Disciples to whom, on their journey to Emmaus, Jesus had joined himself. Her speech and narrative grew ever more inspired; and when we got upon the Hill, we were all so much affected that we knelt down and prayed. This Hill became a Tabor to us."

'At other times she entertained the children with fairy-tales and magic histories. Already while in Lorch she had likewise led the Boy, so far as his power of comprehension and her own knowledge permitted, into the domains of German Poetry. Klopstock's *Messias*, Opitz's Poems, Paul Gerhard's and Gellert's pious Songs, were made known to him in this tender age, through his Mother; and were, for that reason, doubly dear. At one time also the artless Mother made an attempt on him with Hofmannswaldau;[59] but the sugary and windy tone of him hurt the tender poet-feeling of the Boy. With smiling dislike he pushed the Book away; and afterwards was wont to remark, when, at the new year, rustic congratulants with their foolish rhymes would too liberally present themselves, "Mother, there is a new Hofmannswaldau at the door!" Thus did the excellent Mother guide forward the soul of her docile Boy, with Bible-passages and Church-symbols, with tales, histories and poems, into gradual form and stature. Never forgetting, withal, to awaken and nourish his sense for the beauties of Nature. Before long, Nature had become his dearest abode; and only love of that could sometimes tempt him to little abridgments of school-hours. Often, in the pretty region of Lorch, he wished the Sun goodnight in open song; or with childish pathos summoned Stuttgart's Painters to represent the wondrous formation and glorious colouring of the sunset clouds. If, in such a humour, a poor man met him, his overflowing little heart would impel him to the most active pity; and he liberally gave away whatever he had by him and thought he could dispense with. The Father, who, as above indicated, never could approve or even endure such unreasonable giving-up of one's feelings to effeminate impressions, was apt to intervene on these occasions, even with manual punishment, — unless the Mother were at hand to plead the little culprit off.

'But nothing did the Mother forward with more eagerness, by every opportunity, than the kindling inclination of her Son to become a Preacher; which even showed itself in his sports. Mother or Sister had to put a little cowl on his head, and pin round him by way of surplice a bit of black apron; then would he mount a chair and begin earnestly to preach; ranging together in his own way, not without some traces of coherency, all that he had retained from teaching and church-visiting in this kind, and interweaving it with verses of songs. The Mother, who listened attentively and with silent joy, put a higher meaning into this childish play; and, in thought, saw her Son already stand in the Pulpit, and work, rich in blessings, in a spiritual office. The spiritual profession was at that time greatly esteemed, and gave promise of an honourable existence. Add to this, that the course of studies settled for young Würtemberg Theologians not only offered important pecuniary furtherances and advantages, but also morally the fewest dangers. And thus the prudent and withal pious Father, too, saw no reason to object to this inclination of

---

[59] A once-celebrated Silesian of the 17th century, distinguished for his blusterous exaggerations, numb-footed caprioles, and tearing of a passion to rags; — now extinct.

the Son and wish of the Mother.

'It had almost happened, however, that the Latin School, in Ludwigsburg (where our Fritz received the immediately preparatory teaching for his calling) had quite disgusted him with his destination for theology. The Teacher of Religion in the Institute, a narrow-minded, angry-tempered Pietist,' as we have seen, 'used the sad method of tormenting his scholars with continual rigorous, altogether soulless, drillings and trainings in matters of mere creed; nay he threatened often to whip them thoroughly, if, in the repetition of the catechism, a single word were wrong. And thus to the finely-sensitive Boy instruction was making hateful to him what domestic influences had made dear. Yet these latter did outweigh and overcome, in the end; and he remained faithful to his purpose of following a spiritual career.

'When young Schiller, after the completion of his course at the Latin School, 1777, was to be confirmed, his Mother and her Husband came across to Ludwigsburg the day before that solemn ceremony. Just on their arrival, she saw her Son wandering idle and unconcerned about the streets; and impressively represented to him how greatly his indifference to the highest and most solemn transaction of his young life troubled her. Struck and affected hereby, the Boy withdrew; and, after a few hours, handed to his Parents a German Poem, expressive of his feelings over the approaching renewal of his baptismal covenant. The Father, who either hadn't known the occasion of this, or had looked upon his Son's idling on the street with less severe eyes, was highly astonished, and received him mockingly with the question, "Hast thou lost thy senses, Fritz?" The Mother, on the other hand, was visibly rejoiced at that poetic outpouring, and with good cause. For, apart from all other views of the matter, she recognised in it how firmly her Son's inclination was fixed on the study of Theology.'—(This anecdote, if it were of any moment whatever, appears to be a little doubtful.)

'The painfuler, therefore, was it to the Mother's heart when her Son, at the inevitable entrance into the Karl's School, had to give-up Theology; and renounce withal, for a long time, if not forever, her farther guidance and influence. But she was too pious not to recognise by degrees, in this change also, a Higher Hand; and could trustfully expect the workings of the same. Besides, her Son clung so tenderly to her, that at least there was no separation of him from the Mother's heart to be dreaded. The heart-warm attachment of childish years to the creed taught him by his Mother might, and did, vanish; but not the attachment to his Mother herself whose dear image often enough charmed back the pious sounds and forms of early days, and for a time scared away doubts and unbelief.

'Years came and went; and Schiller, at last, about the end of 1780, stept out of the Academy, into the actual world, which he as yet knew only by hearsay. Delivered from that long unnatural constraint of body and spirit, he gave free course to his fettered inclinations; and sought, as in Poetry so also in Life, unlimited freedom! The tumults of passion and youthful buoyancy, after so long an imprisonment, had their sway; and embarrassments in money, their natural consequence, often brought him into very sad moods.

'In this season of time, so dangerous for the moral purity of the young man, his Mother again was his good Genius; a warning and request, in her soft tone of love sufficed to recall youthful levity within the barriers again, and restore the balance. She anxiously contrived, too, that the Son, often and willingly, visited his Father's house. Whenever Schiller had decided to give himself a good day, he wandered out with some friend as far as Solitüde.' (Only some four or five miles.) '"What a baking and a roasting then went on by that good soul," says one who witnessed it, "for the dear Prodigy of a Son and the comrade who had come with him; for whom the good Mother never could do enough! Never have I seen a better maternal heart, a more excellent, more domestic, more womanly woman."

'The admiring recognition which the Son had already found among his youthful friends, and in wider circles, was no less grateful to her heart than the gradual perception that his powerful soul, welling forth from the interior to the outward man, diffused itself into his very features, and by degrees even advantageously altered the curvatures and the form of his body. His face about this time got rid of its freckles and irregularities of skin; and strikingly improved, moreover, by the circumstance that the hitherto rather drooping nose gradually acquired its later aquiline form. And withal, the youthful Poet, with the growing consciousness of his strength and of his worth, assumed an imposing outward attitude; so that a witty Stuttgart Lady, whose house Schiller often walked past, said of him: "Regiment's Dr. Schiller steps out as if the Duke were one of his inferior servants!"

'The indescribable impression which the *Robbers*, the gigantic first-born of a Karl's Scholar, made in Stuttgart, communicated itself to the Mother too; innocently she gave herself up to the delight of seeing her Son's name wondered at and celebrated; and was, in her Mother-love, inventive enough to overcome all doubts and risks which threatened to dash her joy. By Christophine's mediations, and from the Son himself as well, she learned many a disquieting circumstance, which for the present had to be carefully concealed from her Husband; but nothing whatever could shake her belief in her Son and his talent. Without murmur, with faithful trust in God, she resigned herself even to the bitter necessity of losing for a long time her only Son; having once got to see, beyond disputing, that his purpose was firm to withdraw himself by flight from the Duke's despotic interference with his poetical activity as well as with his practical procedures; and that this purpose of his was rigorously demanded by the circumstances. Yet a sword went through her soul when Schiller, for the last time, appeared at Solitüde, secretly to take leave of her.' Her feelings on this tragic occasion have been described above; and may well be pictured as among the painfulest, tenderest and saddest that a Mother's heart could have to bear. Our Author continues:

'In reality, it was to the poor Mother a hard and lamentable time. Remembrance of the lately bright and safe-looking situation, now suddenly rent asunder and committed to the dubious unknown; anxiety about their own household and the fate of her Son; the Father's just anger, and perhaps some tacit self-reproach that she had favoured a dangerous game by keeping it concealed from her honest-hearted Husband,—lay like crushing burdens on her heart. And if many a thing did smooth itself, and many a thing, which at first was to be feared, did not take place, one thing remained fixed continually,—painful anxiety about her Son. To the afflicted Mother, in this heavy time, Frau von Wolzogen devoted the most sincere and beneficent sympathy; a Lady of singular goodness of heart, who, during Schiller's eight hidden months at Bauerbach, frequently went out to see his Family at Solitüde. By her oral reports about Schiller, whom she herself several times visited at Bauerbach, his Parents were more soothed than by his own somewhat excited Letters. With reference to this magnanimous service of friendship, Schiller wrote to her at Stuttgart in February 1783: "A Letter to my Parents is getting on its way; yet, much as I had to speak of you, I have said nothing whatever" (from prudent motives) "of your late appearance here, or of the joyful moments of our conversation together. You yourself still, therefore, have all that to tell, and you will presumably find a pair of attentive hearers." Frau von Wolzogen ventured also to apply to a high court lady, Countess von Hohenheim' (Duke's *finale* in the *illicit* way, whom he at length wedded), 'personally favourable to Schiller, and to direct her attention, before all, upon the heavy-laden Parents. Nor was this without effect. For the Countess's persuasion seems essentially to have contributed to the result that Duke Karl, out of respect for the deserving Father, left the evasion of his own Pupil unpunished.

'It must, therefore, have appeared to the still-agitated Mother, who reverenced the Frau von Wolzogen as her helpful guardian, a flagrant piece of ingratitude, when she learnt that her Son was allowing himself to be led into a passionate love for the blooming young Daughter of his Benefactress. She grieved and mourned in secret to see him exposed to new storms; foreseeing clearly, in this passion, a ready cause for his removal from Bauerbach. To such agitations her body was no longer equal; a creeping, eating misery undermined her health. She wrote to her Son at Mannheim, with a soft shadow of reproof, that in this year, since his absence, she had become ten years older in health and looks. Not long after, she had actually to take to bed, because of painful cramps, which, proceeding from the stomach, spread themselves over breast, head, back and loins. The medicines which the Son, upon express account of symptoms by the Father, prescribed for her, had no effect. By degrees, indeed, these cramps abated or left-off; but she tottered about in a state of sickness, years long: the suffering mind would not let the body come to strength. For though her true heart was filled with a pious love, which hopes all, believes and suffers all, yet she was neither blind to the faults of her Son, nor indifferent to the thought of seeing her Family's good repute and well-being threatened by his non-performances and financial confusions.

'With the repose and peace which the news of her Son's appointment to Jena, and intended marriage, had restored to his Family, there appeared also (beginning of 1790) an improvement to be taking place in the Mother's health. Learning this by a Letter from his Father, Schiller wrote back with lightened heart: "How welcome, dearest Father, was your last Letter to me, and how necessary! I had, the very day before, got from Christophine the sad news that my dearest Mother's state had grown so much worse; and what a blessed turn now has this weary sickness taken! If in the future *regimen vitæ* (diet arrangements) of my dearest Mother, there is strict care taken, her long and many sufferings, with the source of them, may be removed. Thanks to a merciful Providence, which saves and preserves for us the dear Mother of our youth. My soul is moved with tenderness and gratitude. I had to think of her as lost to us forever; and she has now been given back." In reference to his approaching marriage with Lottchen von Lengefeld, he adds, "How did it lacerate my heart to think that my dearest Mother might not live to see the happiness of her Son! Heaven bless you with thousandfold blessings, best Father, and grant to my dear Mother a cheerful and painless life!"

'Soon, however, his Mother again fell sick, and lay in great danger. Not till August following could the Father announce that she was saved, and from day to day growing stronger. The annexed history of the disorder seemed so remarkable to Schiller, that he thought of preparing it for the public; unless the Physician, Court-Doctor Consbruch, liked better to send it out in print himself. "On this point," says Schiller, "I will write to him by the first post; and give him my warmest thanks for the inestimable service he has done us all, by his masterly cure of our dear Mamma; and for his generous and friendly behaviour throughout." "How heartily, my dearest Parents," writes he farther, "did it rejoice us both" (this Letter is of 29th December; on the 20th February of that year he had been wedded to his Lotte), "this good news of the still-continuing improvement of our dearest Mother! With full soul we both of us join in the thanks which you give to gracious Heaven for this recovery; and our heart now gives way to the fairest hopes that Providence, which herein overtops our expectations, will surely yet prepare a joyful meeting for us all once more."

'Two years afterwards this hope passed into fulfilment. The Mother being now completely cured of her last disorder, there seized her so irresistible a longing for her Son, that even her hesitating Husband, anxious lest her very health should suffer, at last gave his consent to the far and difficult journey to Jena. On the 3d Sept. 1792, Schiller, in joyful humour, announces to his friend in Dresden, "Today I have received from home the very welcome tidings that my good Mother, with one of my Sisters, is to visit us here this month. Her arrival falls at a good time, when I hope to be free and loose from labour; and then we have ahead of us mere joyful undertakings." The Mother came in company with her youngest Daughter, bright little Nane, or Nanette; and surprised him two days sooner than, by the Letters from Solitüde, he had expected her. Unspeakable joy and sweet sorrow seized Mother and Son to feel themselves, after ten years of separation, once more in each other's arms. The long journey, bad weather and roads had done her no harm. "She has altered a little, in truth," writes he to Körner, "from what she was ten years ago; but after so many sicknesses and sorrows, she still has a healthy look. It rejoices me much that things have so come about, that I have her with me again, and can be a joy to her."

'The Mother likewise soon felt herself at home and happy in the trusted circle of her children; only too fast flew-by the beautiful and happy days, which seemed to her richly to make amends for so many years of sorrows and cares. Especially it did her heart good to see for herself what a beneficent influence the real and beautiful womanhood of her Daughter-in-law exercised upon her Son. Daily she learnt to know the great advantages of mind and heart in her; daily she more deeply thanked God that for her Son, who, on account even of his weak health, was not an altogether convenient Husband, there had been so tender-hearted and so finely-cultivated a Wife given him as life-companion. The conviction that the domestic happiness of her Son was secure contributed essentially also to alleviate the pain of departure.

'Still happier days fell to her when Schiller, stirred up by her visit, came the year after, with his Wife, to Swabia; and lived there from August 1793 till May 1794. It was a singular and as if providential circumstance, which did not escape the pious Mother, that Schiller, in the same month in which he had, eleven years ago, hurried and in danger, fled out of Stuttgart to Ludwigsburg, should now in peace and without obstruction come, from Heilbronn by the same Ludwigsburg, to the near neighbourhood of his Parents. With bitter tears of sorrow, her eye had then followed the fugitive, in his dark trouble and want of everything; with sweet tears of joy she now received her fame-crowned Son, whom God, through sufferings and mistakes and wanderings, had led to happiness and wisdom. The birth of the Grandson gave to her life a new charm, as if of youth returned. She felt herself highly favoured that God had spared her life to see her dear Son's first-born with her own eyes. It was a touching spectacle to see the Grandmother as she sat by the cradle of the little "Gold Son," and listened to every breath-drawing of the child; or when, with swelling heart, she watched the approaching steps of her Son, and observed his true paternal pleasure over his first-born.

'Well did the excellent Grandmother deserve such refreshment of heart; for all-too soon there came again upon her troublous and dark days. Schiller had found her stronger and cheerfuler than on her prior visit to Jena; and had quitted his Home-land with the soothing hope that his good Mother would reach a long and happy age. Nor could he have the least presentiment of the events which, three years later, burst-in, desolating and destroying, upon his family, and brought the health and life of his dear Mother again into peril. It is above stated, in our sketch of the Husband, in what extraordinary form the universal public misery, under which, in 1796, all South Germany was groaning, struck the Schiller Family at Solitüde. Already on the 21st March of this year, Schiller had written to his Father, "How grieved I am for our good dear Mother, on whom all manner of sorrows have stormed-down in this manner! But what a mercy of God it is, too, that she still has strength left not to sink under these circumstances, but to be able still to afford you so much help! Who would have thought, six or seven years ago, that she, who was so infirm and exhausted, would now be serving you all as support and nurse? In such traits I recognise a good Providence which watches over us; and my heart is touched by it to the core."

'Meanwhile the poor Mother's situation grew ever frightfuler from day to day; and it needed her extraordinary strength of religious faith to keep her from al-together sinking under the pains, sorrows and toils, which she had for so many weeks to bear all alone, with the help only of a hired maid. The news of such misery threw Schiller into the deepest grief. He saw only one way of sending comfort and help to his poor Mother, and immediately adopted it; writing to his eldest Sister in Meiningen, as follows:

"Thou too wilt have heard, dearest Sister, that Luise has fallen seriously ill; and that our poor dear Mother is thereby robbed of all consolation. If Luise's case were to grow worse, or our Father's even, our poor Mother would be left entirely forsaken. Such misery would be unspeakable. Canst thou make it possible, think'st thou, that thy strength could accomplish such a thing? If so, at once make the journey thither. What it costs I will pay with joy. Reinwald might accompany thee; or, if he did not like that, come over to me here, where I would brother-like take care of him.

"Consider, my dear Sister, that Parents, in such extremity of need, have the justest claim upon their children for help. O God, why am not I myself in such health as in my journey thither three years ago! Nothing should have hindered me from hastening to them; but that I have scarcely gone over the threshold for a year past makes me so weak that I either could not stand the journey, or should fall down into sickness myself in that afflicted house. Alas, I can do nothing for them but help with money; and, God knows, I do that with joy. Consider that our dear Mother, who has held up hitherto with an admirable courage, must at last break down under so many sorrows. I know thy childlike loving heart, I know the perfect fairness and equitable probity of my Brother-in-law. Both these facts will teach you better than I under the circumstances. Salute him cordially.—Thy faithful Brother,

"SCHILLER."

Christophine failed not to go, as we saw above. 'From the time of her arrival there, no week passed without Schiller's writing home; and his Letters much contributed to strengthen and support the heavy-laden Mother. The assurance of being tenderly loved by such a Son was infinitely grateful to her; she considered him as a tried faithful friend, to whom one, without reluctance, yields his part in one's own sorrows. Schiller thus expressed himself on this matter in a Letter to Christophine of 9th May. "The last Letter of my dear good Mother has deeply affected me. Ah, how much has this good Mother already undergone; and with what patience and courage has she borne it! How touching is it that she opened her heart to me; and what woe was mine that I cannot immediately comfort and soothe her! Hadst thou not gone, I could not have stayed here. The situation of our dear ones was horrible; so solitary, without help from loving friends, and as if forsaken by their two children, living far away! I dare not think of it. What did not our good Mother do for *her* Parents; and how greatly has she deserved the like from us! Thou wilt comfort her, dear Sister; and me thou wilt find heartily ready for all that thou canst propose to me. Salute our dear Parents in the tenderest way, and tell them that their Son feels their sorrows."

'The excellent Christophine did her utmost in these days of sorrow. She comforted her Mother, and faithfully nursed her Father to his last breath; nay she saved him and the house, with great presence of mind, on a sudden inburst of French soldiers. Nor did she return to Meiningen till all tumult of affairs was past, and the Mother was again a little composed. And composure the Mother truly needed; for in a short space she had seen a hopeful Daughter and a faithful Husband laid in their graves; and by the death of her Husband a union severed which, originating in mutual affection, had for forty-seven years been blessed with the same mutual feeling. To all which in her position was now added the doubly-pressing care about her future days. Here, however, the Son so dear to her interposed with loving readiness, and the tender manner natural to him:

"You, dear Mother," he writes, "must now choose wholly for yourself what your way of life is to be; and let there be, I charge you, no care about me or others in your choice. Ask yourself where you would like best to live,—here with me, or with Christophine, or in our native country with Luise. Whithersoever your choice falls, there will we provide the means. For the present, of course, in the circumstances given, you would remain in Würtemberg a little while; and in that time all would be arranged. I think you might pass the winter months most easily at Leonberg" (pleasant Village nearest to Solitüde); "and then with the Spring you would come with Luise to Meiningen; where, however, I would expressly advise that you had a household of your own. But of all this, more next time. I would insist upon your coming here to me, if I did not fear things would be too foreign and too unquiet for you. But were you once in Meiningen, we will find means enough to see each other, and to bring your dear Grandchildren to you. It were a great comfort, dearest Mother, at least to know you, for the first three or four weeks after Christophine's departure, among people of your acquaintance; as the sole company of our Luise would too much remind you of times that are gone. But should there be no Pension granted by the Duke, and the Sale of Furniture, &c. did not detain you too long, you might perhaps travel with both the Sisters to Meiningen; and there compose yourself in the new world so much the sooner. All that you need for a convenient life must and shall be yours, dear Mother. It shall be henceforth my care that no anxiety on that head be left you. After so many sorrows, the evening of your life must be rendered cheerful, or at least peaceful; and I hope you will still, in the bosom of your Children and Grandchildren, enjoy many a good day." In conclusion, he bids her send him everything of Letters and MSS. which his dear Father left; hereby to fulfil his last wish; which also shall have its uses to his dear Mother.

'The Widow had a Pension granted by the Duke, of 200 gulden' (near 20*l.*); 'and therein a comfortable proof that official people recognised the worth of her late Husband, and held him in honour. She remained in her native country; and lived the next three years, according to her Son's counsel, with Luise in the little village of Leonberg, near to Solitüde, where an arrangement had been made for her. Here a certain Herr Roos, a native of Würtemberg, had made some acquaintance with her, in the winter 1797-8; to whom we owe the following sketch of portraiture. "She was a still-agreeable old person of sixty-five or six, whose lean wrinkly face still bespoke cheerfulness and kindliness. Her thin hair was all gray; she was of short" (middle) "stature, and her attitude slightly stooping; she had a pleasant tone of voice; and her speech flowed light and cheerful. Her bearing generally showed native grace, and practical acquaintance with social life."

'Towards the end of 1799, there opened to the Mother a new friendly outlook in the marriage of her Luise to the young Parson, M. Frankh, in Clever-Sulzbach, a little town near Heilbronn. The rather as the worthy Son-in-law would on no account have the Daughter separated from the Mother.' Error on Saupe's part. The Mother Schiller continued to occupy her own house at Leonberg till near the end of her life; she naturally made frequent little visits to Clever-Sulzbach; and her death took place there.[60] 'Shortly before the marriage, Schiller wrote, heartily wishing Mother and Sister happiness in this event. It would be no small satisfaction to his Sister, he said, that she could lodge and wait upon her good dear Mother in a well-appointed house of her own; to his Mother also it must be a great comfort to see her children all settled, and to live up again in a new generation.

'Almost contemporary with the removal of the Son from Jena to Weimar was the Mother's with her Daughter to Clever-Sulzbach. The peaceful silence which now environed them in their rural abode had the most salutary influence both on her temper of mind and on her health; all the more as Daughter and Son-in-law vied with each other in respectful attention to her. The considerable distance from her Son, when at times it fell heavy on her, she forgot in reading his Letters; which were ever the unaltered expression of the purest and truest child-love. She forgot it too, as often, over the immortal works out of which his powerful spirit spoke to her. She lived to hear the name of Friedrich Schiller celebrated over all Germany with reverent enthusiasm; and ennobled by the German People sooner and more gloriously than an Imperial Patent could do it. Truly a Mother that has had such joys in her Son is a happy one; and can and may say, "Lord, now let me depart in peace; I have lived enough!"

'In the beginning of the year 1802, Schiller's Mother again fell ill. Her Daughter Luise hastened at once to Stuttgart, where she then chanced to be, and carried her home to Clever-Sulzbach, to be under her own nursing. So soon as Schiller heard of this, he wrote, in well-meant consideration of his Sister's frugal economies, to Dr. Hoven, a friend of his youth at Ludwigsburg; and empowered him to take his Mother over thither, under his own medical care: he, Schiller, would with pleasure pay all that was necessary for lodging and attendance. But the Mother stayed with her Daughter; wrote, however, in her last Letter to Schiller: "Thy unwearied love and care for me God reward with thousandfold love and blessings! Ah me! another such Son there is not in the world!" Schiller, in his continual anxiety about the dear Patient, had his chief solace in knowing her to be in such tender hands; and he wrote at once, withal, to his Sister: "Thou wilt permit me also that on my side I try to do something to lighten these burdens for thee. I therefore make this agreement with my Bookseller Cotta that he shall furnish my dear Mother with the necessary money to make good, in a convenient way, the extra outlays which her illness requires."

'Schiller's hope, supported by earlier experiences, that kind Nature would again help his Mother, did not find fulfilment. On the contrary, her case grew worse; she suffered for months the most violent pains; and was visibly travelling towards Death. Two days before her departure, she had the Medallion of her Son handed down to her from the wall; and pressed it to her heart; and, with tears, thanked God, who had given her such good children. On the 29th April 1802, she passed away, in the 69th year of her age. Schiller, from the tenor of the last news

[60] *Beziehungen*, p. 197, n.

received, had given up all hope; and wrote, in presentiment of the bitter loss, to his Sister Frankh at Clever-Sulzbach:

"Thy last letter, dearest Sister, leaves me without hope of our dear Mother. For a fortnight past I have looked with terror for the tidings of her departure; and the fact that thou hast not written in that time, is a ground of fear, not of comfort. Alas! under her late circumstances, life was no good to her more; a speedy and soft departure was the one thing that could be wished and prayed for. But write me, dear Sister, when thou hast recovered thyself a little from these mournful days. Write me minutely of her condition and her utterances in the last hours of her life. It comforts and composes me to busy myself with her, and to keep the dear image of my Mother living before me.

"And so they are both gone from us, our dear Parents; and we Three alone remain. Let us be all the nearer to each other, dear Sister; and believe always that thy Brother, though so far away from thee and thy Sister, carries you both warmly in his heart; and in all the accidents of this life will eagerly meet you with his brotherly love.

"But I can write no more today. Write me a few words soon. I embrace thee and thy dear Husband with my whole heart; and thank him again for all the love he has shown our departed Mother.

"Your true Brother,
"SCHILLER."

'Soon after this Letter, he received from Frankh, his Brother-in-law, the confirmation of his sad anticipations. From his answer to Frankh we extract the following passage: "May Heaven repay with rich interest the dear Departed One all that she has suffered in life, and done for her children! Of a truth she deserved to have loving children; for she was a good Daughter to her suffering necessitous Parents; and the childlike solicitude she always had for them well deserved the like from us. You, my dear Brother-in-law, have shared the assiduous care of my Sister for Her that is gone; and acquired thereby the justest claim upon my brotherly love. Alas, you had already given your spiritual support and filial service to my late Father, and taken on yourself the duties of his absent Son. How cordially I thank you! Never shall I think of my departed Mother without, at the same time, blessing the memory of him who alleviated so kindly the last days of her life." He then signifies the wish to have, from the effects of his dear Mother, something that, without other worth, will remain a continual memorial of her. And was in effect heartily obliged to his Brother, who sent him a ring which had been hers. "It is the most precious thing that he could have chosen for me," writes he to Luise; "and I will keep it as a sacred inheritance." Painfully had it touched him, withal, that the day of his entering his new house at Weimar had been the death-day of his Mother. He noticed this singular coincidence, as if in mournful presentiment of his own early decease, as a singular concatenation of events by the hand of Destiny.

'A Tree and a plain stone Cross, with the greatly-comprehensive short inscription, "Here rests Schiller's Mother," now mark her grave in Clever-Sulzbach Churchyard.'

III. THE SISTERS.

Saupe has a separate Chapter on each of the three Sisters of Schiller; but most of what concerns them, especially in relation to their Brother, has been introduced incidentally above. Besides which, Saupe's flowing pages are too long for our space; so that instead of translating, henceforth, we shall have mainly to compile from Saupe and others, and faithfully abridge.

Christophine (born 4 Sept. 1757; married 'June 1786;' died 31 August 1847).[61]

Till Schiller's flight, in which what endless interest and industries Christophine had we have already seen, the young girls,—Christophine 25, Luise 16, Nanette a rosy little creature of 5,—had known no misfortune; nor, except Christophine's feelings on the death of the two little Sisters, years ago, no heavy sorrow. At Solitüde, but for the general cloud of anxiety and grief about their loved and gifted Brother and his exile, their lives were of the peaceablest description: diligence in household business, sewing, spinning, contented punctuality in all things; in leisure hours eager reading (or at times, on Christophine's part, drawing and painting, in which she attained considerable excellence), and, as choicest recreation, walks amid the flourishing Nurseries, Tree-avenues, and fine solid industries and forest achievements of Papa. Mention is made of a Cavalry Regiment stationed at Solitüde; the young officers of which, without society in that dull place, and with no employment except parade, were considerably awake to the comely Jungfers Schiller and their promenadings in those pleasant woods: one Lieutenant of them (afterwards a Colonel, 'Obrist von Miller of Stuttgart') is said to have manifested honourable aspirations and intentions towards Christophine,—which, however, and all connection with whom or his comrades, the rigorously prudent Father strictly forbade; his piously obedient Daughters, Christophine it is rather thought with some regret, immediately conforming. A Portrait of this Von Miller, painted by Christophine, still exists, it would appear, among the papers of the Schillers.[62]

The great transaction of her life, her marriage with Reinwald, Court Librarian of Meiningen, had its origin in 1783; the fruit of that forced retreat of Schiller's to Bauerbach, and of the eight months he spent there, under covert, anonymously and in secret, as 'Dr. Ritter,' with Reinwald for his one friend and adviser. Reinwald, who commanded the resources of an excellent Library, and of a sound under-

---

[61] Here, from Schiller Senior himself (*Autobiography*, called *"Curriculum Vitæ,"* in *Beziehungen,* pp. 15-18), is a List of his six Children;—the two that died so young we have marked in italics:

1. 'ELISABETH CHRISTOPHINE FRIEDERICKE, born 4 September 1757, at Marbach.

2. 'JOHANN CHRISTOPH FRIEDRICH, born 10 November 1759, at Marbach.

3. 'LUISE DOROTHEA KATHARINA, born 24 January 1766, at Lorch.

4. '*Maria Charlotte, born 20 November 1768, at Ludwigsburg: died 29 March 1774; age 5 gone.*

5. '*Beata Friedericke, born 4 May 1773, at Ludwigsburg: died 22 December, same year.*

6. 'CAROLINE CHRISTIANE, born 8 September 1777, at Solitüde;'—(this is she they call, in fond diminutive, *Nane* or *Nanette.*)

[62] *Beziehungen,* p. 217 n.

standing, long seriously and painfully cultivated, was of essential use to Schiller; and is reckoned to be the first real guide or useful counsellor he ever had in regard to Literature. One of Christophine's Letters to her Brother, written at her Father's order, fell by accident on Reinwald's floor, and was read by him,—awakening in his over-clouded, heavy-laden mind a gleam of hope and aspiration. "This wise, prudent, loving-hearted and judicious young woman, of such clear and salutary principles of wisdom as to economics too, what a blessing she might be to me as Wife in this dark, lonely home of mine!" Upon which hint he spake; and Schiller, as we saw above, who loved him well, but knew him to be within a year or two of fifty, always ailing in health, taciturn, surly, melancholy, and miserably poor, was rebuked by Papa for thinking it questionable. We said, it came about all the same. Schiller had not yet left Mannheim for the second and last time, when, in 1784, Christophine paid him a visit, escorted thither by Reinwald; who had begged to have that honour allowed him; having been at Solitüde, and, either there or on his road to Mannheim, concluded his affair. Streicher, an eyewitness of this visit, says, "The healthy, cheerful and blooming Maiden had determined to share her future lot with a man whose small income and uncertain health seemed to promise little joy. Nevertheless her reasons were of so noble a sort, that she never repented, in times following, this sacrifice of her fancy to her understanding, and to a Husband of real worth."[63] They were married "June 1786;" and for the next thirty, or indeed, in all, sixty years, Christophine lived in her dark new home at Meiningen; and never, except in that melancholy time of sickness, mortality and war, appears to have seen Native Land and Parents again.

What could have induced, in the calm and well-discerning Christophine, such a resolution, is by no means clear; Saupe, with hesitation, seems to assign a religious motive, "the desire of doing good." Had that abrupt and peremptory dismissal of Lieutenant Miller perhaps something to do with it? Probably her Father's humour on the matter, at all times so anxious and zealous to see his Daughters settled, had a chief effect. It is certain, Christophine consulted her Parish Clergyman on the affair; and got from him, as Saupe shows us, an affirmatory or at least permissive response. Certain also that she summoned her own best insight of all kinds to the subject, and settled it calmly and irrevocably with whatever faculty was in her.

To the candid observer Reinwald's gloomy ways were not without their excuse. Scarcely above once before this, in his now longish life, had any gleam of joy or success shone on him, to cheer the strenuous and never-abated struggle. His father had been Tutor to the Prince of Meiningen, who became Duke afterwards, and always continued to hold him in honour. Father's death had taken place in 1751, young Reinwald then in his fourteenth year. After passing with distinction his three-years curriculum at Jena, Reinwald returned to Meiningen, expecting employment and preferment;—the rather perhaps as his Mother's bit of property got much ruined in the Seven-Years War then raging. Employment Reinwald got, but of the meanest *Kanzlist* (Clerkship) kind; and year after year, in spite of his merits, patient faithfulness and undeniable talent, no preferment whatever.

---

[63] *Schwab*, p. 173, citing Streicher's words.

At length, however, in 1762, the Duke, perhaps enlightened by experience as to Reinwald, or by personal need of such a talent, did send him as *Geheimer Kanzlist* (kind of Private Secretary) to Vienna, with a view to have from him reports "about politics and literary objects" there. This was an extremely enjoyable position for the young man; but it lasted only till the Duke's death, which followed within two years. Reinwald was then immediately recalled by the new Duke (who, I think, had rather been in controversy with his Predecessor), and thrown back to nearly his old position; where, without any regard had to his real talents and merits, he continued thirteen years, under the title of *Consistorial Kanzlist*; and, with the miserablest fraction of yearly pay, 'carried on the slavish, spirit-killing labours required of him.' In 1776,—uncertain whether as promotion or as mere abridgment of labour,—he was placed in the Library as now; that is to say, had become *Sub*-Librarian, at a salary of about 15*l.*, with all the Library duties to do; an older and more favoured gentleman, perhaps in lieu of pension, enjoying the Upper Office, and doing none of the work.

Under these continual pressures and discouragements poor Reinwald's heart had got hardened into mutinous indignation, and his health had broken down: so that, by this time, he was noted in his little world as a solitary, taciturn, morose and gloomy man; but greatly respected by the few who knew him better, as a clear-headed, true and faithful person, much distinguished by intellectual clearness and veracity, by solid scholarly acquirements and sterling worth of character. To bring a little help or cheerful alleviation to such a down-pressed man, if a wise and gentle Christophine could accomplish it, would surely be a bit of well-doing; but it was an extremely difficult one!

The marriage was childless; not, in the first, or in any times of it, to be called unhappy; but, as the weight of years was added, Christophine's problem grew ever more difficult. She was of a compassionate nature, and had a loving, patient and noble heart; prudent she was; the skilfulest and thriftiest of financiers; could well keep silence, too, and with a gentle stoicism endure much small unreason. Saupe says withal, 'Nobody liked a laugh better, or could laugh more heartily than she, even in her extreme old age.'—Christophine herself makes no complaint, on looking back upon her poor Reinwald, thirty years after all was over. Her final record of it is: "for twenty-nine years we lived contentedly together." But her rugged hypochondriac of a Husband, morbidly sensitive to the least interruption of his whims and habitudes, never absent from their one dim sitting-room, except on the days in which he had to attend at the Library, was in practice infinitely difficult to deal with; and seems to have kept her matchless qualities in continual exercise. He belonged to the class called in Germany *Stubengelehrten* (Closet Literary-men), who publish little or nothing that brings them profit, but are continually poring and studying. Study was the one consolation he had in life; and formed his continual employment to the end of his days. He was deep in various departments, Antiquarian, Philological, Historical; deep especially in Gothic philology, in which last he did what is reckoned a real feat,—he, Reinwald, though again it was another who got the reward. He had procured somewhere, 'a Transcript of the famous Anglo-Saxon Poem *Heliand* (Saviour) from the Cotton Library in England,' this he, with unwearied labour and to great perfection, had at last got ready for the press; Translation, Glossary, Original all in readiness;—but could find no Publisher, nobody that would print without a premium. Not to earn *less* than nothing by his labour, he sent the Work to the München Library; where, in after years, one Schmeller found it, and used it for an *editio princeps* of his own. *Sic vos non vobis;* heavy-laden Reinwald![64] —

To Reinwald himself Christophine's presence and presidency in his dim household were an infinite benefit,—though not much recognised by him, but accepted rather as a natural tribute due to unfortunate down-pressed worth, till towards the very end, when the singular merit of it began to dawn upon him, like the brightness of the Sun when it is setting. Poor man, he anxiously spent the last two weeks of his life in purchasing and settling about a neat little cottage for Christophine; where accordingly she passed her long widowhood, on stiller terms, though not on less beneficent and humbly beautiful, than her marriage had offered.

Christophine, by pious prudence, faith in Heaven, and in the good fruits of real goodness even on Earth, had greatly comforted the gloomy, disappointed, pain-stricken man; enlightened his darkness, and made his poverty noble. *Simplex munditiis* might have been her motto in all things. Her beautiful Letters to her Brother are full of cheerful, though also, it is true, sad enough, allusions to her difficulties with Reinwald, and partial successes. Poor soul, her hopes, too, are gently turned sometimes on a blessed future, which might still lie ahead: of her at last coming, as a Widow, to live with her Brother, in serene affection, like that of their childhood together; in a calm blessedness such as the world held no other for her! But gloomy Reinwald survived bright Schiller for above ten years; and she had thirty more of lone widowhood, under limited conditions, to spend after him, still in a noble, humbly-admirable, and even happy and contented manner. She was the flower of the Schiller Sisterhood, though all three are beautiful to us; and in poor Nane, there is even something of poetic, and tragically pathetic. For one blessing, Christophine 'lived almost always in good health.' Through life it may be said of her, she was helpful to all about her, never hindersome to any; and merited, and had, the universal esteem, from high and low, of those she had lived among. At Meiningen, 31st August 1847, within a few days of her ninety-first year, without almost one day's sickness, a gentle stroke of apoplexy took her suddenly away, and so ended what may be called a *Secular* Saintlike existence, mournfully beautiful, wise and noble to all that had beheld it.

Nanette (born 8th September 1777, died 23d March 1796; age not yet 19).

Of Nanette we were told how, in 1792, she charmed her Brother and his Jena circle, by her recitations and her amiable enthusiastic nature; and how, next year, on Schiller's Swabian visit, his love of her grew to something of admiration, and practical hope of helping such a rich talent and noble heart into some clear development,—when, two years afterwards, death put, to the dear Nanette and his hopes about her, a cruel end. We are now to give the first budding-out of those fine talents and tendencies of poor Nanette, and that is all the history the dear little

[64] *Schiller's Beziehungen* (where many of Christophine's *Letters*, beautiful all of them, are given).

Being has. Saupe proceeds:

'Some two years after Schiller's flight, Nanette as a child of six or seven had, with her elder Sister Luise, witnessed the first representation of Schiller's *Kabale und Liebe* in the Stuttgart theatre. With great excitement, and breath held-in, she had watched the rolling-up of the curtain; and during the whole play no word escaped her lips; but the excited glance of her eyes, and her heightened colour, from act to act, testified her intense emotion. The stormy applause with which her Brother's Play was received by the audience made an indelible impression on her.

'The Players, in particular, had shone before her as in a magic light; the splendour of which, in the course of years, rather increased than diminished. The child's bright fancy loved to linger on those never-to-be-forgotten people, by whom her Brother's Poem had been led into her sight and understanding. The dawning thought, how glorious it might be to work such wonders herself, gradually settled, the more she read and heard of her dear Brother's poetic achievements, into the ardent but secret wish of being herself able to represent his Tragedies upon the stage. On her visit to Jena, and during her Brother's abode in Swabia, she was never more attentive than when Schiller spoke occasionally of the acting of his Pieces, or unfolded his opinion of the Player's Art.

'The wish of Nanette, secretly nourished in this manner, to be able, on the stage, which represents the world, to contribute to the glory of her Brother, seized her now after his return with such force and constancy, that Schiller's Sister-in-law, Caroline von Wolzogen, urged him to yield to the same; to try his Sister's talent; and if it was really distinguished, to let her enter this longed-for career. Schiller had no love for the Player Profession; but as, in his then influential connections in Weimar, he might steer clear of many a danger, he promised to think the thing over. And thus this kind and amiable protectress had the satisfaction of cheering Nanette's last months with the friendly prospect that her wishes might be fulfilled.—Schiller's hope, after a dialogue with Goethe on the subject, had risen to certainty, when with the liveliest sorrow he learnt that Nanette was ill of that contagious Hospital Fever, and, in a few days more, that she was gone forever.'[65]

Beautiful Nanette; with such a softly-glowing soul, and such a brief tragically-beautiful little life! Like a Daughter of the rosy-fingered Morn; her existence all a sun-gilt soft auroral cloud, and no sultry Day, with its dusts and disfigurements, permitted to follow. Father Schiller seems, in his rugged way, to have loved Nanette best of them all; in an embarrassed manner, we find him more than once recommending her to Schiller's help, and intimating what a glorious thing for her, were it a possible one, education might be. He followed her in few months to her long home; and, by his own direction, 'was buried in the Churchyard at Gerlingen by her side.'

Luise (born 24th January 1766; married 20th October 1799; died 14th September 1836).

Of Luise's life too, except what was shown above, there need little be said. In the dismal pestilential days at Solitüde, while her Father lay dying, and poor Nanette caught the infection, Luise, with all her tender assiduities and household

[65] *Saupe,* pp. 150-5.

talent, was there; but, soon after Nanette's death, the fever seized her too; and she long lay dangerously ill in that forlorn household; still weak, but slowly recovering, when Christophine arrived.

The Father, a short while before his death, summoned to him that excellent young Clergyman, Frankh, who had been so unweariedly kind to them in this time of sickness when all neighbours feared to look in, To ask him what his intentions towards Luise were. It was in presence of the good old man that they made solemn promise to each other; and at Leonberg, where thenceforth the now-widowed Mother's dwelling was, they were formally betrothed; and some two years after that were married.

Her Mother's death, so tenderly watched over, took place at their Parsonage at Clever-Sulzbach, as we saw above. Frankh, about two years after, was promoted to a better living, Möckmühl by name; and lived there, a well-doing and respected Parson, till his death, in 1834; which Luise's followed in September of the second year afterwards. Their marriage lasted thirty-five years. Luise had brought him three children; and seems to have been, in all respects, an excellent Wife. She was ingenious in intellectuals as well as economics; had a taste for poetry; a boundless enthusiasm for her Brother; seems to have been an anxious Mother, often ailing herself but strenuously doing her best at all times.

A touching memorial of Luise is Schiller's last Letter to her, Letter of affectionate apology for long silence, — apology, and hope of doing better, — written only a few weeks before his own death. It is as follows:

"Weimar, 27th March 1805.

"Yes, it is a long time indeed, good dear Luise, since I have written to thee; but it was not for amusements that I forgot thee; it was because in this time I have had so many hard illnesses to suffer, which put me altogether out of my regular way; for many months I had lost all courage and cheerfulness, and given up all hope of my recovery. In such a humour one does not like to speak; and since then, on feeling myself again better, there was, after the long silence, a kind of embarrassment; and so it was still put off. But now, when I have been anew encouraged by thy sisterly love, I gladly join the thread again; and it shall, if God will, not again be broken.

"Thy dear Husband's promotion to Möckmühl, which I learned eight days ago from our Sister" (Christophine), "has given us great joy, not only because it so much improves your position, but also because it is so honourable a testimony for my dear Brother-in-law's deserts. May you feel yourselves right happy in these new relations, and right long enjoy them! We too are got thereby a few miles nearer you; and on a future journey to Franconia, which we are every year projecting, we may the more easily get over to you.

"How sorry am I, dear Sister, that thy health has suffered so much; and that thou wert again so unfortunate with thy confinement! Perhaps your new situation might permit you, this summer, to visit some tonic watering-place, which might do thee a great deal of good."—

"Of our Family here, my Wife will write thee more at large. Our Children, this winter, have all had chicken-pox; and poor little Emilie" (a babe of four months) "had much to suffer in the affair. Thank God, things are all come round with us again, and my own health too begins to confirm itself.

"A thousand times I embrace thee, dear Sister, and my dear Brother-in-law as well, whom I always wish from the heart to have more acquaintance with. Kiss thy Children in my name; may all go right happily with you, and much joy be in store! How would our dear Parents have rejoiced in your good fortune; and especially our dear Mother, had she been spared to see it! Adieu, dear Luise. With my whole soul,

"Thy faithful Brother,

"SCHILLER."

Schiller's tone and behaviour to his Sisters is always beautifully human and brotherlike, as here. Full of affection, sincerity and the warmest truest desire to help and cheer. The noble loving Schiller; so mindful always of the lowly, from his own wildly-dangerous and lofty path! He was never rich, poor rather always; but of a spirit royally munificent in these respects; never forgets the poor "birthdays" of his Sisters, whom one finds afterwards gratefully recognising their "beautiful dress" or the like!—

Of date some six weeks after this Letter to Luise, let us take from Eyewitnesses one glimpse of Schiller's own deathbed. It is the eighth day of his illness; his last day but one in this world:

'*Morning of 8th May 1805.*— —Schiller, on awakening from sleep, asked to see his youngest Child. The Baby' Emilie, spoken of above, 'was brought. He turned his head round; took the little hand in his, and, with an inexpressible look of love and sorrow, gazed into the little face; then burst into bitter weeping, hid his face among the pillows; and made a sign to take the child away.'—This little Emilie is now the Baroness von Gleichen, Co-editress with her Cousin Wolzogen of the clear and useful Book, *Beziehungen*, often quoted above. It was to that same Cousin Wolzogen's Mother (Caroline von Wolzogen, Authoress of the Biography), and in the course of this same day, that Schiller made the memorable response, "Calmer, and calmer."—'Towards evening he asked to see the Sun once more. The curtain was opened; with bright eyes and face he gazed into the beautiful sunset. It was his last farewell to Nature.

'*Thursday 9th May.* All the morning, his mind was wandering; he spoke incoherent words, mostly in Latin. About three in the afternoon, complete weakness came on; his breathing began to be interrupted. About four, he asked for naphtha, but the last syllable died on his tongue. He tried to write, but produced only three letters; in which, however, the character of his hand was still visible. Till towards six, no change. His Wife was kneeling at the bedside; he still pressed her offered hand. His Sister-in-law stood, with the Doctor, at the foot of the bed, and laid warm pillows on his feet, which were growing cold. There now darted, as it were, an electrical spasm over all his countenance; the head sank back; the profoundest repose transfigured his face. His features were as those of one softly sleeping,'—wrapt in hard-won Victory and Peace forevermore![66]—

---

[66] *Schwab*, p. 627, citing Voss, an eyewitness; and Caroline von Wolzogen herself.

APPENDIX I.

NO. 1. DANIEL SCHUBART.

THE enthusiastic discontent so manifest in the *Robbers* has by some been in part attributed to Schiller's intercourse with Schubart. This seems as wise as the hypothesis of Gray's Alderman, who, after half a century of turtle-soup, imputed the ruin of his health to eating two unripe grapes: 'he felt them cold upon his stomach, the moment they were over; he never got the better of them.' Schiller, it appears, saw Schubart only once, and their conversation was not of a confidential kind. For any influence this interview could have produced upon the former, the latter could have merited no mention here: it is on other grounds that we refer to him. Schubart's history, not devoid of interest in itself, unfolds in a striking light the circumstances under which Schiller stood at present; and may serve to justify the violence of his alarms, which to the happy natives of our Island might otherwise appear pusillanimous and excessive. For these reasons we subjoin a sketch of it.

Schubart's character is not a new one in literature; nor is it strange that his life should have been unfortunate. A warm genial spirit; a glowing fancy, and a friendly heart; every faculty but diligence, and every virtue but 'the understrapping virtue of discretion:' such is frequently the constitution of the poet; the natural result of it also has frequently been pointed out, and sufficiently bewailed. This man was one of the many who navigate the ocean of life with 'more sail than ballast;' his voyage contradicted every rule of seamanship, and necessarily ended in a wreck.

Christian Friedrich Daniel Schubart was born at Obersontheim in Swabia, on the 26th of April 1739. His father, a well-meaning soul, officiated there in the multiple capacity of schoolmaster, precentor, and curate; dignities which, with various mutations and improvements, he subsequently held in several successive villages of the same district. Daniel, from the first, was a thing of inconsistencies; his life proceeded as if by fits and starts. At school, for a while, he lay dormant: at the age of seven he could not read, and had acquired the reputation of a perfect dunce. But 'all at once,' says his biographer, 'the rind which enclosed his spirit started asunder;' and Daniel became the prodigy of the school! His good father determined to make a learned man of him: he sent him at the age of fourteen to the Nordlingen Lyceum, and two years afterwards to a similar establishment at Nürnberg. Here Schubart began to flourish with all his natural luxuriance; read classical and domestic poets; spouted, speculated; wrote flowing songs; discovered 'a decided turn for music,' and even composed tunes for the harpsichord! In short, he became an acknowledged *genius*: and his parents consented that he should go to Jena, and perform his *cursus* of Theology.

Schubart's purposes were not at all like the decrees of Fate: he set out towards Jena; and on arriving at Erlangen, resolved to proceed no farther, but perform his *cursus* where he was. For a time he studied well; but afterwards 'tumultuously,' that is, in violent fits, alternating with fits as violent of idleness and debauchery. He became a *Bursche* of the first water; drank and declaimed, rioted and ran in debt; till his parents, unable any longer to support such expenses, were glad to seize the first opening in his *cursus*, and recall him. He returned to them with a mind fevered by intemperance, and a constitution permanently injured; his heart burning with regret, and vanity, and love of pleasure; his head without habits of activity or principles of judgment, a whirlpool where fantasies and hallucinations and 'fragments of science' were chaotically jumbled to and fro. But he could babble college-latin; and talk with a trenchant tone about the 'revolutions of Philosophy.' Such accomplishments procured him pardon from his parents: the precentorial spirit of his father was more than reconciled on discovering that Daniel could also preach and play upon the organ. The good old people still loved their prodigal, and would not cease to hope in him.

As a preacher Schubart was at first very popular; he imitated Cramer; but at the same time manifested first-rate pulpit talents of his own. These, however, he entirely neglected to improve: presuming on his gifts and their acceptance, he began to 'play such fantastic tricks before high Heaven,' as made his audience sink to yawning, or explode in downright laughter. He often preached extempore; once he preached in verse! His love of company and ease diverted him from study: his musical propensities diverted him still farther. He had special gifts as an organist; but to handle the concordance and to make 'the heaving bellows learn to blow' were inconsistent things.

Yet withal it was impossible to hate poor Schubart, or even seriously to dislike him. A joyful, piping, guileless mortal, good nature, innocence of heart, and love of frolic beamed from every feature of his countenance; he wished no ill to any son of Adam. He was musical and poetical, a maker and a singer of sweet songs; humorous also, speculative, discursive; his speech, though aimless and redundant, glittered with the hues of fancy, and here and there with the keenest rays of intellect. He was vain, but had no touch of pride; and the excellencies which he loved in himself, he acknowledged and as warmly loved in others. He was a man of few or no principles, but his nervous system was very good. Amid his chosen comrades, a jug of indifferent beer and a pipe of tobacco could change the earth into elysium for him, and make his brethren demigods. To look at his laughing eyes, and his effulgent honest face, you were tempted to forget that he was a perjured priest, that the world had duties for him which he was neglecting. Had life been all a may-game, Schubart was the best of men, and the wisest of philosophers.

Unluckily it was not: the voice of Duty had addressed him in vain; but that of Want was more impressive. He left his father's house, and engaged himself as tutor in a family at Königsbronn. To teach the young idea how to shoot had few delights for Schubart: he soon gave up this place in favour of a younger brother; and endeavoured to subsist, for some time, by affording miscellaneous assistance to the clergy of the neighbouring villages. Ere long, preferring even pedagogy to starvation, he again became a teacher. The bitter morsel was sweetened with a seasoning of music; he was appointed not only schoolmaster but also organist of Geisslingen. A fit of diligence now seized him: his late difficulties had impressed him; and the parson of the place, who subsequently married Schubart's sister, was friendly and skilful enough to turn the impression to account. Had poor Schubart always been in such hands, the epithet 'poor' could never have belonged to him. In this little village-school he introduced some important reforms and improvements, and in consequence attracted several valuable scholars. Also for his own behoof, he studied honestly. His conduct here, if not irreprehensible, was at least very much amended. His marriage, in his twenty-fifth year, might have improved it still farther; for his wife was a good, soft-hearted, amiable creature, who loved him with her whole heart, and would have died to serve him.

But new preferments awaited Schubart, and with them new temptations. His fame as a musician was deservedly extending: in time it reached Ludwigsburg, and the Grand Duke of Würtemberg himself heard Schubart spoken of! The schoolmaster of Geisslingen was, in 1768, promoted to be organist and band-director in this gay and pompous court. With a bounding heart, he tossed away his ferula, and hastened to the scene, where joys for evermore seemed calling on him. He plunged into the heart of business and amusement. Besides the music which he taught and played, publicly and privately, with great applause, he gave the military officers instruction in various branches of science; he talked and feasted; he indited songs and rhapsodies; he lectured on History and the Belles Lettres. All this was more than Schubart's head could stand. In a little time he fell in debt; took up with virtuosi; began to read Voltaire, and talk against religion in his drink. From the rank of genius, he was fast degenerating into that of profligate: his affairs grew more and more embarrassed; and he had no gift of putting any order in them. Prudence was not one of Schubart's virtues; the nearest approximation he could make to it was now and then a little touch of cunning. His wife still loved him; loved him with that perverseness of affection, which increases in the inverse ratio of its requital: she had long patiently endured his follies and neglect, happy if she could obtain a transient hour of kindness from him. But his endless course of riot, and the straits to which it had reduced their hapless family, at length overcame her spirits: she grew melancholy, almost broken-hearted; and her father took her home to him, with her children, from the spendthrift who had been her ruin. Schubart's course in Ludwigsburg was verging to its close; his extravagance increased, and debts pressed heavier and heavier on him: for some scandal with a young woman of the place, he was cast into prison; and let out of it, with an injunction forthwith to quit the dominions of the Grand Duke.

Forlorn and homeless, here then was Schubart footing the hard highway, with a staff in his hand, and one solitary *thaler* in his purse, not knowing whither he should go. At Heilbronn, the Bürgermeister Wachs permitted him to teach his Bürgermeisterinn the harpsichord; and Schubart did not die of hunger. For a space of time he wandered to and fro, with numerous impracticable plans; now talking for his victuals; now lecturing or teaching music; kind people now attracted to him by his genius and misfortunes, and anon repelled from him by the faults which had abased him. Once a gleam of court-preferment revisited his path: the Elector Palatine was made acquainted with his gifts, and sent for him to Schwetzingen to play before him. His playing gratified the Electoral ear; he would have been provided for, had he not in conversation with his Highness happened to express a rather free opinion of the Mannheim Academy, which at that time was his Highness's hobby. On the instant of this luckless oversight, the door of patronage was slammed in Schubart's face, and he stood solitary on the pavement as before.

One Count Schmettau took pity on him; offered him his purse and home; both of which the way-worn wanderer was happy to accept. At Schmettau's he fell in with Baron Leiden, the Bavarian envoy, who advised him to turn Catholic, and accompany the returning embassy to Munich. Schubart hesitated to become a renegade; but departed with his new patron, upon trial. In the way, he played before the Bishop of Würzburg; was rewarded by his Princely Reverence with gold as well as praise; and arrived under happy omens at Munich. Here for a while fortune seemed to smile on him again. The houses of the great were thrown open to him; he talked and played, and fared sumptuously every day. He took serious counsel with himself about the great Popish question; now inclining this way, now that: he was puzzling which to choose, when Chance entirely relieved him of the trouble. 'A person of respectability' in Munich wrote to Würtemberg to make inquiries who or what this general favourite was; and received for answer, that the general favourite was a villain, and had been banished from Ludwigsburg for denying that there was a Holy Ghost!—Schubart was happy to evacuate Munich without tap of drum.

Once more upon the road without an aim, the wanderer turned to Augsburg, simply as the nearest city, and—set up a Newspaper! The *Deutsche Chronik* flourished in his hands; in a little while it had acquired a decided character for sprightliness and talent; in time it became the most widely circulated journal of the country. Schubart was again a prosperous man: his writings, stamped with the vigorous impress of his own genius, travelled over Europe; artists and men of letters gathered round him; he had money, he had fame; the rich and noble threw their parlours open to him, and listened with delight to his overflowing, many-coloured conversation. He wrote paragraphs and poetry; he taught music and gave concerts; he set up a spouting establishment, recited newly-published poems, read Klopstock's *Messias* to crowded and enraptured audiences. Schubart's evil genius seemed asleep, but Schubart himself awoke it. He had borne a grudge against the clergy, ever since his banishment from Ludwigsburg; and he now employed the facilities of his journal for giving vent to it. He criticised the priesthood of Augsburg; speculated on their selfishness and cant, and took every opportunity of turning them and their proceedings into ridicule. The Jesuits especially, whom he regarded as a fallen body, he treated with extreme freedom; exposing their deceptions, and holding up to public contumely certain quacks whom they patronised. The Jesuitic Beast was prostrate, but not dead: it had still strength enough to lend a dangerous kick to any one who came too near it. One evening an official person waited upon Schubart, and mentioned an *arrest* by virtue of a warrant from the Catholic Bürgermeister! Schubart was obliged to go to prison. The heads of the

Protestant party made an effort in his favour: they procured his liberty, but not without a stipulation that he should immediately depart from Augsburg. Schubart asked to know his crime; but the Council answered him: "We have our reasons; let that satisfy you:" and with this very moderate satisfaction he was forced to leave their city.

But Schubart was now grown an adept in banishment; so trifling an event could not unhinge his equanimity. Driven out of Augsburg, the philosophic editor sought refuge in Ulm, where the publication of his journal had, for other reasons, already been appointed to take place. The *Deutsche Chronik* was as brilliant here as ever: it extended more and more through Germany; 'copies of it even came to London, Paris, Amsterdam, and Petersburg.' Nor had its author's fortune altered much; he had still the same employments, and remunerations, and extravagances; the same sort of friends, the same sort of enemies. The latter were a little busier than formerly: they propagated scandals; engraved caricatures, indited lampoons against him; but this he thought a very small matter. A man that has been three or four times banished, and as often put in prison, and for many years on the point of starving, will not trouble himself much about a gross or two of pasquinades. Schubart had his wife and family again beside him, he had money also to support them; so he sang and fiddled, talked and wrote, and 'built the lofty rhyme,' and cared no fig for any one.

But enemies, more fell than these, were lurking for the thoughtless Man of Paragraphs. The Jesuits had still their feline eyes upon him, and longed to have their talons in his flesh. They found a certain General Ried, who joined them on a quarrel of his own. This General Ried, the Austrian Agent at Ulm, had vowed inexpiable hatred against Schubart, it would seem, for a very slight cause indeed: once Schubart had engaged to play before him, and then finding that the harpsichord was out of order, had refused, flatly refused! The General's elevated spirit called for vengeance on this impudent plebeian; the Jesuits encouraged him; and thus all lay in eager watch. An opportunity ere long occurred. One week in 1778, there appeared in Schubart's newspaper an Extract of a Letter from Vienna, stating that 'the Empress Maria Theresa had been struck by apoplexy.' On reading which, the General made instant application to his Ducal Highness, requesting that the publisher of this 'atrocious libel' should be given up to him and 'sent to expiate his crime in Hungary,' by imprisonment—for life. The Duke desired his gallant friend to be at ease, for that *he* had long had his own eye on this man, and would himself take charge of him. Accordingly, a few days afterwards, Herr von Scholl, Comptroller of the Convent of Blaubeuren, came to Schubart with a multitude of compliments, inviting him to dinner, "as there was a stranger wishing to be introduced to him." Schubart sprang into the *Schlitten* with this wolf in sheep's clothing, and away they drove to Blaubeuren. Arrived here, the honourable Herr von Scholl left him in a private room, and soon returned with a posse of official Majors and Amtmen, the chief of whom advanced to Schubart, and declared him—*an arrested man!* The hapless Schubart thought it was a jest; but alas here was no jesting! Schubart then said with a composure scarcely to be looked for, that "he hoped the Duke would not condemn him unheard." In this too he was deceived; the men of office made him mount a carriage with them, and set off without delay for Hohenasperg. The Duke himself was there with his Duchess, when these bloodhounds and their prey arrived: the princely couple gazed from a window as the group went past them, and a fellow-creature took his farewell look of sun and sky!

If hitherto the follies of this man have cast an air of farce upon his sufferings, even when in part unmerited, such sentiments must now give place to that of indignation at his cruel and cold-blooded persecutors. Schubart, who never had the heart to hurt a fly, and with all his indiscretions, had been no man's enemy but his own, was conducted to a narrow subterraneous dungeon, and left, without book or pen, or any sort of occupation or society, to chew the cud of bitter thought, and count the leaden months as they passed over him, and brought no mitigation of his misery. His Serene Transparency of Würtemberg, nay the heroic General himself, might have been satisfied, could they have seen him: physical squalor, combined with moral agony, were at work on Schubart; at the end of a year, he was grown so weak, that he could not stand except by leaning on the walls of his cell. A little while, and he bade fair to get beyond the reach of all his tyrants. This, however, was not what they wanted. The prisoner was removed to a wholesome upper room; allowed the use of certain books, the sight of certain company, and had, at least, the privilege to think and breathe without obstruction. He was farther gratified by hearing that his wife and children had been treated kindly: the boys had been admitted to the Stuttgard school, where Schiller was now studying; to their mother there had been assigned a pension of two hundred gulden. Charles of Würtemberg was undoubtedly a weak and heartless man, but we know not that he was a savage one: in the punishment of Schubart, it is possible enough that he believed himself to be discharging an important duty to the world. The only subject of regret is, that any duty to the world, beyond the duty of existing inoffensively, should be committed to such hands; that men like Charles and Ried, endowed with so very small a fraction of the common faculties of manhood, should have the destiny of any living thing at their control.

Another mitigating circumstance in Schubart's lot was the character of his gaoler. This humane person had himself tasted the tender mercies of 'paternal' government; he knew the nature of a dungeon better even than his prisoner. 'For four years,' we are told, 'he had seen no human face; his scanty food had been lowered to him through a trap-door; neither chair nor table were allowed him, his cell was never swept, his beard and nails were left to grow, the humblest conveniences of civilised humanity were denied him!'[67] On this man affliction had produced its softening, not its hardening influence: he had grown religious, and merciful in heart; he studied to alleviate Schubart's hard fate by every means within his power. He spoke comfortingly to him; ministered to his infirmities, and, in spite of orders, lent him all his books. These, it is true, were only treatises on theosophy and mystical devotion; but they were the best he had; and to Schubart, in his first lonely dungeon, they afforded occupation and solace.

---

[67] And yet Mr. Fox is reported to have said: *There was one* FREE *Government on the Continent, and that one was — Würtemberg.* They had a parliament and 'three estates' like the English. — So much for paper Constitutions!

Human nature will accommodate itself to anything. The King of Pontus taught himself to eat poison: Schubart, cut out from intemperance and jollity, did not pine away in confinement and abstemiousness; he had lost Voltaire and gay company, he found delight in solitude and Jacob Böhm. Nature had been too good to him to let his misery in any case be unalloyed. The vague unguided ebullience of spirit, which had so often set the table in a roar, and made him the most fascinating of debauchees, was now mellowed into a cloudy enthusiasm, the sable of which was still copiously blended with rainbow colours. His brain had received a slight though incurable crack; there was a certain exasperation mixed with his unsettled fervour; but he was not wretched, often even not uncomfortable. His religion was not real; but it had reality enough for present purposes; he was at once a sceptic and a mystic, a true disciple of Böhm as well as of Voltaire. For afflicted, irresolute, imaginative men like Schubart, this is not a rare or altogether ineffectual resource: at the bottom of their minds they doubt or disbelieve, but their hearts exclaim against the slightest whisper of it; they dare not look into the fathomless abyss of Infidelity, so they cover it over with the dense and strangely-tinted smoke of Theosophy. Schubart henceforth now and then employed the phrases and figures of religion; but its principles had made no change in his theory of human duties: it was not food to strengthen the weakness of his spirit, but an opiate to stay its craving.

Schubart had still farther resources: like other great men in captivity, he set about composing the history of his life. It is true, he had no pens or paper; but this could not deter him. A fellow-prisoner, to whom, as he one day saw him pass by the grating of his window, he had communicated his desire, entered eagerly into the scheme: the two contrived to unfasten a stone in a wall that divided their apartments; when the prison-doors were bolted for the night, this volunteer amanuensis took his place, Schubart trailed his mattress to the friendly orifice, and there lay down, and dictated in whispers the record of his fitful story. These memoirs have been preserved; they were published and completed by a son of Schubart's: we have often wished to see them, but in vain.

By day, Schubart had liberty to speak with certain visitors. One of these, as we have said above, was Schiller. That Schubart, in their single interview, was pleased with the enthusiastic friendly boy, we could have conjectured, and he has himself informed us. 'Excepting Schiller,' said the veteran garreteer, in writing afterwards to Gleim, 'I scarcely know of any German youth in whom the sacred spark of genius has mounted up within the soul like flame upon the altar of a Deity. We are fallen into the shameful times, when women bear rule over men; and make the toilet a tribunal before which the most gigantic minds must plead. Hence the stunted spirit of our poets; hence the dwarf products of their imagination; hence the frivolous witticism, the heartless sentiment, crippled and ricketed by soups, ragouts and sweetmeats, which you find in fashionable balladmongers.'

Time and hours wear out the roughest day. The world began to feel an interest in Schubart, and to take some pity on him: his songs and poems were collected and published; their merit and their author's misery exhibited a shocking contrast. His Highness of Würtemberg at length condescended to remember that a mortal, of wants and feelings like his own, had been forced by him to spend, in sorrow and inaction, the third part of an ordinary lifetime; to waste, and worse than waste, ten years of precious time; time, of which not all the dukes and princes in the universe could give him back one instant. He commanded Schubart to be liberated; and the rejoicing Editor (unacquitted, unjudged, unaccused!) once more beheld the blue zenith and the full ring of the horizon. He joined his wife at Stuttgard, and recommenced his newspaper. The *Deutsche Chronik* was again popular; the notoriety of its conductor made amends for the decay which critics did not fail to notice in his faculties. Schubart's sufferings had in fact permanently injured him; his mind was warped and weakened by theosophy and solitude; bleak northern vapours often flitted over it, and chilled its tropical luxuriance. Yet he wrote and rhymed; discoursed on the corruption of the times, and on the means of their improvement. He published the first portion of his Life, and often talked amazingly about the Wandering Jew, and a romance of which he was to form the subject. The idea of making old *Joannes a temporibus*, the 'Wandering,' or as Schubart's countrymen denominate him the 'Eternal Jew,' into a novel hero, was a mighty favourite with him. In this antique cordwainer, as on a raft at anchor in the stream of time, he would survey the changes and wonders of two thousand years: the Roman and the Arab were to figure there; the Crusader and the Circumnavigator, the Eremite of the Thebaid and the Pope of Rome. Joannes himself, the Man existing out of Time and Space, Joannes the unresting and undying, was to be a deeply tragic personage. Schubart warmed himself with this idea; and talked about it in his cups, to the astonishment of simple souls. He even wrote a certain rhapsody connected with it, which is published in his poems. But here he rested; and the project of the Wandering Jew, which Goethe likewise meditated in his youth, is still unexecuted. Goethe turned to other objects: and poor Schubart was surprised by death, in the midst of his schemes, on the 10th of October 1791.

Of Schubart's character as a man, this record of his life leaves but a mean impression. Unstable in his goings, without principle or plan, he flickered through existence like an *ignis-fatuus*; now shooting into momentary gleams of happiness and generosity, now quenched in the mephitic marshes over which his zig-zag path conducted him. He had many amiable qualities, but scarcely any moral worth. From first to last his circumstances were against him; his education was unfortunate, its fluctuating aimless wanderings enhanced its ill effects. The thrall of the passing moment, he had no will; the fine endowments of his heart were left to riot in chaotic turbulence, and their forces cancelled one another. With better models and advisers, with more rigid habits, and a happier fortune, he might have been an admirable man: as it is, he is far from admirable.

The same defects have told with equal influence on his character as a writer. Schubart had a quick sense of the beautiful, the moving, and the true; his nature was susceptible and fervid; he had a keen intellect, a fiery imagination; and his 'iron memory' secured forever the various produce of so many gifts. But he had no diligence, no power of self-denial. His knowledge lay around him like the plunder of a sacked city. Like this too, it was squandered in pursuit of casual objects. He wrote in gusts; the *labor limæ et mora* was a thing he did not know. Yet his writings have great merit. His newspaper essays abound in happy illustration and brilliant careless thought. His songs, excluding those of a devotional and theosophic cast, are often full of nature, heartiness and true simplicity. 'From his youth upwards,' we are told, 'he studied the true Old-German *Volkslied*; he watched the artisan on the street, the craftsman in his workshop, the soldier in his guardhouse, the maid by the spinning-wheel; and transferred the genuine spirit of primeval Germanism, which he found in them, to his own songs.' Hence their popularity, which many of them still retain. 'In his larger lyrical pieces,' observes the same not injudicious critic, 'we discover fearless singularity; wild imagination, dwelling rather on the grand and frightful than on the beautiful and soft; deep, but seldom long-continued feeling; at times far-darting thoughts, original images, stormy vehemence; and generally a glowing, self-created, figurative diction. He never wrote to show his art; but poured forth, from the inward call of his nature, the thought or feeling which happened for the hour to have dominion in him.'[68]

Such were Schubart and his works and fortunes; the *disjecta membra* of a richly-gifted but ill-starred and infatuated poet! The image of his persecutions added speed to Schiller's flight from Stuttgard; may the image of his wasted talents and ineffectual life add strength to our resolves of living otherwise!

---

[68] *Jördens Lexicon*: from which most part of the above details are taken. — There exists now a decidedly compact, intelligent and intelligible *Life of Schubart*, done, in three little volumes, by Strauss, some years ago. (*Note of* 1857.)

NO. 2. LETTERS OF SCHILLER.

A few Extracts from Schiller's correspondence may be gratifying to some readers. The *Letters to Dalberg*, which constitute the chief part of it as yet before the public, are on the whole less interesting than might have been expected, if we did not recollect that the writer of them was still an inexperienced youth, overawed by his idea of Dalberg, to whom he could communicate with freedom only on a single topic; and besides oppressed with grievances, which of themselves would have weighed down his spirit, and prevented any frank or cordial exposition of its feelings.

Of the Reichsfreiherr von Dalberg himself, this correspondence gives us little information, and we have gleaned little elsewhere. He is mentioned incidentally in almost every literary history connected with his time; and generally as a mild gentlemanly person, a judicious critic, and a warm lover of the arts and their cultivators. The following notice of his death is extracted from the *Conversations-Lexicon*, Part III. p. 12: 'Died at Mannheim, on the 27th of December 1806, in his 85th year, Wolfgang Heribert, Reichsfreiherr von Dalberg; knighted by the Emperor Leopold on his coronation at Frankfort. A warm friend and patron of the arts and sciences; while the German Society flourished at Mannheim, he was its first President; and the theatre of that town, the school of the best actors in Germany, of Iffland, Beck, Beil, and many others, owes to him its foundation, and its maintenance throughout his long Intendancy, which he held till 1803. As a writer and a poet, he is no less favourably known. We need only refer to his *Cora*, a musical drama, and to 'the *Monch von Carmel*.'—These letters of Schiller were found among his papers at his death; rescued from destruction by two of his executors, and published at Carlsruhe, in a small duodecimo, in the year 1819. There is a verbose preface, but no note or comment, though some such aid is now and then a little wanted.

The letters most worthy of our notice are those relating to the exhibition of the *Robbers* on the Mannheim stage, and to Schiller's consequent embarrassments and flight. From these, accordingly, the most of our selections shall be taken. It is curious to see with what timidity the intercourse on Schiller's part commences; and how this awkward shyness gradually gives place to some degree of confidence, as he becomes acquainted with his patron, or is called to treat of subjects where he feels that he himself has a dignity, and rights of his own, forlorn and humble as he is. At first he never mentions Dalberg but with all his titles, some of which to our unceremonious ears seem ludicrous enough. Thus in the full style of German reverence, he avoids directly naming his correspondent, but uses the oblique designation of 'your Excellency,' or something equally exalted: and he begins his two earliest letters with an address, which, literally interpreted, runs thus: 'Empire-free, Highly-wellborn, Particularly-much-to-be-venerated, Lord Privy Coun-sellor!' Such sounding phrases make us smile: but they entirely depend on custom for their import, and the smile which they excite is not by any means a philosophic one. It is but fair that in our version we omit them, or render them by some more grave equivalent.

The first letter is as follows:

[No date.]

'The proud judgment, passed upon me in the flattering letter which I had the honour to receive from your Excellency, is enough to set the prudence of an Au-thor on a very slippery eminence. The authority of the quarter it proceeds from, would almost communicate to that sentence the stamp of infallibility, if I could regard it as anything but a mere encouragement of my Muse. More than this a deep feeling of my weakness will not let me think it; but if my strength shall ever climb to the height of a masterpiece, I certainly shall have this warm approval of your Excellency alone to thank for it, and so will the world. For several years I have had the happiness to know you from the public papers: long ago the splen-dour of the Mannheim theatre attracted my attention. And, I confess, ever since I felt any touch of dramatic talent in myself, it has been among my darling projects some time or other to remove to Mannheim, the true temple of Thalia; a project, however, which my *closer* connection with Würtemberg might possibly impede.

'Your Excellency's very kind proposal on the subject of the *Robbers*, and such other pieces as I may produce in future, is infinitely precious to me; the maturing of it well deserves a narrower investigation of your Excellency's theatre, its special mode of management, its actors, the *non plus ultra* of its machinery; in a word, a full conception of it, such as I shall never get while my only scale of estimation is this Stuttgard theatre of ours, an establishment still in its minority. Unhappily my *economical* circumstances render it impossible for me to travel much; though I could travel now with the greater happiness and confidence, as I have still some *pregnant ideas* for the Mannheim theatre, which I could wish to have the honour of communicating to your Excellency. For the rest, I remain,' &c.

From the second letter we learn that Schiller had engaged to *theatrilise* his orig-inal edition of the *Robbers*, and still wished much to be connected in some shape with Mannheim. The third explains itself:

'Stuttgard, 6th October 1781.

'Here then at last returns the luckless prodigal, the remodelled *Robbers*! I am sorry that I have not kept the time, appointed by myself; but a transitory glance at the number and extent of the changes I have made, will, I trust, be sufficient to excuse me. Add to this, that a contagious epidemic was at work in our military Hospital, which, of course, interfered very often with my *otia poetica*. After fin-ishing my work, I may assure you I could engage with less effort of mind, and certainly with far more contentment, to compose a new piece, than to undergo the labour I have just concluded. The task was complicated and tedious. Here I had to correct an error, which naturally was rooted in the very groundwork of the play; there perhaps to sacrifice a beauty to the limits of the stage, the humour of the pit, the stupidity of the gallery, or some such sorrowful convention; and I need not tell you, that as in nature, so on the stage, an idea, an emotion, can have only one suitable expression, one proper tone. A single alteration in a trait of character may give a new tendency to the whole personage, and, consequently, to his actions, and the mechanism of the piece which depends on them.

'In the original, the Robbers are exhibited in strong contrast with each other; and I dare maintain that it is difficult to draw half a dozen robbers in strong contrast, without in some of them offending the delicacy of the stage. In my first conception of the piece, I excluded the idea of its ever being represented in a theatre; hence came it that Franz was planned as a *reasoning* villain; a plan which, though it may content the thinking Reader, cannot fail to vex and weary the Spectator, who does not come to think, and who wants not philosophy, but action.

'In the new edition, I could not overturn this arrangement without breaking-down the whole economy of the piece. Accordingly I can predict, with tolerable certainty, that Franz when he appears on the stage, will not play the part which he has played with the reader. And, at all events, the rushing stream of the action will hurry the spectator over all the finer shadings, and rob him of a third part of the whole character.

'Karl von Moor might chance to form an era on the stage; except a few speculations, which, however, work as indispensable colours in the general picture, he is all action, all visible life. Spiegelberg, Schweitzer, Hermann, are, in the strictest sense, personages for the stage; in a less degree, Amelia and the Father.

'Written and oral criticisms I have endeavoured to turn to advantage. The alterations are important; certain scenes are altogether new. Of this number, are Hermann's counter-plots to undermine the schemes of Franz; his interview with that personage, which, in the first composition of the work, was entirely and very unhappily forgotten. His interview with Amelia in the garden has been postponed to the succeeding act; and my friends tell me that I could have fixed upon no better act than this, no better time than a few moments prior to the meeting of Amelia with Moor. Franz is brought a little nearer human nature; but the mode of it is rather strange. A scene like his condemnation in the fifth act has never, to my knowledge, been exhibited on any stage; and the same may be said of the scene where Amelia is sacrificed by her lover.

'If the piece should be too long, it stands at the discretion of the manager to abbreviate the speculative parts of it, or here and there, without prejudice to the general impression, to omit them altogether. But in the *printing*, I use the freedom humbly to protest against the leaving out of anything. I had satisfactory reasons of my own for all that I allowed to pass; and my submission to the stage does not extend so far, that I can leave *holes* in my work, and mutilate the characters of men for the convenience of actors.

'In regard to the selection of costume, without wishing to prescribe any rules, I may be permitted to remark, that though in nature dress is unimportant, on the stage it is never so. In this particular, the taste of my Robber Moor will not be difficult to hit. He wears a plume; for this is mentioned expressly in the play, at the time when he abdicates his office. I have also given him a baton. His dress should always be noble without ornament, unstudied but not negligent.

'A young but excellent composer is working at a symphony for my unhappy prodigal: I know it will be masterly. So soon as it is finished, I shall take the liberty of offering it to you.

'I must also beg you to excuse the irregular state of the manuscript, the incorrectness of the penmanship. I was in haste to get the piece ready for you; hence the double sort of handwriting in it; hence also my forbearing to correct it. My copyist, according to the custom of all *reforming* caligraphers, I find, has wofully abused the spelling. To conclude, I recommend myself and my endeavours to the kindness of an honoured judge. I am,' &c.

'Stuttgard, 12th December 1781.

'With the change projected by your Excellency, in regard to the publishing of my play, I feel entirely contented, especially as I perceive that by this means two interests that had become very alien, are again made one, without, as I hope, any prejudice to the results and the success of my work. Your Excellency, however, touches on some other *very* weighty changes, which the piece has undergone from your hands; and these, in respect of myself, I feel to be so important, that I shall beg to explain my mind at some length regarding them. At the outset, then, I must honestly confess to you, I hold the projected transference of the action represented in my play to the epoch of the *Landfried,* and the Suppression of Private Wars, with the whole accompaniment which it gains by this new position, as infinitely better than mine; and must hold it so, although the whole piece should go to ruin thereby. Doubtless it is an objection, that in our enlightened century, with our watchful police and fixedness of statute, such a reckless gang should have arisen in the very bosom of the laws, and still more, have taken root and subsisted for years: doubtless the objection is well founded, and I have nothing to allege against it, but the license of Poetry to raise the probabilities of the real world to the rank of true, and its possibilities to the rank of probable.

'This excuse, it must be owned, is little adequate to the objection it opposes. But when I grant your Excellency so much (and I grant it honestly, and with complete conviction), what will follow? Simply that my play has got an ugly fault at its birth, which fault, if I may say so, it must carry with it to its grave, the fault being interwoven with its very nature, and not to be removed without destruction of the whole.

'In the first place, all my personages speak in a style too modern, too enlightened for that ancient time. The dialect is not the right one. That simplicity so vividly presented to us by the author of *Götz von Berlichingen,* is altogether wanting. Many long tirades, touches great and small, nay entire characters, are taken from the aspect of the present world, and would not answer for the age of Maximilian. In a word, this change would reduce the piece into something like a certain woodcut which I remember meeting with in an edition of Virgil. The Trojans wore hussar boots, and King Agamemnon had a pair of pistols in his belt. I should commit a *crime* against the age of Maximilian, to avoid an *error* against the age of Frederick the Second.

'Again, my whole episode of Amelia's love would make a frightful contrast with the simple chivalry attachment of that period. Amelia would, at all hazards, need to be re-moulded into a chivalry maiden; and I need not tell you that this character, and the sort of love which reigns in my work, are so deeply and broadly tinted into the whole picture of the Robber Moor, nay, into the whole piece, that every part of the delineation would require to be re-painted, before those tints could be removed. So likewise is it with the character of Franz, that speculative, metaphysico-refining knave.

'In a word, I think I may affirm, that this projected transposition of my work, which, prior to the commencement, would have lent it the highest splendour and completeness, could not fail now, when the piece is planned and finished, to change it into a defective *quodlibet*, a crow with peacock's feathers.

'Your Excellency will forgive a father this earnest pleading in behalf of his son. These are but words, and in the long-run every theatre can make of any piece what they think proper; the author must content himself. In the present case, he looks upon it as a happiness that he has fallen into such hands. With Herr Schwann, however, I will make it a condition that, at least, he *print* the piece according to the first plan. In the theatre I pretend to no vote whatever.

'That other change relating to Amelia's death was perhaps even more interesting to me. Believe me, your Excellency, this was the portion of my play which cost me the greatest effort and deliberation, of all which the result was nothing else than this, that Moor *must* kill his Amelia, and that the action is even a *positive beauty*, in his character; on the one hand painting the ardent lover, on the other the Bandit Captain, with the liveliest colours. But the vindication of this part is not to be exhausted in a single letter. For the rest, the few words which you propose to substitute in place of this scene, are truly exquisite, and altogether worthy of the situation. I should be proud of having written them.

'As Herr Schwann informs me that the piece, with the music and indispensably necessary pauses, will last about five hours (too long for any piece!), a second curtailment of it will be called for. I should not wish that any but myself undertook this task, and I myself, *without the sight of a rehearsal, or of the first representation*, cannot undertake it.

'If it were possible that your Excellency could fix the general rehearsal of the piece some time between the twentieth and the thirtieth of this month, and make good to me the main expenses of a journey to you, I should hope, in some few days, I might unite the interest of the stage with my own, and give the piece that proper rounding-off, which, without an actual view of the representation, cannot well be given it. On this point, may I request the favour of your Excellency's decision soon, that I may be prepared for the event.

'Herr Schwann writes me that a Baron von Gemmingen has given himself the trouble and done me the honour to read my piece. This Herr von Gemmingen, I also hear, is author of the *Deutsche Hausvater*. I long to have the honour of assuring him that I liked his *Hausvater* uncommonly, and admired in it the traces of a most accomplished man and writer. But what does the author of the *Deutsche Hausvater* care about the babble of a young apprentice? If I should ever have the honour of meeting Dalberg at Mannheim, and testifying the affection and reverence I bear him, I will then also press into the arms of that other, and tell him how dear to me such souls are as Dalberg and Gemmingen.

'Your thought about the small Advertisement, before our production of the piece, I exceedingly approve of; along with this I have enclosed a sketch of one. For the rest, I have the honour, with perfect respect, to be always,' &c.

This is the enclosed scheme of an Advertisement; which was afterwards adopted:

'THE ROBBERS,

'A PLAY.

'The picture of a great, misguided soul, furnished with every gift for excellence, and lost in spite of all its gifts: unchecked ardour and bad companionship contaminate his heart; hurry him from vice to vice, till at last he stands at the head of a gang of murderers, heaps horror upon horror, plunges from abyss to abyss into all the depths of desperation. Great and majestic in misfortune; and by misfortune improved, led back to virtue. Such a man in the Robber Moor you shall "bewail and hate, abhor and love. A hypocritical, malicious deceiver, you shall likewise see unmasked, and blown to pieces in his own mines. A feeble, fond, and too indulgent father. The sorrows of enthusiastic love, and the torture of ungoverned passion. Here also, not without abhorrence, you shall cast a look into the interior economy of vice, and from the stage be taught how all the gilding of fortune cannot kill the inward worm; how terror, anguish, remorse, and despair follow close upon the heels of the wicked. Let the spectator weep today before our scene, and shudder, and learn to bend his passions under the laws of reason and religion. Let the youth behold with affright the end of unbridled extravagance; nor let the man depart from our theatre, without a feeling that Providence makes even villains instruments of His purposes and judgments, and can marvellously unravel the most intricate perplexities of fate.'

Whatever reverence Schiller entertained for Dalberg as a critic and a patron, and however ready to adopt his alterations when they seemed judicious, it is plain, from various passages of these extracts, that in regard to writing, he had also firm persuasions of his own, and conscientiousness enough to adhere to them while they continued such. In regard to the conducting of his life, his views as yet were far less clear. The following fragments serve to trace him from the first exhibition of his play at Mannheim to his flight from Stuttgard:

'Stuttgard, 17th January 1782.

'I here in writing repeat my warmest thanks for the courtesies received from your Excellency, for your attention to my slender efforts, for the dignity and splendour you bestowed upon my piece, for all your Excellency did to exalt its little merits and hide its weaknesses by the greatest outlay of theatric art. The shortness of my stay at Mannheim would not allow me to go into details respecting the play or its representation; and as I could not say all, my time being meted out to me so sparingly, I thought it better to say absolutely nothing. I observed much, I learned much; and I believe, if Germany shall ever find in me a true dramatic poet, I must reckon the date of my commencement from the past week.' ***

'Stuttgard, 24th May 1782.

*** 'My impatient wish to see the piece played a second time, and the absence of my Sovereign favouring that purpose, have induced me, with some ladies and male friends as full of curiosity respecting Dalberg's theatre and *Robbers* as myself, to undertake a little journey to Mannheim, which we are to set about tomorrow. As this is the principal aim of our journey, and to me a more perfect enjoyment of my play is an exceedingly important object, especially since this would put it in my power to set about *Fiesco* under better auspices, I make it my earnest request of your Excellency, if possible, to procure me this enjoyment on Tuesday the 28th current.' ***

'Stuttgard, 4th June 1782.

'The satisfaction I enjoyed at Mannheim in such copious fulness, I have paid, since my return, by this epidemical disorder, which has made me till today entirely unfit to thank your Excellency for so much regard and kindness. And yet I am forced almost to repent the happiest journey of my life; for by a truly mortifying contrast of Mannheim with my native country, it has pained me so much, that Stuttgard and all Swabian scenes are become intolerable to me. Unhappier than I am can no one be. I have feeling enough of my bad condition, perhaps also feeling enough of my meriting a better; and in both points of view but *one* prospect of relief.

'May I dare to cast myself into your arms, my generous benefactor? I know how soon your noble heart inflames when sympathy and humanity appeal to it; I know how strong your courage is to undertake a noble action, and how warm your zeal to finish it. My new friends in Mannheim, whose respect for you is boundless, told me this: but their assurance was not necessary; I myself in that hour of your time, which I had the happiness exclusively to enjoy, read in your countenance far more than they had told me. It is this which makes me bold to *give* myself without reserve to you, to put my whole fate into your hands, and look to you for the happiness of my life. As yet I am little or nothing. In this Arctic Zone of taste, I shall never grow to anything, unless happier stars and a *Grecian climate* warm me into genuine poetry. Need I say more, to expect from Dalberg all support?

'Your Excellency gave me every hope to this effect; the squeeze of the hand that sealed your promise, I shall forever feel. If your Excellency will adopt the two or three hints I have subjoined, and use them in a letter to the Duke, I have no very great misgivings as to the result.

'And now with a burning heart, I repeat the request, the soul of all this letter. Could you look into the interior of my soul, could you see what feelings agitate it, could I paint to you in proper colours how my spirit strains against the grievances of my condition, you would not, I know you would not, delay one hour the aid which an application from you to the Duke might procure me.

'Again I throw myself into your arms, and wish nothing more than soon, very soon, to have it in my power to show by personal exertions in your service, the reverence with which I could devote to you myself and all that I am.'

The 'hints' above alluded to, are given in a separate enclosure, the main part of which is this:

'I earnestly desire that you could secure my union with the Mannheim Theatre for a specified period (which at your request might be lengthened), at the end of which I might again belong to the Duke. It will thus have the air rather of an excursion than a final abdication of my country, and will not strike them so ungraciously. In this case, however, it would be useful to suggest that means of practising and studying medicine might be afforded me at Mannheim. This will be peculiarly necessary, lest they sham, and higgle about letting me away.'

'Stuttgard, 15th July 1782.

'My long silence must have almost drawn upon me the reproach of folly from your Excellency, especially as I have not only delayed answering your last kind letter, but also retained the two books by me. All this was occasioned by a harassing affair which I have had to do with here. Your Excellency will doubtless be surprised when you learn that, for my last journey to you, I have been confined a fortnight under arrest. Everything was punctually communicated to the Duke. On this matter I have had an interview with him.

'If your Excellency think my prospects of coming to you anywise attainable, my only prayer is to *accelerate the fulfilment of them*. The reason why I now wish this with double earnestness, is one which I dare trust no whisper of to paper. This alone I can declare for certain, that within a month or two, if I have not the happiness of being with you, there will remain no further hope of my ever being there. Ere that time, I shall be forced to take a *step*, which will render it impossible for me to stay at Mannheim.' ***

The next two extracts are from letters to another correspondent. Doering quotes them without name or date: their purport sufficiently points out their place.

'I must haste to get away from this: in the end they might find me an apartment in the Hohenasperg, as they have found the honest and ill-fated Schubart. They talk of better culture that I need. It is possible enough, they might cultivate me differently in Hohenasperg: but I had rather try to make shift with what culture I have got, or may still get, by my unassisted efforts. This at least I owe to no one but my own free choice, and volition that disdains constraint.'

'In regard to those affairs, concerning which they wish to put my spirit under wardship, I have long reckoned my minority to be concluded. The best of it is, that one can cast away such clumsy manacles: me at least they shall not fetter.'

[No date.]

'Your Excellency will have learned from my friends at Mannheim, what the history of my affairs was up to your arrival, which unhappily I could not wait for. When I tell you *that I am flying my country*, I have painted my whole fortune. But the worst is yet behind. I have not the necessary *means* of setting my mishap at defiance. For the sake of safety, I had to withdraw from Stuttgard with the utmost speed, at the time of the Prince's arrival. Thus were my economical arrangements suddenly snapped asunder: I could not even pay my debts. My hopes had been set on a removal to Mannheim; there I trusted, by your Excellency's assistance, that my new play might not only have cleared me of debt, but have permanently put me into better circumstances. All this was frustrated by the necessity for hastening my removal. I went empty away; empty in purse and hope. I blush at being forced to make such disclosures to you; though I know they do not disgrace me. Sad enough for me to see realised in myself the hateful saying, that mental growth and full stature are things denied to every Swabian!

'If my former conduct, if all that your Excellency knows of my character, inspires you with confidence in my love of honour, permit me frankly to ask your assistance. Pressingly as I now need the profit I expect from my *Fiesco*, it will be impossible for me to have the piece in readiness before three weeks: my heart was oppressed; the feeling of my own situation drove me back from my poetic dreams. But if at the specified period, I could make the play not only *ready*, but, as I also hope, *worthy*, I take courage from that persuasion, respectfully to ask that your Excellency would be so obliging as *advance* for me the price that will then become due. I need it now, perhaps more than I shall ever do again throughout my life. I had near 200 florins of debt in Stuttgard, which I could not pay. I may confess to you, that this gives me more uneasiness than anything about my future destiny. I shall have no rest till I am free on *that* side.

'In eight days, too, my travelling purse will be exhausted. It is yet utterly impossible for me to labour with my mind. In my hand, therefore, are at present no resources.

'My actual situation being clear enough from what I have already said, I hold it needless to afflict your Excellency with any *importuning picture* of my want. Speedy aid is all that I can now think of or wish. Herr Meyer has been requested to communicate your Excellency's resolution to me, and to save you from the task of writing to me in person at all. With peculiar respect, I call myself,' &c.

It is pleasing to record that the humble aid so earnestly and modestly solicited by Schiller, was afforded him; and that he never forgot to love the man who had afforded it; who had assisted him, when assistance was of such essential value. In the first fervour of his gratitude, for this and other favours, the poet warmly declared that 'he owed all, all to Dalberg;' and in a state of society where Patronage, as Miss Edgeworth has observed, directly the antipodes of Mercy, is in general 'twice cursed,' cursing him that gives and him that takes, it says not a little for the character both of the obliged and the obliger in the present instance, that neither of them ever ceased to remember their connexion with pleasure. Schiller's first play had been introduced to the Stage by Dalberg, and his last was dedicated to him.[69] The venerable critic, in his eighty-third year, must have received with a calm joy the tragedy of *Tell*, accompanied by an address so full of kindness and respect: it

[69] It clearly appears I am wrong here; I have confounded the Freiherr Wolfgang Heribert von Dalberg, Director of the Mannheim Theatre, with Archduke and *Fürst Primas* Karl Theodor Dalberg, his younger Brother,—a man justly eminent in the Politico-Ecclesiasti-

must have gratified him to think that the youth who was once his, and had now become the world's, could, after long experience, still say of him,

> And fearlessly to thee may *Tell* be shown,
> For every noble feeling is thy own.

Except this early correspondence, very few of Schiller's letters have been given to the world.[70] In Doering's Appendix, we have found one written six years after the poet's voluntary exile, and agreeably contrasted in its purport with the agitation and despondency of that unhappy period. We translate it for the sake of those who, along with us, regret that while the world is deluged with insipid correspondences, and 'pictures of mind' that were not worth drawing, the correspondence of a man who never wrote unwisely should lie mouldering in private repositories, ere long to be irretrievably destroyed; that the 'picture of a mind' who was among the conscript fathers of the human race should still be left so vague and dim. This letter is addressed to Schwann, during Schiller's first residence in Weimar: it has already been referred to in the Text.

'Weimar, 2d May 1788.

'You apologise for your long silence to spare *me* the pain of an apology. I feel this kindness, and thank you for it. You do not impute my silence to decay of friendship; a proof that you have read my heart more justly than my evil conscience allowed me to hope. Continue to believe that the memory of you lives ineffaceably in my mind, and needs not to be brightened up by the routine of visits, or letters of assurance. So no more of this.

'The peace and calmness of existence which breathes throughout your letter, gives me joy; I who am yet drifting to and fro between wind and waves, am forced to envy you that uniformity, that health of soul and body. To me also in time it will be granted, as a recompense for labours I have yet to undergo.

---

cal world of his time, and still more distinguished for his patronage of letters, and other benefactions to his country, than the Freiherr was. Neither is the play of *Tell* 'dedicated' to him, as stated in the text; there is merely a copy presented, with some verses by the Author inscribed in it; at which time Karl Theodor was in his *sixtieth* year. A man of conspicuous station, of wide activity, and high influence and esteem in Germany. He was the personal friend of Herder, Goethe, Schiller, Wieland; by Napoleon he was made *Fürst Primas*, Prince Primate of the Confederation of the Rhine, being already Archbishop, Elector of Mentz, &c. The good and brave deeds he did in his time appear to have been many, public and private. Pensions to deserving men of letters were among the number: Zacharias Werner, I remember, had a pension from him,—and still more to the purpose, Jean Paul. He died in 1817. There was a third Brother also memorable for his encouragement of Letters and Arts. *"Ist kein Dalberg da*, Is there no Dalberg here?" the Herald cries on a certain occasion. (See *Conv. Lexicon*, B. iii.)

To Sir Edward Bulwer, in his *Sketch of the Life of Schiller* (p.c.), I am indebted for very kindly pointing out this error; as well as for much other satisfaction derived from that work. (*Note of* 1845.)

[70] There have since been copious contributions: *Correspondence with Goethe, Correspondence with Madam von Wolzogen*, and perhaps others which I have not seen. (*Note of* 1845.)

'I have now been in Weimar nearly three quarters of a year: after finishing my *Carlos*, I at last accomplished this long-projected journey. To speak honestly, I cannot say but that I am exceedingly contented with the place; and my reasons are not difficult to see.

'The utmost political tranquillity and freedom, a very tolerable disposition in the people, little constraint in social intercourse, a select circle of interesting persons and thinking heads, the respect paid to literary diligence: add to this the unexpensiveness to me of such a town as Weimar. Why should I not be satisfied?

'With Wieland I am pretty intimate, and to him I must attribute no small influence on my present happiness; for I like him, and have reason to believe that he likes me in return. My intercourse with Herder is more limited, though I esteem him highly as a writer and a man. It is the caprice of chance alone which causes this; for we opened our acquaintance under happy enough omens. Besides, I have not always time to act according to my likings. With Bode no one can be very friendly. I know not whether you think here as I do. Goethe is still but *expected* out of Italy. The Duchess Dowager is a lady of sense and talent, in whose society one does not feel constrained.

'I thank you for your tidings of the fate of *Carlos* on your stage. To speak candidly, my hopes of its success on any stage were not high; and I know my reasons. It is but fair that the Goddess of the Theatre avenge herself on me, for the little gallantry with which I was inspired in writing. In the mean time, though *Carlos* prove a never so decided failure on the stage, I engage for it, our public shall see it ten times acted, before they understand and fully estimate the merit that should counterbalance its defects. When one has seen the beauty of a work, and not till then, I think one is entitled to pronounce on its deformity. I hear, however, that the second representation succeeded better than the first. This arises either from the changes made upon the piece by Dalberg, or from the fact, that on a second view, the public comprehended certain things, which on a first, they—did not comprehend.

'For the rest, no one can be more satisfied than I am that *Carlos*, from causes honourable as well as causes dishonorable to it, is no speculation for the stage. Its very length were enough to banish it. Nor was it out of confidence or self-love that I forced the piece on such a trial; perhaps out of self-interest rather. If in the affair my vanity played any part, it was in this, that I thought the work had solid stuff in it sufficient to outweigh its sorry fortune on the boards.

'The present of your portrait gives me true pleasure. I think it a striking likeness; that of Schubart a little less so, though this opinion may proceed from my faulty memory as much as from the faultiness of Lobauer's drawing. The engraver merits all attention and encouragement; what I can do for the extension of his good repute shall not be wanting.

'To your dear children present my warmest love. At Wieland's I hear much and often of *your eldest daughter*; there in a few days she has won no little estimation and affection. Do I still hold any place in her remembrance? Indeed, I ought to blush, that by my long silence I so ill deserve it.

'That you are going to my dear native country, and will not pass my Father without seeing him, was most welcome news to me. The Swabians are a good people; this I more and more discover, the more I grow acquainted with the other provinces of Germany. To my family you will be cordially welcome. Will you take a pack of compliments from me to them? Salute my Father in my name; to my Mother and my Sisters *your daughter* will take my kiss.'

'And with these hearty words,' as Doering says, 'we shall conclude this paper.'

NO. 3. FRIENDSHIP WITH GOETHE.

The history of Schiller's first intercourse with Goethe has been recorded by the latter in a paper published a few years ago in the *Morphologie*, a periodical work, which we believe he still occasionally continues, or purposes to continue. The paper is entitled *Happy Incident*; and may be found in Part I. Volume 1 (pp. 90-96) of the work referred to. The introductory portion of it we have inserted in the text at page 109; the remainder, relating to certain scientific matters, and anticipating some facts of our narrative, we judged it better to reserve for the Appendix. After mentioning the publication of *Don Carlos*, and adding that 'each continued to go on his way apart,' he proceeds:

'His Essay on *Grace and Dignity* was yet less of a kind to reconcile me. The Philosophy of Kant, which exalts the dignity of mind so highly, while appearing to restrict it, Schiller had joyfully embraced: it unfolded the extraordinary qualities which Nature had implanted in him; and in the lively feeling of freedom and self-direction, he showed himself unthankful to the Great Mother, who surely had not acted like a step-dame towards him. Instead of viewing her as self-subsisting, as producing with a living force, and according to appointed laws, alike the highest and the lowest of her works, he took her up under the aspect of some empirical native qualities of the human mind. Certain harsh passages I could even directly apply to myself: they exhibited my confession of faith in a false light; and I felt that if written without particular attention to me, they were still worse; for in that case, the vast chasm which lay between us gaped but so much the more distinctly.

'There was no union to be dreamed of. Even the mild persuasion of Dalberg, who valued Schiller as he ought, was fruitless: indeed the reasons I set forth against any project of a union were difficult to contradict. No one could deny that between two spiritual antipodes there was more intervening than a simple diameter of the sphere: antipodes of that sort act as a sort of poles, and so can never coalesce. But that some relation may exist between them will appear from what follows.

'Schiller went to live at Jena, where I still continued unacquainted with him. About this time Batsch had set in motion a Society for Natural History, aided by some handsome collections, and an extensive apparatus. I used to attend their periodical meetings: one day I found Schiller there; we happened to go out together; some discourse arose between us. He appeared to take an interest in what had been exhibited; but observed, with great acuteness and good sense, and much to my satisfaction, that such a disconnected way of treating Nature was by no means grateful to the exoteric, who desired to penetrate her mysteries.

'I answered, that perhaps the initiated themselves were never rightly at their ease in it, and that there surely was another way of representing Nature, not separated and disunited, but active and alive, and expanding from the whole into the parts. On this point he requested explanations, but did not hide his doubts; he would not allow that such a mode, as I was recommending, had been already pointed out by experiment.

'We reached his house; the talk induced me to go in. I then expounded to him with as much vivacity as possible, the *Metamorphosis of Plants*,[71] drawing out on paper, with many characteristic strokes, a symbolic Plant for him, as I proceeded. He heard and saw all this with much interest and distinct comprehension; but when I had done, he shook his head and said: "This is no experiment, this is an idea." I stopped with some degree of irritation; for the point which separated us was most luminously marked by this expression. The opinions in *Dignity and Grace* again occurred to me; the old grudge was just awakening; but I smothered it, and merely said: "I was happy to find that I had got ideas without knowing it, nay that I saw them before my eyes."

'Schiller had much more prudence and dexterity of management than I: he was also thinking of his periodical the *Horen*, about this time, and of course rather wished to attract than repel me. Accordingly he answered me like an accomplished Kantite; and as my stiff necked Realism gave occasion to many contradictions, much battling took place between us, and at last a truce, in which neither party would consent to yield the victory, but each held himself invincible. Positions like the following grieved me to the very soul: *How can there ever be an experiment that shall correspond with an idea? The specific quality of an idea is, that no experiment can reach it or agree with it.* Yet if he held as an idea the same thing which I looked upon as an experiment, there must certainly, I thought, be some community between us, some ground whereon both of us might meet! The first step was now taken; Schiller's attractive power was great, he held all firmly to him that came within his reach: I expressed an interest in his purposes, and promised to give out in the *Horen* many notions that were lying in my head; his wife, whom I had loved and valued since her childhood, did her part to strengthen our reciprocal intelligence; all friends on both sides rejoiced in it; and thus by means of that mighty and interminable controversy between *object* and *subject*, we two concluded an alliance, which remained unbroken, and produced much benefit to ourselves and others.'

The friendship of Schiller and Goethe forms so delightful a chapter in their history, that we long for more and more details respecting it. Sincerity, true estimation of each other's merit, true sympathy in each other's character and purposes appear to have formed the basis of it, and maintained it unimpaired to the end. Goethe, we are told, was minute and sedulous in his attention to Schiller, whom he venerated as a good man and sympathised with as an afflicted one: when in mixed companies together, he constantly endeavoured to draw out the stores of his modest and retiring friend; or to guard his sick and sensitive mind from annoyances that might have irritated him; now softening, now exciting conversation,

---

[71] A curious physiologico-botanical theory by Goethe, which appears to be entirely unknown in this country; though several eminent continental botanists have noticed it with commendation. It is explained at considerable length in this same *Morphologie*.

guiding it with the address of a gifted and polished man, or lashing out of it with the scorpion-whip of his satire much that would have vexed the more soft and simple spirit of the valetudinarian. These are things which it is good to think of: it is good to know that there *are* literary men, who have other principles besides vanity; who can divide the approbation of their fellow mortals, without quarrelling over the lots; who in their solicitude about their 'fame' do not forget the common charities of nature, in exchange for which the 'fame' of most authors were but a poor bargain.

NO. 4. DEATH OF GUSTAVUS ADOLPHUS.

As a specimen of Schiller's historical style, we have extracted a few scenes from his masterly description of the Battle of Lützen. The whole forms a picture, executed in the spirit of Salvator; and though this is but a fragment, the importance of the figure represented in it will perhaps counterbalance that deficiency.

'At last the dreaded morning dawned; but a thick fog, which lay brooding over all the field, delayed the attack till noon. Kneeling in front of his lines, the King offered up his devotions; the whole army, at the same moment, dropping on their right knees, uplifted a moving hymn, and the field-music accompanied their singing. The King then mounted his horse; dressed in a jerkin of buff, with a surtout (for a late wound hindered him from wearing armour), he rode through the ranks, rousing the courage of his troops to a cheerful confidence, which his own forecasting bosom contradicted. *God with us* was the battle-word of the Swedes; that of the Imperialists was *Jesus Maria*. About eleven o'clock, the fog began to break, and Wallenstein's lines became visible. At the same time, too, were seen the flames of Lützen, which the Duke had ordered to be set on fire, that he might not be outflanked on this side. At length the signal pealed; the horse dashed forward on the enemy; the infantry advanced against his trenches.

'Meanwhile the right wing, led on by the King in person, had fallen on the left wing of the Friedlanders. The first strong onset of the heavy Finland Cuirassiers scattered the light-mounted Poles and Croats, who were stationed here, and their tumultuous flight spread fear and disorder over the rest of the cavalry. At this moment notice reached the King that his infantry were losing ground, and likely to be driven back from the trenches they had stormed; and also that his left, exposed to a tremendous fire from the Windmills behind Lützen, could no longer keep their place. With quick decision, he committed to Von Horn the task of pursuing the already beaten left wing of the enemy; and himself hastened, at the head of Steinbock's regiment, to restore the confusion of his own. His gallant horse bore him over the trenches with the speed of lightning; but the squadrons that came after him could not pass so rapidly; and none but a few horsemen, among whom Franz Albert, Duke of Sachsen-Lauenburg, is mentioned, were alert enough to keep beside him. He galloped right to the place where his infantry was most oppressed; and while looking round to spy out some weak point, on which his attack might be directed, his short-sightedness led him too near the enemy's lines. An Imperial sergeant (*gefreiter*), observing that every one respectfully made room for the advancing horseman, ordered a musketeer to fire on him. "Aim at *him* there," cried he; "that must be a man of consequence." The soldier drew his trigger; and the King's left arm was shattered by the ball. At this instant, his cavalry came galloping up, and a confused cry of *"The King bleeds! The King is shot!"* spread horror and dismay through their ranks. "It is nothing: follow me!" exclaimed the King, collecting all his strength; but overcome with pain, and on the point of fainting, he desired the Duke of Lauenburg, in French, to take him without notice from the tumult. The Duke then turned with him to the right wing, making a wide circuit to conceal this accident from the desponding infantry; but as they rode along, the King received a second bullet through the back, which took from him the last remainder of his strength. "I have got enough, brother," said he with a dying voice: "haste, save thyself." With these words he sank from his horse; and here, struck by several other bullets, far from his attendants, he breathed out his life beneath the plundering hands of a troop of Croats. His horse flying on without its rider, and bathed in blood, soon announced to the Swedish cavalry the fall of their King; with wild yells they rush to the spot, to snatch that sacred spoil from the enemy. A deadly fight ensues around the corpse, and the mangled remains are buried under a hill of slain men.

'The dreadful tidings hasten in a few minutes over all the Swedish army: but instead of deadening the courage of these hardy troops, they rouse it to a fierce consuming fire. Life falls in value, since the holiest of all lives is gone; and death has now no terror for the lowly, since it has not spared the anointed head. With the grim fury of lions, the Upland, Småland, Finnish, East and West Gothland regiments dash a second time upon the left wing of the enemy, which, already making but a feeble opposition to Von Horn, is now utterly driven from the field.

'But how dear a victory, how sad a triumph! Now first when the rage of battle has grown cold, do they feel the whole greatness of their loss, and the shout of the conqueror dies in a mute and gloomy despair. He who led them on to battle has not returned with them. Apart he lies, in his victorious field, confounded with the common heaps of humble dead. After long fruitless searching, they found the royal corpse, not far from the great stone, which had already stood for centuries between Lützen and the Merseburg Canal, but which, ever since this memorable incident, has borne the name of *Schwedenstein*, the Stone of the Swede. Defaced with wounds and blood, so as scarcely to be recognised, trodden under the hoofs of horses, stripped of his ornaments, even of his clothes, he is drawn from beneath a heap of dead bodies, brought to Weissenfels, and there delivered to the lamentations of his troops and the last embraces of his Queen. Vengeance had first required its tribute, and blood must flow as an offering to the Monarch; now Love assumes its rights, and mild tears are shed for the Man. Individual grief is lost in the universal sorrow. Astounded by this overwhelming stroke, the generals in blank despondency stand round his bier, and none yet ventures to conceive the full extent of his loss.'

The descriptive powers of the Historian, though the most popular, are among the lowest of his endowments. That Schiller was not wanting in the nobler requisites of his art, might he proved from his reflections on this very incident, 'striking like a hand from the clouds into the calculated horologe of men's affairs, and directing the considerate mind to a higher plan of things.' But the limits of our Work are already reached. Of Schiller's histories and dramas we can give no farther specimens: of his lyrical, didactic, moral poems we must take our leave without giving any. Perhaps the time may come, when all his writings, transplanted to our own soil, may be offered in their entire dimensions to the thinkers of these Islands; a conquest by which our literature, rich as it is, might be enriched still farther.

APPENDIX II.

GOETHE'S INTRODUCTION TO GERMAN TRANSLATION OF THIS LIFE OF SCHILLER

THE preceding Appendix, which is here marked "Appendix *First*," has hitherto, in all Editions, been the only one, and has ended the Book. As indeed, for the common run of English readers, it still essentially may, or even must. But now, for a more select class, and on inducements that are accidental and peculiar, there is, in this final or farewell Edition, which stands without change otherwise, something to be added as Appendix *Second*, by the opportunity that offers.

Schiller has now many readers of his own in England: perhaps the most and best that read this my poor Account of his *Life* know something of Germany and him at first-hand; and have their curiosity awake in regard to things German:—to such readers, if not to others, I can expect that the following Reprint or Reproduction of a Piece from the greatest of Germans, which connects itself with Schiller and this Book on Schiller, may not be unwelcome. To myself it has become symbolical, touching and memorable; and much invites my insertion of it here, since there happens to be room.

Certainly an interesting little circumstance in the history of this Book, and to me the one circumstance that now has any interest, is, That a German Translation of it had the altogether unexpected honour of an Introductory Preface by Goethe, in the last years of his life. A beautiful small event to me and mine, in our then remote circle; coming suddenly upon us, like a little outbreak of sunshine and azure, in the common gray element there! It was one of the more salient points of a certain individual relation, and far-off personal intercourse, which had arisen some years before, with the great man whom we had never seen, and never saw; and which was very beautiful, high, singular and dear to us,—to myself, and to ANOTHER who is not with me now. A little gleam as of celestial radiancy, miraculous almost, but indisputable, shining out on us always from time to time; somewhat ennobling for us the much of impediment that lay there, and forbidding it altogether to impede. Truly there are few things I now remember with a more bright or pious feeling than our then relation, amid the Scottish moors, to the man whom of all others I the most honoured, and felt that I was the most indebted to. Looking back on all this, through the vista of almost forty years, and what they have brought and have taken, I decide to reproduce this Goethe *Introduction*, as a little pillar of memorial, while time yet is.

Many of my present readers, too, readers especially of this Volume, may have their curiosities about the "Introduction (*Einleitung*)" of so small a thing by so great a man (which withal is a Piece not to be found in the great man's *Collected*

Works, or elsewhere that I know of):—and will good-naturedly allow me to have my own way with it, namely to reprint it here in the original words. And will not even quarrel with me if I reproduce in *facsimile* those poor "*Verzierungen* (Copperplates)" of Goethe's devising, Shadows of Human Dwellings far away; judging well how beautiful and full of meaning the poorest of them now is to me.

Subjoined, on the next page, is Goethe's List or 'special Indication' of these latter; the only words of his which, on this occasion, I translate as well (*Note of 1868*):

'SPECIAL INDICATION OF THE LOCALITIES REPRESENTED.

'*Frontispiece*, Thomas Carlyle's House in the County of Dumfries, South of Scotland.

'*Titlepage Vignette*, The Same in the distance.

'*Upper-side of Cover*, Schiller's House in Weimar.

'*Under-side of Cover*, Solitary small Apartment in Schiller's Garden, over the Leutra Brook in Jena, built by himself; where, in the completest seclusion, he wrote many things, *Maria Stuart* in particular. After his removal from Jena, and subsequent decease, the little Edifice was taken away as threatening to fall ruinous; and we wished here to preserve the remembrance of it.'

NÄHERE BEZEICHNUNG
DER DARGESTELLTEN LOKALITÄTEN.

Titelkupfer, Thomas Carlyles Wohnung in der Graffschaft Dumfries, des südlichen Schottlands.

Titel-Vignette, dieselbe in der Ferne.

Vorderseite des Umschlags, Wohnung Schillers in Weimar.

Rückseite des Umschlags, einsames Häuschen in Schillers Garten, über der Jenaischen Leutra, von ihm selbst errichtet; wo er in vollkommenster Einsamkeit manches, besonders Maria Stuart schrieb. Nach seiner Entfernung und erfolgtem Scheiden, trug man es ab, wegen Wandelbarkeit, und man gedachte hier das Andenken desselben zu erhalten.

THOMAS CARLYLE
Leben Schillers.
AUS DEM ENGLISCHEN.
eingeleitet
durch
GOETHE.
Frankfurt am Main 1830
Verlag von Heinrich Wilmans.

THOMAS CARLYLE
LEBEN SCHILLERS,
AUS DEM ENGLISCHEN;

ein0.1geleitet

durch

GOETHE.

Frankfurt am Main, 1830.
Verlag von Heinrich Wilmans.

Als gegen Ende des vergangenen Jahres ich die angenehme Nachricht erhielt, dass eine mir freundlich bekannte Gesellschaft, welche bisher ihre Aufmerksamkeit inländischer Literatur gewidmet hatte, nunmehr dieselbe auf die ausländische zu wenden gedenke, konnte ich in meiner damaligen Lage nicht ausführlich und gründlich genug darlegen, wie sehr ich ein Unternehmen, bey welchen man auch meiner auf das geneigteste gedacht hatte, zu schätzen wisse.

Selbst mit gegenwärtigem öffentlichen Ausdruck meines dankbaren Antheils geschieht nur fragmentarisch was ich im bessern Zusammenhang zu überliefern gewünscht hätte. Ich will aber auch das wie es mir vorliegt nicht zurückweisen, indem ich meinen Hauptzweck dadurch zu erreichen hoffe, dass ich nämlich meine Freunde mit einem Manne in Berührung bringe, welchen ich unter diejenigen zähle, die in späteren Jahren sich an mich thätig angeschlossen, mich durch eine mitschreitende Theilnahme zum Handeln und Wirken aufgemuntert, und durch ein edles, reines wohlgerichtetes Bestreben wieder selbst verjüngt, mich, der ich sie heranzog, mit sich fortgezogen haben. Es ist der Verfasser des hier übersetzten Werkes, Herr Thomas Carlyle, ein Schotte, von dessen Thätigkeit und Vorzügen, so wie von dessen näheren Zuständen nachstehende Blätter ein Mehreres eröffnen werden.

Wie ich denselben und meine Berliner Freunde zu kennen glaube, so wird zwischen ihnen und ihm eine frohe wirksame Verbindung sich einleiten und beide Theile werden, wie ich hoffen darf, in einer Reihe von Jahren sich dieses Vermächtnisses und seines fruchtbaren Erfolges zusammen erfreuen, so dass ich ein fortdauerndes Andenken, um welches ich hier schliesslich bitten möchte, schon als dauernd gegönnt, mit anmuthigen Empfindungen voraus geniessen kann.

in treuer Anhänglichkeit und Theilnahme.

Weimar April
1830.

J.W.v. Goethe.

Es ist schon einige Zeit von einer allgemeinen Weltliteratur die Rede und zwar nicht mit Unrecht: denn die sämmtlichen Nationen, in den fürchterlichsten Kriegen durcheinander geschüttelt, sodann wieder auf sich selbst einzeln zurückgeführt, hatten zu bemerken, dass sie manches Fremde gewahr worden, in sich aufgenommen, bisher unbekannte geistige Bedürfnisse hie und da empfunden. Daraus entstand das Gefühl nachbarlicher Verhältnisse, und anstatt dass man sich bisher zugeschlossen hatte, kam der Geist nach und nach zu dem Verlangen, auch in den mehr oder weniger freyen geistigen Handelsverkehr mit aufgenommen zu werden.

Diese Bewegung währt zwar erst eine kurze Weile, aber doch immer lang genug, um schon einige Betrachtungen darüber anzustellen, und aus ihr bald möglichst, wie man es im Waarenhandel ja auch thun muss, Vortheil und Genuss zu gewinnen.

Gegenwärtiges, zum Andenken Schillers, geschriebene Werk kann, übersetzt, für uns kaum etwas Neues bringen; der Verfasser nahm seine Kenntnisse aus Schriften, die uns längst bekannt sind, so wie denn auch überhaupt die hier verhandelten Angelegenheiten bey uns öfters durchgesprochen und durchgefochten worden.

Was aber den Verehrern Schillers, und also einem jeden Deutschen, wie man kühnlich sagen darf, höchst erfreulich seyn muss, ist: unmittelbar zu erfahren, wie ein zartfühlender, strebsamer, einsichtiger Mann über dem Meere, in seinen besten Jahren, durch Schillers Productionen berührt, bewegt, erregt und nun zum weitern Studium der deutschen Literatur angetrieben worden.

Mir wenigstens war es rührend, zu sehen, wie dieser, rein und ruhig denkende Fremde, selbst in jenen ersten, oft harten, fast rohen Productionen unsres verewigten Freundes, immer den edlen, wohldenkenden, wohlwollenden Mann gewahr ward und sich ein Ideal des vortrefflichsten Sterblichen an ihm aufbauen konnte.

Ich halte deshalb dafür dass dieses Werk, als von einem Jüngling geschrieben, der deutschen Jugend zu empfehlen seyn möchte: denn wenn ein munteres Lebensalter einen Wunsch haben darf und soll, so ist es der: in allem Geleisteten das Löbliche, Gute, Bildsame, Hochstrebende, genug das Ideelle, und selbst in dem nicht Musterhaften, das allgemeine Musterbild der Menschheit zu erblicken.

Ferner kann uns dieses Werk von Bedeutung seyn, wenn wir ernstlich betrachten: wie ein fremder Mann die Schillerischen Werke, denen wir so mannigfaltige Kultur verdanken, auch als Quelle der seinigen schätzt, verehrt und dies, ohne irgend eine Absicht, rein und ruhig zu erkennen giebt.

Eine Bemerkung möchte sodann hier wohl am Platze seyn: dass sogar dasjenige, was unter uns beynahe ausgewirkt hat, nun, gerade in dem Augenblicke welcher auswärts der deutschen Literatur günstig ist, abermals seine kräftige Wirkung beginne und dadurch zeige, wie es auf einer gewissen Stufe der Literatur immer nützlich und wirksam seyn werde.

So sind z.B. Herders Ideen bey uns dergestalt in die Kenntnisse der ganzen Masse übergegangen, dass nur wenige, die sie lesen, dadurch erst belehrt werden, weil sie, durch hundertfache Ableitungen, von demjenigen was damals von grosser Bedeutung war, in anderem Zusammenhange schon völlig unterrichtet worden. Dieses Werk ist vor kurzem ins Französische übersetzt; wohl in keiner andern Ueberzeugung als dass tausend gebildete Menschen in Frankreich sich immer noch an diesen Ideen zu erbauen haben.

In Bezug auf das dem gegenwärtigen Bande vorgesetzte Bild sey folgendes gemeldet: Unser Freund, als wir mit ihm in Verhältniss traten, war damals in Edinburgh wohnhaft, wo er in der Stille lebend, sich im besten Sinne auszubilden suchte, und, wir dürfen es ohne Ruhmredigkeit sagen, in der deutschen Literatur hiezu die meiste Förderniss fand.

Später, um sich selbst und seinen redlichen literarischen Studien unabhängig zu leben, begab er sich, etwa zehen deutsche Meilen südlicher, ein eignes Besitzthum zu bewohnen und zu benutzen, in die Grafschaft Dumfries. Hier, in einer gebirgigen Gegend, in welcher der Fluss Nithe dem nahen Meere zuströmt, ohnfern der Stadt Dumfries, an einer Stelle welche Craigenputtock genannt wird, schlug er mit einer schönen und höchst gebildeten Lebensgefährtin seine ländlich einfache Wohnung auf, wovon treue Nachbildungen eigentlich die Veranlassung zu gegenwärtigem Vorworte gegeben haben.

Gebildete Geister, zartfühlende Gemüther, welche nach fernem Guten sich bestreben, in die Ferne Gutes zu wirken geneigt sind, erwehren sich kaum des Wunsches, von geehrten, geliebten, weitabgesonderten Personen das Portrait, sodann die Abbildung ihrer Wohnung, so wie der nächsten Zustände, sich vor Augen gebracht zu sehen.

Wie oft wiederholt man noch heutiges Tags die Abbildung von Petrarch's Aufenthalt in Vaucluse, Tasso's Wohnung in Sorent! Und ist nicht immer die Bieler Insel, der Schutzort Rousseau's, ein seinen Verehrern nie genugsam dargestelltes Local?

In eben diesem Sinne hab' ich mir die Umgebungen meiner entfernten Freunde im Bilde zu verschaffen gesucht, und ich war um so mehr auf die Wohnung Hrn. Thomas Carlyle begierig, als er seinen Aufenthalt in einer fast rauhen Gebirgsgegend unter dem 55ten Grade gewählt hatte.

Ich glaube durch solch eine treue Nachbildung der neulich eingesendeten Originalzeichnungen gegenwärtiges Buch zu zieren und dem jetzigen gefühlvollen Leser, vielleicht noch mehr dem künftigen, einen freundlichen Gefallen zu erweisen und dadurch, so wie durch eingeschaltete Auszüge aus den Briefen des werthen Mannes, das Interesse an einer edlen allgemeinen Länder- und Weltannäherung zu vermehren.

THOMAS CARLYLE AN GOETHE.

Craigenputtock den 25. Septbr. 1828.

"Sie forschen mit so warmer Neigung nach unserem gegenwärtigen Aufenthalt und Beschäftigung, dass ich einige Worte hierüber sagen muss, da noch Raum dazu übrig bleibt. Dumfries ist eine artige Stadt, mit etwa 15000 Einwohnern und als Mittelpunct des Handels und der Gerichtsbarkeit anzusehen eines bedeutenden Districkts in dem schottischen Geschäftskreis. Unser Wohnort ist nicht darin, sondern 15 Meilen (zwei Stunden zu reiten) nordwestlich davon entfernt, zwischen den Granitgebirgen und dem schwarzen Moorgefilde, welche sich westwärts durch Gallovay meist bis an die irische See ziehen. In dieser Wüste von Heide und Felsen stellt unser Besitzthum eine grüne Oase vor, einen Raum von geackertem, theilweise umzäumten und geschmückten Boden, wo Korn reift und Bäume Schatten gewähren, obgleich ringsumher von Seemöven und hartwolligen Schaafen umgeben. Hier, mit nicht geringer Anstrengung, haben wir für uns eine reine, dauerhafte Wohnung erbaut und eingerichtet; hier wohnen wir in Ermangelung einer Lehr- oder andern öffentlichen Stelle, um uns der Literatur zu befleissigen, nach eigenen Kräften uns damit zu beschäftigen. Wir wünschen dass unsre Rosen und Gartenbüsche fröhlich heranwachsen, hoffen Gesundheit und eine friedliche Gemüthsstimmung, um uns zu fordern. Die Rosen sind freylich zum Theil noch zu pflanzen, aber sie blühen doch schon in Hoffnung.

Zwei leichte Pferde, die uns überall hintragen, und die Bergluft sind die besten Aerzte für zarte Nerven. Diese tägliche Bewegung, der ich sehr ergeben bin, ist meine einzige Zerstreuung; denn dieser Winkel ist der einsamste in Brittanien, sechs Meilen von einer jeden Person entfernt die mich allenfalls besuchen möchte. Hier würde sich Rousseau eben so gut gefallen haben, als auf seiner Insel St. Pierre.

Fürwahr meine städtischen Freunde schreiben mein Hierhergehen einer ähnlichen Gesinnung zu und weissagen mir nichts Gutes; aber ich zog hierher, allein zu dem Zweck meine Lebensweise zu vereinfachen und eine Unabhängigkeit zu erwerben, damit ich mir selbst treu bleiben könne. Dieser Erdraum ist unser, hier können wir leben, schreiben und denken wie es uns am besten däucht, und wenn Zoilus selbst König der Literatur werden sollte.

Auch ist die Einsamkeit nicht so bedeutend, eine Lohnkutsche bringt uns leicht nach Edinburgh, das wir als unser brittisch Weimar ansehen. Habe ich denn nicht auch gegenwärtig eine ganze Ladung von französischen, deutschen, amerikanischen, englischen Journalen und Zeitschriften, von welchem Werth sie auch seyn mögen, auf den Tischen meiner kleinen Bibliothek aufgehäuft!

Auch an alterthümlichen Studien fehlt es nicht. Von einigen unsrer Höhen entdeck' ich, ohngefähr eine Tagereise westwärts, den Hügel, wo Agrikola und seine Römer ein Lager zurückliessen; am Fusse desselben war ich geboren, wo Vater und Mutter noch leben um mich zu lieben. Und so muss man die Zeit wirken lassen. Doch wo gerath ich hin! Lassen Sie mich noch gestehen, ich bin ungewiss über meine künftige literarische Thätigkeit, worüber ich gern Ihr Urtheil vernehmen möchte; gewiss schreiben Sie mir wieder und bald, damit ich mich immer mit

Ihnen vereint fühlen möge."

Wir, nach allen Seiten hin wohlgesinnten, nach allgemeinster Bildung strebenden Deutschen, wir wissen schon seit vielen Jahren die Verdienste würdiger schottischer Männer zu schätzen. Uns blieb nicht unbekannt, was sie früher in den Naturwissenschaften geleistet, woraus denn nachher die Franzosen ein so grosses Uebergewicht erlangten.

In der neuern Zeit verfehlten wir nicht den lichen Inflows anzuerkennen, den ihre Philosophie auf die Sinnesänderung der Franzosen ausübte, um sie von dem starren Sensualism zu einer geschmeidigern Denkart auf dem Wege des gemeinen Menschenverstandes hinzuleiten. Wir verdankten ihnen gar manche gründliche Einsicht in die wichtigsten Fächer brittischer Zustände und Bemühungen.

Dagegen mussten wir vor nicht gar langer Zeit unsre ethisch-ästhetischen Bestrebungen in ihren Zeitschriften auf eine Weise behandelt sehen, wo es zweifelhaft blieb, ob Mangel an Einsicht oder böser Wille dabey obwaltete; ob eine oberflächliche, nicht genug durchdringende Ansicht, oder ein widerwilliges Vorurtheil im Spiele sey. Dieses Ereigniss haben wir jedoch geduldig abgewartet, da uns ja dergleichen im eignen Vaterlande zu ertragen genügsam von jeher auferlegt worden.

In den letzten Jahren jedoch erfreuen uns aus jenen Gegenden die liebevollsten Blicke, welche zu erwiedern wir uns verpflichtet fühlen und worauf wir in gegenwärtigen Blättern unsre wohldenkenden Landsleute, insofern es nöthig seyn sollte, aufmerksam zu machen gedenken.

Herr Thomas Carlyle hatte schon den Wilhelm Meister übersetzt und gab sodann vorliegendes Leben Schillers im Jahre 1825 heraus.

Im Jahre 1827 erschien *German Romances* in 4 Bänden, wo er, aus den Erzählungen und Mährchen deutscher Schriftsteller als: Musäus, La Motte Fouqué, Tieck, Hoffmann, Jean Paul und Goethe, heraushob, was er seiner Nation am gemässesten zu seyn glaubte.

Die einer jeden Abtheilung vorausgeschickten Nachrichten von dem Leben, den Schriften, der Richtung des genannten Dichters und Schriftstellers geben ein Zeugniss von der einfach wohlwollenden Weise, wie der Freund sich möglichst von der Persönlichkeit und den Zuständen eines jeden zu unterrichten gesucht, und wie er dadurch auf den rechten Weg gelangt, seine Kenntnisse immer mehr zu vervollständigen.

In den Edinburgher Zeitschriften, vorzüglich in denen welche eigentlich fremder Literatur gewidmet sind, finden sich nun, ausser den schon genannten deutschen Autoren, auch Ernst Schulz, Klingemann, Franz Horn, Zacharias Werner, Graf Platen und manche andere, von verschiedenen Referenten, am meisten aber von unserm Freunde, beurtheilt und eingeführt.

Höchst wichtig ist bey dieser Gelegenheit zu bemerken, dass sie eigentlich ein jedes Werk nur zum Text und Gelegenheit nehmen, um über das eigentliche Feld und Fach, so wie alsdann über das besondere Individuelle, ihre Gedanken zu eröffnen und ihr Gutachten meisterhaft abzuschliessen.

Diese *Edinburgh Reviews*, sie seyen dem Innern und Allgemeinen, oder den auswärtigen Literaturen besonders gewidmet, haben Freunde der Wissenschaften aufmerksam zu beachten; denn es ist höchst merkwürdig, wie der gründlichste Ernst mit der freysten Uebersicht, ein strenger Patriotismus mit einem einfachen reinen Freysinn, in diesen Vorträgen sich gepaart findet.

Geniessen wir nun von dort, in demjenigen was uns hier so nah angeht, eine reine einfache Theilnahme an unsern ethisch-ästhetischen Bestrebungen, welche für einen besondern Charakterzug der Deutschen gelten können, so haben wir uns gleichfalls nach dem umzusehen, was ihnen dort von dieser Art eigentlich am Herzen liegt. Wir nennen hier gleich den Namen Burns, von welchem ein Schreiben des Herrn Carlyle's folgende Stelle enthält.

"Das einzige einigermassen Bedeutende, was ich seit meinem Hierseyn schrieb, ist ein Versuch über Burns. Vielleicht habt Ihr niemals von diesem Mann gehört, und doch war er einer der entschiedensten Genies; aber in der tiefsten Classe der Landleute geboren und durch die Verwicklungen sonderbarer Lagen zuletzt jammervoll zu Grunde gerichtet, so dass was er wirkte verhältnissmässig geringfügig ist; er starb in der Mitte der Manns-Jahre (1796)."

"Wir Engländer, besonders wir Schottländer, lieben Burns mehr als irgend einen Dichter seit Jahrhunderten. Oft war ich von der Bemerkung betroffen, er sey wenig Monate vor Schiller, in dem Jahr 1759 geboren und keiner dieser beiden habe jemals des andern Namen vernommen. Sie glänzten als Sterne in entgegengesetzten Hemisphären, oder, wenn man will, eine trübe Erdatmosphäre fing ihr gegenseitiges Licht auf."

Mehr jedoch als unser Freund vermuthen mochte, war uns Robert Burns bekannt; das allerliebste Gedicht *John Barley-Corn* war anonym zu uns gekommen, und verdienter Weise geschätzt, veranlasste solches manche Versuche unsrer Sprache es anzueignen. *Hans Gerstenkorn*, ein wackerer Mann, hat viele Feinde, die ihn unablässig verfolgen und beschädigen, ja zuletzt gar zu vernichten drohen. Aus allen diesen Unbilden geht er aber doch am Ende triumphirend hervor, besonders zu Heil und Fröhlichkeit der leidenschaftlichen Biertrinker. Gerade in diesem heitern genialischen Anthropomorphismus zeigt sich Burns als wahrhaften Dichter.

Auf weitere Nachforschung fanden wir dieses Gedicht in der Ausgabe seiner poetischen Werke von 1822, welcher eine Skizze seines Lebens voransteht, die uns wenigstens von den Aeusserlichkeiten seiner Zustände bis auf einen gewissen Grad belehrte. Was wir von seinen Gedichten uns zueignen konnten, überzeugte uns von seinem ausserordentlichen Talent, und wir bedauerten, dass uns die Schottische Sprache gerade da hinderlich war, wo er des reinsten natürlichsten Ausdrucks sich gewiss bemächtigt hatte. Im Ganzen jedoch haben wir unsre Studien so weit geführt, dass wir die nachstehende rühmliche Darstellung auch als unsrer Ueberzeugung gemäss unterschreiben können.

Inwiefern übrigens unser Burns auch in Deutschland bekannt sey, mehr als das Conversations-Lexicon von ihm überliefert, wüsste ich, als der neuen literarischen Bewegungen in Deutschland unkundig, nicht zu sagen; auf alle Fälle jedoch gedenke ich die Freunde auswärtiger Literatur auf die kürzesten Wege zu weisen: *The Life of Robert Burns. By J.G. Lockhart. Edinburgh 1828*, rezensirt von unserm Freunde im *Edinburgh Review*, December 1828.

Nachfolgende Stellen daraus übersetzt, werden den Wunsch, das Ganze und den genannten Mann auf jede Weise zu kennen, hoffentlich lebhaft erregen.

"Burns war in einem höchst prosaischen Zeitalter, dergleichen Brittanien nur je erlebt hatte, geboren, in den aller ungünstigsten Verhältnissen, wo sein Geist nach hoher Bildung strebend ihr unter dem Druck täglich harter körperlicher Arbeit nach zu ringen hatte, ja unter Mangel und trostlosesten Aussichten auf die Zukunft; ohne Förderniss als die Begriffe, wie sie in eines armen Mannes Hütte wohnen, und allenfalls die Reime von Ferguson und Ramsay, als das Muster der Schönheit aufgesteckt. Aber unter diesen Lasten versinkt er nicht; durch Nebel und Finsterniss einer so düstern Region entdeckt sein Adlerauge die richtigen Verhältnisse der Welt und des Menschenlebens, er wächst an geistiger Kraft und drängt sich mit Gewalt zu verständiger Erfahrung. Angetrieben durch die unwiderstehliche Regsamkeit seines inneren Geistes strauchelt er vorwärts und zu allgemeinen Ansichten, und mit stolzer Bescheidenheit reicht er uns die Frucht seiner Bemühungen, eine Gabe dar, welche nunmehr durch die Zeit als unvergänglich anerkannt worden."

"Ein wahrer Dichter, ein Mann in dessen Herzen die Anlage eines reinen Wissens keimt, die Töne himmlischer Melodien vorklingen, ist die köstlichste Gabe, die einem Zeitalter mag verliehen werden. Wir sehen in ihm eine freyere, reinere Entwicklung alles dessen was in uns das Edelste zu nennen ist; sein Leben ist uns ein reicher Unterricht und wir betrauern seinen Tod als eines Wohlthäters, der uns liebte so wie belehrte."

"Solch eine Gabe hat die Natur in ihrer Güte uns an Robert Burns gegönnt; aber mit allzuvornehmer Gleichgültigkeit warf sie ihn aus der Hand als ein Wesen ohne Bedeutung. Es war entstellt und zerstört ehe wir es anerkannten, ein ungünstiger Stern hatte dem Jüngling die Gewalt gegeben, das menschliche Daseyn ehrwürdiger zu machen, aber ihm war eine weisliche Führung seines eigenen nicht geworden. Das Geschick – denn so müssen wir in unserer Beschränktheit reden – seine Fehler, die Fehler der Andern lasteten zu schwer auf ihm, und dieser Geist, der sich erhoben hatte, wäre es ihm nur zu wandern geglückt, sank in den Staub; seine herrlichen Fähigkeiten wurden in der Blüthe mit Füssen getreten. Er starb, wir dürfen wohl sagen, ohne jemals gelebt zu haben. Und so eine freundlich warme Seele, so voll von eingebornen Reichthümern, solcher Liebe zu allen lebendigen und leblosen Dingen! Das späte Tausendschönchen fällt nicht unbemerkt unter seine Pflugschar, so wenig als das wohlversorgte Nest der furchtsamen Feldmaus, das er hervorwühlt. Der wilde Anblick des Winters ergötzt ihn; mit einer trüben, oft wiederkehrenden Zärtlichkeit, verweilt er in diesen ernsten Scenen der Verwüstung; aber die Stimme des Windes wird ein Psalm in seinem Ohr; wie gern mag er in den sausenden Wäldern dahin wandern: denn er fühlt seine Gedanken erhoben zu dem, der auf den Schwingen des Windes einherschreitet. Eine wahre Poetenseele! sie darf nur berührt werden und ihr Klang ist Musik."

"Welch ein warmes allumfassendes Gleichheitsgefühl! welche vertrauenvolle, gränzenlose Liebe! welch edelmuthiges Ueberschätzen des geliebten Gegenstandes! Der Bauer, sein Freund, sein nussbraunes Mädchen sind nicht länger gering und dörfisch, Held vielmehr und Königin, er rühmt sie als gleich würdig des Höchsten auf der Erde. Die rauhen Scenen schottischen Lebens sieht er nicht im arkadischen Lichte, aber in dem Rauche, in dem unebenen Tennenboden einer solchen rohen Wirthlichkeit findet er noch immer Liebenswürdiges genug. Armuth fürwahr ist sein Gefährte, aber auch Liebe und Muth zugleich; die einfachen Gefühle, der Werth, der Edelsinn, welche unter dem Strohdach wohnen, sind lieb und ehrwürdig seinem Herzen. Und so über die niedrigsten Regionen des menschlichen Daseyns ergiesst er die Glorie seines eigenen Gemüths und sie steigen, durch Schatten und Sonnenschein gesänftigt und verherrlicht, zu einer Schönheit, welche sonst die Menschen kaum in dem Höchsten erblicken."

"Hat er auch ein Selbstbewusstseyn, welches oft in Stolz ausartet, so ist es ein edler Stolz, um abzuwehren, nicht um anzugreifen, kein kaltes misslaunisches Gefühl, ein freyes und geselliges. Dieser poetische Landmann beträgt sich, möchten wir sagen, wie ein König in der Verbannung; er ist unter die Niedrigsten gedrängt und fühlt sich gleich den Höchsten; er verlangt keinen Rang, damit man ihm keinen streitig mache. Den Zudringlichen kann er abstossen, den Stolzen demüthigen, Vorurtheil auf Reichthum oder Altgeschlecht haben bey ihm keinen Werth. In diesem dunklen Auge ist ein Feuer, woran sich eine abwürdigende Herablassung nicht wagen darf; in seiner Erniedrigung, in der äussersten Noth vergisst er nicht für einen Augenblick die Majestät der Poesie und Mannheit. Und doch, so hoch er sich über gewöhnlichen Menschen fühlt, sondert er sich nicht von ihnen ab, mit Wärme nimmt er an ihrem Interesse Theil, ja er wirft sich in ihre Arme und, wie sie auch seyen, bittet er um ihre Liebe. Es ist rührend zu sehen, wie in den düstersten Zuständen dieses stolze Wesen in der Freundschaft Hülfe sucht, und oft seinen Busen dem Unwürdigen aufschliesst; oft unter Thränen an sein glühendes Herz ein Herz andrückt, das Freundschaft nur als Namen kennt. Doch war er scharf und schnellsichtig, ein Mann vom durchdringendsten Blick, vor welchem gemeine Verstellung sich nicht bergen konnte. Sein Verstand sah durch die Tiefen des vollkommensten Betrügers, und zugleich war eine grossmüthige Leichtgläubigkeit in seinem Herzen. So zeigte sich dieser Landmann unter uns: Eine Seele wie Aeolsharfe, deren Saiten vom gemeinsten Winde berührt, ihn zu gesetzlicher Melodie verwandelten. Und ein solcher Mann war es für den die Welt kein schicklicher Geschäft zu finden wusste, als sich mit Schmugglern und Schenken herumzuzanken, Accise auf den Talg zu berechnen und Bierfässer zu visiren. In solchem Abmühen ward dieser mächtige Geist kummervoll vergeudet, und hundert Jahre mögen vorüber gehen, eh uns ein gleicher gegeben wird, um vielleicht ihn abermals zu vergeuden."

Und wie wir den Deutschen zu ihrem Schiller Glück wünschen, so wollen wir in eben diesem Sinne auch die Schottländer segnen. Haben diese jedoch unserm Freunde so viel Aufmerksamkeit und Theilnahme erwiesen, so wär' es billig, dass wir auf gleiche Weise ihren Burns bey uns einführten. Ein junges Mitglied der hochachtbaren Gesellschaft, der wir gegenwärtiges im Ganzen empfohlen haben, wird Zeit und Mühe höchlich belohnt sehen, wenn er diesen freundlichen Gegendienst einer so verehrungswürdigen Nation zu leisten den Entschluss fassen und das Geschäft treulich durchführen will. Auch wir rechnen den belobten Robert Burns zu den ersten Dichtergeistern, welche das vergangene Jahrhundert hervorgebracht hat.

Im Jahr 1829 kam uns ein sehr sauber und augenfällig gedrucktes Octavbändchen zur Hand: *Catalogue of German Publications, selected and systematically arranged for W.H. Koller and Jul. Cahlmann. London.*

Dieses Büchlein, mit besonderer Kenntniss der deutschen Literatur, in einer die Uebersicht erleichternden Methode verfasst, macht demjenigen der es ausgearbeitet und den Buchhändlern Ehre, welche ernstlich das bedeutende Geschäft übernehmen eine fremde Literatur in ihr Vaterland einzuführen, und zwar so dass mann in allen Fächern übersehen könne was dort geleistet worden, um so wohl den Gelehrten den denkenden Leser als auch den fühlenden und Unterhaltung suchenden anzulocken und zu befriedigen. Neugierig wird jeder deutsche Schriftsteller und Literator, der sich in irgend einem Fache hervorgethan, diesen Catalog aufschlagen um zu forschen: ob denn auch seiner darin gedacht, seine Werke, mit andern Verwandten, freundlich aufgenommen worden. Allen deutschen Buchhändlern wird es angelegen seyn zu erfahren: wie man ihren Verlag über dem Canal betrachte, welchen Preis man auf das Einzelne setze und sie werden nichts verabsäumen um mit jenen die Angelegenheit so ernsthaft angreifenden Männern in Verhältniss zu kommen, und dasselbe immerfort lebendig erhalten.

Wenn ich nun aber das von unserm Schottischen Freunde vor soviel Jahren verfasste Leben Schillers, auf das er mit einer ihm so wohl anstehenden Bescheidenheit zurücksieht, hiedurch einleite und gegenwärtig an den Tag fördere, so erlaube er mir einige seiner neusten Aeusserungen hinzuzufügen, welche die bisherigen gemeinsamen Fortschritte am besten deutlich machen möchten.

THOMAS CARLYLE AN GOETHE.

den 22. December 1829.

"Ich habe zu nicht geringer Befriedigung zum zweitenmale den Briefwechsel gelesen und sende heute einen darauf gegründeten Aufsatz über Schiller ab für das *Foreign Review.* Es wird Ihnen angenehm seyn zu hören, dass die Kentniss und Schätzung der auswärtigen, besonders der deutschen Literatur, sich mit wachsender Schnelle verbreitet so weit die englische Zunge herrscht; so dass bey den Antipoden, selbst in Neuholland, die Weisen Ihres Landes ihre Weisheit predigen. Ich habe kürzlich gehört, dass sogar in Oxford und Cambridge, unsern beiden englischen Universitäten, die bis jetzt als die Haltpuncte der insularischen eigenthümlichen Beharrlichkeit sind betrachtet worden, es sich in solchen Dingen zu regen anfängt. Ihr Niebuhr hat in Cambridge einen geschickten Uebersetzer gefunden und in Oxford haben zwei bis drei Deutsche schon hinlängliche Beschäftigung als Lehrer ihrer Sprache. Das neue Licht mag für gewisse Augen zu stark seyn; jedoch kann Niemand an den guten Folgen zweifeln, die am Ende daraus hervorgehen werden. Lasst Nationen wie Individuen sich nur einander kennen und der gegenseitige Hass wird sich in gegenwärtige Hülfleistung verwandeln, und anstatt natürlicher Feinde, wie benachbarte Länder zuweilen genannt sind, werden wir alle natürliche Freunde seyn."

Wenn uns nach allen diesem nun die Hoffnung schmeichelt, eine Uebereinstimmung der Nationen, ein allgemeineres Wohlwollen werde sich durch nähere Kentniss der verschiedenen Sprachen und Denkweisen, nach und nach erzeugen; so wage ich von einem bedeutenden Inflows der deutschen Literatur zu sprechen, welcher sich in einem besondern Falle höchst wirksam erweisen möchte.

Es ist nämlich bekannt genug, dass die Bewohner der drei brittischen Königreiche nicht gerade in dem besten Einverständnisse leben, sondern dass vielmehr ein Nachbar an dem andern genügsam zu tadeln findet, um eine heimliche Abneigung bey sich zu rechtfertigen.

Nun aber bin ich überzeugt, dass wie die deutsche ethisch-ästhetische Literatur durch das dreifache Brittanien sich verbreitet, zugleich auch eine stille Gemeinschaft von Philogermanen sich bilden werde, welche in der Neigung zu einer vierten, so nahverwandten Völkerschaft, auch unter einander, als vereinigt und verschmolzen sich empfinden werden.

SCHILLERS LEBEN.

Erster Abschnitt.

Seine Jugend (1759-1784.)

Unter allen Schriftstellern ist am Schluss des letzten Jahrhunderts wohl keiner der Aufmerksamkeit würdiger, als Friedrich Schiller. Ausgezeichnet durch glänzenden Geist, erhabenes Gefühl und edlen Geschmack liess er den schönsten Abdruck dieser selten vereinigten Eigenschaften in seinen Werken zurück. Der ausgebreitete Ruhm, welcher ihm dadurch geworden,...

... es sind neue Formen der Wahrheiten, neue Grundsätze der Weisheit, neue Bilder und Scenen der Schönheit, die er dem leeren formlosen unendlichen Raum abgenommen; zum κτημα εις αει oder zum ewigen Eigenthum aller Geschlechter dieses Erdballs.[s. 301.]

... die unsere Literatur, so reich sie auch schon an sich ist, noch ungleich mehr bereichern würde. [*Anhang*, s. 54.]

SUMMARY AND INDEX.

SUMMARY

PART I.
SCHILLER'S YOUTH.
(1759-1784.)

Introductory remarks: Schiller's high destiny. His Father's career: Parental example and influences. Boyish caprices and aspirations. (p. 3.)—His first schoolmaster: Training for the Church: Poetical glimmerings. The Duke of Würtemberg, and his Free Seminary: Irksome formality there. Aversion to the study of Law and Medicine. (9.)—Literary ambition and strivings: Economic obstacles and pedantic hindrances: Silent passionate rebellion. Bursts his fetters. (13.)—*The Robbers*: An emblem of its young author's baffled, madly struggling spirit: Criticism of the Characters in the Play, and of the style of the work. Extraordinary ferment produced by its publication: Exaggerated praises and condemnations: Schiller's own opinion of its moral tendency. (17.)—Discouragement and persecution from the Duke of Würtemberg. Dalberg's generous sympathy and assistance. Schiller escapes from Stuttgard, empty in purse and hope: Dalberg supplies his immediate wants: He finds hospitable friends. (28.)—Earnest literary efforts. Publishes two tragedies, *Fiesco* and *Kabale und Liebe*. His mental growth. Critical account of the Conspiracy of Fiesco: Fiesco's genial ambition: The Characters of the Play nearer to actual humanity. How all things in the Drama of Life hang inseparably together. (35.)—*Kabale und Liebe*, a domestic tragedy of high merit: Noble and interesting characters of hero and heroine. (42.)—The stormy confusions of Schiller's youth now subsiding. Appointed poet to the Mannheim Theatre. Nothing to fear from the Duke of Würtemberg. The Public, his only friend and sovereign. A Man of Letters for the rest of his days. (46.)

PART II.
FROM HIS SETTLEMENT AT MANNHEIM
TO HIS SETTLEMENT AT JENA.
(1784-1790:)

Reflections: Difference between knowing and doing: Temptations and perils of a literary life: True Heroism. Schiller's earnest and steadfast devotion to his Ideal Good: Misery of idleness and indecision. (p. 51.)—German esteem for the Theatre. Theatrical, and deeper than theatrical activities: The *Rheinische Thalia* and *Philosophische Briefe*. The two Eternities: The bog of Infidelity surveyed but not crossed. (56.)—Insufficiency of Mannheim. A pleasant tribute of regard. Letter to

Huber: Domestic tastes. Removes to Leipzig. Letter to his friend Schwann: A marriage proposal. Fluctuations of life. (63.)—Goes to Dresden. *Don Carlos*: Evidences of a matured mind: Analysis of the Characters: Scene of the King and Posa. Alfieri and Schiller contrasted. (73.)—Popularity: Crowned with laurels, but without a home. Forsakes the Drama. Lyrical productions: *Freigeisterei der Leidenschaft*. The *Geisterseher*, a Novel. Tires of fiction. Studies and tries History. (95.)—Habits at Dresden. Visits Weimar and Bauerbach. The Fraülein Lengefeld: Thoughts on Marriage. (102.)—First interview with Goethe: Diversity in their gifts: Their mistaken impression of each other. Become better acquainted: Lasting friendship. (106.)—History of the *Revolt of the Netherlands*. The truest form of History-writing. Appointed Professor at Jena. Friendly intercourse with Goethe. Marriage. (112.)

PART III.
FROM HIS SETTLEMENT AT JENA TO HIS DEATH.
(1790-1805.)

Academical duties. Study of History: Cosmopolitan philosophy, and national instincts. History of the *Thirty-Years War*. (p. 119.)—Sickness, and help in it. Heavy trial for a literary man. Schiller's unabated zeal. (125.)—Enthusiasm and conflicts excited by Kant's Philosophy. Schiller's growing interest in the subject: Letters on *Æsthetic Culture*, &c. Claims of Kant's system to a respectful treatment. (129.)—Fastidiousness and refinement of taste. Literary projects: Epic poems: Returns to the Drama. Outbreak of the French Revolution. (137.)—Edits the *Horen*: Connexion with Goethe. A pleasant visit to his parents. Mode of life at Jena: Night-studies, and bodily stimulants. (143.)—*Wallenstein*: Brief sketch of its character and compass: Specimen scenes, Max Piccolomini and his Father; Max and the Princess Thekla; Thekla's frenzied grief: No nobler or more earnest dramatic work. (152.)—Removes to Weimar: Generosity of the Duke. Tragedy of *Maria Stuart*. (178.)—The *Maid of Orleans*: Character of Jeanne d'Arc: Scenes, Joanna and her Suitors; Death of Talbot; Joanna and Lionel. Enthusiastic reception of the play. (181.)—Daily and nightly habits at Weimar. The *Bride of Messina*. *Wilhelm Tell*: Truthfulness of the Characters and Scenery: Scene, the Death of Gossler. (201.)—Schiller's dangerous illness. Questionings of Futurity. The last sickness: Many things grow clearer: Death. (219.)—General sorrow for his loss. His personal aspect: Modesty and simplicity of manner: Mental gifts. (222.)—Definitions of genius. Poetic sensibilities and wretchedness: In such miseries Schiller had no share. A fine example of the German character: No cant; no cowardly compromising with his own conscience: Childlike simplicity. Literary Heroism. (227.)

SUPPLEMENT OF 1872.

Small Book by Herr Saupe, entitled *Schiller and his Father's Household*. Really interesting and instructive. Translation, with slight corrections and additions. (p. 241.)

SCHILLER'S FATHER.

Johann Caspar Schiller, born in Würtemberg, 27th October 1723. At ten years a fatherless Boy poorly educated, he is apprenticed to a barber-surgeon. Becomes 'Army Doctor' to a Bavarian regiment. Settles in Marbach, and marries the daughter of a respectable townsman, afterwards reduced to extreme poverty. The marriage, childless for the first eight years. Six children in all: The Poet Schiller the only Boy. (p. 243.)—Very meagre circumstances. At breaking-out of the Seven-Years War returns to the Army. At the Ball of Fulda; at the Battle of Leuthen. Cheerfully undertakes anything useful. Earnestly diligent and studious. Greatly improves in general culture, and even saves money. (244.)—Boards his poor Wife with her Father. His first Daughter and his only Son born there. At the close of the War he carries his Wife and Children to his own quarters. A just man; simple, strong, expert; if also somewhat quick and rough. (246.) Solicitude for his Son's education. Appointed Recruiting Officer, with permission to live with his Family at Lorch. The children soon feel themselves at home and happy. Little Fritz receives his first regular school instruction, much to the comfort of his Father. Holiday rambles among the neighbouring hills: Brotherly and Sisterly affection. Touches of boyish fearlessness: Where does the lightning come from? (248.)—The Family run over to Ludwigsburg. Fritz to prepare for the clerical profession. At the Latin School, cannot satisfy his Father's anxious wishes. One of his first poems. (253.)—The Duke of Würtemberg notices his Father's worth, and appoints him Overseer of all his Forest operations: With residence at his beautiful Forest-Castle, Die Solitüde. Fritz remains at the Ludwigsburg Latin School: Continual exhortations and corrections from Father and Teacher. Youthful heresy. First acquaintance with a Theatre. (255.)—The Duke proposes to take Fritz into his Military Training-School. Consternation of the Schiller Family. Ineffectual expostulations: Go he must. Studies Medicine. Altogether withdrawn from his Father's care. Rigorous seclusion and constraint. The Duke means well to him. (258.)—Leaves the School, and becomes Regimental-Doctor at Stuttgard. His Father's pride in him. Extravagance and debt. His personal appearance. (260.)—Publication of the *Robbers*. His Father's mingled feelings of anxiety and admiration. Peremptory command from the Duke to write no more poetry, on pain of Military Imprisonment. Prepares for flight with his friend Streicher. Parting visit to his Family at Solitüde: His poor Mother's bitter grief. Escapes to Mannheim. Consternation of his Father. Happily the Duke takes no hostile step. (263.)—Disappointments and straits at Mannheim. Help from his good friend Streicher. He sells *Fiesco*, and prepares to leave Mannheim. Through the kindness of Frau von Wolzogen he finds refuge in Bauerbach. Affectionate Letter to his Parents. His Father's stern solicitude for his welfare. (268.)—Eight months in Bauerbach, under the name of Doctor Ritter. Unreturned attachment to Charlotte Wolzogen. Returns to Mannheim. Forms a settled engagement with Dalberg, to whom his Father writes his thanks and anxieties. Thrown on a sickbed: His Father's admonitions. He vainly urges his Son to petition the Duke for permission to return to Würtemberg; the poor Father earnestly wishes to have him near him again. Increasing financial difficulties. More earnest fatherly admonition and advice. Enthusiastic reception of *Kabale und Liebe*. *Don Carlos* well in hand. A friend in trouble through mutual debts. Applies to his Father for unreasonable help. Annoyance at the inevitable refusal. His Father's loving and faithful expostulation. His Sister's proposed marriage with Reinwald. (273.)—Beginning of his friendly intimacy with the excellent Körner. The Duke of Weimar bestows on him the title of Rath. No farther risk for him from Würtemberg. At Leipzig, Dresden, Weimar. Settles at last as Professor in Jena. Marriage and comfortable home: His Father well satisfied, and joyful of heart. Affectionate Letter to his good Father. (282.)—Seized with a dangerous affection of the chest. Generous assistance from Denmark. Joyful visit to his Family, after an absence of eleven years. Writes a conciliatory Letter to the Duke. Birth of a Son. The Duke's considerateness for Schiller's Father. The Duke's death. (286.)—Schiller's delight in his Sisters, Luise and Nanette. Letter to his Father. Visits Stuttgard. Returns with Wife and Child to Jena. Assists his Father in publishing the results of his long experiences of gardens and trees. Beautiful and venerable old age. (290.)—Thick-coming troubles for the Schiller Family. Death of the beautiful Nanette in the flower of her years: Dangerous illness of Luise: The Father bedrid with gout. The poor weakly Mother bears the whole burden of the household distress. Sister Christophine, now Reinwald's Wife, hastens to their help. Schiller's anxious sympathy. His Father's death. Grateful letters to Reinwald and to his poor Mother. (296.)

HIS MOTHER.

Elizabetha Dorothea Kodweis, born at Marbach, 1733. An unpretending, soft and dutiful Wife, with the tenderest Mother-heart. A talent for music and even for poetry. Verses to her Husband. Troubles during the Seven-Years War. Birth of little Fritz. The Father returns from the War. Mutual helpfulness, and affectionate care for their children. She earnestly desires her Son may become a Preacher. His confirmation. Her disappointment that it was not to be. (p. 300.)—Her joy and care for him whenever he visited his Home. Her innocent delight at seeing her Son's name honoured and wondered at. Her anguish and illness at their long parting. Brighter days for them all. She visits her Son at Jena. He returns the visit with Wife and Child. Her strength in adversity. Comfort in her excellent Daughter Christophine. Her Husband's death. Loving and helpful sympathy from her Son. (307.)—Receives a pension from the Duke. Removes with Luise to Leonberg. Marriage of Luise. Happy in her children's love and in their success in life. Her last illness and death. Letters from Schiller to his Sister Luise and her kind husband. (318.)

HIS SISTERS.

Till their Brother's flight the young girls had known no misfortune. Diligent household occupations, and peaceful contentment. A love-passage in Christophine's young life. Her marriage with Reinwald. His unsuccessful career: Broken down in health and hope. Christophine's loving, patient and noble heart. For twenty-nine years they lived contentedly together. Through life she was helpful to all about her; never hindersome to any. (p. 324.)—Poor Nanette's brief history. Her excitement, when a child, on witnessing the performance of her Brother's *Kabale und Liebe*. Her ardent secret wish, herself to represent his Tragedies on the Stage. All her young glowing hopes stilled in death. (331.)—Luise's betrothal and marriage. An anxious Mother, and in all respects an excellent Wife. Her Brother's last loving Letter to her. His last illness, and peaceful death. (333.)

APPENDIX I.

No. 1. DANIEL SCHUBART.

Influence of Schubart's persecutions on Schiller's mind. His Birth and Boyhood. Sent to Jena to study Theology: Profligate life: Returns home. Popular as a preacher: Skilful in music. A joyful, piping, guileless mortal. (p. 341.)—Prefers pedagogy to starvation. Marries. Organist to the Duke of Würtemberg. Headlong business, amusement and dissipation. His poor Wife returns to her Father: Ruin and banishment. A vagabond life. (343.)—Settles at Augsburg, and sets up a Newspaper: Again a prosperous man: Enmity of the Jesuits. Seeks refuge in Ulm: His Wife and Family return to him. The Jesuits on the watch. Imprisoned for ten years: Interview with young Schiller. (346.)—Is at length liberated. Joins his Wife at Stuttgard, and reëstablishes his Newspaper. Literary enterprises: Death. Summary of his character. (351.)

No. 2. LETTERS OF SCHILLER TO DALBERG.

Brief account of Dalberg. Schiller's desire to remove to Mannheim. Adaptation of the *Robbers* to the stage. (p. 354.)—Struggles to get free from Stuttgard and his Ducal Jailor: Dalberg's friendly help. Friendly letter to his friend Schwann. (362.)

No. 3. FRIENDSHIP WITH GOETHE.

Goethe's feeling of the difference in their thoughts and aims: Great Nature *not* a phantasm of her children's brains. Growing sympathy and esteem, unbroken to the end. (p. 371.)

No. 4. DEATH OF GUSTAVUS ADOLPHUS.

Schiller's historical style. A higher than descriptive power. (p. 375.)

APPENDIX II.

Schiller's Life into German; Author's Note thereon. (p. 380.)—Goethe's introduction (in German), with Four Prints. (393.)

INDEX

G

H

I

J

K

L

M

O

P

R

S

T

V

W

X

Y

Z

Lector House believes that a society develops through a two-fold approach of continuous learning and adaptation, which is derived from the study of classic literary works spread across the historic timeline of literature records. Therefore, we aim at reviving, repairing and redeveloping all those inaccessible or damaged but historically as well as culturally important literature across subjects so that the future generations may have an opportunity to study and learn from past works to embark upon a journey of creating a better future.

This book is a result of an effort made by Lector House towards making a contribution to the preservation and repair of original ancient works which might hold historical significance to the approach of continuous learning across subjects.

HAPPY READING & LEARNING!

LECTOR HOUSE LLP
E-MAIL: lectorpublishing@gmail.com